WEBSTER'S FAMILY ENCYCLOPEDIA

WEBSTER'S FAMILY ENCYCLOPEDIA

VOLUME 4

1995 Edition

This book is not published by the original publishers of **WEBSTER'S DICTIONARY**, or by their successors.

Exclusively distributed by
Archer Worldwide, Inc.
Great Neck, New York, USA

Worldwide distribution rights assigned to Archer Worldwide, Inc.
Great Neck, New York 11021

Printed in the United States of America.

Abbreviations Used in Webster's Family Encyclopedia

AD	After Christ
Adm.	Admiral
Ala.	Alabama
Apr	April
AR	Autonomous Republic
at no	atomic number
at wt	atomic weight
Aug	August
b.	born
BC	Before Christ
bp	boiling point
C	Celsius, Centigrade
c.	circa
Calif.	California
Capt.	Captain
CIS	Commonwealth of Independent States
cm	centimeters
Co.	Company
Col.	Colonel
Conn.	Connecticut
d.	died
Dec	December
Del.	Delaware
E	east, eastern
EC	European Community
e.g.	for example
est	estimated
F	Fahrenheit
Feb	February
Fl. Lt.	Flight Lieutenant
Fla.	Florida
ft	feet
Ga.	Georgia
Gen.	General
Gov.	Governor
ht	height
i.e.	that is
in	inches
Ind.	Indiana
Ill.	Illinois
Jan	January
K	Kelvin
Kans.	Kansas
kg	kilograms
km	kilometers
kph	kilometers per hour
kW	kilowatts
lb	pounds
Lt.	Lieutenant
Lt. Gen.	Lieutenant General
m	meters
M. Sgt.	Master Sergeant
Mar	March
Mass.	Massachusetts
Md.	Maryland
mi	miles
Mich.	Michigan
Minn.	Minnesota
Miss.	Mississippi
mm	millimeters
Mo.	Missouri
MP	Member of Parliament
mp	melting point
mph	miles per hour
N	north, northern
NATO	North Atlantic Treaty Organization
NE	northeast
Neb.	Nebraska
N.H.	New Hampshire
N.J.	New Jersey
N.M.	New Mexico
NNE	north-northeast
NNW	north-northwest
Nov	November
NW	northwest
N.Y.	New York
OAS	Organization of American States
Oct	October
Okla.	Oklahoma
OPEC	Organization of Petroleum Exporting Countries
Pa.	Pennsylvania
PLO	Palestine Liberation Organization
Pres.	President
R.I.	Rhode Island
S	south, southern
S.C.	South Carolina
SE	southeast
Sen.	Senator
Sept	September
Sgt.	Sergeant
sq mi	square miles
SSE	south-southeast
SSW	south-southwest
SW	southwest
Tenn.	Tennessee
Tex.	Texas
UN	United Nations
US	United States
USSR	Union of Soviet Socialist Republics
Va.	Virginia
Vt.	Vermont
W	west, western
wt	weight

ellipse A closed curve having the shape of an elongated *circle. The sum of the distances from any point on the circumference to each of two fixed points, known as the foci, is a constant. In the Cartesian *coordinate system its equation is $(x - h)^2/a^2 + (y - k)^2/b^2 = 1$, where (h,k) is the center of the ellipse and a and b are the largest and shortest radii, which are parallel to the coordinate axes. In the case of a and b being equal, the ellipse becomes a *circle of radius a. The ellipse is one of a family of curves known as *conic sections.

Ellis, (Henry) Havelock (1859–1939) British psychologist and essayist, noted for his studies of human sexual behavior. His major work, *Studies in the Psychology of Sex* (7 vols, 1897–1928), was among the first to deal frankly with sexual problems and met with legal opposition. He was also concerned with women's rights, edited publications in both the arts and sciences, and wrote *Impressions and Comments* (3 vols, 1914–24), a series of essays on art.

Ellis Island 40 42N 74 03W A small island in New York Harbor. It served as an entry center for immigrants to the US (1892–1943).

Ellison, Ralph (Waldo) (1914–94) US author. Educated at Tuskegee Institute (1933–36), he wrote of African Americans and the opportunities presented in the US and taught at New York University. His *Invisible Man* (1952) won a National Book Award in 1953. Other works include *Shadow and Act* (1964).

Ellora Caves A cluster of rock-cut Hindu, Buddhist, and Jaina temples in Maharashtra state (W India). They were made mainly between the mid 7th and the early 10th centuries AD. The most sumptuous temple is the Kailashanatha, dedicated to Shiva.

Ellsworth, Lincoln (1880–1951) US explorer. After graduation from Yale and Columbia universities he worked as an engineer in Canada and Alaska and led a geological expedition to Peru. In 1926 he was part of the first successful crossing of the Arctic (with Roald *Amundsen and Umberto *Nobile) from Spitsbergen, Norway, to Teller, Alaska, in the dirigible *Norge*. By 1935 he had become the first to fly across Antarctica. Ellsworth Land is named for him.

Ellsworth, Oliver (1745–1807) US politician, lawyer, and jurist; Chief Justice of the US Supreme Court (1796–1800). A practicing lawyer in Connecticut from 1771, he was a delegate to the Continental Congress in 1777 and coauthored (with Roger Sherman) the *Connecticut Compromise at the Constitutional Convention in 1787. He served in the US Senate (1789–96) and was a principal author of the Bill of Rights (1791). In 1796 he was appointed chief justice of the Supreme Court by President *Washington, a position he held until 1800 when he was forced resign due to ill health.

Ellsworth Land An area in Antarctica, at the base of the Antarctic Peninsula. It contains the highest peak in Antarctica, *Vinson Massif. UK claims to the area are contested by Argentina and Chile.

elm A □tree of the genus *Ulmus* (about 30 species), widely distributed in N temperate regions. Up to 131 ft (40 m) high, elms have oval, pointed, toothed leaves, clusters of small reddish flowers, and rounded or heart-shaped winged nuts. Elms are widely planted for shade and ornament and for their strong durable timber. Unfortunately the number of elm trees in Europe and North America has been greatly reduced by *Dutch elm disease. Species include the English elm (*U. procera*), the Eurasian wych elm (*U. glabra*), and the American elm (*U. americana*). Family: *Ulmaceae*. *See also* slippery elm.

elm bark beetle A wood-boring beetle, *Scolytus scolytus, S. multistriatus*, or *Hylurgopinus rufipes*, that tunnels under the bark of elm trees and carries the fungus *Ceratostomella ulni*, which causes *Dutch elm disease. Family: *Scolytidae* (*see* bark beetle).

El Obeid 13 15N 30 45E A city in the Sudan. It is a trading center for gum arabic, cereals, and cattle. Population (1984): 140,000.

Elohim One of the Hebrew names of God. It occurs often in the Old Testament and is strictly the plural of *eloah* (which can also be a name of God) but it is used with a singular verb when it denotes God rather than gods.

El Paso 31 45N 106 30W A city in the US, in W Texas on the Rio Grande. Situated on the Mexican border, it is the commercial and industrial center of a mining and cattle-raising area. It is also a major base for the armed forces. Manufactures include refined oil and food products. Population (1990): 515,342.

Elphanta Island 18 58N 72 54E An islet off the W coast of India, in Bombay Harbor. It is famous for its cave temples and a three-headed bust, 20 ft (6 m) high, of the god Shiva.

El Salvador, Republic of A country in Central America, on the Pacific Ocean. Narrow coastal lowlands rise to a fertile plateau, which is enclosed by volcanic mountains. The country is frequently subject to earthquakes. Most of the population is of mixed European and Indian descent. *Economy*: mainly agricultural, the economy has been dominated by coffee since the late 19th century. Cotton is the second main commercial crop. Forests produce not only valuable hardwoods, such as mahogany and walnut, but also dye woods and balsam of which El Salvador is the world's principal source. Most of the cultivated land is controlled by a few families, which has led to considerable movement and even emigration (especially in the 1960s) among the country's farmers, most of whom rent their land. El Salvador has few mineral resources and the main source of power is hydro-electricity. Traditional industries, such as food processing and textiles, remain important, but tourism is also being developed. *History*: the Aztec population was conquered by the Spaniards in 1526 and after the overthrow of Spanish rule the region formed part of the Central American Federation (1823–38). In 1841 it became an independent republic. Tension arising from the emigration of Salvadoreans to Honduras culminated in warfare between the two countries in 1965 and again in 1969, following El Salvador's defeat of Honduras in a World Cup soccer game. In 1978–79 considerable internal unrest occurred in response to the repressive regime of Gen. Carlos Humberto Romero with kidnappings of foreigners by left-wing guerrillas, occupations of foreign embassies, and assassinations. Romero was deposed in 1979 and a junta took control but the violence continued. Following inconclusive elections in 1981 Alvaro Magaña was appointed interim president (1982). Despite substantial US aid, the government was not able to defeat rebel forces, and right-wing "death squads" murdered thousands of citizens suspected of liberal sympathies. In 1984 a moderate, José Napoleón Duarte, was elected president with US support, ending the immediate threat of a right-wing takeover, and in 1985 his party won a majority in parliamentary elections. Economic problems remained severe, and a devastating earthquake in 1986 added to the burden. Duarte lost the presidential election in 1989 and was succeeded by Alfredo Cristiani. Cristiani worked with rebel leaders to achieve a preliminary peace settlement in 1991; a formal treaty was signed in early 1992. It provided for UN supervision of a cease-fire, disarmament, and an investigation of human rights violations. El Salvador is a member of the OAS, the Organization of Central American States, and the Central American Common Market. Official language: Spanish. Official religion: Roman Catholic. Official currency: colón of 100 centavos. Area 8236 sq mi (21,393 sq km). Population (1989): 5,900,000. Capital: San Salvador. Main port: Acajutla.

Elysium (*or* Elysian Fields) In Greek mythology, the field on the banks of the *Oceanus River where those favored by the gods live in eternal happiness. They are also called (by Hesiod) the Isles of the Blessed. In Roman mythology Elysium is part of the underworld.

Emancipation Act (1861) The edict issued by *Alexander II that freed the serfs of Russia (a third of the country's population). The peasants were to receive land from the landlord and pay for it in labor and crops but inequities in land distribution caused considerable discontent.

Emancipation Proclamation (1863) The edict issued by Pres. Abraham *Lincoln that freed slaves in the rebellious southern states of the US. It was promulgated in part to weaken the Confederate war effort by depriving the South of laborers, but Lincoln considered it "the central act" of his administration. The proclamation's limited provisions were extended and confirmed by the 13th Amendment, which abolished *slavery throughout the nation (1865).

Emba River A river in Kazakhstan, flowing mainly SW from the Mugodzhar Hills, through the Emba oilfield, to the Caspian Sea. Length: 380 mi (611 km).

embalming The techniques for preserving dead bodies from decay. Embalming was frequent in ancient Egypt (*see* mummy). In medieval Europe it was usually carried out by removing the corpse's internal organs, bathing it in spirits of wine, filling cavities made in the flesh with herbs, and finally wrapping it in waxed or tarred sheets. Since the 18th century arterial injections of preservative solutions, now generally a mixture of formaldehyde, alcohols, and salts, have been used.

embargo A resolution by a country or countries not to supply another country with certain goods, or not to import certain goods from another country, for political reasons. For example, in 1979 the Arab countries imposed an oil embargo on Egypt, after Egypt had signed a peace treaty with Israel.

Embargo Act (1807) A US law that banned trade with Europe for the duration of the Napoleonic Wars. Because both Britain and France had blockaded US trade with Europe, the US decided to end trade with Europe temporarily rather than be brought into the fighting. Passed during the administration of Thomas *Jefferson, it was not successful and was repealed in 1809. *See also* Non-Intercourse Act.

embolism The sudden blocking of an artery by a clot or other material that has come from another part of the body via the bloodstream (the material is called an embolus). The commonest example is when a clot forms in the leg and pieces break away and lodge in the arteries of the lung—a **pulmonary embolism**. A clot may sometimes come from the heart and lodge in the brain, causing a *stroke. Air and fat can also cause embolism. *See also* thrombosis.

embroidery The decoration of fabrics with needlework, usually in silk but occasionally in gold and silver thread. It was practiced by the ancient Egyptians, but the first important western embroidery was the *Bayeux tapestry. From about the 13th century embroidery was chiefly used for state and church vestments. Gros point and petit point are two common kinds of stitch used to form elaborate overall pictures, and from the 17th century such embroidered fabric was much used for curtains, bed hangings, and seat covers.

embryo An animal or plant in the earliest stages of its development. In vertebrate animals the embryonic stage lasts from the first division of the fertilized egg until the young animal either hatches from the egg or is expelled from the womb at birth. A human embryo is called a *fetus from the eighth week of pregnancy. In invertebrate animals the embryo is generally called a *larva. In plants, the embryo lies within the *seed and consists of a root (radicle), shoot (plumule), and cotyledons for nourishment. **Embryology** is the study of the development of embryos.

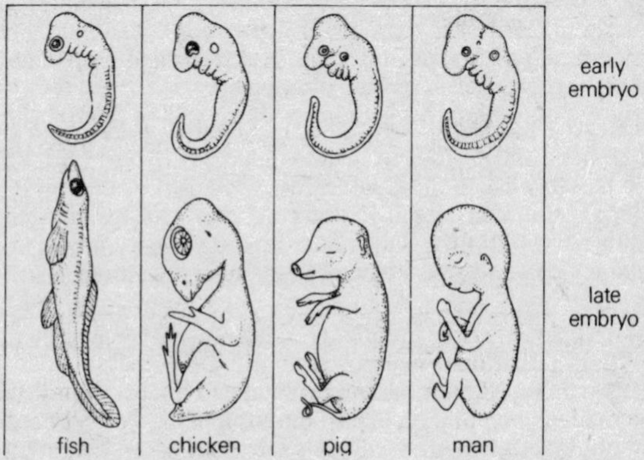

various vertebrate embryos *The different species are hard to distinguish in the early stages of development; later they develop individual characteristics.*

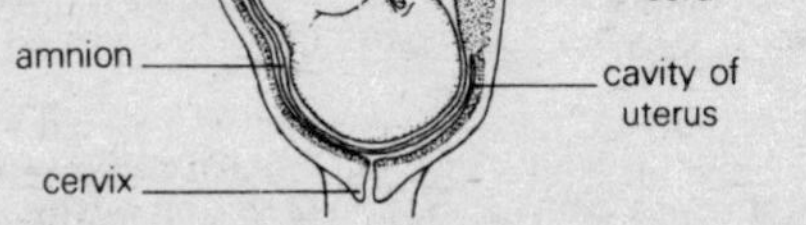

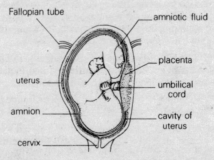

human embryo *A few weeks before birth this fetus is practically fully formed.*

EMBRYO

emerald A green variety of *beryl, the color being due to the presence of small amounts of chromium. Used as a gemstone, it occurs mainly in metamorphic rocks, particularly mica schists, the finest specimens coming from Muzo, Colombia. It is less resistant to wear than most gemstones. Birthstone for May.

Emerson, Ralph Waldo (1803–82) American essayist and poet. Born in Boston, Emerson was educated at Harvard and ordained as a Unitarian minister in 1829, but his wife's death in 1831 provoked a radical re-evaluation of his beliefs. After a tour of Europe, during which he met *Wordsworth, *Coleridge, and *Carlyle, he settled in Concord, Mass. where he was one of the founders of the *Transcendentalist movement. His essay *Nature* (1836) was quickly recognized as the most eloquent exposition of the transcendentalist philosophy. A prolific lecturer, poet, and essayist, he expressed his optimistic humanism in his *Poems* (1847), *Representative Men* (1850), and *The Conduct of Life* (1860). The latter work expressed his opposition to slavery and was written during his active participation in the Abolition movement.

emery A granular, grayish-black rock composed of *corundum with magnetite, hematite, or spinel. It occurs mainly in metamorphic rocks or sediments, particularly metamorphosed ferruginous bauxite, and altered limestones. It is used as an abrasive, in grinding wheels, emery cloth, and glass polishes, and in the manufacture of certain concrete floors. The principal producers are Turkey and Greece.

emigration. *See* migration, human.

Emilia-Romagna A region in N Italy. It consists of the fertile lowlands of the Po River in the N and E, bounded by the Apennines in the S. It is an important agricultural region producing sugar beets, cereals, vegetables, wine, rice, and fruit. Traditional manufacturing industries associated with agriculture are being replaced by modern chemical and oil-based industries and engineering. Area: 8542 sq mi (22,122 sq km). Population (1991): 3,984,055. Capital: Bologna.

Éminence Grise. *See* Joseph, Père.

Emin Paşa, Mehmed (Eduard Schnitzer; 1840–92) German-born physician and naturalist, who became a Muslim and took employment in Egypt. In 1878 *Gordon appointed him chief medical officer in the S Sudan, a post he held until "rescued" (1888) by *Stanley, who thought he was in danger after Gordon's death in Khartoum. He was murdered by Arabs on his way to explore Lake Victoria, but not before making notable contributions to natural history, anthropology, and geography.

Emmen 52 47N 6 55E A city in the NE Netherlands, in Drenthe province. It was formerly a peat-digging center. Industries include metallurgy, timber processing, and chemicals. Population (1981 est): 90,450.

Emmental (*or* Emmenthal) The valley of the upper Emme River, in W central Switzerland. It is famous for its cheese.

Emmet, Robert (1778–1803) Irish nationalist, who led a rebellion in Dublin for Irish independence in 1803. It amounted to little more than a riot, but Emmet's speech before his execution ensured his immortality.

Empedocles (c. 490–430 BC) Sicilian Greek philosopher. He modified the teachings of *Pythagoras and opposed *Parmenides' view of reality as one and unchanging. Empedocles founded the doctrine that earth, air, fire, and water make up the world, and that love and strife (attraction and antipathy) govern their distribution in a cycle of four stages.

emperor moth A large Eurasian *saturniid moth, *Saturnia pavonia*. Males fly by day, attracted by scent to the stationary females. The caterpillars spin a cocoon with an opening that allows easy exit but prevents entrance by predators.

emperor penguin A large *penguin, *Aptenodytes forsteri*. 3.9 ft (1.2 m) tall and 75 lb (34 kg) in weight, it is the largest seabird and has a blue-gray plumage with a black head and throat, a white belly, and orange patches on the neck.

emphysema A disease of the lungs characterized by destruction of lung tissue and distension of the air spaces. It is most commonly caused by cigarette smoking and is often accompanied by chronic *bronchitis. Patients become very breathless on exertion. It is a progressive condition, but the symptoms may be relieved by giving up smoking, breathing exercises, and administration of oxygen.

Empire, British. *See* British Empire.

Empire style The neoclassical style in the decorative arts developed during the Napoleonic empire (1804–14). It was inspired by classical Greek, Roman, and Egyptian models and reflected contemporary interest in archeology (e.g. *Pompeii). Dark woods, such as rosewood, were favored, sparsely ornamented with *ormolu. Shapes tended to be plain but caryatids were used as supports. The effect was of restrained but opulent elegance. The **Second Empire style** was the official architectural style of the French Government under Emperor Napoleon III (1852–70). Grandiose and ideally suited to public buildings, it became popular throughout Europe and America.

empiricism The philosophical belief that all knowledge is ultimately based on experience, that is, information received through the senses. It is opposed to *rationalism and denies that we have any *a priori knowledge or innate ideas: we owe all our concepts to experience of the world. Concepts only have meaning if they can be associated with some (actual or possible) experience, and statements asserted to be true can only be justified by appealing to experience. (Mathematical and logical knowledge are often exempted from this requirement by being classified as analytically true—true in virtue of syntax and the meaning of symbols alone.) Since the British empiricists, *Locke, *Berkeley, and *Hume, empiricism has been an influential force in much of western philosophy.

Ems telegram (July 13, 1870) A communication from *William I of Prussia to his chancellor *Bismarck, the edited and published version of which precipitated the *Franco-Prussian War. The telegram described a disagreement between William and the French ambassador concerning the succession of the Spanish throne. Bismarck altered the telegram to make it read as if each party had insulted the other.

emu A large, flightless, long-legged Australian bird, *Dromaius novaehollandiae*, found in open plains and forests. Up to 60 in (150 cm) tall and 100 lb (45 kg) in weight, it has a dark-brown, hairlike plumage with a naked blue spot on each side of the neck, and can run at speeds of up to 30 mph (50 km per hr). It is the only member of its family (*Dromaiidae*). *See also* ratite.

emulsion. *See* colloid.

emu wren An Australian *wren of the genus *Stipiturus* (3 species). About 3 in (7.5 cm) long, it has a brownish plumage and a long 3.5 in (9 cm) cocked tail consisting of six wispy gray feathers.

enamel A glaze that is fused onto the surface of metal. Enameled gold jewelry dating back to the 13th century BC has been found, and various methods of enameling have developed since then. Generally, a clear flux made from melted sand, soda potash, and red lead is stained with a metal oxide and left to harden. The resultant enamel cakes are ground and spread on the metal object, which is then placed in a furnace to fuse the enamel with the metal. Painted enamels are applied after the ground enamel has been fired and are not, therefore, true enamels.

enamelwork The art of decorating metal surfaces with colored glass that is fused by heat onto the metal. There are three main kinds: *cloisonné, *champlevé, and painted enamelwork. The technique of painted enamelwork involves painting powdered, wet enamel all over the metal before firing. Painted enamel is particularly associated with Limoges, France, (15th and 16th centuries) and with England (18th century).

encaustic painting A method of painting using ground pigments emulsified in hot wax, which are applied thickly with a spatula or brush. Heat is then directed onto the paint to fuse it with the picture surface. Although revived by various artists, it was most successfully employed by ancient Greek and Roman painters.

encephalins (*or* enkephalins) Short peptide molecules, found in parts of the brain and spinal cord, that are thought to relieve pain. These and similar compounds are called **endorphins**. In the spinal cord encephalins are believed to inhibit painful sensations by reacting with specific receptor sites on the sensory nerve endings. In the brain their function is less certain but may be associated with mood. The pain-relieving effects of acupuncture may be due to the release of the body's encephalins.

encephalitis Inflammation of the brain. It usually occurs as a result of a virus infection, but can be caused by malaria, fungi, or parasites (rarely by bacteria). The patient is often drowsy and fevered and has a bad headache. There is no specific treatment for viral encephalitis but the patient usually recovers. *See also* sleepy sickness.

Encke's comet A comet that has a period of only 3.3 years (decreasing by 2.5 hours/revolution) and has been very closely studied during its numerous apparitions. Its period was first established by the German astronomer J. F. Encke (1791–1865).

enclosure The fencing in of open land to make more efficient use of it. Enclosure has occurred in most parts of Europe but is associated particularly with England, where it reached a peak in the 15th–16th and 18–19th centuries. The enclosing by landlords, without prior agreement, of land to which tenants had enjoyed traditional grazing rights encountered much opposition and in the 16th century a series of acts against enclosure was passed. The movement again intensified in the 18th century, contributing to the *agricultural revolution. The General Enclosure Acts (1801, 1836, 1845) established procedures to safeguard tenant rights.

encyclical, papal A decree of the pope addressed to the whole Roman Catholic Church. The term referred originally to a letter to all the churches in a particular area, such as a diocese. The most famous example of an encyclical in recent times is *Humanae Vitae* (1968), which was issued by Paul VI and expressed the teaching of the Church on contraception.

encyclopedia A reference book summarizing all human knowledge or comprehensively surveying a particular subject. Greek and Roman encyclopedias, such as *Pliny the Elder's *Historia naturalis* (77 AD), were thematically arranged, as were the medieval Latin compilations, such as Vincent of Beauvais' influential *Speculum maius* (c. 1250). After the Renaissance, alphabetical arrangement with articles written in vernacular languages to facilitate use by the layman became accepted. Ephraim Chambers' *Cyclopaedia* (1728) was the earliest to use cross-references. Diderot's 35-volume *Encyclopédie* (1751–65) used specialist contributors and editors (*see* Encyclopedists), but its ideological bias left gaps that the first *Encyclopedia Britannica* (1768–71) sought to fill. Major encyclopedias that first appeared in the 19th century and are still published in some form include the German *Brockhaus* (1809), the *Encyclopedia Americana* (1833), *Chamber's Encyclopaedia* (1859), and the French *Grand Dictionnaire Universel* (1865–76) of Larousse. In the 20th century the expansion of scientific knowledge has posed particular problems for compilers; in particular the need to keep pace with technology requires frequent updating of reference works. For this reason some modern encyclopedias, including this one, are compiled on computer-based systems and typeset by computer.

Encyclopedists (French name: Encyclopédistes) The French intellectuals who contributed to *Diderot's monumental *Encyclopédie*, published in 28 volumes between 1751 and 1772. Five more volumes were published in 1776–77. Over 200 scholarly experts, including such leading figures of the *Enlightenment as Voltaire, Rousseau, and d'Alembert, contributed articles that combined scientific facts and radical philosophical thinking. By their appeal to reason, rather than faith, the Encyclopedists threatened the authority of church and state.

Enderby Land An area in Antarctica, on the Indian Ocean E of Queen Maud Land. The coast is mountainous and the interior consists of an ice-capped plateau. The site of a Russian research station, it is claimed by Australia.

Enders, John Franklin (1897–1985) US microbiologist, who shared the 1954 Nobel Prize with Frederick *Robbins and Thomas Weller (1915–) for their work on *viruses. In 1948 they discovered a method of growing virus cultures by adding penicillin to prevent the growth of bacteria, a problem that had plagued previous attempts. Their work paved the way for the development of vaccines to prevent viral diseases.

endive An annual or biennial plant, *Cichorium endivia*, probably native to S Asia and N China and cultivated widely. It has a rosette of shiny leaves, either curled and narrow (var. *crispa*), used for salads, or broad (*latifolia*), used for cooking. The pale-blue, daisy-like flowers grow on spikes up to 40 in (100 cm) high. Family: **Compositae*. *See also* chicory.

Endlicher, Stephan Ladislaus (1804–49) Hungarian botanist, who proposed a system of plant classification based on two groups: thallophytes (algae, fungi, and lichens) and cormophytes (mosses, ferns, and seed plants). Although based on erroneous principles, his system was adopted throughout Europe for a time.

endocrine glands Ductless glands that produce and secrete *hormones into the bloodstream. Most are regulated by hormones from the *pituitary gland, which is itself controlled by neurohormones secreted by the *hypothalamus. Other endocrine glands include the *thyroid, *adrenal, and *parathyroid glands, parts of the *pancreas (the islets of Langerhans), and the ovaries and testes. The wall of the intestine also contains many endocrine cells that release hormones, such as secretin and gastrin, controlling the secretion of digestive enzymes. The study of the endocrine glands in health and disease is called **endocrinology**.

endorphins. *See* encephalins.

endoscopy Examination of the interior of the body by means of a viewing instrument (endoscope) as an aid to diagnosis. There are many types of endoscopes, specialized for viewing different organs. The modern endoscope for examining the stomach and intestine is a flexible *fiberoptic instrument, which is swallowed by the patient. It enables all areas to be observed and photographed and often has attachments for removing tissue specimens for *biopsy. Endoscopy of the gastrointestinal tract is particularly useful for identifying sites of intestinal bleeding and for diagnosing peptic ulcers and tumors.

Endymion In Greek legend, a beautiful youth, either a shepherd of Caria or a king of Elis, who was put into an everlasting sleep by Selene, goddess of the moon, so that she could enjoy his beauty forever.

energy A property of a system that enables it to do work, i.e to move the point of application of a force. The several forms of energy can be converted into each other under appropriate conditions. *Kinetic energy is energy of motion, whereas *potential energy is stored energy, for example the energy stored in a body by virtue of its position in a gravitational or electric field. Other forms of energy include heat (the kinetic energy of the atoms and molecules in a body), chemical energy (the potential energy stored in the chemical bonds between atoms in a substance), nuclear energy (the potential energy stored in the atomic nucleus), and radiant energy (the energy associated with electromagnetic waves).

As a consequence of the special theory of relativity, mass (*m*) has also to be regarded as a special form of energy (*E*), in accordance with the equation $E = mc^2$, where *c* is the velocity of light. Thus the production of nuclear energy involves a loss of mass in the fuel. However, the sum of the mass and the energy is conserved (*see* conservation of mass and energy). Energy is measured in joules (SI units), calories or ergs (c.g.s. units), kilowatt-hours or British thermal units (Imperial units).

Energy sources: man's first use of energy (other than that of his own body or the body of animals) came with the discovery of fire. For combustion is a process in which chemical energy is converted into heat energy. The first fuel was wood; but fossil fuels (asphalt, coal, oil, natural gas) have been in use for about 8000 years. However, it was the *industrial revolution and the later advent of motorized transport that brought explosive increases in the demand for energy and consequently for fossil fuels. These demands have steadily increased during the 20th century, especially with the spread of technology throughout the world. There is now great concern over the remaining reserves of fossil fuels, which some experts believe will be exhausted in less than a hundred years. Nuclear fission reactors (*see* nuclear energy), a source independent of fossil fuels, now provide some 10% of the world's energy needs and alternative sources, such as solar, tidal, wind, and geothermal power, are being actively explored. However, if it can be successfully harnessed, nuclear fusion (*see* thermonuclear reactor) will be the most abundant energy source in the next century.

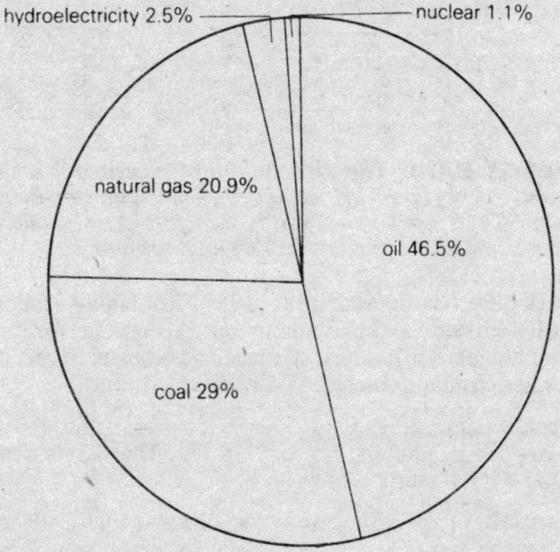

ENERGY *World primary sources.*

Energy, Department of (DOE) US cabinet-level agency that provides the framework for a comprehensive and balanced national energy plan. Headed by the secretary of energy, it researches and develops energy technology and conservation programs and markets federal power. Established in 1977, it took over certain functions of the departments of Commerce and the Interior.

energy band A concept used to explain the electrical properties of solids, particularly *semiconductors. Electrons need to have a minimum energy, E_V, to free them from the atoms of the solid. Below this energy they are said to be in the valence band. To be able to move through the solid, so that they constitute a current, they need to be above another energy level, E_c, in the so-called conduction band. In an insulator, E_c is significantly greater than E_V and there are effectively no electrons in the conduction band. In a conductor, there are many electrons with energy greater than E_c, and E_c may be less than E_V, i.e., the conduction and valence bands are very close or overlap. A pure semiconductor at *absolute zero behaves like an insulator, but the difference between E_c and E_V is small. With an increase in temperature (a measure of the average energy of the particles in the material), some electrons enter the conduction band. Also, the presence of impurities in a semiconductor crystal brings electrons of an intermediate energy level with it, since E_V and E_c vary from one material to another. Depending on the type of impurity, the number of electrons in either the conduction band or the valence band at a particular temperature, will increase, changing the electrical properties of the solid.

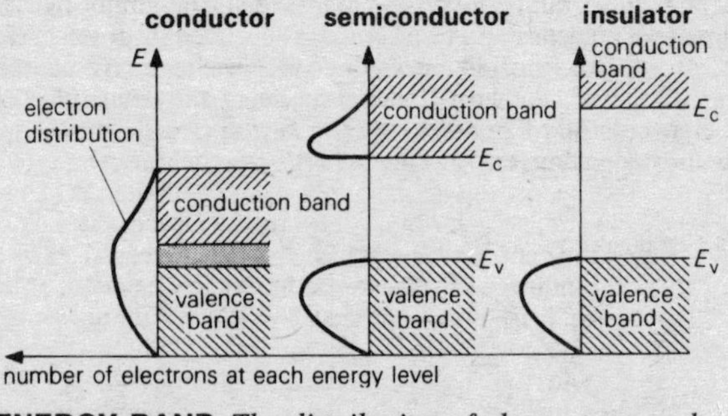

ENERGY BAND *The distribution of electrons over the various energy levels in a conductor, semiconductor, and insulator. There are no electrons in the "forbidden" band between E_c and E_v in semiconductors and insulators.*

Enesco, Georges (G. Enescu; 1881–1955) Romanian violinist and composer. He settled in Paris and had a long and brilliant performing career; he composed symphonies, sonatas, and nationalistic Romanian rhapsodies. A distinguished teacher, his pupils included Menuhin.

Engadin (French name: Engadine) The Swiss part of the upper Inn Valley, divided into Upper Engadin and Lower Engadin. Tourism is important and it contains several winter-sports centers.

Engels, Friedrich (1820–95) German socialist and chief collaborator of Karl *Marx. For a time he managed a factory in Manchester, England. In 1844 he met Marx, and was able to introduce him to English economic conditions and the British working-class movement. They wrote the *Communist Manifesto* (1848), in which they predicted the eventual overthrow of capitalism in favor of a classless society. Among Engels' other works are the *Condition of the Working Class in England in 1844* (1845). His *Anti-Dühring* (1878) systematizes *dialectical materialism. After Marx's death, he edited the last volume of *Das Kapital* (1885).

engineering The systematic application of scientifc knowledge to the design, creation, and use of structures and machines. Engineering has its roots in the constructions in classical times by military engineers of harbors, roads, aqueducts, tunnels, canals, and siege machines. *Civil engineering arose from the study and design of such static structures as bridges, dams, buildings, etc., whereas *mechanical engineering is concerned with dynamical systems, such as machinery and engines. Other important branches of engineering are *electrical engineering, aeronautical engineering, and *chemical engineering.

engineering drawing A systematic method of producing a drawing to scale of machines, their components, or other technical structures to convey the shape, dimensions, and other information to the constructor. They usually consist of a series of orthogonal projections, side elevations, plans, and other views or details depending on the complexity of the object.

England The largest political division in the *United Kingdom. With Wales to the W and Scotland to the N, it is separated from the mainland of Europe by the North Sea and the English Channel and from Ireland by the Irish Sea. It consists of two main zones: the lowlands, which extend across the Midlands, the SE, East Anglia, and the Fens, and the highlands of the Pennines and the Lake District in the N and the granite uplands of Dartmoor and Exmoor in the SW. The chief rivers are the Thames and the Severn. The center of government and administration of the UK, England is also the wealthiest and most populous of the UK countries. *Economy*: the development of industry has been a major contributor to England's wealth. Mineral extraction has historically been of importance and the recent exploitation of North Sea oil and gas continues to make an important contribution to the economy. The main English coalfields are situated in the East Midlands, Yorkshire, and Northumberland and Durham. The production of iron ore has declined in recent years and there is an increased reliance on imports. Manufacturing industries are centered in Greater London, Birmingham, Lancashire, Yorkshire, Tyneside, and Teeside, although there has been a dramatic decline in manufacturing employment in London in recent years. The production of motor vehicles faces strong competition from oversees competitors. Other major industries include heavy engineering, petrochemicals, and pharmaceuticals (Manchester), food processing (Liverpool), and steel processing (Sheffield). Despite the expansion of industries based on advanced technology, together with the reorganization and modernization of older industries, the decline of heavy industry (including shipbuilding) has led to high levels of unemployment in these areas. Agriculture has increased in productivity, although the number of people employed in this sector has decreased. The greatest proportion of crop land is in the E and SE, producing chiefly cereals, potatoes, and sugar beet. Fishing and tourism are also important sources of revenue. *History*: there is much archeological evidence of prehistoric settlement in England but historical records begin with the Roman occupation, from 43 AD until the early 5th century. Christianity was introduced in the 4th century, and conquests between the 3rd and 7th centuries by *Angles, *Saxons, and *Jutes led to the establishment of independent kingdoms (*see* Mercia; Northumbria; Wessex), which were united in the 9th century under Wessex. By the late 800s the Danes had established themselves and from 1016 to 1042 the English were ruled successively by the Danish kings *Canute and *Hardecanute. The *Norman conquest (1066) ended the *Anglo-Saxon period of English history and established a new dynasty of Norman kings. In 1455 the rival claims of the Houses of *Lancaster and *York precipitated the Wars of the *Roses, which lasted until Richard III's defeat (1485) by Henry *Tudor. The 16th century saw the establishment of Protestantism in England (*see* Reformation), the formal union of England and Wales (*see* Union, Acts of), and, under Elizabeth I, a significant development in overseas exploration and trade. The consequent rivalry with Spain culminated in the English defeat of the *Armada (1588). The Tudors were succeeded by the *Stuarts in 1603, when James VI of Scotland ascended the English throne as *James I. The unpopularity of James and his son Charles I brought about the *Civil War, which ended with Charles' execution (1649) and the establishment of republican government. The Stuart *Restoration (1660) followed the fall of Oliver Cromwell's *Protectorate but the authoritarian and pro-Catholic policies of James II brought about his deposition in 1688 and the succession of William of Orange and his Stuart wife Mary. The 18th century saw union with Scotland (1707), the development of *cabinet government during the administration of Sir Robert Walpole, and the loss of the American colonies (1783; *see* American Revolution). Following union with Ireland in 1801, England, Wales, Scotland, and Ireland became the United Kingdom of Great Britian and Ireland. With the *industrial revolution the UK evolved from an agricultural to an industrial economy, and political influence shifted from the landowners to the urban middle class. The growing labor movement led to the formation in 1900 of the *Labour Party, which was subsequently to replace the Liberals as one of the two chief political parties. The 19th century also saw the heyday of the British *Empire and the beginning of colonial rivalry with Germany, which was a significant factor in the outbreak of *World War I. The interwar years were dominated by the Depression and the growing threat of fascist governments abroad, which culminated in *World War II. Successive governments have failed to deal effectively with Britain's post-war economic decline and with the prolonged crisis in Northern *Ireland. Area: 50,332 sq mi (130,360 sq km). Population (1990): 48,750,000. Capital: London. *See also* Great Britain.

Engler, Gustav Heinrich Adolf (1844–1930) German botanist, who proposed a system of plant classification that is still widely accepted. Engler adapted *Eichler's system (1883) to encompass the whole plant kingdom. Engler held several important administrative posts in plant science and was an expert on plant geography.

English A West Germanic language spoken originally in Britain but now also in the US, Canada, New Zealand, Australia, and many other parts of the world. It is the world's most widely known and used language. Its history may be divided into three periods. In the Old English period (c. 450–1100 AD), four dialects were spoken: Northumbrian, Mercian, Kentish, and West Saxon. The last became the standard form. Middle English refers to the period from 1100 to 1500, when five dialects were spoken: Northern (developed from Northumbrian), West and East Midlands (diverging from Mercian), South Western (from West Saxon) and South Eastern (from Kentish). Each developed in characteristic ways but in general the influence of French after the Norman conquest brought new vocabulary and sound patterns. Modern English covers the period from 1500 and was much influenced by the speech of London. English slowly became a relatively uninflected language with great flexibility in the way words may function. Its vocabulary is about half Germanic and half Romance with many other borrowings.

English art and architecture The styles of art and architecture found in England. Before the Norman conquest the art of the British Isles was identified with *Celtic art, Roman art and architecture, and Anglo-Saxon art. Illuminated manuscripts constituted the outstanding contribution of Anglo-Saxon artists, and manuscripts of a high quality continued to be produced in the later Middle

Ages. The Normans introduced *Romanesque art and architecture (e.g. Durham Cathedral). In the 12th century, *Gothic architecture was introduced, which developed into several distinct styles and became the indigenous church architecture of the Middle Ages. In the early 17th century the architect Inigo *Jones introduced *Palladianism to England, and, among painters, the Flemings *Rubens and *Van Dyck towered above their English comtemporaries. Architecture in the late 17th century was dominated by *Wren, Vanbrugh, and Hawksmoor, exponents of the *baroque. The 18th and early 19th centuries saw the great era of town architecture; this was followed by the *Gothic revival. Notable painters of the 18th century were *Hogarth, *Reynolds, and *Gainsborough. Romanticism found expression in the work of *Turner and *Constable and the 19th century also witnessed the formation of the *Pre-Raphaelite Brotherhood, which, with the work of William *Morris, influenced *Art Nouveau in England. The philosophy of "art for art's sake" was articulated by *Sickert. The 20th century has produced outstanding sculptors, including *Epstein *Hepworth, and Henry *Moore, and painters, such as Augustus *John, Graham *Sutherland, Stanley *Spencer, L. S. *Lowry, and Francis *Bacon.

English Channel (French name: La Manche) An arm of the Atlantic Ocean in NW Europe, between England and France. It is one of the busiest shipping lanes in the world. Many attempts at swimming the Channel (usually across the Strait of *Dover) have been made; the first successful one was by Capt Webb (1875). *See also* Channel Tunnel.

English literature The earliest works of the Old English period (407–1066 AD) are heroic poems, notably the epic *Beowulf*, which belong to a Germanic oral tradition of alliterative unrhymed verse and were not put into written form until the 7th century. There are also a number of remarkable, shorter poems, such as the elegies *The Wanderer* and *The Seafarer*, and many poems on Christian subjects. Major Old English religious writers, such as Bede and Alcuin, wrote in Latin: English prose started with the translations from Latin made by King Alfred and developed in the *Anglo-Saxon Chronicle*, the compilation of which he initiated.

Norman-French displaced Old English as the dominant written language after the Conquest, but the native language, enriched by French, was firmly re-established in the 14th century in the Middle English poetry of Chaucer, whose works were indebted to Italian Renaissance authors, especially Dante, Petrarch, and Boccaccio. The native alliterative tradition continued in such poems as *Piers Plowman, Pearl*, and *Gawain and the Green Knight*. Printing was introduced in 1476 by Caxton.

Although Chaucer had introduced Renaissance influences, it was not until the 16th century that the full effects of humanism were felt. The sonnet was introduced, and Spenser produced the Elizabethan allegorical epic *The Faerie Queene* (1590). The blank-verse plays of Kyd and Marlowe prepared the way for the dramas of Shakespeare, Jonson, and their 17th-century successors. Donne and the Metaphysical school are the most important poets of the early 17th century, while Milton dominates the latter part. Among the most influential prose works were the Authorized Version of the Bible and Bunyan's *The Pilgrim's Progress* (1678).

During the Restoration (from 1660), Dryden developed the heroic couplet in his satires and made an important contribution to modern English prose in his criticism. The classical ideals of the Augustan Age (c. 1690–1740) were embodied in the satirical verse of Pope and the essays of Addison and Steele and were maintained by later writers, such as Johnson, Goldsmith, and Sheridan. Swift was the outstanding prose satirist of the period.

Various economic and social factors during the early 18th century contributed to the emergence of the novel, pioneered by Richardson, Fielding, Defoe, Smollett, Sterne, and various authors of the "Gothic" novel of horror. It reached its full development in the works of Jane Austen, Walter Scott, Thackeray, the Brontës, Dickens, George Eliot, Trollope, Meredith, Hardy, Conrad, and the American Henry James.

In the early 19th century the classicism of the previous period was challenged by the Romantic movement. Its precursor was Blake and its leading figures were Wordsworth, Coleridge, Keats, Shelley, and Byron. Their chief successors in the Victorian era were Tennyson, Browning, Matthew Arnold, and Swinburne. Macaulay, John Stuart Mill, Carlyle, Ruskin, and Pater were among the influential prose writers. At the turn of the century the comedies of Wilde and Shaw enlivened the English theater; prior to World War I Kipling, Hardy, Yeats, Belloc, Chesterton, Wells, Housman, and de la Mare produced a distinguished body of verse as well as fiction and criticism. Postwar poetry was dominated by Eliot, Auden, MacNeice, Spender, and the later work of Yeats. Among the leading novelists and prose writers were Forster, Joyce, D. H. Lawrence, Woolf, Aldous Huxley, Orwell, Isherwood, Greene, and Evelyn Waugh. Between World War II and the present appeared the poems of Dylan Thomas and Philip Larkin; the plays of Osborne, Pinter, and Tom Stoppard; and the novels of Kingsley Amis, Muriel Spark, Iris Murdoch, Anthony Powell, and Anthony Burgess.

English-Speaking Union An organization, based in London, that promotes friendship and understanding between English-speaking countries. It was founded by Sir Evelyn Wrench (1882–1966) in 1918 and now has 160 branches in the UK, North America, Australasia, India, and the Caribbean.

engraving A method of producing a reproductive plate by chiseling, carving, or biting the design onto a metal or wood plate. Intaglio engraving denotes such methods as *etching, *mezzotint, and soft- or hard-ground engraving, in which the printed impression pulls ink from inside the carved grooves. By contrast, relief engraving denotes methods, such as *woodcut, in which the carved-away areas are not inked. Intaglio engraving allows for extreme delicacy and detail; relief engraving is often exploited for illustrations, where force and clarity are needed.

Enlightenment (*or* Age of Reason) An 18th-century philosophical movement that sought to replace orthodox, authoritarian beliefs with rational, scientific inquiry. During the 17th century, as scientific knowledge increased, such scholars as Newton, Locke, Pascal, and Descartes questioned accepted beliefs, and criticism of established society and assumptions spread throughout Europe. In France the *Philosophes (e.g. Voltaire) attacked established religion (*see* deism) and the Enlightenment beliefs in individual liberty and equality were embodied in the work of Rousseau and other *Encyclopedists. The movement came to an end with the French Revolution.

Enlightened despots were those European monarchs (e.g. Emperor *Joseph II, Frederick the Great of Prussia, and Catherine the Great of Russia) who introduced reforms, based on the ideas of the Enlightenment, by authoritarian means.

Enlil The Sumerian god of the sky and storms. He was the patron deity of *Nippur and, with *Anu and *Ea, formed the supreme trinity in the Sumerian pantheon.

Ennius, Quintus (238–169 BC) Roman poet. After service in the second Punic War, he was brought to Rome by the elder Cato in 204 and became a Roman citizen in 184. His works include tragic dramas adapted from the Greek, philosophical poems, epigrams, and the *Annals*, a national epic in 18 books narrating the history of Rome from Aeneas to his own time. Only fragments of his works survive.

Enoch An Old Testament patriarch. **The Books of Enoch** are two biblical books ascribed to him; they were in fact written in the 2nd century BC and 1st century AD respectively. The first, a composite work of Jewish origin, is a series of apocalyptic visions. The second is of Hellenistic origin and records revelations supposedly given to Enoch, his journey to heaven, and advice to his children.

enosis. *See* EOKA.

Enragés (French: Madmen) Members of an extremist French Revolutionary group (1793). Led by Jacques Roux (d. 1794), they demanded direct government action to alleviate food shortages and to help the poor. Actively encouraging food riots, their leaders were arrested by the Committee of *Public Safety and their extremist role was adopted by the Hébertists (*see* Hébert).

Enschede 52 13N 6 55E A city in the E Netherlands, in Overijssel province. It is an important center of the Dutch cotton industry. Population (1991 est): 147,000.

Ensor, James Sydney, Baron (1860–1949) Belgian painter; his father was English but he was born and spent most of his life in Ostend. He was initially condemned for what was thought his crude technique, but the originality of his grotesque imagery of masks and skeletons, as in the symbolic representation of modern social evils in *Entry of Christ into Brussels* (1888), received popular recognition in the 1920s.

Entebbe 0 05N 39 29E A city in Uganda, in Buganda on the NW shore of Lake Victoria. It was the administrative center of Uganda until 1958 but is now largely residential. It contains Uganda's international airport, where, in 1976, Israeli hostages taken from a hijacked French plane by Palestinian guerrillas were rescued by Israeli troops. Population: 21,000.

entellus. *See* langur.

Entente Cordiale (1904) An agreement between France and Britain. During the 19th century, colonial expansion, especially in Africa, caused tension between France, Britian, and Germany. France feared a German war and Britain and France, partly through Edward VII's efforts to reconcile their traditional enmity, signed the Entente Cordiale. This was not an alliance but a mutual recognition of each other's colonial interests, especially France's in Morocco and Britain's in Egypt. The agreement brought greater diplomatic cooperation against German pressure.

enthalpy (H) A thermodynamic property of a system equal to its internal energy plus the product of its pressure and volume. The change in enthalpy (ΔH) when a chemical reaction takes place is equal to the heat given out or absorbed. By convention ΔH is negative if heat is evolved by the reaction.

entomology The study of insects. Entomology probably has its origins in the observations of *Aristotle. Modern entomology dates from the 17th century, when the introduction of microscopy enabled fine details of insect anatomy to be described; for instance, in the work of the Dutch naturalist Jan *Swammerdam. Today attention is focused especially on insect pests, since knowledge of their physiology and ecology is of prime importance in their control or eradication.

entrepreneur An individual in a capitalist economy who is prepared to commit capital and to initiate a commercial venture. Entrepreneurship is often counted as a fourth factor of production (the others being land, labor, and capital), providing the spark that sets the others off. With the development of large corporations and a large public sector in most economies, the role of the individual entrepreneur has somewhat diminished.

entropy A measure of the disorder of a system, used in *thermodynamics. Thus a solid has less entropy than a liquid since the constituent particles in a solid are in a more ordered state. Originally defined in connection with the second law of thermodynamics, the change in entropy of a reversible system is equal to the energy absorbed by the system divided by the thermodynamic temperature at which the change takes place. The entropy of a closed system never decreases during a thermodynamic process: if it increases the process is irreversible; if it remains unchanged it is reversible. *See also* heat death of the universe.

Enugu 6 20N 7 29E A city in S Nigeria. It developed following the discovery of nearby coal in 1909 and is an important mining, manufacturing, and trade center. It contains part of the University of Nigeria (1962). Population (1992 est): 286,000.

Enver Pasha (1881–1922) Turkish soldier and politician, who was a leader of the *Young Turk revolution of 1908. During World War I he was one of the three real rulers of the Ottoman Empire. His aim was to unite the Turks of central Asia with those of Turkey in one state. He was killed in a rising in central Asia against the Bolsheviks.

Environmental Protection Agency (EPA) US executive branch agency that protects and enhances the environment under laws enacted by Congress. It controls and abates pollution in the areas of air, water, solid waste, pesticides, radiation, and toxic substances. Established in 1970, its headquarters are in Washington, D.C.

enzymes An important group of proteins that act as biological catalysts, i.e. they speed up (or slow down) the rate of chemical reactions in living organisms. Enzymes are manufactured by cells according to the *genetic code carried by the chromosomes; because each enzyme catalyzes a specific reaction, it is the enzymes that determine the function of the cell. The structure of enzymes and the nature of their active sites (where they bind to reacting molecules) can be determined by such techniques as X-ray diffraction. Control of *metabolism is largely exerted through regulation of enzyme production and activity, which are inhibited by such poisons as cyanide. Many enzymes require associated nonprotein *coenzymes to function properly.

Eocene epoch. *See* Tertiary period.

eohippus An extinct ancestor of the *horse, also called *Hyracotherium* or dawn horse, that lived in the Eocene epoch (about 55 million to 40 million years ago). About 11 in (28 cm) tall, it was a browsing, forest dweller with a short neck and had four toes on the forefoot and three on the hindfoot. *See also* Hipparion.

Eos. *See* Aurora.

Epaminondas (c. 418–362 BC) Theban general and military strategist, who defeated Sparta at *Leuctra in 371, thereby ending the military supremacy of Sparta in Greece. He was the first to use cavalry to support infantry in a coordinated attack and his military innovations influenced both Philip II and Alexander the Great of Macedon. He died in the battle of Mantinea, in which the Spartans were defeated.

Épernay 49 02N 3 58E A city in NE France, in the Marne department on the Marne River. A center for the wine industry of Champagne, it has famous underground wine cellars. Population (1975): 31,108.

ephedrine A drug with effects resembling those of *adrenaline. It stimulates the heart, dilates the bronchi (air passages to the lungs), and has marked effects on the nervous system. Ephedrine is used mainly to treat asthma. Side effects include trembling and feelings of anxiety.

ephemeral A plant that completes its life cycle—from germination to seed production—in under a year, enabling more than one generation to be produced within a single year. Many common weeds, such as groundsel and chickweed, are ephemerals.

ephemeris (Greek: diary) A reference manual, usually published annually, that is used in astronomical observation and navigation. It lists the predicted positions of the sun, moon, and planets in the forthcoming year and also gives times of eclipses, stellar positions, and other similar information.

Ephesians, Epistle of Paul to the A New Testament book that originated as a circular letter from the Apostle Paul to churches in Asia Manor. Written about 60 AD, it deals with a number of religious and moral points and stresses the equality of Jewish and Gentile Christians.

Ephesus An ancient Greek city and trading center on the Ionian coast of *Asia Minor. *Croesus of *Lydia captured it in 550 BC. It maintained its prosperity under the Persians and Alexander the Great. In Roman times Ephesus was rivaled only by *Alexandria as a commercial center. It was sacked by the *Goths in 262 AD. *See also* Artemis, Temple of.

Ephraim, tribe of One of the 12 *tribes of Israel. It claimed descent from Ephraim, the son of Joseph and grandson of Jacob and Rachel. It occupied mountainous territory NW of the Dead Sea.

epic A long narrative poem concerning a heroic theme and written in an appropriately dignified style. The *Iliad* and the *Odyssey* of Homer (8th century BC) are the earliest epics in western literature and are the models of Virgil's *Aeneid* (c. 29–19 BC), in which the hero Aeneas is seen as representing the national spirit of Rome. The *Aeneid* inspired later national epics, such as Camões' *Os Lusíadas* (1572) and Ronsard's *Franciade* (1572). In English literature, examples include the Old English *Beowulf* (8th century AD), Spenser's *Faerie Queene* (1589–96), a mixture of epic and romance, and Milton's *Paradise Lost* (1667).

epicenter. *See* earthquake.

Epictetus (c. 60–110 AD) Stoic philosopher. A freed slave, Epictetus was banished, with other philosophers, from Rome in 89 AD and settled in Epirus. He taught that loving one's enemies, repudiating pleasure, and understanding that all men are brothers are ways to serenity. Epictetus' teachings were preserved by his pupil *Arrian. *See also* Stoicism.

Epicureanism A school of philosophy founded by *Epicurus around 300 BC in Athens. He taught that the highest good was pleasure and the avoidance of pain, based on tranquility of mind and conscience. Many seeking a license for the pursuit of pleasure have styled themselves Epicureans, giving the term its common sense of "unashamed sensualist." True Epicureans, however, seek serenity through detachment from worldly affairs.

Epicurus (341–270 BC) Greek philosopher and founder of the school of *Epicureanism. In 306 BC he began teaching in a garden in Athens. Virtuous and temperate, he was a good friend and citizen but avoided politics, following his maxim "Live unseen and unknown." His surviving works are few and fragmentary but his philosophy, especially his *atomism, was expounded by *Lucretius.

Epidauros A city state of ancient Greece, situated across the Saronic Gulf from *Athens. Its sanctuary of *Asclepius was famous in antiquity. Patients asleep in the temple were visited by the god in their dreams and treated by his priests next morning; grateful inscriptions record numerous cures. The 4th-century BC theater (part of the temple complex) is sufficiently preserved to be still used for plays.

epidemiology The science that investigates the incidence and causative factors of diseases that are associated with a particular environment or way of life. Epidemiologists have enlarged their studies from the classical epidemics of communicable diseases, such as smallpox and cholera, to include noncommunicable diseases associated with modern societies. Thus they have demonstrated the connection between cigarette smoking and lung cancer, diet and coronary heart disease, etc.

epidermis The outermost layer of cells in animals and plants. In lower animals (invertebrates) it often secretes a protective *cuticle. In higher animals (including mammals) it forms the outer layer of the □skin. In plants the epidermis usually consists of a single layer of cells, but aerial organs have extra protection in the form of a noncellular waxy cuticle. Both layers prevent dehydration of internal tissues, lessen damage by bacteria and fungi, and reduce attack by such pests as aphids.

epididymis. *See* testis.

epiglottis A leaf-shaped flap of cartilage at the root of the tongue that prevents food and fluid from entering the windpipe during swallowing. As it is swallowed, the food presses the epiglottis down against the opening of the larynx (at the top of the windpipe). This, combined with the reflex upward movement of the larynx that occurs during swallowing, effectively seals off the entrance to the windpipe.

epilepsy A disease characterized by fits or sudden loss of consciousness. Epilepsy is common—Dostoievski, Van Gogh, Julius Caesar, and Byron all suffered from it. There are several different forms. In grand mal epilepsy the patient suddenly becomes stiff, loses consciousness, and has convulsions. The fit lasts only a few minutes but afterward he is sleepy and confused. Petit mal is a mild form seen only in children, who suddenly lose consciousness but usually do not fall down. Petit mal attacks last only a few seconds. Temporal lobe epilepsy is characterized by peculiar forms of behavior and strange sensations. All forms are treated with anticonvulsant drugs.

Épinal 48 10N 6 28E A city in E France, the capital of the Vosges department on the Moselle River. It is the center for a region manufacturing cotton goods and artificial fibers. Population (1975): 42,810.

epinephrine. *See* adrenaline.

Epiphany (*or* Twelfth Day) A Christian feast celebrated on Jan 6. In Eastern Orthodox Churches it commemorates the baptism of Jesus. Introduced to the West in the 4th century, it developed as a celebration of the coming of the *Magi to Bethlehem, representing the manifestation (Greek: *epiphaneia*) of Christ to the Gentiles. **Twelfth Night** is the night preceding Epiphany and traditionally devoted to festivities and entertainments. In several countries gifts are exchanged on Epiphany rather than at Christmas.

epiphyte A plant that grows on another plant for support. Epiphytes are not parasites: some obtain nourishment from decaying plant remains and many solve the problem of obtaining water by developing such structures as aerial roots. Some orchids are epiphytic.

Epirus (*or* Ípiros) A coastal region of NW Greece and S Albania, bordering on the Ionian Sea. Its tribes were united in the 4th century BC in a kingdom that reached its peak under *Pyrrhus in the early 3rd century BC. Sacked by the Romans in 167, it became part of the province of Macedonia in 148 BC. In the 13th century AD it briefly formed an independent kingdom before falling to the Serbs and Albanians and then (1430) to the Ottoman Turks. It was divided between Greece and Albania in 1913.

episcopacy In Christian Churches, government by bishops. The biblical basis of episcopacy is equivocal, and many Protestant Churches, for example the Congregational and Presbyterian, have adopted different methods. In the Roman Catholic and Orthodox Churches the episcopal hierarchy is seen as a continuation of the original group of apostles chosen by Christ (*see* Apostolic Succession). Among the Reformed Churches episcopal government is retained in whole or in part by Anglicans, Methodists, and Lutherans.

epistemology The philosophical discipline that considers the nature, basis, and limits of knowledge. Ancient Greek philosophers examined the relations between knowledge, truth, and belief, and the question of whether knowledge exists independently of a knower. *Locke and *Kant, however, first treated epistemology as fundamental to all philosophical and scientific enquiry. It is one of the three main branches of modern *philosophy.

Epistles The 21 books of the *New Testament that were written as letters. These are arranged in two groups, those by Paul (13) and those by others (7), divided by the Epistle to the Hebrews, of which the author is unknown. Of Paul's letters, nine are to specific churches and four to individuals. The remainder are attributed to James, Peter (2), John (3), and Jude. In the liturgy of many Christian Churches, the Epistle is the name of the first of two passages of Scripture recited or sung at the celebration of the Eucharist, the second being the Gospel. It is usually a passage from the New Testament Epistles but may be a passage from the Old Testament, Acts, or Revelation.

epithelium A tissue that forms the linings of the mouth, nose, pharynx, intestines, respiratory tract, and the skin. There are different types of epithelia specialized for different functions. For example, the cells of the intestinal epithelium are glandular, secreting digestive enzymes, while the skin epithelium produces a tough protective layer of keratin.

epoch. *See* geological time scale.

epoxy resin A type of synthetic *resin made by polymerizing groups containing a three-membered ring that includes the –O– atom (epoxy group). They are themselves viscous liquids but set to hard clear solids on the addition of such curing agents as amines. Epoxy resins are extensively used as adhesives, the resin and the curing agent being mixed immediately before use.

Epstein, Sir Jacob (1880–1959) British sculptor, born in the US. Working in London after 1905, he achieved notoriety with his nude figures for the British Medical Association (1907–08) and his memorial tomb to Oscar Wilde (1912). After 1912 he briefly experimented with avant-garde sculpture, influenced by primitive art, and continued to provoke public criticism with such sculptures as *Rima*, a memorial to the author William Hudson (1925), and *Genesis* (1931). However, his bronze portrait busts of such celebrities as Conrad (1924), Einstein (1933), and T. S. □Eliot were more favorably received.

Equal Rights Amendment (ERA) Proposed amendment to the US Constitution. Reading "equality of rights under the law shall not be denied or abridged by the United States nor by any State on account of sex" and "Congress shall have the power to enforce, by appropriate legislation, the provisions of this article," its purpose is to ban sex discrimination. Passed by Congress in 1971 and 1972, the controversial issue failed to achieve ratification by the necessary 38 states by the extended deadline (June 1982). It was reintroduced in Congress (July 1982), but was defeated in the House of Representatives (1983).

equation A mathematical statement in which two expressions, usually containing at least one variable or unknown quantity, are equated. For example, the simple algebraic expression $2x + 4 = 8$ is an equation that can be simplified, or solved, to give a value of 2 for the unknown quantity x: this is known as the root of the equation. Equations are also used to show the general interdependence of several quantities, without necessarily finding their specific values. The degree of an equation is equal to the highest value of the exponent of the variable. A **linear equation** is of the first degree and has the form $y = mx + c$. A *graph of such an equation is a straight line, which (in the Cartesian *coordinate system) has a *gradient equal to m and cuts the y-axis at c. A *quadratic equation is of the second degree, i.e. contains terms in x^2.

Two or more equations in which all the variables must obey all the equations are called **simultaneous equations**. For a complete solution of simultaneous equations there must be as many equations as there are variables.

equation of time. *See* sundial.

equator The great circle around the earth at latitude 0°, lying midway between the poles in a plane at right angles to the earth's axis. It is 24,902 mi (40,076 km) long and divides the N from the S hemisphere.

Equatorial Guinea, Republic of A small country in W central Africa, on the Gulf of Guinea. It consists of two provinces: mainland Mbini (formerly Río Muni), which includes several offshore islands; and the island of Bioko (formerly Macías Nguema), which includes the island of Piagalu (formerly Annobón) about 100 miles to the SW. Mbini is mainly tropical forest, with a coastal plain rising gradually to over 3000 ft (1000 m) in the interior; Bioko is dominated by three extinct volcanoes, the highest of which reaches 9865 ft (3007 m). The inhabitants are mainly *Fang, Fernandinos, and the indigenous Bubi (descendants of slaves from West Africa), who inhabit Bioko. *Economy*: chiefly agricultural, the main crops being cocoa on Bioko, and coffee in Mbini, where timber is also produced. There is little industry, apart from fish processing on Bioko; the main exports are coffee and cocoa. *History*: formerly a Spanish colony, the area became two Spanish provinces in 1959. The country attained some internal self-government in 1964 and was one of the last of the African colonial territories to become independent (in 1968). In 1975 Nigerian immigrant workers were expelled after 50 years in the country, and this has had an adverse effect on the economy. In 1979 the life president Francisco Macías Nguema (1924–79) was overthrown and executed in a coup led by Lt. Col. Teodoro Obiang Nguema Mbasogo. In 1982 voters approved a constitution, hailed as one of the most liberal in Africa, with guarantees of human rights and universal suffrage. In 1983 an abortive coup was mounted against the Obiang government, indicative of unrest in the country. The government subsequently held the country's first elections in 19 years. Obiang was reelected in 1989, but there was still only one slate of candidates on the ballot. Official language: Spanish. Official currency: ekuele of 100 céntimos. Area: 10,831 sq mi (28,051 sq km). Population (1988 est): 336,000. Capital and main port: Malabo (formerly Santa Isabel).

equestrianism The art of horsemanship. As a sport, governed by the Fédération équestre internationale (founded 1921), it involves *dressage, *showjumping, and *horse trails.

equinox Either of the two points at which the *ecliptic intersects the celestial equator (*see* celestial sphere). The ecliptic represents the apparent annual path of the sun around the celestial sphere. The sun crosses the celestial equator from S to N at the **vernal** (*or* spring) **equinox**, usually on Mar 21. It crosses from N to S at the **autumnal equinox**, usually on Sept 23. At the equinoxes the center of the sun is above and below the horizon for equal lengths of time, and night and day are then of almost equal duration.

equity In law, the body of rules applied by the courts to achieve a fair result in cases in which the application of ordinary law would fail to do so. The system developed in England and is followed in the US. The historical distinction between the *common law and equity is due to the failure of the common law to provide a remedy in certain cases, bringing about the custom of applying for redress to the king, who referred the question to the Lord Chancellor's court, the Court of Chancery. Here the rules of equity developed separately from, but by the same method (judicial precedent) as the common law. Now all courts administer both law and equity, the rules of equity prevailing if in conflict with the common law.

equivalence The relationship between two mathematical or logical statements linked so that one is true if and only if the other is true. For example "*a* is greater than *b*" is equivalent to "*b* is less than *a*."

era. *See* geological time scale.

Era of Good Feeling (1817–25) A phrase used to describe the mood of the US during James *Monroe's administration. There were no political conflicts, isolationism was predominant, and the US no longer worried as much about European affairs.

Erasistratus of Ceos (3rd century BC) Greek physician, who discovered the difference between sensory and motor nerves and described the heart as part of a system carrying both air and blood to various parts of the body.

Erasmus, Desiderius (1466–1536) Christian humanist and writer, born at Rotterdam. He was perhaps the most influential of Renaissance thinkers and studied and taught all over Europe. His enthusiasm for learning was matched by his zeal for writing, and he produced many original works and compilations, including *Encomium Moriae* (*Praise of Folly*; 1509), written to amuse his host in England, Thomas *More. His translation of the Greek New Testament, the first ever, conclusively exposed the Vulgate as a secondhand document. He opposed dogmatism and priestly power, yet he never rejected Roman Catholic theology and steadfastly remained impartial throughout the Lutheran conflict with the papacy.

Erastianism The subjection of ecclesiastical affairs to secular authority. It is named for Thomas Erastus (1524–83), a Swiss theologian who opposed the strict views of *Calvinists. He argued that the civil authority has complete power in affairs both of church and state. Richard Hooker defended the argument in England in his *Ecclesiastical Polity* (1594). The *Church of England's subjection to the crown is sometimes described as Erastian.

Eratosthenes of Cyrene (c. 276–c. 194 BC) Greek astronomer; a close friend of *Archimedes. His greatest achievement was his calculation of the earth's circumference. His result, obtained by measuring the sun's position at the summer solstice at two different places, was accurate to within 600 miles.

Erbil. *See* Irbil.

erbium (Er) A lanthanide element, which like *yttrium, *ytterbium, and *terbium is named for Ytterby, a village in Sweden near which lanthanide-rich ores are found. It forms an oxide (Eb_2O_3) and halides (e.g. $EbCl_3$. It is added to phosphores, glasses, and alloys. At no 68; at wt 167.26; mp 881°F (1529°C); bp 1425°F (2510°C).

Ercilla, Alonso de (1533–94) Spanish poet. A courtier of *Philip II, he fought the Araucanian Indians in Chile. His epic *La Araucana* (Part I, 1569; Part 2, 1578; Part 3, 1589–90) is noted for its realistic descriptive passages and its sympathetic treatment of the Indians.

Erebus, Mount 77 40S 167 20E An active volcano on Ross Island, in the Antarctic. Discovered in 1841, it was climbed in 1908. Height: 12,520 ft (3794 m).

Eretria An ancient Greek city in *Euboea. An early leader in commerce and colonization, Eretria was defeated by *Chalcis about 700 BC, after which it declined in importance. The Persians sacked Eretria in 490 BC. It was rebuilt and later joined the *Delian League, but it never regained its former significance.

Erevan. *See* Yerevan.

Erfurt 50 59N 11 00E A city in S Germany, on the Gera River. One of the oldest German cities, it became a member of the Hanseatic League in the 15th century and was of great commercial importance in the 16th century. Notable buildings include the cathedral (1154–1476) and the 13th-century Church of St Severus. Its university, established in 1392, was closed in 1816. Martin Luther studied there (1501–05). Industries include the manufacture of machinery, electrical equipment, textiles, and footwear. Population (1990): 217,000.

erg The unit of energy in the *c.g.s. system equal to the work done when a force of one dyne acts through a distance of one centimeter. 1 erg = 10^{-7} joule.

ergonomics The study of the psychological and physical factors that can be used to improve the design of both machines and systems for human use. In the US the term human-factors engineering is widely used and in other parts of the world ergonomics is known as psychological engineering. The study finds application in many fields, including astronautics, the design of aircraft and cars, and a wide variety of industrial processes. Although it is a young science, having largely grown up since World War II, most university engineering courses now include it.

ergosterol. *See* vitamin D.

ergot A disease caused by the fungus *Claviceps purpurea*, which affects cereals and grasses, especially rye. In affected plants a hard black fungal body develops in place of the grain. Consumption of bread made with diseased grain produces the symptoms of **ergotism**—gangrene of the fingers and toes or convulsions. The gangrenous form of ergotism is accompanied by inflammation and pain in the affected part and in the Middle Ages it was called St Anthony's fire, since a pilgrimage to St Anthony's tomb was believed to result in a cure. Drugs obtained from ergot include ergometrine, used to induce childbirth, and ergotamine, for relieving migraine.

Erhard, Ludwig (1897–1977) West German statesman and economist; Christian Democratic chancellor (1963–66). As minister of economic affairs (1949–63), he was largely responsible for the recovery of German industry after World War II. He succeeded Adenauer as chancellor and subsequently became honorary chairman of the Christain Democratic Party.

Erica. *See* heath.

Ericsson, John (1803–89) US naval engineer, born in Sweden, who in 1836 invented the screw propeller, which replaced paddle wheels in ships. Ericsson also designed the *ironclad *Monitor*, launched in 1862, which was the first warship to have an armored revolving turret. The *Monitor* defeated the Confederate ship *Merrimack* in the first battle between ironclads.

Eridanus A large constellation in the S sky, named for a river in ancient mythology. The only bright star is *Achernar.

Eridu A city of ancient *Sumer, SW of *Ur (S Iraq), continuously occupied from around 5000 to 600 BC. Excavations (1946–49) revealed a *ziggurat, probably devoted to the worship of Eridu's patron deity *Ea.

Erie North American, Iroquoian-speaking Indian tribe found in W New York and N Ohio. Known as the Cat Nation or Panther People, the approximately 15,000 Erie were basically an agricultural people. Spurred on by their neighbors, the Hurons, who had been devastated by the Iroquois, and by threats of Iroquois expansion, the Erie waged an unsuccessful war (1656) against the Iroquois. Severely reduced in numbers, the tribe's remaining members were taken in by the Seneca.

Erie 42 07N 80 05W A city in the US, in Pennsylvania on Lake Erie. Founded in 1753, it is a Great Lakes port and ships coal, timber, iron, and grain. Its manufactures include paper and electrical equipment. Population (1990): 108,718.

Erie, Lake The fourth largest of the Great Lakes in North America, between Canada and the US. Linked with Lake Ontario via the Welland Ship Canal, it forms part of the St Lawrence Seaway system. Its shallow depth causes rapid freezing and it is closed to navigation during winter. Area: 9930 sq mi (25,718 sq km).

Erie Canal A canal that crosses central New York from Albany in the E to Buffalo in the W. Built between 1817 and 1825, the canal was 363 mi (585 km) long, 40 ft (13 m) wide and 4 ft (1.3 m) deep, and had 83 locks and 18 aqueducts. It begins on the Hudson River and runs along one of its tributaries, the Mohawk. The early canal revolutionized the freight business, lowering rates 90%. Competition from railroads forced enlargement of the canal, but it was not until after 1909 that the canal was large enough for barges and became the principal part of the New York State Barge Canal System. Today, due to rerouting through Lake Oneida, the canal is 340 mi (548 km) long; it is 150 ft (46 m) wide and 12 ft (3.7 m) deep.

Erigena, John Scotus (c. 800–c. 877 AD) Medieval philosopher, probably born in Ireland. He is said to have traveled widely and after about 846 lived under the protection of Charles the Bald in France, where he was appointed head of the court school at Paris. He defied ecclesiastical orthodoxy in his writings on predestination and cosmology, which show leanings toward *Neoplatonism, *Pelagianism, and *pantheism.

Erik the Red (late 10th century) Norwegian explorer. Exiled as a child with his father he was brought up in Iceland. In 982 he set out from Iceland on an exploration westward and reached Greenland, where he established the first European colony (c. 986). He was the father of *Leif Eriksson.

Erik XIV (1533–77) King of Sweden (1560–68), whose ambitions in the Baltic led to an inconclusive war with Denmark (1563–70). He unsuccessfully sought marriage with Elizabeth I of England. After becoming insane, he was deposed and imprisoned.

Eriksson, Leif (11th century) Icelandic explorer, the son of *Eric the Red. He was converted to Christianity by Olaf I Tryggvason of Norway around 1000. According to tradition, Eriksson, on his way to promote the faith in Greenland, off course, became the first European to reach America. He landed in a region he called Vinland (Newfoundland or Nova Scotia). His story is told in Icelandic sagas.

Erinyes (*or* Furies) In Greek legend, spirits of vengeance who lived in the underworld and ruthlessly pursued all evildoers. They were three in number and were named (in later writers) Allecto, Tisiphone, and Megaera. In Roman legend they were known as the Furies (Latin *Furiae* or *Dirae*). *See also* Eumenides.

Eris A Greek goddess personifying strife. She was the sister of *Ares. She threw a golden apple inscribed "To the Fairest" among the gods at the wedding feast of Peleus and Thetis. Aphrodite, Hera, and Athena each claimed the apple. The decision was referred to *Paris, who chose Aphrodite because she offered him in return the most beautiful woman as his wife. This myth, known as the Judgment of Paris, explains the origin of the *Trojan War.

Eritrea A country in E Africa, bordering on the Red Sea. A province of Ethiopia until 1993, it consists of a narrow coastal plain rising inland to the Ethiopian plateau. Locusts and water shortage limit agricultural production, which has also been adversely affected by recent political upheavals. *History*: made an Italian colony in 1890, it became the base for the Italian invasions of Ethiopia. The area came under British administration in 1941 and was federated as an autonomous unit of Ethiopia in 1952. In 1962 it became an integral part of the Ethiopian empire, giving rise to political discontent. During the 1970s this developed into a bloody civil war; many major towns, as well as most of the countryside, fell into the hands of the secessionists but the Ethiopian government, anxious to retain its only two ports (Assab and Massawa), was unwilling to yield to demands for complete independence. In May 1978, a major government offensive backed by Soviet and Cuban aid was carried out, in which most towns were recaptured. The separatists continued to operate from their bases in the countryside, however, and the rebels became more successful as Ethiopia's problems accelerated in the late 1980s. In 1991, Eritrean rebels forced out all Ethiopian troops, and in April 1993 a referendum overwhelmingly endorsed Eritrean independence. In May independence was formally declared, with Issaias Afwerki as the nation's first president, and UN membership was granted. Area: 45,405 sq mi (117,600 sq km). Population (1992 est): 3,200,000. Capital: Asmara.

Erlangen 49 36N 11 02E A city in S Germany, in Bavaria on the Regnitz River. The university, shared with Nuremburg, was moved here from Bayreuth in 1743. Its manufactures include electrical equipment and textiles. Population (1990 est): 104,000.

Erlanger, Joseph (1874–1965) US physiologist, who, with Herbert *Gasser, developed techniques for recording the electrical impulses in nerve fibers using a cathode-ray oscilloscope. They demonstrated that the conduction rate of impulses depends on the thickness of the fiber and its function and that different fibers transmit different types of impulses, represented by different waveforms. Erlanger and Gasser shared the 1944 Nobel Prize for this work.

ermine A *stoat in its white winter coat. At the onset of winter in northern latitudes, the brown coat is molted, leaving a pure white coat except for the tip of the tail: excellent camouflage on snow-covered ground.

Ernst, Max (1891–1976) German artist, born in Brühl. At first a philosophy and psychiatric student at Bonn University, he achieved artistic prominence in 1919 as a founder of the Cologne *dada movement. He excelled in collage, particularly of cut-out illustration, and became a leading practitioner of *surrealism in Paris. He invented the technique of frottage, whereby pencil rubbings of leaves, wood graining, cloth, etc., were used to suggest images of the unconscious mind. In 1941 he moved to the US.

Eros (astronomy) An asteroid (about 12 mi [20 km] diameter) that moves in a highly elliptical orbit and in 1975 passed within 14 million mi (23 million km) of earth.

Eros (mythology) The Greek god of love, the son of Aphrodite by Zeus, Hermes, or Ares. He was usually portrayed as a winged youth armed with bow and arrows. He was identified with the Roman Cupid.

Erté (Romain de Tirtoff; 1892–1990) French fashion illustrator and designer, born in Russia. He worked for the US magazine *Harper's Bazaar* (1916–37) and designed extravagant costumes and tableaux for the Folies-Bergère (1919–30) and other theaters. He later produced lithographs and sculpture.

erysipelas A skin infection caused by *Streptococcus* bacteria. It starts suddenly and usually on the face, which is red and hot, and the patient has a high fever. Penicillin quickly cures the infection.

erythrocyte (*or* red blood cell) A disk-shaped □blood cell, about 0.0003 in (0.007 mm) in diameter, that lacks a nucleus and contains *hemoglobin—a complex iron-bearing pigment responsible for the color of blood. Hemoglobin combines reversibly with oxygen and is the means by which blood transports oxygen from the lungs to the tissues. There are normally about 4.5 million erythrocytes per cubic millimeter of blood. A deficiency of red blood cells or hemoglobin is called *anemia.

Erzgebirge (English name: Ore Mountains; Czech name: Krušné Hory) A range of mountains extending about 80 mi (130 km) along the Czech-German border between the Fichtelgebirge in the W and the Elbe River in the E. They have been heavily worked for silver, copper, lead, uranium, zinc, iron, and tin ores as well as coal and other minerals. They are also a popular tourist area.

Erzurum 39 57N 41 17E A city in NE Turkey, on the route from Ankara and Trabzon to Iran. Local products include handmade jewelry, and there is a university (1957). Population (1990): 242,391.

Esarhaddon King of Assyria (680–669 BC) in succession to his father *Sennacherib after defeating rivals for the throne. In about 674 he attacked Egypt, conquering it in 671.

Esbjerg 55 28N 8 28E The largest fishing port in Denmark, in the SW on the North Sea coast. It exports include fish, fish products, meat, and dairy products. Population (1988 est): 81,400.

escalation clause A provision in an industrial contract that allows the contractor to increase his price if his costs exceed a stated limit. Escalation clauses are widely used for long-term projects in a time of inflation.

escalator An automatic, moving stairway for transporting passengers from one level to another. Escalators consist of a continuous moving belt of metal stairs, usually driven by an electric motor. The stairs move on tracks between two handrails moving at the same speed. At the top and bottom landings the stairs flatten out and pass through metal combs to dislodge small objects. They are generally about 5 ft (1.6 m) wide and move at 10–12 ft (3–3.5 m) per second.

escape velocity The initial velocity required by a projectile to enable it, without any further source of power, to escape from the gravitational field of the earth or a celestial body. The escape velocity varies with the mass and diameter of the body but not with the mass of the projectile. It is also independent of the angle of launch. For the earth the escape velocity is 36,745 ft (11,200 m) per second and for the moon, 7776 ft (2370 m) per second.

Escaut River. *See* Scheldt River.

eschatology (Greek *eschatos*: last) The part of Christian theology concerned with the last things, often summarized as death, judgment, heaven, and hell. It refers to the ultimate fate of both the individual and of human society. Eschatological writing is common to both Old and New Testaments, where it is linked with the expectation of a coming Messiah. The teaching of Christ has also been explained as based on the assumption that the end of the world was imminent and that consequently a concern with the last things was urgent. Recent theological work has attempted to restore the relevance of these concepts in a less mythologically inclined world.

Esch-Cummins Act (1920) A US act that consolidated the railroads under private operation. The US government had controlled the railroads during World War I. Although the railroads returned to private hands, the Interstate Commerce Commission controlled the rate structure, the sale of stocks in the lines, and profit spending under the terms of the act.

Escobedo v. Illinois (1964) US Supreme Court decision that ruled that an accused person who is refused right of counsel has been denied constitutional rights. Danny Escobedo, accused of murder, was not allowed to consult with his lawyer and was not informed of his right to remain silent. A statement given by him during this period was used in court as major evidence that led to his conviction. The court ruled that the statement could not be used as evidence.

Escoffier, Auguste (1846–1935) French chef. He gained an international reputation while supervising the kitchens at the Savoy and the Carlton hotels in London. He was made a member of the Légion d'Honneur in 1920.

Escorial, El A royal palace, mausoleum, and monastery near Madrid. Built for Philip II between 1563 and 1584, El Escorial is an austere, square, granite building, measuring 530 ft (162 m) by 670 ft (204 m). Philip himself was probably actively concerned in the design, which was begun by Juan Bautista de Toledo (d. 1567) and completed by Juan de *Herrera. El Escorial houses a magnificent collection of books and paintings.

Esdraelon, Plain of (*or* Valley of Jezreel; Hebrew name; 'Emeq Yizre'el) A lowland area in N Israel, stretching SE from Mount Carmel. In ancient times it was a major commercial route and contains the ancient site of Megiddo. It was swampy until drainage and settlement began in 1921.

Esdras, Books of Two books of the *Apocrypha purporting to be by *Ezra. The first is a compilation of various documents, giving a largely parallel account of events recorded in Chronicles, Ezra, and Nehemiah, but adding a legend explaining how King Darius of Persia was persuaded to permit the rebuilding of the Temple at Jerusalem. The second contains details of several visions consoling the Jews in their suffering and promising them a glorious future.

Esfahan. *See* Isfahan.

esker An elongated ridge consisting chiefly of sands and gravels deposited by glaciers. Once the bed of a stream flowing beneath or in a glacier, eskers are left behind once the ice has melted or retreated. They may extend for hundreds of miles.

Eskilstuna 59 22N 16 31E A city in SE Sweden. A center of the iron and steel industries, its manufactures include machinery, precision instruments, electrical equipment, and cutlery. Population: 90,354.

Eskimo A Mongoloid people of the Arctic region of North America and Greenland. Traditionally, the men are hunters of seals, whales, walrus, and caribou, using harpoons, canoes (*or* kayaks), dogs, and sleds. Fishing is also important. Their clothes, made by the women, are of animal skins. Only some of the many different groups build the familiar snow dwellings (igloos). Others construct semisubterranean sod shelters or use snow-covered skin tents. There is no overall sense of identity among them and the main units are small family bands.

Their small ivory or stone carvings are highly prized. Modern Eskimo have abandoned much of their traditional ways, adopting the life styles of the Americans and Canadians.

Eskimo-Aleut languages A language group, sometimes included in the classification of American Indian language. It consists of two distinct languages: Eskimo, spoken in Greenland and in many dialects along the N coast of Canada, and *Aleut, spoken in the Aleutian Islands.

Eskimo dog. *See* husky.

Eskişehir 39 46N 30 30E A city in W Turkey, W of Ankara. Its warm springs are well known, and pipes are made from the local meerschaum deposits. There is a university (1973). Population (1990): 413,082.

esophagus The gullet: a muscular tube, about 10 in (25 cm) long, running from the pharynx at the back of the mouth to the stomach. Contractions of the esophagus propel swallowed food toward the stomach: the food is lubricated with mucus secreted by the walls of the esophagus.

ESP. *See* extrasensory perception.

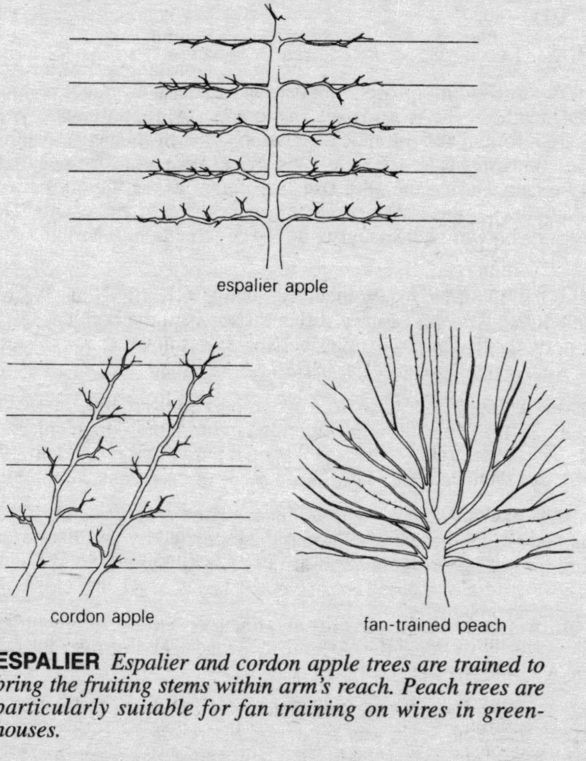

ESPALIER *Espalier and cordon apple trees are trained to bring the fruiting stems within arm's reach. Peach trees are particularly suitable for fan training on wires in greenhouses.*

espalier A shrub or tree, especially a fruit tree, that is trained to grow flat against a wall or a framework of wood, iron, or wire to support the fruit-laden branches and facilitate picking the crop. The branches are usually arranged in ladder-like tiers. Other methods result in a fanlike arrangement of branches or a single stem (cordon).

esparto A perennial *grass, *Stipa tenacissima*, also known as alfa or halfa, native to Spain and N Africa, where it is cultivated. It grows in sharp pointed tufts, up to 40 in (1 m) high, and is used to make paper, cord, and rope.

Esperanto An artificial language invented by a Polish philologist, L. L. Zamenhof (1859–1917), in 1887. It was intended to be a universal medium of communication and is indeed the most successful artificial language, being spoken by over 100,000 people. Grammatically it is entirely regular, its pronunciation is consistent with its spelling, and as well as grammatical rules it has the potential for the formation of new words. The rules of the language are laid down in Zamenhof's *Fundamento de Esperanto* (1905).

Espionage Act (1917) An act of Congress to punish any acts intended to interfere with the US effort during World War I. The Department of Justice was given the authority to censor, to survey and confiscate the mails, and to deport those it felt were undesirable.

Espoo (Swedish name: Esbo) 60 10N 24 42E A city in S Finland, just W of Helsinki. It serves mainly as a dormitory town for the capital. Population (1992 est): 176,000.

ESRO. *See* European Space Research Organization.

essay A short literary prose composition in which a subject is discussed in a personal manner. The word *essai* was coined by *Montaigne, whose *Essais* (1580) are informal and intimate discussions of such subjects as vanity and idleness. In contrast, Francis Bacon's *Essays* (1597) were formal treatments of weighty topics. During the 18th and 19th centuries the literary periodicals provided an outlet for the essays of *Addison, *Steele, *Lambe, and *De Quincey. Among well-known later essayists are Max *Beerbohm, Virginia *Woolf, and Aldous *Huxley.

Essen 51 27N 6 57E A city in W Germany, in North Rhine-Westphalia near the Ruhr River. The 9th-century cathedral survived the bombing of World War II. Formerly the site of the Krupp steelworks, it is now the administrative center of the *Ruhr. Population (1991): 626,973.

Essenes An ancient Jewish sect active between the 2nd century BC and the 2nd century AD in Palestine. Information about them is fragmentary and inconsistent. They seem to have stressed personal purity and asceticism. Many scholars think that the *Dead Sea Scrolls are relics of an Essene community.

essential oils Substances with a characteristic scent produced by the glands of aromatic plants. Essential oils may be extracted by distillation, mechanical pressing, or organic solvents and are used in perfumes, food flavorings, and medicines. Examples include attar of roses, lavender oil, and clove oil.

Essequibo River A river in Guyana, rising on the Brazilian border and flowing generally N to enter the Atlantic Ocean, draining over half of Guyana. Length: 630 mi (1014 km).

Essex, Robert Devereux, 2nd Earl of (?1566–1601) English soldier and courtier to Elizabeth I. He was appointed Master of the Horse (1587) after distinguishing himself against Spain. He commanded an expedition (1591–92) sent to aid Henry IV of France and in 1593 became a privy councillor; he took part in the sack of Cádiz (1596). He was dismissed (1600) after failing to suppress an Irish rebellion and in 1601 raised a riot in London, for which he was executed.

Esslingen 48 45N 9 19E A city in SW Germany, in Baden-Württemberg on the Neckar River. It is noted for its Gothic church (1321–1516) and its wines. Population (1990 est): 89,000.

estate The total property owned by an individual upon his death. Consisting of both real and personal property, it is distributed, often in accordance with the terms of a will, after the owner's death.

Este An Italian princely family of Lombard origin, which under **Obizzo II** (1264–93) gained control of Ferrara, Modena, and Reggio. His successors maintained control of these three regions in spite of papal opposition and were a dominant force in Italian Renaissance politics and culture until Ferrara was incorporated into the papal states in 1598. The Estensi continued to hold Reggio until the French invasion of 1796 and Modena until the unification of Italy in the mid 19th century.

The **Villa d'Este**, at Tivoli, near Rome, was designed (1550) for Cardinal Ippolito II d'Este (1509–72).

Esterházy A family prominent in Hungarian affairs from the 16th to 19th centuries. **Miklós Esterházy** (1582–1645) became imperial governor of Hungary in 1625. His son **Prince Pál Esterházy** (1635–1713) held command against the Turks and became a prince of the Holy Roman Empire (1687). Pál's grandson **Prince Miklós József Esterházy** (1714–90) rebuilt the family castle, Esterháza, and employed Haydn for 30 years. Miklós Józef's grandson **Prince Miklós Esterházy** (1765–1833) fought against the French in the Napoleonic Wars and accumulated an outstanding art collection. Miklós' son **Prince Pál Antal Esterházy** (1786–1866), a diplomat, was foreign minister in 1848.

esters Organic compounds produced by the reaction of an alcohol with an acid, with the elimination of water. Common organic esters are formed from carboxylic acids. The lighter ones often have a pleasant smell and taste and are widely used in perfumes and flavorings. Fats are triesters of long-chain carboxylic acids and glycerol. *See* saponins; soaps.

Esther An Old Testament woman who became the queen of the Persian King Ahasuerus. **The Book of Esther** recounts an event in Persia during the reign of *Xerxes I (called Ahasuerus in the text), when Esther used her influence to frustrate a plot to massacre the Jews. The deliverance led to the establishment of the Jewish feast of *Purim.

Estonian A language of the Baltic-Finnic branch of the Finno-Ugric division of the Uralic language family. It is spoken by the Estonians, who number about one million people in Estonia. It is related to Finnish with which it shares the distinctive characteristic of distinguishing three degrees of consonant and vowel length. The written language is based on a northern dialect, Tallinn, and has a literature dating from the 16th century.

Estonia, Republic of (*or* Estonia) A republic in N Europe. Estonia has many lakes and includes numerous islands in the Baltic Sea. Some 70% of the population are Estonians. Fishing is an important occupation, the main catch being herring. Other industries include machine building, radio, engineering, and the processing of shale—the most important mineral deposit, from which gas is produced, supplying St. Petersburg. Pig breeding is the chief agricultural activity, and the main crops are barley, oats, and potatoes. *History*: in the 13th century the N was occupied by the Danes and the S by the Livonian Knights (a German order of knighthood). The Danes withdrew in 1346 and the Knights were replaced by the Swedes in the 16th and 17th centuries. Estonia was ceded to Russia in 1721. Rebellions in the 19th century culminated in a declaration of independence (1918), which was recognized by Soviet Russia in 1920. It was assigned to the Soviet Union by the Nazi-Soviet Pact (1939) and became an SSR in 1940. It was occupied by Germany in World War II. Its status was not accepted by the US. In 1991, when communism in the Soviet Union collapsed, Estonia declared its independence. It was admitted to the UN the same year. Estonia, with Latvia and Lithuania, pursued policies that kept the Baltic republics distinct from other former Soviet republics. Area: 17,410 sq mi (45,100 sq km). Population (1990 est): 1,573,000. Capital: Tallinn.

Estoril 38 42N 9 23W A seaside resort in W Portugal, on the Atlantic Ocean. It has an outstanding avenue of palm trees between its casino and the seafront. Population (1981): 16,000.

estrogen A group of steroid hormones that function principally as female sex hormones. The most important estrogens in mammals are estradiol and estrone. Produced by the ovaries under the influence of pituitary *gonadotrophins, they promote the development of the reproductive organs and secondary sexual characteristics (such as enlargement of breasts) at puberty and regulate the changes of the menstrual cycle (*see* menstruation). Estrogens are also produced by the placenta, adrenal glands, and testes. Synthetic estrogens are used in medicine to treat menstrual and menopausal disorders; they are also constituents of *oral contraceptives.

estrus The period of "heat" in the sexual cycle of female mammals, when the female will attract males and permit copulation. It corresponds to the time of ovulation, so that mating is most likely to result in pregnancy. The estrous cycle is similar to the menstrual cycle of women, except that the lining of the womb is not shed during estrus.

etching A method of making prints from a metal plate covered with an acid-resistant ground, on which a design is drawn with a needle. The plate is then placed in acid, the exposed lines being eaten away. These recessed lines retain ink and the design is transferred to the paper by rolling under pressure. Although the first dated etching was made in 1513, it was *Rembrandt who freed the medium from its technical and formal dependence on *engraving. The process continues to be widely used, with *Picasso among the leading 20th-century exponents.

Eteocles. *See* Polyneices.

ethane (C_2H_6) A colorless gas, the second member of the *alkane series. It occurs in *natural gas.

ethanol (*or* ethyl alcohol; C_2H_5OH) A colorless flammable liquid that is the active constituent of alcoholic drinks. It is prepared by fermentation or by the catalytic hydration of *ethylene. It is used as a solvent, a raw material for producing other chemicals, and a fuel. *See also* alcohol strength.

Ethelbert (c. 552–616 AD) King of Kent, who became overlord of all England south of the Humber. Encouraging the conversion of his people to Christianity, he received Augustine's mission from Rome. He wrote the first extant English code of laws.

Ethelred I (d. 871 AD) King of England (866–71), in whose reign the Vikings launched a full-scale invasion of England. Ethelred died after his victory at Ashdown, leaving his brother *Alfred the Great to fight on.

Ethelred the Unready (968–1016) King of England (978–1016). In the face of Danish raids, he was forced to pay huge tributes (Danegeld) to the enemy. He was driven into exile by *Sweyn in 1013 but returned after Sweyn's death (1014), dying during *Canute's invasion of England (1015–16).

Ethelwulf (d. 858 AD) King of Wessex (839–58). Renowned for his military prowess, he reputedly defeated 350 Viking ships (851). Ethelwulf reduced taxation, endowed the Church, made lay lands heritable, and provided a system of poor relief.

ether Any member of the group of organic compounds with the general formula R–O–R″, which are formed by the condensation of two alcohols. Diethyl ether, $C_2H_5OC_2H_5$, often known simply as ether, is a volatile liquid made by treating *ethanol with concentrated sulfuric acid. It is used as an anesthetic and solvent.

Etherege, Sir George (c. 1635–c. 1692) English dramatist. A diplomat in Turkey from 1668 to 1671, he fled to Paris after the accession of William III. In his comedies of fashionable London life, *The Comical Revenge* (1664), *She Wou'd If She Cou'd* (1668), and *The Man of Mode* (1674), he introduced the comedy of manners to the British theater.

Ethical Culture movement A movement originating in New York in the late 19th century, developed by Felix Adler, to promote the importance of morality in all aspects of life. Adler hoped to encourage ethical behavior independent of religious belief, and thereby promote social reform.

ethics The science of morality, also called moral philosophy. It is one of the three main branches of modern *philosophy and seeks to discover a consistent principle by which human actions and character can be judged. Until about a century ago, ethics was prescriptive, aiming to guide men's conduct. Now it is more descriptive, attempting to discover how moral decisions are actually made. In ancient philosophy, *hedonism, which held that the greatest goal was happiness, and rationalism, which held that it was reason, were the rival schools. Plato and Aristotle combined hedonism and *rationalism. Medieval scholasticism took God's will as the sole ethical standard and grafted this onto Aristotelian ethics. After the Renaissance, pragmatists like *Hobbes, *Bentham, and John Stuart Mill (*see* Mill, James) developed *utilitarianism, in which the good of society rather than of the individual is the criterion. *Kant and other idealists were intuitionists, believing that conscience is to ethics as intelligence is to logic. Today utilitarianism is the implicit basis of commercial, legal, and social ethics, but conscience remains the guide of most individuals.

Ethiopia (former name: Abyssinia) A country in NE Africa, on the Red Sea. Ethiopia may be divided into four physiographical regions. The SE consists mostly of desert forming the Ogaden Plateau; further toward the center an elevated plateau region rises to heights of more than 14,000 ft (4250 m) and joins the Great Rift Valley, which constitutes a desert area; the Ethiopian Plateau extends across the NW, consisting of highlands reaching over 15,000 ft (4570 m). The Blue Nile crosses the Ethiopian Plateau, where the majority of the population lives. The population consists of many ethnic groups, including the Galla and *Amhara. *Economy*: Ethiopia remains one of the poorest countries in the world and agriculture is chiefly at subsistence level. The situation has been worsened in recent years by serious crop failures, causing famines. All land was nationalized in 1975 and much of it is now farmed cooperatively, the main emphasis being on the development of the rural areas. Mineral resources are sparse, though there are small amounts of gold and platinum as well as salt in Eritrea. The disrupted *Ogaden region is thought to be a potential source of mineral wealth. Gas and oil are being explored and exploitation of the country's considerable potential for hydroelectricity has already begun. Some industries, such as textiles, cement, and food processing, are being encouraged. The main export is coffee. *History*: Ethiopia has a longer known history than any other country in Africa apart from Egypt and legend claimed the descent of its rulers from

Solomon and the Queen of Sheba. From the 2nd to the 9th century AD the Aksumite Empire enjoyed considerable prosperity and expansion, in the 4th century Ethiopia became the first Christian country in Africa. This period was followed by centuries of struggles (especially with the Muslims) and of internal divisions. It was not until the 19th century that the country was once more reunited under Emperor Tewodros II. In 1896 Italian attempts to conquer it were defeated by *Menelik II. However, in 1935 Italy (under Mussolini) invaded Ethiopia. In spite of Anglo-French attempts (Hoare-Laval Pact) to arrange a settlement and League of Nations sanctions against Italy, in 1936 Addis Ababa fell and the emperor, *Haile Selassie, fled to England. For the next five years Ethiopia formed part of Italian East Africa (with Eritrea and Italian Somaliland). In 1941 the Allies liberated Ethiopia, and Haile Selassie returned to the throne. Eritrea again became part of Ethiopia, becoming fully integrated in 1962. Haile Selassie was deposed in 1974 and a provisional military government came to power. After the execution of members of the ruling military council in 1977, the government became known as the Derg (Provisional Military Administrative Council) with Mengistu Haile Mariam as president. During this unsettled period liberation movements in Eritrea and the Somali-speaking Ogaden area seized the opportunity to increase their armed struggle against the government. By the end of 1977 Somali troops had occupied most of the Ogaden region but with the help of Soviet weapons and Cuban troops, Ethiopia regained control of the area. Encouraged by their victories over Somalia, the government launched a temporarily successful offensive against Eritrean secessionists in 1978. In the early 1980s drought led to crop failures, reaching a crisis in 1984, when famine became widespread. An international airlift was organized to bring food to the starving nation, and in 1985 the government began an unpopular resettlement program for famine-struck areas. Successes by rebel forces in Tigre and *Eritrea in 1989–91 led to Mengistu's overthrow in 1991 and Eritrea's independence in 1993. Official language: Amharic; English is widely spoken. Official religion: Ethiopian Orthodox (Coptic). Official currency: birr of 100 cents. Area: 386,000 sq mi (1,000,000 sq km). Population (1992 est): 54,000,000. Capital: Addis Ababa.

ethnology The comparative study and theory of contemporary cultures. In most current usages it is synonymous with cultural *anthropology. However, it has also been used to refer to the historical study of cultures, especially preliterate cultures, and sometimes as a synonym for social anthropology. It may be distinguished from ethnography, which is the descriptive study of culture and is less concerned with the development of theory.

ethology The study of animal behavior. Ethologists are concerned with how animals respond to signals or stimuli (whether from other animals, from their own bodies, or from the environment in which they live), how they sense these signals, and what their response means to other animals and to themselves. They demonstrate the interactions between the inherited (instinctive) aspects of behavior and those determined by experience (learning).

Ethology was founded in Europe in the 1930s by the work of Konrad *Lorenz and Niko *Tinbergen, who studied animals in their natural states. In the US the approach was one of comparative psychology, using laboratory animals under strict experimental conditions. The work of ethologists has provided insights into some aspects of human behavior.

ethylene (*or* ethene; C_2H_4) A colorless flammable gaseous *alkene. It is made by *cracking petroleum and is used to make *polythene (polyethylene). It is also used to ripen fruit artificially.

Etna, Mount 37 45N 15 00E A volcano in E Sicily, having a central crater and over 200 subsidiaries. The first recorded eruption was in 476 BC and significant eruptions this century have occurred in 1928, 1949, and 1971. The coastal town of Catania, 17 mi (28 km) away, has been engulfed twice. Height: 10,705 ft (3263 m).

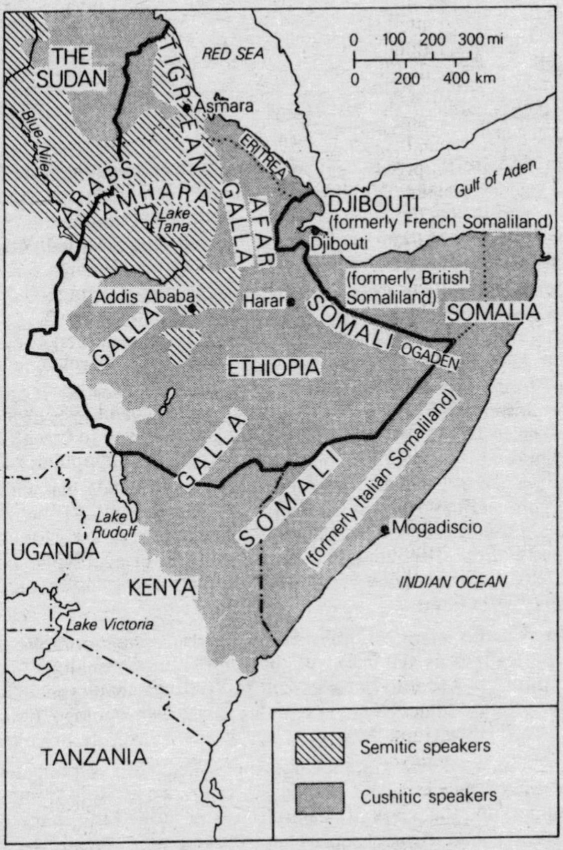

ETHIOPIA *Distribution of main ethnic groups.*

Eton 51 31N 0 37W A town in SE England, in Berkshire opposite Windsor on the River Thames. Eton College, the famous private school, was founded by Henry VI in 1440. Population (1981): 3523.

Etruria The region of ancient Italy N of Rome, approximating modern Tuscany. Occupied first by *Villanovan peoples, Etruria was inhabited by the *Etruscans from the 8th century BC but by the 3rd century BC had come under Roman control.

Etruscans The ancient inhabitants of Etruria (now Tuscany) in central Italy. From the 8th to the 5th centuries BC their cities, forming a loose political confederacy, dominated their neighbors but after 396 they were rapidly absorbed by the Romans. The Etruscans' origins are mysterious; certain Oriental traits in their artifacts and the frescoes decorating their tombs suggest that they were invaders from Asia Minor, but such traits may have arisen through their extensive trading links. Their language was non-Indo-European and although many inscriptions are known and the alphabet is not dissimilar to ancient Greek, it is still untranslated.

etymology The study of the history of words, in which words are traced back to their earliest recorded forms and, where sufficient evidence exists, even beyond these to hypothetical reconstructed forms. Most English words are derived either from Proto-Germanic (*see* Germanic languages) or from Latin and French. Many learned English words were taken from Greek or made up from Greek elements, while in the past 200 years English has come to borrow words from languages in every part of the world.

Euboea (Modern Greek name: Évvoia; former English name: Negropont) The second largest Greek island, in the W Aegean Sea. It is separated from the mainland for most of its length by only a narrow channel and rises to 5719 ft (1743 m) at Mount Delphi. Sheep and cattle are raised and grapes, figs, olives, and cereals, grown. Area: 1509 sq mi (3908 sq km). Chief town: Chalcis.

Eucalyptus A genus of tropical and subtropical evergreen trees (about 600 species) native to Australia but widely cultivated elsewhere. Eucalypts—also known as gum trees and stringybarks—are among the tallest trees in the world, 300–325 ft (90–100 m) high. The blue-gray bark is smooth and often peeling and the mature leaves are long and narrow (young leaves are rounded or oblong). The flowers are showy, with tiny petals and a fluffy mass of red or white stamens. The fruit is a woody pod. Fast-growing and drought-resistant, eucalypts are important sources of timber. The wood is used as fuel and for buildings and fencing; the bark for paper making and tanning. The best-known species are the *blue gum and the red gum (*E. ficifolia*). Because they take up much water, eucalypts are used to reclaim marshy land. They are also used for street planting. All parts of the trees contain essential oils (oil of eucalyptus comes from blue gum leaves). Some species are shrubby and are known as *mallees. Family: *Myrtaceae* (myrtle family).

Eucharis A genus of bulb-forming South American plants (10 species), called Amazon lilies. Up to 24 in (60 cm) tall, they have clusters of large fragrant white flowers, up to 5 in (13 cm) across, with protruding, slender stamens and six backward-curling white sepals. The plants are grown for ornament in greenhouses. Family: *Amaryllidaceae*.

Eucharist (Greek *eucharistia*: thanksgiving) The chief *sacrament and central act of worship of the Christian Churches. Also known as Holy Communion, the Lord's Supper, and the Mass, its institution is described in the three Synoptic Gospels. At the last meal of Christ and the apostles, bread and wine were blessed by Christ and shared, representing his death on the cross and the subsequent redemption of mankind. Differing interpretations have been placed on the sense in which Christ is held to be present in the sacrament (*see* consubstantiation; transubstantiation).

Eucken, Rudolf Christoph (1846–1926) German writer. He upheld idealist metaphysics against 19th-century positivism and materialism and sought to isolate the spiritual content of historical movements. He won the Nobel Prize for literature in 1908.

Euclid (c. 300 BC) Greek mathematician, famous for his book entitled *Elements* in which he derived all that was known of geometry from a few simple axioms. The geometry that obeys Euclid's axioms is known as *Euclidean geometry, all other kinds being called *non-Euclidean.

Euclidean geometry A system of geometry based on the axioms contained in *Euclid's *Elements*. In Euclidean geometry, parallel lines never meet and the angles in a triangle always add up to 180°. The geometry of physical space can be assumed for most purposes to be Euclidean. The surface of a sphere, however, is non-Euclidean. *Compare* non-Euclidean geometry.

Eudoxus of Cnidus (c. 408–c. 355 BC) Greek astronomer and mathematician, who studied under Plato and later founded a school, first on the NW coast of Asia Minor and then in Athens. He studied the motions of the planets and derived many geometric proofs, some of which were later incorporated by *Euclid in his *Elements*.

Eugene 44 02N 123 05W A city in W central Oregon, on the W bank of the Willamette River. The University of Oregon, established in 1872, is here. Lumber and food products are its main produce. Population (1990): 112,669.

Eugène of Savoy, Prince (1663–1736) Austrian general. Born in Paris, he was refused a commission by Louis XIV and entered the service of Emperor Leopold I. He fought outstandingly against the Turks, winning victories at Zenta (1697), which freed Hungary of Turkish domination, Peterwardein (1716), and Belgrade (1717). In the War of *Austrian Succession (1701–14), he won, with Marlborough, the victories of *Blenheim (1704), Oudenaarde (1708), and Malplaquet (1709).

eugenics The science that studies the inheritable factors that determine the physical and mental qualities of the human race, with the aim of improving the quality of life for future generations. The term was first coined by Sir Francis *Galton in 1883. Eugenics is now concerned primarily with the detection and—where possible—elimination of such genetic diseases as Down's syndrome with the aid of *prenatal diagnosis.

Eugénie (1826–1920) The influential wife (1853–73) of *Napoleon III of France. She several times acted as his regent and encouraged French intervention in Mexico. After the fall of the Empire (1870) she retired to England.

Euglena A genus of single-celled microorganisms found chiefly in fresh water. They are spindle-shaped, with a flexible cell wall (pellicle) and a gullet from which protrudes a long, whiplike flagellum, used for locomotion. Some species contain chlorophyll or other pigments and can manufacture food by photosynthesis; others feed on small organisms, such as bacteria. Euglenas are regarded by some authorities as algae and by others as protozoans of the class *Flagellata*. □Protozoa.

Eulenspiegel, Till A German peasant folk hero, a crafty and often savage joker whose exploits inspired numerous folktales and many literary and musical works, notably the epic poem by Gerhard *Hauptmann (1928) and the tone poem by Richard *Strauss.

Euler, Leonhard (1707–83) German mathematician, widely regarded as the greatest mathematician of the 18th century and certainly the most prolific of all time, writing some 800 papers during his lifetime. Many more were published posthumously. He did much work on the number e, the base of natural *logarithms, which is often known as **Euler's number**. He gave that number its symbol, and introduced the symbol i for the square root of −1 and also the notation $f(x)$ for a function of the variable x.

Eumenides (Greek: the kindly ones) In Greek legend, spirits identical with the *Erinyes. After *Orestes was acquitted by the Areopagus of his mother's murder, the pursuing Erinyes became known as the Eumenides.

Euonymus A genus of widely distributed trees, shrubs, and woody climbers (176 species), often grown as ornamentals for their attractive foliage (often with striking autumn colors) and fruits, which are surrounded by a bright-pink or orange, fleshy coat (aril). The genus includes the *spindle tree. Family: *Celastraceae*.

euphonium Brass instrument with a wide, conical bore, a cup-shaped mouthpiece, four valves, and a range of about three and a half octaves above the B flat below middle C. Its range is equivalent to that of a tenor *tuba and it is much used in the brass band.

Euphorbia A worldwide genus of herbs and small trees (1600 species), having clusters of small flowers each surrounded by conspicuous, petal-like bracts. The genus includes some ornamental shrubs (*see* crown of thorns; poinsettia; snow-on-the-mountain). The herbaceous euphorbias are known as *spurges. Family: *Euphorbiaceae*.

Euphrates River A river in SW Asia, rising in E Turkey and flowing SE through Syria into Iraq. 118 mi (190 km) from the Persian Gulf, it joins the Tigris River to form the Shatt al-Arab. It flows past the historic sites of Babylon, Ur, Nippur, and Sippara. Length: 1678 mi (2700 km).

Euphronios (late 6th–early 5th centuries BC) Athenian red-figure potter and vase painter. He signed some 15 surviving vases and is mentioned as a rival by another painter. His drawing shows skill in composition and an interest in characterization.

Eupolis (late 5th century BC) Greek dramatist, a rival of *Aristophanes. His lively and scurrilous comedies satirized contemporary politicians and socialites. Only fragments of his works survive.

Eurasia Europe and Asia considered as one land mass. Geographically, Europe is a peninsula of the Asian continent, with the Ural Mountains generally taken as the dividing line.

EURATOM. *See* European Atomic Energy Community.

eurhythmics A system of teaching music by developing the student's physical response to rhythm. Devised by *Jaques-Dalcroze in about 1905, it has since been used in physical education, *ballet and *modern dance training, and even in mental education because it improves the student's concentration. The student is taught a series of body movements to express different musical rhythms; he is then encouraged to improvise his movements.

Euripides (c. 480–406 BC) Greek dramatist, the third (after *Aeschylus and *Sophocles) of the three major writers of Attic tragedy. According to tradition he was born in Salamis on the day Xerxes' fleet was defeated in the famous battle. In 408 he went to the court of Archelaus in Macedonia, where he remained for the rest of his life. Of approximately 90 plays, 19 survive, including the tragedies *Medea* (431), *Hippolytus* (428), *Electra* (415), *The Trojan Women* (415), *The Bacchae* (405), and *Iphigenia at Aulis* (405). His technical innovations included naturalistic dialogue and a diminution of the role of the chorus. He had a deep interest in feminine psychology and his women, both virtuous and evil, are strongly characterized. His critical attitude toward traditional religion in some of the plays, which offended his contemporaries, is balanced by incidents portraying real heroism and lyrical passages of great beauty.

Eurodollars An international currency based on US dollar balances held by banks outside the US. The Eurodollar market developed from 1957 onward as persistent US *balance-of-payments deficits (largely due to foreign aid and investment programs) led to a large outflow of dollars, which were put to use in

Europe often to finance international trade. Oil-producing countries often have large holdings of Eurodollars, which they may move between investment centers in order to take advantage of the highest interest rates. Eurodollars and other expatriate currencies together make up the Eurocurrency market, which deals in large amounts of short-term funds the volatility and freedom from government control of which may at times pose a threat to the stability of international money markets.

Europa In Greek legend, the daughter of King Agenor of Tyre. She was carried to Crete by Zeus in the form of a bull and bore him three sons: Minos, Rhadamanthus, and Sarpedon.

Europe A continent bordering on the Arctic Ocean (N), the Atlantic Ocean (W), and the Mediterranean Sea (S); the Ural Mountains, the Ural River, and the Caspian Sea form its E boundary. Europe is the second (after Australasia) smallest continent but owing perhaps to its latitude and geography has exerted a disproportionate influence on the rest of the world. It comprises a peninsula of the land mass of Eurasia and all geological eras have contributed to its formation. Its long coastline is much indented with several peninsulas (e.g. Scandinavia, Italy) and offshore islands (e.g. the British Isles, Iceland). A central plain, extending from the Ural Mountains to the Atlantic Ocean and divided by uplands and the English Channel, comprises two thirds of the continent. It rises in the S to a series of mountain systems (e.g. the Pyrenees, Alps, Apennines, Carpathian Mountains), and in the N to the mountainous region of Scandinavia and Scotland. The chief rivers flow from the Valdai Hills (e.g. Volga, Don, Dnieper) or the Alps (e.g. Danube, Rhine, Rhône, Po). Its four **climatic zones** are characterized by mild winters, cool summers, and rain all the year round (NW); mild winters, hot summers, and chiefly spring and autumn rain (Mediterranean); cold winters, warm summers, and chiefly summer rain (Central Europe); and very cold winters (E Europe). **Vegetation zones** comprise, from N to S: tundra; a coniferous forest belt, predominantly of Scots pine and Norway spruce; a deciduous forest belt, notably of oak and hornbeam in the E and of oak, birch, and holly in the W, with beech in the central lowlands; and the mainly evergreen and scrub vegetation of the Mediterranean. Steppe and semidesert characterize the SE. Forest once covered some 80% of Europe but intense agriculture since the Middle Ages and industrialization since the 19th century have reduced it to 30% of the land mass. Europe possesses important mineral resources. Coalfields, especially in the UK, Germany, France, Belgium, Russia, and other former Soviet republics, continue to be an important source of power, and oil and natural-gas reserves are found in Russia, Romania, Albania, and beneath the North Sea. Iron-ore deposits are found on a large scale only in Russia and other former Soviet republics which also have reserves of nickel, tin, and manganese, but nonmetallic minerals, including kaolinite and rock salt, occur widely. Europe's high-density population is concentrated in its industrial regions, which are found chiefly in a central belt extending from England, through N France, the Netherlands, and Germany, to Moscow; N Italy, however, is also densely populated. Most of the unusually large number of national groups in Europe speak an *Indo-European language. The European peoples may be subdivided into racial types (e.g. Nordic, Germanic, Alpine, and Mediterranean) but extensive intermixing has occurred. Christianity, in its various forms, is the dominant religion and has exerted a profound influence on European culture, which also continues to bear the imprint of the civilizations of ancient *Greece and Rome (*see* Roman Republic; Roman Empire). Nevertheless Europe's medieval and modern history is that of its diverse nations, conflicts between which culminated in the 20th century in the two World Wars. The postwar period witnessed a split between the communist countries of E Europe, dominated by the Soviet Union, and the countries of W Europe, which sought to resolve their rivalries by means of economic and, increasingly, political union (*see* European Community). The disintegration of communist governments in E Europe in the late 1980s–early 1990s and the breakup of the Soviet Union in 1991 led to signs of greater European unity. Area: about 4,000,000 sq mi (10,400,000 sq km). Population (1990 est): 725,000,000.

European Atomic Energy Community (EURATOM) An international organization founded in 1958 by the Treaty of Rome (1957) to promote and develop the peaceful uses of atomic energy in Europe. In 1967 the merger of EURATOM and the *European Coal and Steel Community with the EEC was begun.

European Coal and Steel Community (ECSC) A body established in 1952 to coordinate the production of coal and steel in France, Italy, West Germany, and the *Benelux countries. In 1967 the merger of the ECSC and the *European Atomic Energy Community with the EEC was begun.

European Community (EC *or* Common Market) An organization of W European States created by the Treaty of Rome (1957) to foster economic cooperation and common development with the eventual aim of economic, and a measure of political, unity. Agreements have been reached on the removal of customs tariffs between members, the setting of a Common Customs Tariff for imports from nonmember states, and the abolition of barriers to free movement of labor, services, and capital between member states. The original six signatories were Belgium, France, Italy, Luxembourg, the Netherlands, and West Germany. In 1973 the UK, Denmark, and the Republic of Ireland became members; Greece joined in 1981; and Spain and Portugal joined in 1986. After the collapse of communist regimes in E Europe at the end of the 1980s and the breakup of the Soviet Union in 1991, prospects for an expanded EC including some of these countries increased. In 1967 the merger of the *European Atomic Energy Community and the *European Coal and Steel Community with the EC was initiated. The EC implemented a *Common Agricultural Policy (CAP) in 1962 (modified in 1968) and a Common Fisheries Policy in 1983.

The Commission of the European Communities is in Brussels and consists of 14 members; its president is elected for a two-year term. The Commission acts as an advisory body to, and is responsible for implementing policy decided upon by, the Council of Ministers. Also in Brussels, the Council comprises ministers from the governments of the ten member countries. The 10 heads of state meet triannually as the European Council. The European Parliament at Strasbourg comments on the Commission's legislative proposals; it must be consulted on the annual budgets and may dismiss the Commission. Members are (since 1979) elected by direct vote in the member countries and sit as political groups (e.g. Christian Democrats, Socialists) in the Parliament. The Court of Justice, at Luxembourg, ensures the observance of law in the treaties establishing the Communities.

European Free Trade Association (EFTA) An association of seven states (Austria, Finland, Iceland, Norway, Portugal, Sweden, and Switzerland) founded in 1960 to foster free trade of industrial goods between members. Individual countries may negotiate independent trade agreements with nonmember states. In 1992 an agreement with the European Community brought EFTA closer to its former rival.

European Space Agency (ESA) An organization responsible for Europe's space program, formed in 1975 from the merger of the European Space Research Organization and the European Launcher Development Organization. All ESA *satellites were launched by NASA before completion of the ESA launcher **Ariane**, the first successful launching of which took place in 1979.

European Space Research Organization (ESRO) An organization founded in 1962 to encourage space reserach among European states with particular emphasis on its exploitation for peaceful purposes. Activities include the development of scientific, meterological, and telecommunications programs.

europium (Eu) A *lanthanide element, used in television-tube phosphors. It forms oxides (EuO, Eu_2O_3), and chlorides ($EuCl_2$, $EuCl_3$). At no 63; at wt 151.96; mp 488°F (822°C); 918°F (1597°C).

Europoort. *See* Rotterdam.

Eurydice In Greek legend, a *dryad, the wife of *Orpheus. She died of a snake bite. Orpheus descended to the underworld to recover her but lost her forever when he violated the condition of her release and turned to look at her before emerging.

eurypterid An extinct *arthropod, also called water scorpion, belonging to a subclass (*Eurypterida*) of the Ordovician and Permian periods, i.e. 500–225 million years ago. Its tapering, segmented body, up to 10 ft (3 m) long, bore several pairs of oarlike appendages at the head end. Eurypterids, which lived in salt or brackish waters, were predators of worms and small fish or bottom-dwelling scavengers. □fossil.

Eusebius of Caesarea (4th century AD) Christian churchman and historian. As Bishop of Caesarea from 313, he took a moderate position with regard to *Arianism and sought a compromise between the conflicting views of Arius and Athanasius; he finally accepted the creed proposed by the Council of *Nicaea. He is famous for his *Ecclesiastical History*, an account of the Church from apostolic times to his own day.

Eustace, St (2nd century AD) Roman martyr and the patron saint of hunters. According to tradition, he was a general who was converted to Christianity through experiencing a miraculous vision of a stag with a crucifix between its antlers. Feast Day: Sept 20.

Eustachio, Bartolommeo (?1520–74) Italian anatomist and physician, who gave his name to the canal connecting the ear and throat (the Eustachian tube) although this had already been discovered by the Greek physician Alcmaeon of Croton (5th century BC). Eustachio's anatomical studies included the ear, kidney, and nervous system but his *Tabulae anatomicae* was not published until 1714.

eustasy Worldwide changes in sea level, attributed mainly to the accumulation and release of water in the form of ice during the ice ages. Since the last Ice Age sea level has risen gradually.

Euterpe In Greek legend, one of the *Muses, the patron of tragedy, flute playing, or lyric poetry.

euthanasia (Greek: easy death) The taking of life to relieve suffering. Euthanasia is a controversial issue concerned with whether or not those with painful and incurable diseases should be provided with a painless means of dying if they ask for it. This is voluntary euthanasia and includes both active steps for taking life (e.g. administration of drugs) and the withholding of life-supporting treatment (passive euthanasia). Even more unacceptable to some people is the concept of compulsory euthanasia, in which the patient—for example, a severely deformed baby—is unable to express his or her own wishes and the responsibility for deciding to terminate life rests on society or a person acting on authority. Many societies exist to promote the cause of voluntary euthanasia, but in no country has either voluntary or compulsory euthanasia been legalized.

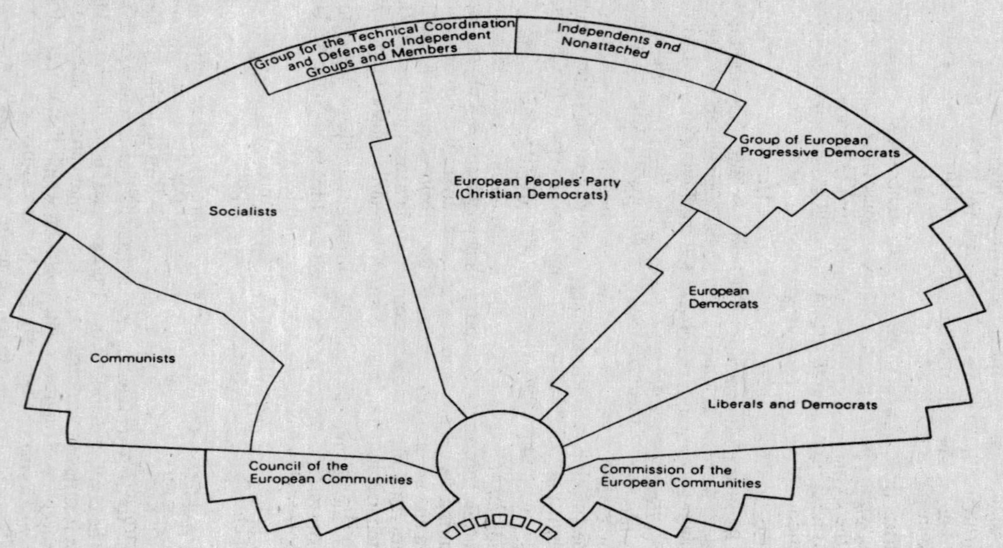

EUROPEAN COMMUNITY *The plan of the chamber of the European Parliament, showing political groups and their relative strengths.*

eutrophication The overfertilization of lakes, due chiefly to pollution by sewage, runoff from the land, and industrial wastes (inorganic nitrates and phosphates). These compounds act as nutrients, stimulating algal growth to produce huge blooms. Their subsequent decomposition reduces the oxygen content in the water, so killing animals with a high oxygen requirement. Much of the nitrate and phosphate settles to the bottom, to promote further growth at a later stage.

Evangelicalism A movement within Protestant Churches that advocates adherence to traditional concepts of biblical belief. Evangelicals reject the Catholic and Orthodox view of authority residing in the traditions of the Church and the *Apostolic Succession, while remaining faithful to Trinitarian orthodoxy. They resist the liberalizing trend apparent in nonevangelical Protestant circles, concentrating on the importance of personal salvation and the consequences of accepting the divine inspiration of the Bible.

Evans, Sir Arthur John (1851–1941) British archeologist. His interest in Cretan sealstones, while Keeper of the Ashmolean Museum, Oxford, led him to his life's work, the excavation of *Knossos (1899–1935). In *The Palace of Minos* (1921–36) he firmly established the chronology and main features of *Minoan civilization.

Evans, Dame Edith (1888–1976) British actress. Her long career included many celebrated performances in Shakespearean roles and in classic comedies such as *The Rivals* and *The Importance of Being Earnest*. She gave some of her most acclaimed stage and film performances during her eighties.

Evans, Oliver (1755–1819) American engineer, who conceived the principle of the continuous production line. In 1784 Evans put his ideas into practice in a flour mill: grain entered one end of an automated production line, was processed, and then discharged as flour at the other end. He also patented a high-pressure steam engine in 1790.

Evans, Walker (1903–75) US photographer. He worked for the Farm Securities Administration and photographed everyday life during the Depression. He also documented New England's architecture of the 19th century in photographs from 1930 on. During the 1940s he photographed the living conditions of Southern sharecroppers and included them in *Let Us Now Praise Famous Men* (1941), with text by James Agee. He was an editor of *Fortune* magazine (1945–65). His works are collected in *American Photographs* (1938), *Message from the Interior* (1966), and *Many Are Called* (1966).

Evanston 42 03N 87 42W A city in the US, in NE Illinois, on Lake Michigan, N of Chicago. Northwestern University, around which the community grew, opened in 1855. Economic activities include publishing, food processing, and the production of chemicals and communications equipment. Population (1990): 73,233.

Evansville 38 00N 87 33W A city in the US, in SW Indiana, on the Ohio River. Its industries include plastics, meat packing, refrigeration equipment, flour milling, pharmaceuticals, and aluminum. Population (1990): 126,272.

evaporation The conversion of a liquid into a vapor at temperatures below its boiling point. As it is the most energetic atoms and molecules that escape from the surface in evaporation, the average energy of those that remain is reduced, and consequently the liquid is cooled.

evening primrose A herbaceous plant of the genus *Oenothera* (100 species), 35–40 in (90–100 cm) tall, native to the Americas but widespread in Europe. The fragrant, yellow flowers, 1–2 in (2–5 cm) in diameter, open in the evening.

The leaves are spirally arranged and the fruit is a long capsule. Family: *Onagraceae* (willowherb family).

Everest, Mount 27 59N 86 56E The highest mountain in the world, on the Nepal-Tibet (China) border in the Himalayas. It was recognized as the highest in 1852, but the height itself was not established until 1955. Climbing attempts started in 1920 and the 12th expedition was the first to succeed: (Sir) Edmund *Hillary and Sherpa *Tenzing Norgay reached the summit on May 29, 1953. On May 5, 1978, two Austrians became the first to reach the top without the aid of oxygen breathing equipment. Height: 29,028 ft (8848 m).

Everglades A subtropical swampy area in Florida, extending S of Lake Okeechobee. The natural vegetation of sawgrass and rushes is preserved in the Everglades National Park but elsewhere large areas have been drained for agriculture. It was the home of the Seminole Indians until the 1830s.

evergreen plants Plants, the foliage of which is retained throughout the year. The leaves of evergreens, which are tough and waxy, are produced and shed at different times all year round, individual leaves often remaining on the tree for several years. Most conifers and many tropical, broad-leaved trees are evergreen. **Deciduous plants** produce softer leaves, which are all shed before winter, leaving only the woody parts and protected buds exposed. Deciduous trees generally occur in temperate regions in which there are seasonal fluctuations in climate.

everlasting flowers Any flowers that can be dried without losing their shape or color and are used in floral arrangements and pictures. They include many members of the *Compositae* (daisy family), such as the true everlastings, or immortelles (*Helichrysum* species), the flower heads of which may be dyed various colors. One of the most popular of these is the strawflower of Australia (*H. bracteatum*). Other plants used include *Anaphalis margaritacea* (the pearly everlasting) and *Gnaphalium* and *Helipterum* species, and striking shapes are supplied by *teasels (*Dipsacus* species). Grasses with showy panicles are often used, especially wild oats and barley.

Everson v. Board of Education (1947) US Supreme Court decision that upheld as constitutional tax-supported school bussing to parochial schools. The court ruled that such a policy did not violate separation of church and state.

Evert, Christine (1954–) US tennis player. She won the US singles title 1975–78, 1980, and 1982 and was Wimbledon singles champion in 1974, 1976 and 1981 and doubles champion in 1976. She also won the Australian Open twice (1982, 1984) and the French Open seven times (1974–75, 1979–80, 1983, 1985–86). She was married to British tennis player John Lloyd from 1979 to 1987. She became a television commentator after her retirement.

evolution In biology, the gradual and continuous process by which the first and most primitive of living organisms have developed into the diversity of plant and animal life known today. Speculations about the origin of living things go back to the Greek philosophers, notably Aristotle, but until the 18th century it was generally believed that each group of organisms was separately and divinely created. In the 1760s *Linnaeus—in his work on the classification and naming of organisms—recognized the possibility of relationship between similar groups, and his contemporary *Buffon suggested that the differences he observed in fossil organisms were brought about by changes in the environment in which they lived.

The first theory of evolution was published by Lamarck, in 1809 (*see* Lamarckism). His explanation of the process—that changes in form acquired during the lifetime of an animal could be inherited—lacked definite proof, although it has had its supporters. A more satisfactory theory was put forward by Charles *Darwin and A. R. *Wallace in 1858: they proposed that new species arose by a process of natural selection acting on individual inheritable variations in a population (*see* Darwinism). Later work has proved that these heritable changes result from spontaneous genetic mutations, and Darwin's theory—with some modifications—is now generally accepted.

evzones Members of a Greek infantry regiment, originally from Epirus, who fought with distinction in the Balkan Wars and World War II. Evzones wear a distinctive, white-skirted uniform; their name derives from the Greek word meaning "dressed for exercise."

Ewe A people of SE Ghana and S Togo, numbering approximately one million, who originated from *Oyo in Nigeria. Their language belongs to the *Kwa subgroup of the Niger-Congo family. They practice shifting agriculture and, in coastal areas, seafishing. They are divided into independent groups, which form temporary alliances for war.

Excalibur King Arthur's magic sword. In one legend Arthur succeeds, where others had failed, in drawing it from a stone, thereby proving his claim to the English throne. In another he receives it from the Lady of the Lake, to whom it is thrown back at his death. *See also* Arthurian legend.

excavator A self-propelled vehicle equipped with a hydraulically powered movable boom and shovel used for excavating trenches, loading earth, etc. Larger models are used for mining and quarrying and usually consist of a crawler vehicle on which is mounted a boom with one or several digging buckets controlled by cables from a winch.

exchange control Government regulations to control the extent to which a foreign currency can be purchased to prevent a large outflow of foreign exchange, which might precipitate a *balance-of-payments crisis. By controlling foreign exchange a government can restrict imports or limit them to those considered desirable by the government.

exchange rates The value of one country's currency in terms of another's. Foreign trade and tourism make it essential for currencies to be convertible at a stable rate of exchange. Until World War I, and again briefly between 1925 and 1931, international currencies were backed by, and convertible into, gold (*see* gold standard). Between 1931 and 1947 various systems were in use.

In 1947 the *International Monetary Fund (IMF) came into operation, as a result of the *Bretton Woods Conference (1944). The IMF fixed par values for members' currencies in terms of gold and these values could not be changed without consulting the IMF. *Special Drawing Rights were introduced in 1970 in an attempt to increase world liquidity, but were unable to maintain the stability of the system: the suspension of convertibility from US dollars to gold in 1971 led to an agreement to allow currencies to float (i.e. to find their own value as a result of market forces). Floating rates avoid the problem of large, destabilizing devaluation, which took place under the Bretton Woods fixed-rate system.

excise tax. *See* customs and excise duties.

excitation In physics, the raising of a system from its lowest energy level (the ground state) to a higher energy level (the excited state). The term is usually confined to atoms, molecules, ions, and nuclei and is most frequently caused by the absorption of a *photon. In an atom, ion, or nucleus the photon is absorbed by an electron or *nucleon causing it to move to a higher energy level. Molecules can also be excited into higher states of rotational or vibrational energy.

excommunication The exclusion of a Christian from the community of the Church for misconduct. There are biblical precedents for various forms of excommunication, especially in the Pauline epistles. In the later Chruch, exclusions from the sacraments was frequently used as a means of censure, and in the Middle Ages the papacy used it to apply political pressure against sovereigns. It is still used by the Roman Catholic Church as a form of discipline and is theoretically available in some Protestant Churches.

excretion The elimination of the waste products of metabolism by the body. In higher animals and man this includes the excretion of nitrogenous waste in the form of urine by the *kidneys, the egestion of feces—the waste products of digestion—from the bowel, and the exhalation of carbon dioxide from the lungs in breathing. A small amount of urea is also excreted in sweat. Lower animals have various simple organs for the excretion of waste products (*see* nephridium).

Executive Privilege The right of a US president to withhold information from Congress and the courts if such information would endanger national security. It was first used by Pres. George *Washington in 1796.

Exekias (6th century BC) Athenian potter and vase painter, known from his signatures on several vases. One of the last black-figure painters, Exekias painted dignified symmetrical compositions in painstaking but fluent detail.

Exeter 50 43N 3 31W A city in SW England, on the Exe River. Its 13th-century cathedral, a fine example of Gothic architecture, was damaged by bombing in World War II along with many other buildings. Exeter's Guildhall is said to be the oldest municipal building in the country. Industries include tourism, printing, the manufacture of agricultural machinery, and leather goods. Population (1981): 95,621.

existentialism A philosophical movement that rejects metaphysics and concentrates on the individual's existence in the world. The forerunner of existentialism, *Kierkegaard, reacting against German *idealism and the complacency of established Christianity, developed a pragmatic psychologically realistic philosophy of existence. This was adapted by French intellectuals, especially Sartre, after World War II. Sartre's existentialism allows individuals freedom in a nihilistic universe: "All human activities are equivalent, all are destined by principle to defeat." But a man is responsible for his effect on others, though only *his* existence is real to him and he is ultimately his own judge. Sartre expounded existentialism chiefly in *Being and Nothingness* (1943), but his plays and novels (and those of *Camus) present existentialist ideas more accessibly.

exobiology (or astrobiology) The branch of biology that investigates the possibility of life on other planets. Exobiologists monitor the electromagnetic spectrum, including light and radio waves, emitted by the stars for evidence of the organic molecules that are a prerequisite of life on earth. They are also involved in designing life-detecting experiments carried to planets in our own solor system by space probes, such as the Viking series.

Exodus (Greek: going out) The second book of the bible, traditionally ascribed to Moses. It recounts the events culminating in the departure of the Israelites from Egypt, where they had lived as slaves since the time of Joseph, and their arrival at Mount Sinai, where the *Ten Commandments are given to Moses. The narrative also includes the story of the birth of Moses, the establishment of the *Passover, and the miraculous crossing of the Red Sea. The events themselves perhaps date from the 15th century BC; the book was probably compiled between the 9th and 4th centuries BC.

exorcism The religious practice of driving out evil spirits by means of prayers and other ritual acts. It is a common rite in a number of religions, including ancient Judaism, and was adopted by Christianity on the basis that it was performed by Christ and the apostles in the New Testament. It refers specifically to the prayers, etc., used to expel evil spirits that supposedly possess a person. Although still available in some Churches, the rite may only be performed by a priest with a bishop's permission.

exosphere. *See* atmosphere.

expanding universe The theory that the universe is expanding was first proposed by Edwin *Hubble in 1929 following observations that the light from distant galaxies is subject to a *redshift, which arises from the recession of the galaxies from us (and from each other). The expansion can be explained by the *big-bang theory. *See also* Hubble constant.

expansion The general increase in dimensions of a substance with increasing temperature. In solids it is caused by the greater vibrational energy of the atoms leading to increased interatomic distances. In liquids and gases the expansion is caused by the greater velocities of the atoms or molecules. The thermal expansion of an ideal gas is described by *Charles's law. The **coefficient of linear expansion** of a substance is the increase in length per unit length of the substance caused by a rise in temperature of 33°F (1°C).

Ex Parte McCardle (1869) The US Supreme Court decision ruling that Congress regulated the right of the Supreme Court to hear appeals from lower (appellate) courts. Although the Supreme Court is granted the right to hear appeals from lower courts by the Constitution, it is "with such exceptions and under such regulations as Congress shall make." In this case, it was feared that a decision in favor of William McCardle, accused of sedition by the military in the South, would overturn the Reconstruction Acts.

Ex Parte Milligan (1866) The US Supreme Court decision that a civilian could not be tried by a military court outside of a war area. Lambdin P. Milligan, a civilian from Indiana, had been tried for treason by the military and sentenced to death. He appealed to the Supreme Court, contending it unconstitutional for the military to try a civilian when civil courts operated in the same area. This decision overruled President Lincoln's previous Civil War proclamation, issued without approval of Congress, that civilians were subject to military rule.

explosives Substances that can be made to produce a large volume of gas very suddenly. The energy of the expanding gases may be used for a number of industrial or military purposes. There are three main types. **Mechanical explosives** depend on a physical reaction, such as overloading a container of gas until it bursts. They are little used except in specialized mining applications where the release of gas from chemicals is undesirable. In **nuclear explosives**, a nuclear chain reaction (*see* nuclear energy) takes place in a sudden uncontrolled manner, releasing energy almost instantaneously. This is used for bombs and occasionally for mining. Most explosives used are **chemical explosives**. These include *TNT, *nitroglycerin, and *dynamite. Modern high explosives are often in the form of water gels, which are plastic, water resistant, and easy to handle safely.

exponential function A mathematical function of the general form Ae^{Bx} where A and B are constants and e is the base of natural *logarithms. Bx is called the exponent; if the exponent is a complicated expression, $f(x)$ say, then the function is often written as $\exp[f(x)]$. The function e^x has the important property that its differential is always equal to the function itself. *See also* calculus.

exposure meter A device for measuring the intensity of light falling on a photographic *camera, used to determine the film exposure time and lens *f-number needed to suit the lighting conditions. It often consists of a *photocell that is directed at the subject from the camera, registering light as a reading on an electric current meter. In some cameras this current is used to control the aperture or shutter speed automatically.

expressionism A movement in modern art covering a variety of schools, the common aim of which was to convey the crude force of human emotion. The bright colors and distorted forms of *Van Gogh and *Munch foreshadow expressionism proper. An even earlier forerunner was the German painter *Grünewald. The chief exponents of expressionism were Die *Brücke and Der *Blaue Reiter groups in Germany but independent figures, such as *Rouault, *Soutine, *Schiele, and *Kokoschka also worked in an expressionist style.

extrasensory perception (ESP) Acquisition of information not accessible through normal perceptual processes. Three phenomena are usually classified under this heading: clairvoyance (knowledge of distant events and concealed objects), telepathy (thought transference between people), and precognition (knowledge of future events). Evidence for all three tends to be anecdotal, but some experiments in which subjects have been asked to guess symbols on cards of which they can see only the backs or to reproduce, without having seen it, a simple sketch done by another person show a statistically significant success rate. *See also* Rhine, Joseph.

extroversion (*or* extraversion) The tendency to be interested in the outside world more than in oneself. Extroversion is a quality of personality, first described by Carl *Jung and still used in modern theories of personality. Extroverts are gregarious and outgoing. They prefer frequent changes of activity; their interests tend to be practical and scientific rather than philosophical; and they tend to be resistant to permanent *conditioning. *Compare* introversion.

extrusive rock. *See* igneous rock.

Exxon Valdez Oil Spill Most extensive oil spill in the United States, occurring in March 1989 in Prince William Sound, Alaska. More than 250,000 gallons of oil were spilled after the *Exxon Valdez* ran aground, polluting important fishing waters and some 1000 miles of shore and killing fish, birds, and sea mammals such as sea otters. The oil cleanup operation began slowly, complicating pollution hazards, and Exxon ultimately agreed (1991) to fines and other payments of more than $1,000,000,000, in addition to the cleanup costs. Litigation on various issues continued into the mid-1990s.

eye The organ of sight. The human eyes lie within two bony sockets in the skull and are attached by six muscles, which produce eye movements. At the front of the eye the white, fibrous outer layer (sclera) is replaced by a transparent curve layer (*see* cornea). A delicate membrane (the conjunctiva) covers the front of the eye and lines the eyelids: it is liable to become inflamed (*see* conjunctivitis). Light entering the eye is refracted by the cornea and passes through the watery aqueous humor and pupil to the lens. The pigmented *iris controls the amount of light entering the eye. The shape of the lens can be adjusted by means of the ciliary muscles so that an image is focused through the jelly-like vitreous humor onto the *retina. Contraction of the ciliary muscles causes the lens to become flattened for focusing distant objects; relaxation of the muscles increases the curvature of the lens for focusing near objects. Light-sensitive cells in the retina send impulses to the brain via the optic nerve. *See also* blindness; farsightedness; ophthalmology; nearsightedness.

eyebright A semiparasitic, annual herb of the genus *Euphrasia* (over 130 species), of temperate regions. Eyebrights have small, toothed leaves and small, unstalked, two-lipped flowers, usually white with violet and yellow markings. They grow to a height of 6 in (15 cm). Family: *Scrophulariaceae*.

Eyre, Lake A shallow salt lake of NE South Australia. It is normally dry except during the rainy season when heavy rains from N Queensland and the Northern Territory are fed into the lake by *Cooper Creek and other streams. The last time it was full was in 1950. Lowest point: about 36 ft (10 m) below sea level. Area: about 3500 sq mi (9100 sq km).

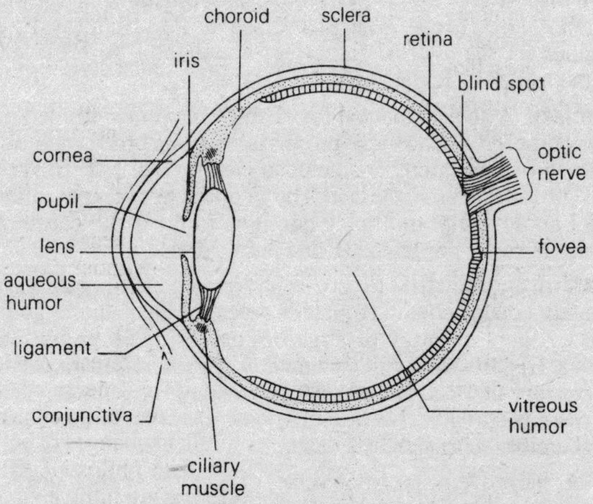

EYE *The structure of the human eye is revealed in this section. The blind spot, where the optic nerve leaves the eye, contains no visual cells and is therefore insensitive to light. The fovea is the area of acutest vision.*

Eyre Peninsula A peninsula of South Australia, situated between the Great Australian Bight and Spencer Gulf. Iron ore is mined in the Middleback Range in the NE.

Eysenck, Hans Jürgen (1916–) German-born British psychologist. A critic of conventional psychoanalysis, he developed an alternative treatment—*behavior therapy—for neurosis and other mental disorders. Eysenck also developed scientifically based methods of evaluating personality and intelligence, partly based on the distinction between introverts and extroverts. His findings on racial differences in intelligence (*Race, Intelligence and Education*, 1971) caused much controversy.

Ezekiel An Old Testament prophet, the successor of *Isaiah and *Jeremiah. **The Book of Ezekiel** records his prophecies, probably written during the *Babylonian exile (6th century BC). The prophecies concern the coming destruction of Jerusalem and Israel, denunciations of various foreign states, the renewal of the people, and finally the ideal society and the rebuilding of the Temple at Jerusalem.

Ezra In the Old Testament, a religious reformer, who was sent by the Persian king, possibly *Artazerxes II (c. 436–358 BC), to regulate Jewish affairs in Jerusalem.

The Book of Ezra in the Old Testament is a sequel to *Chronicles and was compiled by the author of Chronicles and the Book of *Nehemiah. It records the return of the Jews after the *Babylonian exile in about 537 BC, the rebuilding of the Temple, and legal and religious reforms introduced by Ezra.

F

Fabergé, Peter Carl (1846–1920) Russian goldsmith and jeweler. He designed elegant *objets d'art* and was patronized by European royalty. He was especially famous for the jeweled Easter eggs containing surprise gifts given by the tsars to the tsarinas. He died in exile.

Fabian Society A society, named for *Fabius Maximus, formed in London in 1884 for the purpose of peacefully promoting socialist ideas and establishing a socialist state in Britain. Members included George Bernard *Shaw, Sidney and Beatrice *Webb, and Annie *Besant. The Fabians were active in the establishment of the Labour Party and today continue to press the cause of socialism through public lectures, conferences, and publications.

Fabius Maximus, Quintus (d. 203 BC) Roman general of the second *Punic War. Appointed dictator after *Hannibal's defeat of the Romans at Trasimene in 217, Fabius adopted a policy of attrition, harassing Hannibal but avoiding pitched battles. His derogatory title Cunctator (Delayer) became honorable after Hannibal's victory at *Cannae proved the wisdom of Fabius's tactics. It was *Scipio Africanus's aggressive policies, however, that achieved the final triumph over Hannibal, after Fabius's death.

fable A short narrative in prose or verse, often with animal characters, which illustrates a moral truth. The western literary form had its origins in the collection of fables attributed to *Aesop (6th century BC) and later expanded by the Roman poet *Phaedrus (1st century AD). The medieval genre of *beast epic developed from this form, which reached its highest degree of sophistication in the work of *La Fontaine. Authors of children's literature, notably Rudyard *Kipling, Lewis *Carroll, and Beatrix *Potter, have used this form extensively. Other modern examples are by George *Orwell and James Thurber.

fabliau A medieval French comic and satiric narrative poem, a type that flourished between 1150 and 1400. About 150 examples survive, mostly simple tales the humor of which is usually broad and obscene. Among known authors is Rutebeuf (*see* trouvères). Chaucer's *Miller's Tale* and *Reeve's Tale* (in the *Canterbury Tales*) are the outstanding examples in English.

Fabre, Jean Henri (1823–1915) French entomologist, noted for his studies of bees, wasps, and other insects. From his observations, Fabre realized the importance of inherited instinct in insect behavior. He wrote many popular books about his researches, including *Souvenirs entomologiques* (1879–1907).

Fabricius ab Aquapendente, Hieronymus (1537–1619) Italian physician. Fabricius was a student of *Fallopius and himself became an eminent teacher, one of his pupils being William *Harvey. Among Fabricius' contributions were studies of embryology and fetal development (*De formata foetu*, 1600) and his discovery of one-way valves in veins.

Fabry, Charles (1867–1945) French physicist, who while working at the Sorbonne discovered *ozone in the upper atmosphere (1913). This discovery was made with the Fabry-Pérot interferometer, an instrument that he had designed in collaboration with Alfred Pérot (1863–1925) in 1896.

factoring The commercial practice of buying trade debts and collecting them on behalf of clients. If a manufacturer sells his products to a number of customers, some of whom may be slow payers, he can sell these debts to a factor, who will usually pay 80% of the debt immediately and the balance (less a service charge) when the debt has been collected. This service is often combined (for an extra charge) with credit insurance, enabling the debt to be guaranteed even if the debtor fails.

Fadden, Sir Arthur William (1895–1973) Australian statesman; prime minister (1941) following Menzies' resignation. He was leader of the Country Party (1941–58).

Faenza 44 19N 11 54E A city in N Italy, in Emilia-Romagna. During the 15th and 16th centuries it was famous for the manufacture of majolica earthenware, especially *faience, and a ceramics museum was founded here in 1908. Iron goods and textiles are manufactured. Population (1985): 55,000.

Faeroe Islands (*or* Faroe Islands; Danish name: Faerøerne) A Danish group of self-governing islands in the N Atlantic Ocean, between the Shetland Islands and Iceland; 17 of the 22 islands are inhabited, the chief ones being Strømø, Østerø, and Vaagø. Chiefly hilly, the terrain limits agriculture to sheep raising and the production of hay and potatoes. Fishing and fish processing is important. Area: 540 sq mi (1400 sq km). Population (1986): 46,000. Capital Thorshavn, on Strømø.

Fahd, King (ibn Abdul al-Aziz al-Saud) (1922–) Saudi Arabian king (1982–). The Son of *Ibn Saud, founder of Saudi Arabia, and half brother of *Khalid Ibn Abdul Aziz, he served as minister of education (1953–60) and of the interior (1962–75). Named crown prince in 1975, he strengthened Saudi Arabia's petroleum and natural gas industries, planned the construction of two new cities and an airport (1981), and proposed a peace plan for the Middle East. As king, he sought to bolster Saudi Arabia's economy and its role in the *Organization of Petroleum Exporting Countries (OPEC), to settle Middle-East conflicts, and to maintain close ties with Western countries. During the Persian Gulf crisis and war (1990–91) he mediated attempts to reach a peaceful solution between Iraq and Kuwait and supported the US-led UN troops in his country.

Fahrenheit scale A temperature scale in which the temperature of melting ice is taken as 32 degrees and the temperature of boiling water, as 212 degrees. Named for the German physicist Gabriel Daniel Fahrenheit (1686–1736).

Fa-hsien. *See* Fa Xian.

faience Several kinds of tin-glazed earthenware made in France. Strictly, *faience* is French shorthand for *porzellana di Faenza*, a species of *majolica made in Italy, and the technique of coating fragile porous earthenware with impervious hard white opaque tin glaze derives from majolica. Italian potters were using the method in France in the 16th century. Centers of production during the 17th and 18th centuries were Lyons, Marseilles, Moustiers, Nevers, and Rouen. Designs drawn from local history (*faience parlante*) and revolutionary events (*faience patriotique*) were popular variations. Richly painted baroque and *rococo styles are common.

Fairbanks 64 51N 147 43W A city in E central Alaska, at the confluence of the Tanana and Chena rivers. It was established in 1902 during the gold rush and gold and silver mining are still economically important, as well as coal mining and processing. Lumbering is also carried on. The University of Alaska is in the nearby town of College. Population (1990): 30,843.

Fairbanks, Charles Warren (1852–1918) US politician, US vice president (1905–09). He served as Republican senator from Ohio (1897–1905) until becoming vice president under Theodore Roosevelt. He ran unsuccessfully as the vice presidential candidate with Charles Evans Hughes in 1916.

Fairbanks, Douglas (Julius Ullman; 1883–1939) US film actor. With D. W. *Griffith, Charlie *Chaplin, and his wife Mary *Pickford he founded United Artists Corporation in 1919. His films, in which he played the roles of handsome athletic heroes, include *The Mark of Zorro* (1920) and *The Black Pirate* (1926). His son **Douglas Fairbanks Jr** (1909–) also became a film actor. He played roles similar to those of his father, in films such as *The Prisoner of Zenda* (1937) and *Sinbad the Sailor* (1947).

Fair Deal The legislative program proposed by President *Truman (1945–1953). First presented in Truman's 1949 inaugural address, the Fair Deal was essentially a continuation of the Roosevelt *New Deal, including expanded social security benefits, federal regulation of working conditions, and ambitious housing programs. Strong opposition by Republicans and southern Democrats in Congress, however, prevented the implementation of most of the Fair Deal proposals.

Fairfax, Thomas, 3rd Baron (1612–71) English general, who as commander in chief of the *New Model Army defeated Charles I at *Naseby. Fairfax subsequently opposed the king's execution and resigned his command in 1650 in protest against the planned invasion of Scotland. After Cromwell's death he participated in the restoration of Charles II.

fairies Supernatural beings that are half man, half spirit. Folklore depicts them as enigmatic beings skilled in magic and illusion, benevolent or harmful in turn. Some tales tell of their aid to, and even intermarriage with, humans, but others of their abduction of humans, especially children, for whom changelings were substituted. It has been suggested that they represent memories of extinct indigenous peoples, such as the Picts. Modern fairies are usually shown as small, but in folklore they were frequently tall and awesomely beautiful.

Fair Labor Standards Act (1938) A US law that regulated the minimum wage and maximum working hours allowed interstate commerce workers. It provided for overtime pay and banned child labor. Passed during the New Deal, it has long been upheld.

Fair Oaks A battlefield in E central Virginia, E of Richmond. During the Civil War's Peninsular Campaign in 1862, Union Gen. George B. McClellan's forces defeated Confederate Gen. Joseph E. Johnston's troops in 1862. Fair Oaks is also called the Battle of Seven Pines.

fairy bluebird A songbird of the genus *Irena* (2 species), occurring in tropical evergreen forests and feeding chiefly on fruit and nectar. The blue-backed fairy bluebird (*I. puella*) of Indomalaysia has a glossy black plumage with a bright-blue back and tail and red eyes. Family: *Irenidae* (leafbirds).

fairy penguin The smallest of the *penguins, *Eudyptula minor*, also called little penguin. About 12 in (30 cm) tall, it is the only penguin commonly occurring on Australian coasts, breeding in dense colonies and nesting in crevices or disused burrows.

fairy shrimp A *crustacean, belonging to the order *Anostraca*, that occurs in mainly freshwater pools and ponds of arid regions (*compare* brine shrimp). It has an elongated body, up to 1 in (25 mm) long, without a carapace and swims on its back using 11–19 pairs of appendages. Subclass: **Branchiopoda*.

fairy stories Tales for children of a more or less simple kind, involving fantastic or supernatural elements. Most originate in oral tradition, although some are rewritten in sophisticated form, as with *Perrault's *Tales of Mother Goose* (1697); others, like Oscar *Wilde's *The Happy Prince* (1888), are purely literary in origin. The most famous collection of oral tales is *Kinder- und Hausmärchen*

(1812–13) by the brothers *Grimm. Probably the most famous writer of original tales is the Dane Hans Christian *Andersen. Fairy tales often transcend national boundaries; similar tales are found throughout the world.

Faisalabad 31 25N 73 09E A city in NE Pakistan, called Lyallpur until 1979. It is the commercial and manufacturing center of an agricultural region specializing in cotton and wheat. Population (1981): 1,104,210.

Faisal I (1885–1933) King of Iraq (1921–33). He played an important part in the Arab revolt during World War I. After the war he was briefly King of Syria before the French occupation (1920). In 1921 the British installed him as king in the mandate of Iraq.

Faisal II (1935–58) King of Iraq (1939–58). Until he came of age in 1953, his uncle acted as regent. He was killed in the 1958 revolution led by *Kassem.

Faisal Ibn Abdul Aziz (1905–75) King of Saudi Arabia (1964–75). A son of *Ibn Saud, Faisal represented Saudi Arabia at the UN. In 1958 he became the real ruler of Saudi Arabia, although his brother *Saud was still nominally king until abdicating in 1964. His reign saw economic development and the increased international importance of Saudi Arabia as an oil-producing country. He was assassinated by his nephew.

faith healing (*or* spiritual healing) The curing of illness or disability by supernatural means. The temple of *Asclepius at *Epidauros was a famous faith-healing center in antiquity. Christ is credited with several miraculous cures (Matthew 9.2–7, etc.). Some charismatic healers apparently achieve cures unaccountable to science, particularly at mass rallies where powerful emotional effects operate upon the patients, but the possibilities for deception by callous tricksters are obvious and frauds frequently occur.

Fakhr ad-Din II (c. 1572–1635) Ruler of Lebanon (1593–1633). He took advantage of the weakness of the Ottomans to expand into Syria and Palestine, but in 1635 was captured and executed in Istanbul. He is sometimes seen as a forerunner of Lebanese nationalists.

fakir (Arabic: poor man) A Muslim mendicant who practices ascetic and religious exercises, often a member of a Muslim sect or of a Sufi religious brotherhood (*compare* dervishes). In India the term is applied more generally to any (Muslim or Hindu) ascetic or yogi.

Falabella The smallest breed of pony, developed by the Falabella family in Argentina using Shetland pony stock. It has a fine soft coat of any color and is popular as a mount for small children. Height: $3\frac{1}{3}$–$7\frac{1}{2}$ hands (38–76 cm).

Falaise 48 54N 0 11W A small town in NW France, in the Calvados department. It is best known as the site of the castle of the Dukes of Normandy, in which William the Conqueror was born. The town was virtually destroyed during the Normandy campaign (*see* World War II).

Falange Española The Spanish Fascist party, created in 1933 by José António *Primo de Rivera. The Falange wanted to regenerate Spain by means of revolution but rejected socialism as atheistic and alien to Spanish traditions. In 1937 Franco merged the Falange with the various Nationalist parties to create the National Movement, which became Spain's only legal party after the Civil War.

Falashas An Ethiopian tribe, who practice an early form of Judaism. They adhere closely to the Bible but do not have the postbiblical Jewish literature or observances. In recent years many Falashas have been introduced to modern Judaism and some have emigrated to Israel.

falcon A ground-nesting bird of prey belonging to a widely distributed family (*Falconidae*; 58 species); 6–24 in (15–60 cm) long, falcons are characterized by long pointed wings and a notched hooked bill. True falcons belong to the genus *Falco* and are fast, powerful fliers killing small birds in flight with their claws or seizing small mammals from the ground. The small falconets occur in tropical regions and usually feed on insects. Order: *Falconiformes* (falcons, hawks, etc.). *See also* caracara; gyrfalcon; hobby; kestrel; lanner; merlin; peregrine.

falconry (*or* hawking) The sport of hunting small animals or birds with falcons, other hawks, or sometimes eagles. It was practiced in Asia from the 8th century BC and was very popular in Europe from late medieval times to the 17th century. Traditionally the birds are either taken as fledglings (eyasses) or caught as one-year-old birds (passagers) or fully mature birds (haggards), but because many hunting birds are now protected species, they are often bred in captivity. They are then trained to sit hooded on the gloved fist and, by the use of a lure (an imitation bird with meat attached), to hunt and kill (but not retrieve). Large species, such as the peregrine falcon, need very open country, while smaller species are used in wooded country.

Falkirk 56 00N 3 48W A city in Scotland, in Central Region of the Forth-Clyde Canal. Here Bonnie Prince Charlie defeated General Hawley in 1746. Formerly a prominent market town, Falkirk is now important industrially, particularly for iron founding and aluminum rolling. Population (1973 est): 36,901.

FALKLAND ISLANDS *An Argentinian armored personnel carrier patrols the streets of Stanley, the islands' capital, during the Argentinian occupation.*

Falkland Islands (Argentine name: Islas Malvinas) An island group and British crown colony in the S Atlantic Ocean. The main islands of the group of about 100 are East and West Falkland; its dependencies to the SE are *South Georgia and the South Sandwich group. The population is almost entirely of British origin. Sheep farming is the main occupation on the islands' rough moorland, producing wool for export (chiefly to the UK). *History*: the first landing was by Capt. John Strong in 1690. In the early 19th century the islands became a British colony. During World War I the naval battle of the Falkland Islands, in which the Germans were decisively defeated by the British, was fought off East Falkland (December 1914). Argentina has long made claims to the group, and on Apr 2, 1982, invaded the islands. US and UN attempts to mediate a diplomatic settlement failed and a task force sent by the UK recaptured South Georgia (Apr 25) and the Falkland Islands themselves on June 14, after considerable loss of life on both sides. Area: 4700 sq mi (12,173 sq km). Population (1980 est): 1813. Capital: Stanley.

Falla, Manuel de (1876–1946) Spanish nationalist composer. He lived in Paris (1907–14), where he met Ravel and Debussy, and spent his last years in Argentina. His music was heavily influenced by Spanish folksong and he is best known for his ballet scores *Love the Magician* (1915) and *The Three-Cornered Hat* (1919), *Nights in the Gardens of Spain* (for piano and orchestra; 1909–15), and a concerto for harpsichord and chamber ensemble.

Fallen Timbers, Battle of (1794) Army victory over the Indians. General Anthony *Wayne attacked Indian tribesmen, who had been aided by the British at Fort Miami, near Toledo, Ohio, in an area of many fallen trees. Victorious, the US signed (1795) with the Indians the Treaty of Greenville, which provided more peaceful opportunities for US exploration of the Northwest Territory.

Fallopian tubes. *See* ovary.

Fallopius, Gabriel (1523–62) Italian anatomist, who discovered the tubes leading from the ovaries to the uterus, which were named for him (Fallopian tubes). A pupil of the great anatomist *Vesalius, Fallopius described the semicircular canals of the ear and many features of the reproductive system in his *Observationes anatomicae* (1561).

fallout Radioactive particles deposited from the atmosphere after a nuclear explosion. If large, the particles are deposited within a radius of a few hundred miles during the first few hours after the explosion. This is known as local fallout. Tropospheric fallout may occur anywhere along the same line of latitude as the explosion during the first week after the explosion. If the particles are drawn high up into the atmosphere, stratospheric fallout may result, which can last for several years.

fallow deer A *deer, *Dama dama*, native to Mediterranean forests but widely kept in parks and woodlands. About 3 ft (90 cm) high at the shoulder, fallow deer are fawn with white spots in summer, becoming grayish in winter; males have flattened antlers with numerous points. They feed mainly on grass but also browse on leaves.

Falmouth 41 34N 70 38W A resort town in SE Massachusetts, on the S shore of E Cape Cod. The Woods Hole Oceanographic Institution is here. Besides tourism, industries include cranberry growing and processing. Population (1990): 27,960.

False Decretals A collection of mostly forged decrees compiled in 9th-century France, but incorporated into *Isidore of Seville's compilation of decrees of Church councils. They were used to establish the authority of the papacy at the time of its ascendancy up to the 11th century and were accepted as genuine throughout the Middle Ages, being finally discredited only in 1558.

False Dimitrii. *See* Time of Troubles.

Falwell, Jerry (1933–) US fundamentalist minister; Moral Majority, Inc. leader (1979–87). He founded the Thomas Road Baptist Church (1956) in Lynchburg, Va., and that same year started broadcasting his *Old-Time Gospel Hour* program daily on radio; it was televised on Sundays from 1971. By 1980 church membership numbered 17,000 and television listeners 18 million. Moral Majority, disbanded in 1989, promoted conservatism and dealt with education, lobbying, candidate endorsement, and legal aid. In 1986, he founded the Liberty Federation, a conservative group to fight communism and to support a strong national defense.

Famagusta 35 07N 33 57E A port in Cyprus, on the E coast. Founded in the 3rd century BC, it did not develop until the 13th century AD, when Christians fled here from Palestine. It has an old walled town and a gothic cathedral (now a mosque). Its port handles most of the island's freight cargo. Population (1985): 20,000.

family planning. *See* contraception.

fandango A Spanish dance with three beats to the bar performed by a man and a woman to the accompaniment of guitar and castanets. The dance begins slowly and becomes gradually faster; the dancers freeze when the music stops.

Faneuil, Peter (1700–43) US businessman. Raised in New Rochelle, N.Y., of French Huguenot parents, he settled in Boston as a young man. He started his own business and eventually inherited his uncle's fortune. In 1740, wishing to give a gift to the city, he built Faneuil Hall, a marketplace and meeting hall. Although it burned down in 1761 it was rebuilt in 1763 and served as a meeting place during the American Revolution—thus, its name "Cradle of American Liberty." Charles *Bulfinch designed an addition in 1805.

Fang A Bantu people of West Africa comprising a number of tribes in N Gabon, Equatorial Guinea, and S Cameroon. They were originally a warlike hunting people but became ivory traders and craftsmen under colonial rule. Cocoa farming is now important and the Fang have prospered in the postindependence period.

Fangio, Juan Manuel (1911–) Argentinian automobile racer, who won 24 Grand Prix races and was world champion a record five times (1951, 1954–57).

Fa Ngum (c. 1316–c. 1373) King of Lan Xang (*or* Lang Chang), which embraced most of present-day Laos, Thailand, and part of Cambodia (1354–73). He proclaimed himself king after forcing the Lao chiefs of the upper Mekong to accept his sovereignty. He then launched further conquests to the S and W. Wearied by constant warfare, his subjects rebelled in 1373, forcing him to abdicate.

Fanning Island 03 52N 159 22W A coral atoll in the W central Pacific Ocean, in Kiribati in the Line Islands. Copra is exported. Area: 13 sq mi (33 sq km).

fantail A *flycatcher of the genus *Rhipidura* (24 species), of S Asia and Australasia, having a long fan-shaped tail. Fantails are 6–9 in (16–22 cm) long with a gray, black, or reddish-brown plumage, often with patches of white on the breast, tail, and face.

fantasia (*or* fantasy) In the 16th and 17th centuries, a piece of music (typically for viols or a keyboard instrument) having a polyphonic character. The name was applied by such composers as Mozart and Beethoven to extended compositions that did not follow the *sonata form. It is also a piece of music constructed from themes from an opera or a number of well-known tunes, such as Liszt's fantasia on Mozart's opera *Don Giovanni*.

Fantin-Latour, (Ignace) Henri (Joseph Théodore) (1836–1904) French painter, born in Grenoble. He is best known for his flower paintings and portrait groups, particularly of his impressionist friends in *Studio in the Batignolles Quarter* and *Homage to Delacroix* (both in the Louvre).

fanworm A marine *annelid worm belonging to the family *Sabellidae*, also called peacock or feather-duster worm. Fanworms build a parchmentlike tube, up to 18 in (45 cm) long, from which protrudes a feathery crown of tentacles that trap food particles and absorb oxygen. Class: *Polychaeta*.

FAO. *See* Food and Agriculture Organization.

farad (F) The *SI unit of electrical capacitance equal to the capacitance of a parallel-plate capacitor with a potential difference of one volt across its plates when the capacitor is charged with one coulomb. Named for Michael *Faraday.

Faraday, Michael (1791–1867) British chemist and physicist. Apprenticed to a bookbinder, he found the books to excite his first interest in science. He persuaded Sir Humphry *Davy to take him on as his assistant (1813), eventually succeeding Davy at the Royal Institution as professor of chemistry (1833). His earliest scientific work was on the liquefaction of gases (1823) and his first major contribution to science was the discovery of benzene (1825). However, it is with electricity and electrochemistry that his name is permanently linked. After discovering the process of electrolysis (1832) he went on to work out the laws that control it (*see* Faraday's laws of electrolysis). In electricity, he discovered the connection between electricity and magnetism and, independently of Joseph *Henry, first showed that electromagnetic induction was possible. He used induction to produce the first electrical generator (1831) and also the first transformer.

Faraday constant The quantity of electricity equivalent to one mole of electrons, i.e. the product of *Avogadro's number and the electronic charge. It has the value 96,487 coulombs per mole.

Faraday effect The rotation of the plane of polarization of plane-polarized light when it travels through certain substances in a direction parallel to the lines of force of an applied magnetic field. The effect occurs in quartz and water and is named for Michael *Faraday.

Faraday's laws of electrolysis Two laws formulated by M. Faraday in 1813–14. (1) The mass of a substance produced by an electrolytic reaction varies directly with the amount of electricity passed through the cell. (2) The masses of substances produced by a given amount of electricity are proportional to the equivalent masses of the substances.

These empirical laws are now understood to hold simply because electricity is composed of uniform discrete particles (electrons). *See also* electrolysis.

farce (from Latin *farcire*: to stuff) A dramatic genre intended only to amuse its audience, a less sophisticated and less intellectual form than pure comedy. Elements common to most farce include peculiar situations, improbable coincidences, and ridiculous exaggerations of character and physical action. The term originally described comic interludes—"stuffing"—in medieval French religious plays. Some of the best farces were written in the late 19th century, notably those of Feydeau and Labiche in France and Pinero and W. S. Gilbert in England.

Far East The countries and areas of E and SE Asia bordering on the Pacific Ocean. It includes Siberia (Russia), China, North and South Korea, and Japan and sometimes Indonesia, Malaysia, and the Philippines. The term is often generally applied to all the countries of E and SE Asia.

Fareham 50 51N 1 10W A city in S England, in Hampshire on Portsmouth Harbour. Its industries include boatbuilding, engineering, and horticulture (particularly strawberry growing). It is also a market town and sailing center. Population (1981): 88,274.

Farel, Guillaume (1489–1565) French Protestant reformer. Forced to leave France in 1524 because of his beliefs, he settled in Geneva. Although banished from the city, he later returned and succeeded in establishing Protestantism there in 1536. From 1537 he worked with *Calvin, having persuaded him to stay in Geneva.

Farewell, Cape 59 50N 43 40W The S tip of Greenland, on Egger Island. A headland rising to 2000 ft (600 m), it is edged with rocks and is known for its bad weather.

Fargo 46 52N 96 49W A city in North Dakota, on the Red River. Named for the pioneer expressman W. G. Fargo, it is the trading center of an agricultural region. The North Dakota State University was established here in 1890. Population (1990): 74,111.

Fargo, William. *See* Wells, Henry.

Farnese, Alessandro, Duke of Parma (1545–92) Italian general in the service of *Philip II of Spain (his uncle). In 1571 he fought the Turks at *Lepanto and from 1577 served against the *Revolt of the Netherlands. As governor general of the Netherlands (1578–92), he regained the S provinces, making peace at *Arras (1579). In 1585 he captured Antwerp following a 13-month siege.

Faroe Islands. *See* Faeroe Islands.

Farouk I (1920–65) The last king of Egypt (1936–52). His inability to prevent British intervention in Egyptian affairs, and defeat in the first Arab-Israeli War (1948–49), led to his overthrow and exile in Monaco.

Farquhar, George (1678–1707) Irish dramatist. After studying and acting in Dublin he won immediate success in London with his first play, *Love and a Bottle* (1699). His two best-known plays, *The Recruiting Officer* (1706) and *The Beaux' Stratagem* (1707), replaced the highly mannered and cynical conventions of Restoration drama with a more natural sentimental style.

Farragut, David (Glasgow) (1801–70) US admiral. As a young man he became a ship's officer and by 1824 was commander of his own ship. His service during the Civil War involved command of a Union fleet that blockaded parts of the Mississippi River and prevented the Confederates from receiving needed aid. New Orleans (1862) and Vicksburg (1863) fell with his help, and several forts on Mobile Bay, Ala., were captured (1864) due to his daring run through the mined harbor.

Farrell, James T(homas) (1904–79) US writer. He wrote about his native Chicago and the middle-class Irish-Americans there. His trilogy, *Young Lonigan* (1932), *The Young Manhood of Studs Lonigan* (1934), and *Judgment Day* (1935), followed one man's life and early death. He also wrote about young Danny O'Neill and would-be writer Bernard Clare (Carr) in a series of novels (1963–68), and authored the novels *Invisible Swords* (1971) and *The Death of Nora Ryan* (1978), and the essay collections *A Note on Literary Criticism* (1936) and *Literature and Morality* (1947).

farsighted(ness) (*or* hypermetropia) Inability to see close objects clearly, because the lens of the eye focuses light to a point behind the retina (light-sensitive layer). This is less common than nearsightedness among young people, but, owing to changes in the lens with age, many people need glasses for reading by the time they are 50. This type of farsightedness is known as presbyopia.

Fasciola. *See* liver fluke.

fascism A 20th-century political movement. Taking its name from the *fasces*, the bound bundles of rods that symbolized the authority of ancient Roman magistrates, fascism first became an organized movement in Italy in 1919 under *Mussolini. Social and economic backwardness, fear of communist revolution, and frustrated national ambitions following World War I encouraged its growth, and in 1922 Mussolini's *Blackshirts came to power. Fascism became more doctrinaire, rejecting ideas of individual liberty and equality, emphasizing national or racial superiority, and concentrating authority on a dictatorial cult figure. In Germany Hitler, who came to power in 1933 as leader of the *Nazi Party, added anti-Semitism to fascist militarism and anticommunism. World War II destroyed Mussolini's and Hitler's dictatorships and fascism won little support in other countries, except in Spain, where Franco's regime survived almost 40 years. The term fascist is now often used pejoratively to describe any advocate of extreme right-wing views.

Fashoda incident (1898) A confrontation between Britain and France at Fashoda in the Egyptian Sudan over their rival claims to the area. French forces under Jean-Baptiste Marchand (1863–1914) occupied the fort at Fashoda, which quickly brought *Kitchener and his Anglo-Egyptian force to the spot. After several months of diplomatic wrangling, which brought the two countries to the brink of a major war, France was forced to withdraw and Britain's claims were recognized.

Fassbinder, Rainer Werner (1946–82) German film director. Working with a small group of actors in Munich, he produced a rapid succession of bleak realistic films on contemporary social themes. These include *The Bitter Tears of Petra von Kant* (1972) and *Fear Eats the Soul* (1974).

Fast, Howard Melvin (1914–) US writer. A member of the Communist Party (1943–57), he served a prison term (1950) for concealing his membership from the House Un-American Activities Committee (HUAC) and was awarded the Stalin International Peace Prize (1954). His break with the party is related in *Naked God* (1957). His works include *Two Valleys* (1933), *Citizen Tom Paine* (1943), *Freedom Road* (1944), *Spartacus* (1952), *The Immigrants* (1977), *Second Generation* (1978), *The Establishment* (1979), and *The Legacy* (1981).

fast reactor A nuclear reactor (*see* nuclear energy) in which natural uranium enriched with uranium-235 or plutonium-239 is used without a moderator, the chain reaction being sustained by fast neutrons. In these reactors the core is surrounded by a blanket of natural uranium into which neutrons escape. These neutrons collide with U-238 nuclei to form U-239 nuclei, which decay to the fissionable isotope Pu-239. By suitable design, more Pu-239 can be produced in the blanket than is required to enrich the fuel in the core. These reactors are therefore called **breeder reactors** and they are 50 times more economical in uranium usage than *thermal reactors.

Their main disadvantage is that the temperature is so high that a liquid metal (usually sodium) has to be used as coolant: any leakage of sodium could be disastrous. Also, plutonium is both extremely toxic and can be used to make *nuclear weapons. For these reasons fast breeder reactors, although under development in several countries, are somewhat unpopular.

Fatah, al- (Arabic: the victory) A Palestinian organization, also known as the Palestine National Liberation Movement, established in the late 1950s. Led by Yasser *Arafat, al-Fatah began guerrilla warfare and terrorism against Israel in the mid-1960s. It is a component of the *Palestine Liberation Organization.

Fatehpur Sikri 27 06N 77 39E A deserted city in Uttar Pradesh (N India). Founded (1569) by *Akbar, it was the Mogul capital until Akbar's move to *Lahore (1585). Its palaces, mosques, and gateways are masterpieces of *Mogul architecture, notably the Buland Darwaza (Victory Gate).

Fates In Greek mythology, three goddesses who determine human destinies. The daughters of Zeus and Themis, they are: Lachesis, who assigns a person's position at birth; Clotho, who spins out the thread of his existence; and Atropos, who cuts the thread at death.

Fathers of the Church The title given to certain writers of the early Christian Church whose works were regarded as carrying special weight in matters of doctrine and who were noted for their great learning and holiness. The period in which they lived extends from the 1st–7th centuries, and they are classified as ante-Nicene or post-Nicene according to whether they lived before or after the Council of *Nicaea (325). They include Tertullian, Athanasius, Ambrose, Augustine, Jerome, and Gregory the Great.

fathom A unit used to express depths of water. Originally intended to be the distance between a man's fingertips with his arms outstretched, it is equal to six feet. It has now largely been replaced by the meter.

Fátima 39 37N 8 39W A village in central Portugal. It was here that three children allegedly saw a vision of the Virgin Mary (1917); it is now a place of pilgrimage.

Fatimah (d. 632) The daughter of *Mohammed. She married *Ali and was the mother of his sons, Hasan and Husayn, from whom most of the Shiite *imams were descended. She died shortly after her father. The Fatimid caliphs claimed descent from her.

Fatimids A dynasty of *caliphs ruling in N Africa and Egypt (909–1171). The Fatimids claimed descent from *Fatimah, Mohammed's daughter, and formed a subsect of the *Ismaili. They seized power in Tunisia in 909 and conquered Egypt in 969. In the 11th century their power declined and the caliphs became puppets in the hands of their soldiers. In 1171 they were finally overthrown by *Saladin.

fats and oils *Lipid substances formed by the combination of glycerol with *fatty acids. Fats occur widely in animals and plants as an energy store and as insulating material. Vegetable fats and oils are used in making soaps, margarines, cooking oils, paints, and lubricants. Animal fats are used in foods, soaps, and candles. Oils are distinguished from fats by being liquid at 43°F (20°C), whereas fats are solid. Mineral oils are hydrocarbons rather than lipids (*see* oil).

fatty acid (*or* carboxylic acid) An organic acid that comprises one or more carboxyl groups (–COOH) attached to an alkyl group. Fatty acids combine with glycerol to form glycerides, the main constituents of *fats and oils. Animal fats tend to be hard because they contain a high proportion of saturated fatty acids; soft fats, such as vegetable and fish oils, contain greater proportions of unsaturated and polyunsaturated fatty acids (containing one or more double bonds). There is evidence to suggest that the risk of heart disease associated with dietary fat is reduced if the fat consumed is rich in polyunsaturated fatty acids. Certain essential fatty acids are normally required in small amounts in the diet.

Faulkner, William (1897–1962) US novelist. Born in Mississippi, he abandoned his university education to write. He supported himself with various jobs before publishing his first poetry collection, *The Marble Faun*, in 1924. His first novel, *Soldier's Pay*, appeared in 1926. *Sartoris* (1929), the hero of which is based on Faulkner's great-grandfather, also an author, was the first of his stories set in the fictitious Yoknapatawpha County, based on his native N Mississippi. Faulkner's characters and their personal tragedies acquire an epic universal grandeur, despite the decaying society within which they occasionally find themselves. His major novels, usually experimental in form and technique, include *The Sound and the Fury* (1929), *As I Lay Dying* (1930), *Light in August* (1932), *Absalom, Absalom!* (1936), and *The Reivers* (1966). He was awarded the Nobel Prize in 1949.

WILLIAM FAULKNER *Writer whose works, usually set in fictional Yoknapatawpha County, Mississippi, portrayed universal man.*

fault A fracture plane in the rocks of the earth's crust, the rocks on each side being displaced relative to one another, either vertically, horizontally, or obliquely. Faulting occurs as a result of accumulated strain in the rocks, usually at plate margins (*see* plate tectonics). The extent of vertical displacement of the strata is called the throw; the horizontal displacement is the heave. A horst is an upstanding feature between two parallel faults; conversely a graben or rift valley is downthrown between parallel faults.

Fauré, Urbain (Gabriel) (1845–1924) French composer and organist, a pupil of Saint-Saëns. He became organist at the Madeleine (1877) and director of the Paris conservatory (1905). He was afflicted with deafness in later life. His works include the well-known *Requiem* (1886–87), incidental music for Maeterlincke's play *Pelléas and Mélisande* (1898), the opera *Pénélope* (1913), the orchestral *Pavane* (1887), and much piano music and chamber music. Fauré is probably best known for his songs, such as those in the cycle *La Bonne Chanson* (1891–92).

Faust A legendary medieval German scholar and magician who sold his soul to the Devil in exchange for knowledge and power. Stories of magicians in league with the Devil (often personified by Mephistopheles) combined with the historical Johann Faust (c. 1480–c. 1539), a vagrant scholar and mountebank, to produce a figure who has inspired numerous literary works, notably by *Marlowe (1592), *Lessing (1784), *Goethe (1808, 1832), and Thomas *Mann (1947), as well as musical works, including operas by *Gounod and *Boito. The character of Faust has varied from that of Marlowe's power-seeking magician to that of Goethe's rationalist philosopher.

fauvism A movement in French painting at the turn of the 19th century, characterized by the aggressive use of strong colors. The fauves (French: wild beasts, so called by a critic of their work) included, under the leadership of *Matisse, Raoul *Dufy, Georges *Braque, Georges *Rouault, and Maurice de *Vlaminck. Most of the fauves had become interested in *cubism by 1908.

Fawkes, Guy (1570–1606) English conspirator. A convert to Roman Catholicism, he served in the Spanish army in the Netherlands during the 1590s and on his return to England became involved in the Gunpowder Plot, led by Robert Catesby (1573–1605), to blow up James I and Parliament. The conspirators were informed upon and Fawkes was discovered (Nov 5, 1605) with the gunpowder in a cellar of the Palace of Westminister. Catesby was killed while resisting arrest and Fawkes was executed. Nov 5 continues to be celebrated with fireworks and the burning of a bonfire of effigies of Fawkes (so-called "guys").

Fa Xian (*or* Fa-hsien; 5th century AD) Chinese Buddhist monk. He traveled to India and Ceylon in about 402 returning to China in about 413 with a large collection of early Sanskrit Buddhist texts. His translation of these and his account of his journey provide important documentation of the beginning of relations between China and India.

FBI. *See* Federal Bureau of Investigation.

feathers The specialized body covering of birds. Thought to have evolved from the scales of reptilian ancestors, feathers arise from definite tracts over the body surface and are of several types: the down feathers of chicks are short and soft, whereas the quill feathers of adult birds typically have a stiff shaft bearing two vanes with interlocking barbs and are specialized for flight as wing and tail feathers. As well as its role in flight, the plumage has several other functions. Like the hair of mammals, it helps to regulate body temperature and provides protection against the environment. It is also responsible for the bird's distinctive coloration, which is particularly important in courtship or aggressive displays. In order to maintain their function the feathers must be periodically renewed, and most birds undergo at least two molts a year. Molting is controlled partly by hormones and partly by environmental factors.

feather star. *See* crinoid.

February Second month of the year. The name is derived from Februus, the Roman god of purification. It has 28 days with 29 every fourth, or leap, year, to equate the calendar year with the solar year. The zodiac signs for February are Aquarius and Pisces; the flowers are violets and primroses, and the birthstone is the amethyst.

feces The material that is expelled from the bowels through the anus. It is a solid or semisolid mass consisting of undigested food (chiefly cellulose and other fibers), mucus, bacteria, and material from the liver, including bile pigments (which are responsible for the color of feces). Any persistent change in the appearance of the feces may be an indication of disease. *See also* constipation; diarrhea.

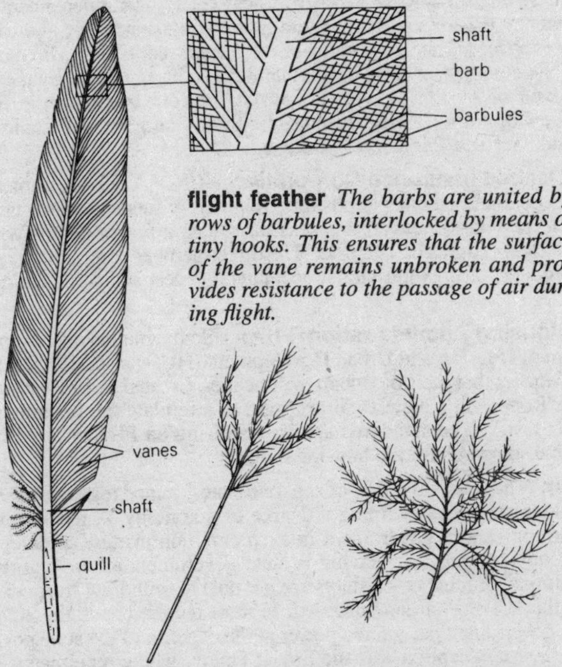

flight feather *The barbs are united by rows of barbules, interlocked by means of tiny hooks. This ensures that the surface of the vane remains unbroken and provides resistance to the passage of air during flight.*

filoplume *This small hair-like feather, which has very few barbs, is found in large numbers between and beneath the quill feathers.*

down feather *This type of feather forms the insulating body covering of nestlings. Its fluffy appearance is due to the lack of interlocking hooks on the barbules.*

FEATHERS

Fechner, Gustav Theodor (1801–87) German physicist, noted for his work in experimental psychology. Fechner developed techniques for investigating the sensations experienced by human subjects exposed to stimuli of varying strengths. He also proposed a mathematical expression (later shown to be inaccurate) of the theory concerning the just noticeable difference between two stimuli, advanced by E. H. *Weber.

Federal Aviation Administration (FAA) US Department of Transportation agency that oversees aviation. It regulates commercial and civil aviation and coordinates air traffic of both with that of military aircraft. Formerly the Federal Aviation Agency, it took its present name in 1967.

Federal Bureau of Investigation (FBI) The organization within the Department of Justice that carries out investigations into possible breaches of federal law, especially those related to security. Founded as the Bureau of Investigation in 1908, it became the FBI in 1935; under J. Edgar *Hoover (director 1924–72) it developed considerable autonomy. It was prominent in campaigns against organized crime in the 1930s and from the 1970s; and in anticommunist campaigns from the 1950s.

Federal Communications Commission (FCC) An independent US government agency that oversees interstate radio, television, wire, and cable communication services. The Communications Act, passed in 1934, directed the formation of the commission with seven members to be appointed by the president and approved of by the Senate. It consists of four bureaus: the Broadcast Bureau, the Common Carrier Bureau, the Safety and Special Radio Services Bureau, and the Field Engineering Bureau.

Federal Deposit Insurance Corporation (FDIC) A US government agency that insures commercial bank depositors from loss of funds. It was established in 1933 when the Glass-Steagall Act was passed as a future defensive measure against the bank failures of 1929–33. The three-member commission, appointed by the president, insures individual accounts and sets standards for qualifying banks.

Federal Housing Administration (FHA) US government agency, part of the Department of Housing and Urban Development (HUD) since 1965, that insures mortgage lenders that their payments will be met. Created in 1934, it was part of President *Roosevelt's New Deal program to stimulate the housing and construction industry. The standards set for acquiring an FHA-insured mortgage have become standards for the housing industry.

federalism The political union of separate states, joined together to serve their common interests while retaining a degree of autonomy. A federation usually provides strong central government in such common matters as defense, a national currency system, etc., leaving to state government affairs that depend on local conditions. In most cases states are not able to withdraw from a federation at will, as the *Civil War demonstrated. In most federations in the 20th century the central government has gained power at the expense of the state government, as in the US. An exception was the Soviet Union, where republics were given greater control over their budgets and in the management of industry. Canada is a federation that is under severe strain owing to the separatist elements in the province of *Quebec. Other federations include those of Malaysia and Australia.

Federalist Papers (1787–88) A series of essays published in New York newspapers, urging ratification of the US Constitution. The authors of the essays, using the name Publius, were Alexander *Hamilton, James *Madison, and John *Jay. They explained in detail the new federal government and its various departments. The essays were later published (1788) in two volumes, *The Federalist.*

Federalist Party US political party, led by John *Adams and Alexander *Hamilton, that advocated the establishment of a strong central government for the newly independent US. The Federalists emerged in 1787 as those who supported the ratification of the proposed *Constitution, explaining their position in a series of political essays known as the *Federalist Papers. They were opposed by the Republicans led by Thomas *Jefferson, who feared encroachments on individual liberty by a centralized government. With the ratification of the Constitution in 1788 and the election of George *Washington, the Federalist candidate, as the first president, the Federalists emerged as the majority party. During the administration of Washington and his successor, Adams, the Federalists were responsible for establishing a national administration. Their political power declined, however, with the defeat of John Adams and the election of Jefferson as president in 1800. After the *War of 1812, the Federalist Party lost much of its national influence, and many of its members joined the *Whig Party headed by John Quincy *Adams and Henry *Clay.

Federal Reserve System The *central bank of the US, established in 1913, which implements the government's monetary policy. There are 12 Federal Reserve Districts each of which has its own Federal Bank, controlled by the Federal Reserve Board in Washington.

Federal Trade Commission (FTC) A US government agency that regulates competition in interstate commerce. Established in 1914, its five commissioners, appointed by the president, look into unfair competition practices, such as monopolies, restraint of trade practices, and false advertising. Working closely with the Justice Department, the commission enforces antitrust legislation.

feedback In electronics and communications theory, the process of returning to the input of a device a fraction of the output signal. **Negative feedback**, in which the feedback opposes and therefore reduces the input, is often used in *amplifier circuits. It compensates for noise and distortion in the output signal, although it also reduces the overall amplification. **Positive feedback** reinforces the input signal. If it becomes too high, the circuit oscillates and the output becomes independent of the input. This is the cause of the singing noise heard in a public-address system when the microphone picks up feedback from the loudspeakers.

Feininger, Lyonel (Charles Adrian) (1871–1956) US painter and illustrator, born in New York. He studied painting in Germany and Paris and first worked as an illustrator and cartoonist for various German and French periodicals before concentrating on painting in 1907. His works were exhibited with the *Blaue Reiter group and he taught at the *Bauhaus (1919–33), eventually returning to the US in 1937. He developed a personal form of *cubism in his oils and watercolors, his favorite subjects being architectural forms, boats, and the sea.

feldspars The most important group of rock-forming minerals and the major constituents of igneous rocks. There are four components of feldspars: anorthite (calcium plagioclase, $CaAl_2SI_2O_8$); albite (sodium plagioclase, $NaAlSi_3O_8$); orthoclase (potassium feldspar, $KAlSi_3O_8$); and celsian (barium feldspar, $BaAl_2Si_2O_8$, which is rare). Feldspars ranging between albite and anorthite in composition are plagioclase feldspars; those ranging between albite and orthoclase are alkali feldspars. Calcic plagioclase includes anorthite, bytownite, and labradorite; sodic plagioclase includes andesine, oligoclase, and albite. Alkali feldspars include sanidine, anorthoclase, orthoclase, microcline, and adularia.

Felidae The *cat family: a family of mammals of the order **Carnivora*. It includes the cats, lion, tiger, leopard, and cheetah.

Felix V (antipope). *See* Amadeus VIII.

Feller, Bob (Robert William Andrew F.; 1918–) US baseball pitcher. He pitched for the Cleveland Indians (1936–41; 1945–56). Nicknamed "Rapid Robert," he had 348 strikeouts in one year (1946) and 266 career wins. During his career he pitched three no-hit games. He was elected to the Baseball Hall of Fame (1962).

Fellini, Federico (1920–93) Italian film director. He began working in films as an actor and scriptwriter. His films, many of which are characterized by their autobiographical elements and their use of baroque imagery and fantasy, include *La strada* (1954), *8½* (1963), *Roma* (1972), and *Amarcord* (1974).

felony A more serious offense than a misdemeanor, involving such crimes as burglary and murder. Conviction for a felony can result in imprisonment for one year or more.

feminism. *See* women's movement.

femur The thigh bone: the longest bone in the human body. It extends from the pelvis, where it forms part of the ball-and-socket hip joint, to the joint of the knee. The head of the femur is commonly fractured in the elderly after falls.

fencing The art of combat with a sword, of which there are three main forms in sport: foil, épée, and saber. Bouts for all three weapons are fought on a *piste*, or marked-out area 6.5 × 46 ft (2 × 14 m) for foil and épée or 6.5 × 78.5 ft (2 × 24 m) for saber. A hit is scored against a competitor who crosses the rear limit. The winner is the first to score five hits (for men) or four (for women) in a time limit of six minutes (for men) or five (for women), the form of the hit varying between the three weapons. For competitions the electric foil and épée are used for automatic judging of hits.

FENCING

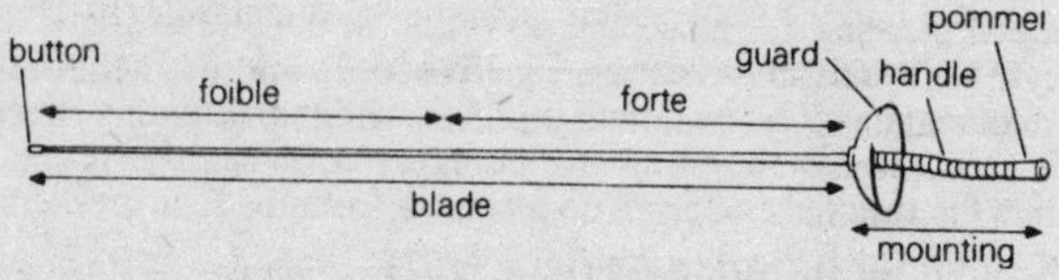

Parts of a sword

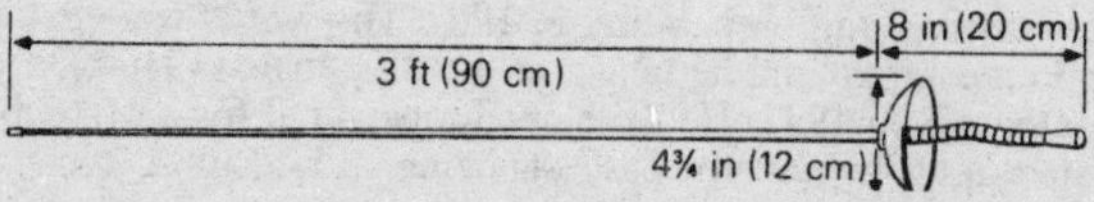

Foil *The foil weighs a maximum of 17.6 oz (500 g). Its blade is quadrangular and very flexible.*

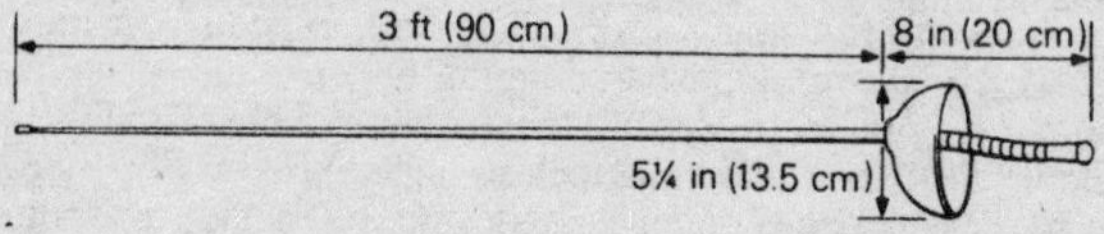

Épée *The épée weighs a maximum of 27.2 oz (770 g). Its blade is triangular and stiffer than that of the foil.*

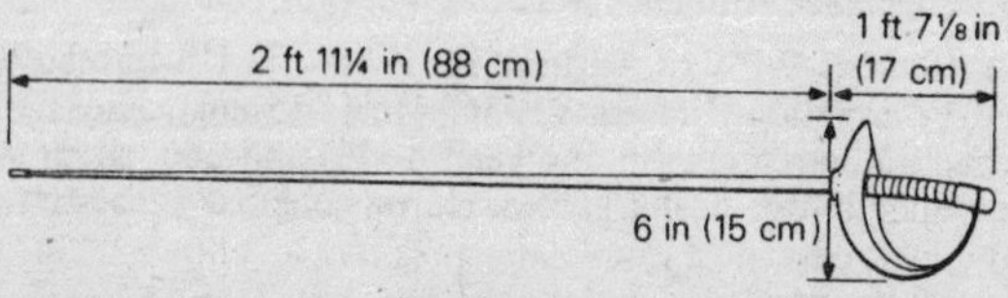

Saber *The saber weighs a maximum of 17.6 oz (500 g). Its blade is a flattened V-shape.*

Fénelon, François de Salignac de la Mothe (1651–1715) French Roman Catholic prelate and theologian. As director (from 1678) of an institution for recent Roman Catholic converts, he wrote *Traité de l'éducation des filles* (1687), criticizing the coercive conversion of Huguenots. In 1689 he became tutor to

Louis XIV's grandson, the Duke of Burgundy, and in 1695 Archbishop of Cambrai. His famous *Aventures de Télémaque* (1699), written for the duke's instruction, alienated the king and his *Explication des maximes des saints* (1697), containing a defense of *Quietism, was condemned by the pope.

Fenian cycle Irish Gaelic tales and ballads of the Fianna, a legendary band of warrior-poets named for their leader, *Finn MacCool, who was said to have flourished in the 3rd century AD. Many of the tales are collected in *The Colloquy of the Ancient Men* (c. 1200) in which Oisin (*see* Ossian) and Caoilte, members of the Fianna, return to Ireland from the Land of Youth and recount their youthful adventures to St Patrick, and in the manuscripts *The Book of the Dun Cow* (c. 1100) and *The Book of Leinster* (c. 1160).

Fenians Members of a secret Irish-American revolutionary society, the Irish Republican Brotherhood (IRB), formed in 1858 by James Stephens (1825–1901). The Fenians staged an unsuccessful uprising in Ireland in 1867 but the IRB's influence continued into the 20th century, when it was superseded by the IRA.

fennec A desert *fox, *Fennecus zerda*, of Africa and the Middle East. It is sandy-colored and has large pointed ears. Measuring up to 28 in (70 cm) including the tail 12 in (30 cm), it spends the day in a burrow and hunts at night, finding lizards, birds, and insects by ear. □mammal.

fennel A strong-smelling perennial herb, *Foeniculum vulgare*, native to S Europe and cultivated throughout temperate Eurasia;. 20 in–5 ft (0.5–1.5 m) high, it has feathery dark-green leaves and clusters of small yellow flowers. The leaves are used mostly to flavor foods and sauces. The greenish seeds taste of aniseed and are used to flavor liqueurs, candies, pastries, and sweet pickles. The seed oil is used to scent soaps and perfumes. Florence, or sweet, fennel (*F. dulce*) is cultivated for its bulblike leafstalks, which may be eaten cooked as a vegetable or raw in salads. Family: **Umbelliferae*.

fenugreek An annual herb, *Trigonella foenum-graecum*, native to the Mediterranean but widely cultivated. About 24 in (60 cm) high, it has toothed compound leaves and small white flowers that develop into slender curved pods. The brownish seeds are used to flavor curry and chutney. Family: **Leguminosae*.

Ferber, Edna (1887–1968) US novelist. She worked as a reporter in Wisconsin and Chicago before she started writing short stories and novels in 1911. Emma McChesney, a saleswoman, was one of her most popular early characters and appeared in many short stories. *So Big* (1924) brought her the Pulitzer Prize in 1925 and *Showboat* (1926) was adapted for the musical stage. Other works, most of which were made into motion pictures, include *Cimarron* (1930), *Saratoga Trunk* (1941), *Giant* (1952), and *Ice Palace* (1958). She also wrote plays, including *Dinner at Eight* (1932) and *Stage Door* (1936), with George S. Kaufman.

fer-de-lance A common extremely venomous tropical American *pit viper, *Bothrops atrox*. It is much feared by plantation workers and often visits houses in search of rodents; 4–7 ft (1.2–2 m) long, it has a broad triangular head, is gray or brown with black-edged diamond patterning and a yellowish chin, and generally feed on small mammals, frogs, and lizards.

Ferdinand (1865–1927) King of Romania (1914–27), who in 1916 joined the Allies in *World War I. In 1918 he annexed Bessarabia from Russia and in 1919 intervened in Hungary to destroy Kun's communist government.

Ferdinand (I) the Great (?1016–65) King of Castile (1037–65). He conquered León (1039) and resumed the offensive against the Moorish border kingdoms, reducing the rulers of Toledo, Saragossa, and Seville to tributaries.

Ferdinand I (1503–64) Holy Roman Emperor (1558–64). His elder brother, Emperor *Charles V, gave him the Hapsburg possessions in Germany in 1521 and in 1526 he became King of Bohemia and of Hungary, although his title to the Hungarian crown was challenged by John Zápolya (1487–1540) until 1538. Ferdinand negotiated the religious Peace of *Augsburg (1555).

Ferdinand I (1751–1825) King of Naples and Sicily (Two Sicilies; 1816–25). As Ferdinand IV he was King of Naples (1759–99, 1799–1806), being twice driven into exile in Sicily by the French. He ruled the Two Sicilies despotically.

Ferdinand I (1793–1875) Emperor of Austria (1835–48) and King of Hungary (1830–48). Feebleminded and epileptic, he was dominated by *Metternich. He abdicated during the Revolution of 1848.

Ferdinand I (1861–1948) Prince (1887–1908) and king (1908–18) of Bulgaria. In 1908 Ferdinand declared Bulgaria independent from Turkey but was forced to abdicate in 1918 after supporting the Central Powers.

Ferdinand II (1578–1637) King of Bohemia (1617–37) and Hungary (1618–37) and Holy Roman Emperor (1619–37), who championed the *Counter-Reformation. In 1619 the predominantly Protestant diet (assembly) of Bohemia offered the Bohemian crown to the Protestant *Frederick V of the Palatinate. The ensuing dispute developed into the *Thirty Years' War. Initially successful, Ferdinand suffered reverses with the intervention into the war of France and Sweden, forcing him to accept the compromise Peace of Prague (1635).

Ferdinand III (1608–57) King of Bohemia and of Hungary (1625–57) and Holy Roman Emperor (1637–57). He created a standing army, reformed the imperial council, and helped conclude the *Thirty Years' War by signing the Peace of *Westphalia (1648).

Ferdinand (V and II) the Catholic (1452–1516) King of Castile as Ferdinand V (1474–1504) and of Aragon as Ferdinand II (1479–1516). He ruled Castile jointly with his wife *Isabella I of Castile and after her death was regent for their daughter Joanna the Mad. Ferdinand's accession to the Aragonese throne effected the union of Castile and Aragon, to which Granada, taken from the Moors in 1492, was added. The introduction of the Inquisition (1480) and the expulsion of the Jews (1492) aimed to strengthen both church and monarchy, to which Ferdinand's reforms in Aragon contributed. His ambitions abroad led to wars with France for hegemony in Italy.

Ferdinand VII (1784–1833) King of Spain (1808, 1814–33). In 1808 Ferdinand was forced by Napoleon to abdicate but returned to the throne in 1814. His repressive policies caused a liberal uprising (1820) and the establishment of a liberal government until 1823, when it was ousted with French help. Alfonso repudiated the Salic Law of succession to enable his daughter *Isabella to succeed him, an act that led to the emergence of *Carlism.

Fergana (*or* Ferghana) 40 23N 71 19E A city in Uzbekistan. It is the industrial and cultural center of the fertile Fergana Valley, one of the country's main cotton-, silk-, and fruit-growing districts. Population (1987): 203,000.

Feriae The sacred festival days of ancient Rome, which were usually marked by a public holiday, feasts, prayers, and sacrifices to the gods. Feriae were normally held on fixed annual dates.

Ferlinghetti, Lawrence (1919–) US poet. His public readings and his publishing business, the City Lights Bookshop in San Francisco, promoted *Beat movement poetry. His own poetry, published in *Pictures from the Gone World* (1955), *A Coney Island in the Mind* (1958), *Tyrannus Nix?* (1969), and other collections, is largely political satire. A journal, *Back Roads to Far Places*, was published in 1971.

Fermanagh A historic county in SW Northern Ireland, bordering on the Republic of Ireland. It consists of hilly country contained chiefly in the Erne Basin and is divided by the Upper and Lower Lough Erne. It is predominantly agricultural producing livestock and potatoes. Industries include the production of clothing, cotton thread, and tweeds. Area: 715 sq mi (1851 sq km). County town: Enniskillen.

Fermat, Pierre de (1601–65) French mathematician. Professionally a lawyer, Fermat studied mathematics in his spare time. He founded *number theory and, with Blaise *Pascal, *probability theory. He is best known for *Fermat's last theorem and *Fermat's principle.

Fermat's last theorem A theorem first proposed by Pierre *Fermat, that there are no natural numbers x, y, z, and n such that $x^n + y^n = z^n$ when n is greater than two. The theorem has never been proved for the general case, only for particular examples of n. Fermat himself claimed to have proved it but he never recorded his proof.

Fermat's principle When light travels between two points its path is such that the time taken is a minimum. The principle holds when the light is reflected or refracted between the two points. It is also known as the principle of least time and is named for P. *Fermat.

fermentation The process by which microorganisms and tissues respire in the absence of oxygen (i.e. anaerobically). The fermentation of carbohydrates by yeasts to form alcohol is the basis of making wines and beers (*see* beer and brewing; wine) and the production of industrial alcohol. Other types of fermentation produce lactic acid, as in the souring of milk by bacteria. Fermentation can cause the decomposition of organic materials under anaerobic conditions but the organisms concerned are able to use only a small proportion of the available energy compared to aerobic organisms.

Fermi, Enrico (1901–54) US physicist, born in Italy. His early work in Italy was concerned with the mathematical statistics of nuclear particles; independently of *Dirac he produced the form of statistics known as *Fermi-Dirac statistics. For his work on the bombardment of uranium by thermal neutrons he was awarded the 1938 Nobel Prize. Because of his antifascism and because his wife was Jewish, Fermi and his family sailed directly from the Stockholm Nobel ceremony to the US, where he remained for the rest of his life. He was the first person to achieve a controlled nuclear chain reaction, in a converted squash court at Chicago University (1942). He later played a central role in the development of the atom bomb at Los Alamos. After his return to Chicago (1946) he bitterly opposed *Teller in the development of the hydrogen bomb.

Fermi-Dirac statistics A quantum-statistical method of analyzing a system of indistinguishable particles to determine the probability of the energy distribution. Unlike *Bose-Einstein statistics it assumes that these particles, which are known as fermions, obey the *Pauli exclusion principle. Named for E. *Fermi and P. A. M. *Dirac.

fermion Any elementary particle that obeys *Fermi-Dirac statistic. These particles, which have half-integral spin, include *leptons and *baryons. *Compare* boson.

fermium (Fm) An artificial transuranic element, named for Fermi. Like *einsteinium it was found in debris from the 1952 hydrogen-bomb explosion. The most stable isotope, ^{257}Fm, has a half-life of 80 days. At no 100; at wt 257.

fern A perennial leafy *pteridophyte plant of the class *Pteropsida* (or *Filicinae* according to some classification schemes; about 9000–15,000 species), most abundant in shady damp tropical regions but also widely distributed elsewhere. The life cycle of a fern shows *alternation of generations. The fern plant itself is the asexual (sporophyte) generation, which has a creeping underground stem (rhizome) bearing roots and aerial fronds, which reach a height of 80 ft (25 m) in the *tree ferns. The fronds are featherlike and usually divided one or more times into leaflets. Asexual spores are produced in spore capsules, which usually occur in clusters (sori) protected by a covering (indusium) on the underside of the leaflets. The spores develop into the inconspicuous sexual (gametophyte) generation—a tiny heart-shaped plant (called a prothallus) producing egg and sperm cells. The fertilized egg cell develops into a new sporophyte plant, which grows up from the prothallus. Many tropical and subtropical ferns are cultivated as house plants for their attractive foliage.

Fernandel (Fernand Joseph Desire Contandin; 1903–71) French comedian. Originally a music-hall singer and comedian, he later acted in numerous films, notably a series in the 1950s in which he played a village priest, Don Camillo, in conflict with the communist mayor.

Fernando Po. *See* Equatorial Guinea.

Ferrara 44 50N 11 38E A city in N Italy, in Emilia-Romagna. Important in Renaissance times as the seat of the Este family, it has a cathedral, castle, citadel, and university (1391). The religious reformer Savonarola was born here. Ferrara has wine, fruit, and grain trades and its manufactures include plastics, sugar, and chemicals. Population (1991 est): 141,000.

Ferrara-Florence, Council of (1438–45) The Church council at which the last concerted attempt was made to resolve the schism between Eastern and Western Churches. The council endeavored to reach agreement on doctrinal differences, such as the *Filioque clause, and to provide assistance for Constantinople against the Turks. Agreement was reached in 1439 but was short lived.

Ferraro, Geraldine Anne (1935–) US politician; Democratic candidate for vice president (1984). After graduation from Fordham Law School (1960) she became a Queens, N.Y., assistant district attorney (1974). The first woman from her district to be elected to the US House of Representatives (1978), she served on the Public Works and Transportation Committee and on the Budget Committee. As the running mate of Democratic presidential candidate Walter *Mondale in the 1984 election, she was the first woman chosen for that role. A frank and engaging speaker, she waged a spirited campaign, despite allegations of financial improprieties lodged against her husband, John A. Zaccaro. After the Democratic defeat, she returned to private life.

ferret A domesticated form of *polecat, *Mustela putorius*, that is slightly smaller than the European polecat and lighter in color (sometimes albino). Ferrets were probably bred from an Asian race (sometimes called *M. eversmanni*) and have been domesticated since at least 400 BC; they are used to drive rats and rabbits from their burrows.

ferrimagnetism A form of magnetism occurring in those *antiferromagnetic materials in which the microscopic *magnetic moments are aligned antiparallel but are not equal. The behavior is weakly *ferromagnetic below the Néel temperature and *paramagnetic above it.

ferrite **1.** A compound of iron with the general chemical formula MFe_2O_4, where M is a metal. Most ferrites are *ferromagnetic or *ferrimagnetic ceramic materials and they are used in transformers and computer memories. **2.** Iron in its body-centered cubic crystal structure, either pure or as a constituent of *steel.

FERNANDEL *In one of his famous roles, as the priest Don Camillo.*

Ferrol del Caudillo, El 43 29N 8 14W A city in NW Spain, in Galicia on the Atlantic Ocean. A port and naval base, it has ship-building and ship-repairing industries. General Franco was born here. Population: 87,736.

ferromagnetism The property of a material that enables it to become a permanent magnet, i.e. ferromagnetic materials when placed in a *magnetic field develop a very strong internal field and retain some of it when the external field is removed. The most common ferromagnetic substances are iron, cobalt, nickel, and alloys of these metals. Ferromagnetism, like *paramagnetism, is caused by the unbalanced spin of atomic electrons, which creates a magnetic dipole moment having the effect of a tiny magnet. In ferromagnetic substances, the application of an external field causes groups of these tiny magnets, called domains, to become aligned; many of them remain aligned when the field is removed. Above a certain temperature, called the Curie point, thermal agitation destroys the domain structure and the substance becomes paramagnetic. The response of a ferromagnetic material to changes in magnetic field is known as the hysteresis effect; the internal field strength remaining after the external field has been reduced to zero is called the remanence.

Fertile Crescent A strip of land in the Middle East roughly comprising the lower Nile Valley, the E Mediterranean coast, Syria, and *Mesopotamia. Formerly enjoying a wetter climate, it was the cradle of civilization, with sites showing evidence of settled communities from at least 9000 BC.

fertility drugs Drugs given to infertile women to stimulate the release of an egg cell from the ovary. The best known are the *gonadotrophins—hormones normally released by the pituitary gland to control activity of the ovary. Another fertility drug is clomiphene. The dosage of these drugs is carefully controlled in order to prevent multiple pregnancies.

fertilization The union of a male and a female *gamete, involving the fusion of hereditary material: it is the essential process of sexual *reproduction. The resulting cell, called a zygote, undergoes division (*see* cleavage), growth, and development to form a new individual, in which half the chromosomes (and therefore the genes) are of paternal origin and half of maternal origin. In **self-fertilization** both gametes are produced by the same individual; in **cross-fertilization** they derive from different individuals (these terms are applied particularly to the processes in flowering plants). In most aquatic animals the gametes are expelled into the water and fertilization is external; in most terrestrial animals the sperms are introduced into the body of the female, where fertilization takes place.

fertilizers Substances added to soils to maintain or improve soil fertility. Natural farmyard manures have long been used as a source of plant nutrients and humus, which maintains the physical structure of the soil. Other traditional fertilizers have included bone meal, dried blood, and other animal products. Modern artificial fertilizers, dating from the 19th century, provided the means for dramatic increases in crop yields. The major plant nutrients required are nitrogen (chiefly provided as ammonium nitrate derived from fixation of atmospheric nitrogen), phosphate (derived from naturally occurring rock phosphate), and potassium (from mined potash deposits). These fertilizers are used either individually as "straights" or in combined or "compound" form to provide ratios of plant nutrients matched to the crop requirements.

Artificial fertilizers have been of immense benefit in helping to feed a rapidly expanding human population. The view that they are inferior to natural fertilizers is largely unfounded. Plants take in nitrogen ions, etc., in solution through their roots whether the source is a sack of fertilizer or farmyard manure. However, excessive application of artificial fertilizers can lead to pollution of streams, rivers, and even drinking water.

Fès (*or* Fez; Arabic name: Fas) 34 05N 5 00W A city in N Moroçco. In the 14th century the Islamic city reached its peak as a major center for commerce and learning. It remains important for Arabic and Islamic teaching and has two mosques; the Qarawiyin Mosque is the oldest in Africa and contains a university (859 AD). The city gave its name to the traditional red felt hat worn by Muslims. It is a trade center for hides and leather, fruit, and traditional crafts. Population (1982): 448,823.

fescue A *grass of the genus *Festuca* (about 100 species), native to temperate and cold regions of the N hemisphere. It grows in tufts, 19–61 in (46–152 cm) high. Meadow fescue (*F. pratensis*) is sown as a pasture grass and used for livestock fodder; sheep's fescue (*F. ovina*) grows on mountains and in dry and exposed soil and the variety *F. ovina glauca* is used on ornamental borders. Red or creeping fescue (*F. rubra*) is common in grass mixtures for lawns.

fetishism **1.** In anthropology, the practice of using charms magically. The term derives from the Portuguese *feitico*, something made. Fetishism is found among W African tribes and, hence, in the West Indies. Auguste *Comte characterized primitive religion as essentially fetishism, by which he meant the attribution of human qualities to nonhuman bodies. Later *Tylor reserved the term for the idea of spirits embodied in or associated with material objects. The term is not very common in modern sociology or anthropology. **2.** In psychiatry, the abnormal condition in which sexual satisfaction is obtained by handling or otherwise using nongenital objects (fetishes). The fetish may be an article of clothing (such as shoes or underwear), rubber objects, leather, fur, or hair, and in some cases normal sexual relationships are impossible unless the fetish is present.

fetus (*or* foetus) The developing baby in the womb from the beginning of the ninth week of pregnancy until birth. The fetus is protected by a series of membranes enclosing a fluid (amniotic fluid), which can be extracted and used for diagnostic purposes. The fetus is connected through the *umbilical cord and *placenta to the mother's bloodstream. ☐embryo. *See also* prenatal diagnosis.

Feuchtwanger, Lion (1884–1958) German novelist and dramatist. Exiled in 1933, he fled to the US in 1940. His best-known novels are historical romances, notably *Jew Süss* (1925) and *The Pretender* (1936). He collaborated with *Brecht on plays and translations.

feudalism The type of land tenure, characteristic of medieval Europe, in which property was held by a vassal of a lord in return for military service and a pledge of homage. Feudalism originated with the collapse of public order in W Europe during the 8th and 9th centuries. Both kings and great lords distributed life grants of lands and offices in return for promises of loyalty and service. This practice developed into the grant of hereditary fiefs or fees (Latin word: *feoda*, from which the word feudalism is derived) in return for military service. The resulting fragmentation of authority was reflected in the rapid growth of feudal armies, often engaged in private wars, the development of the castle as an administrative and military center, and the growth of private justice administered by local lords rather than by a central authority. From the 12th century these implications of feudal tenure were challenged by the growing power of western rulers, especially in England, where it was abolished in 1661. Their governments increasingly depended on a royal bureaucracy and an army of mercenaries rather than the feudal bands. The growth of towns, outside the feudal framework, also contributed to the decline of feudalism.

Feuerbach, Ludwig Andreas (1804–72) German philosopher. Critical of Hegelian *idealism, Feuerbach saw the power of history not as a nebulous succession of spirits of the ages but as the total material conditions in any given period that caused people to behave as they did. This view and also his writings on religion, in which he argued that people lost their essential selves by applying their own attributes to imaginary beings, impressed *Marx and *Engels.

Feuillants, Club of the A moderate French Revolutionary political group that met at the former monastery of the Feuillants in Paris. Founded in 1791, the Feuillants opposed extremism, favoring constitutional monarchy. They disbanded in 1792, when the monarchy was abolished.

fever A body temperature greater than 98.6°F (37°C). This is most commonly due to *infection, but other causes include tumors, drugs, a heart attack, and a blood clot in the leg. Sometimes no cause can be found. The patient usually has a headache, shivers, and feels ill.

feverfew A perennial aromatic Eurasian herb, *Tanacetum* (or *Chrysanthemum*) *parthenium*, about 20 in (50 cm) high, with heads of yellow and white daisylike flowers. Formerly a popular medicinal herb, it was used to reduce fever. Family: **Compositae*.

Feydeau, Georges (1862–1921) French playwright, famous for his many farces, written between 1881 and 1916. They are characterized by fast-moving, intricate, and cheerfully immoral plots, witty dialogue, and complicated stage sets. They include *The Lady from Maxim's* (1889), *Hotel Paradiso* (1894), and *A Flea in Her Ear* (1907).

Feynman, Richard Phillips (1918–88) US physicist, who shared the 1965 Nobel Prize with Julian Schwinger and Shinitiro Tomonaga for their development of quantum electrodynamics. He is best known for his invention of Feynman diagrams, which illustrate the interactions between charged particles by the exchange of virtual photons.

Fez. *See* Fès.

Fezzan (*or* Fazzan; Latin name: Phazania) An area in SW Libya, forming part of the Sahara. It was a province until provinces were abolished in 1963.

Fianna Fáil (Irish: Soldiers of Destiny) Irish political party, founded in 1926 by Eamon *De Valera from moderate *Sinn Féin members. The ruling party in the years 1932–48, 1951–54, 1957–73, 1977–81, and 1982–, its leaders have included the legendary De Valera (until 1959), Sean Lemass, Jack *Lynch, and Charles Haughey.

fiber (*or* dietary fiber) The constituent of the human diet that is not digested. It consists of the cell walls of plants, i.e. cellulose, lignin, hemicellulose, and pectic substances. Significant amounts are present in whole wheat cereals and flour, root vegetables, nuts, and fruit: highly refined foods, such as sugar, have a low fiber content. Dietary fiber is considered helpful in preventing constipation, diverticular disease, obesity, diabetes mellitus, and colonic cancer: societies with high-fiber diets rarely suffer from these conditions.

fiberglass (glass fiber *or* spun glass) Material made from glass drawn into fine threads. Fiberglass has excellent heat- and fire-resistant properties and is a good electrical insulator. It is spun and woven into curtain material; made into glass wool for heat, electrical, and sound insulation; woven into coarse mats for filters; and used in reinforcing molded plastics for boats, car bodies, etc.

fiber optics The use of flexible glass fibers for transmitting light. Each fiber, which may be used singly or in bunches, is usually less than a millimeter thick and has a high refractive index. The light inside the fiber is totally internally reflected and travels through the fiber with little loss of intensity. The fibers are highly polished and coated with a substance of lower refractive index to reduce dispersion further. Glass fibers are used for examining otherwise inaccessible places, for example in medical diagnosis and in specialized industrial processes.

fibers Threadlike substances of animal, vegetable, or man-made origin. *Wool and *silk are the most widely used animal fibers. Vegetable fibers include cotton, flax, hemp, jute, and sisal. Man-made fibers fall into two categories: **modified natural fibers**, including *rayon made from wood cellulose, and **synthetic fibers**, most of which are made by the polymerization of petrochemicals. They include *polyesters, nylon, and *acrylics. Some inorganic substances are also used in the form of fibers: examples include glass (*see* fiberglass; fiber optics), *asbestos, and *carbon fibers.

Fibonacci, Leonardo (c. 1170–c. 1230) Italian mathematician. He traveled widely, especially in North Africa, where he learned the *decimal system of numerals and the use of zero, which al-Khwarizmi had, in turn, learned from the Indians. Fibonacci published the system in Europe, but mathematicians were slow to adopt it. In the **Fibonacci series** (0, 1, 1, 2, 3, 5, 8, . . .) each number is the sum of the preceding two.

fibrositis Inflammation of fibrous tissue, usually of the back muscles and muscle sheaths. This causes sudden pain and stiffness (muscular rheumatism). It is best relieved by rest, but aspirin or similar analgesics may help.

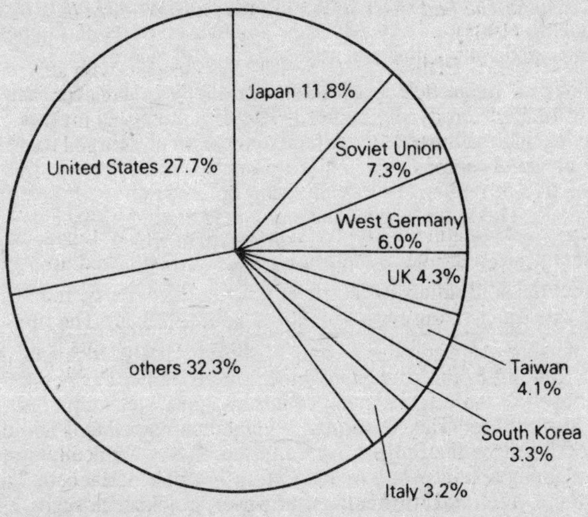

FIBERS *World production of synthetic fibers in the 1980s.*

fibula. *See* leg.

Fichte, Johann Gottlieb (1762–1814) German philosopher and follower of *Kant. Fichte, however, debunked Kant's world of numinous "things-in-themselves," holding that practical reason and man's autonomously good will originated all that is worthwhile in the world, as well as creating the highest type of human personality. The outer world, a passive place, is the field of action for this human consciousness; by contrast, the ego, or self, is the only basic reality. The existence of other egos was, however, essential for the individual's pursuit of moral perfection. Fichte's philosophical works include *Foundation of the Laws of Nature* (1796) and *System of Moral Philosophy* (1798). His popular works strove to kindle German nationalism against Napoleon.

Fichtelgebirge A mountain range in E Germany, between Bayreuth and the Czech border. It is mainly wooded (the name means "spruce mountains") and rises to 3448 ft (1051 m) at the Schneeberg. The minerals obtained from it include lead, copper, and marble.

Ficino, Marsilio (1433–99) Italian Platonist scholar. In 1462, under *Medici patronage, he founded the Platonic Academy to disseminate *Platonism and reconcile it with Christianity. His system was a blend of Neoplatonic metaphysics and Augustinian theology expressed in a hierarchical universe, with strata ranging from body to angels and God. Experience consisted of the ascent of man's immortal soul toward God. Ficino's translations of Plato (1484) remained standard for many years.

fiddler crab A small burrowing *crab, 1–1.2 in (25–30 mm) long, belonging to the genus *Uca* (about 65 species). The brightly colored male has an enlarged claw, which it holds somewhat like a violin. Fiddler crabs are found on salt marshes and sandy beaches of tropical and temperate regions, feeding on algae and other organic material. Tribe: *Brachyura.*

Fiedler, Arthur (1894–1979) US conductor; director of the Boston Pops Orchestra (1930–79). After studying in Berlin, Germany, he played for the Boston Symphony Orchestra (1915–30) and, drawing from its members, formed the

Boston Pops in 1930. Playing all sorts of music from symphonic to rock, Fiedler and his orchestra became known for free summer concerts on the banks of the Charles River, radio and television appearances, and recordings.

field In physics, a region of space in which a body possessing certain properties can exert a force on similar bodies, when they are not in contact. For example, a body having mass exerts an attractive force on all other massive bodies as a result of its gravitational field. Similarly, an electrically charged body exerts a force (attractive or repulsive, depending on polarity) on other charged bodies and a magnetized body will have a magnetic field around it. A field is often represented by lines of force to indicate the direction in which the force acts at that point. The closeness together of the lines represents the strength of the force, and therefore the field, in that area.

Field, Cyrus West (1819–92) US financier and entrepreneur. Largely self-educated, he amassed a fortune by age 32 through persistence and shrewd investments. Retiring from active involvement in his earlier business interests, he devoted himself to the establishment of a transatlantic telegraph link, first suggested to him by Frederick Gisborne, a Canadian engineer. Field ultimately raised $1,500,000 for the project from a group of New York investors and the first transatlantic cable was laid in 1858 from Valentia, Ireland, to Trinity Bay, Newfoundland. Technical difficulties, however, quickly ended its use. Undeterred by the severe financial losses he had suffered by this failure, Field persisted with the project after the Civil War. He secured the services of the steamboat *Great Eastern* for the laying of an improved cable that went into service in 1866. Although the transatlantic cable project was his most important achievement, Field also invested heavily in railroads and newspapers later in life.

Field, Marshall (1834–1906) US businessman. As a young man he became a partner in a wholesale firm in 1856 in Chicago. After a series of partnerships, Field bought out his partners and established in 1881 Marshall Field and Company, which became the world's largest and most innovative retail store. He revolutionized retailing with one-price marking, liberal credit, a merchandise return system, and a department store restaurant. He supported the University of Chicago and was a founder of the Art Institute of Chicago (1878) and the Columbian Museum (1893), now the Field Museum of Natural History.

field emission The emission of electrons from the surface of certain materials when they are subjected to a very high electric field. Typically, fields of about 10^{10} volts per meter are required. The effect is also known as cold emission or autoemission. It is utilized in the **field-emission microscope**, in which a magnified image of a surface is obtained by subjecting it to a high electric field and observing the distribution of emitted electrons on a cathode-ray screen.

fieldfare A *thrush, *Turdus pilaris*, of N Europe and Siberia, migrating to S and W Europe. It is about 10 in (25 cm) long with a speckled brown breast, brown back, white underwings, and blue-gray head.

field hockey An 11-a-side field game for men and women, the object of which is to score goals. It has been played in various forms for at least 4000 years and is an Olympic sport. A team comprises a goalkeeper, two fullbacks, three halfbacks, and five forwards (left wing, inside left, center, inside right, and right wing), each of which carries a curved stick for hitting the ball. Play is started at the beginning of the two 35-minute periods (and after each goal) with a face-off in the center of the field. In this brief ritual two opposing players cross their sticks and tap the ground three times. Play proceeds by dribbling the ball with the stick and passing it by hitting it along the ground or through the air. *See also* ice hockey.

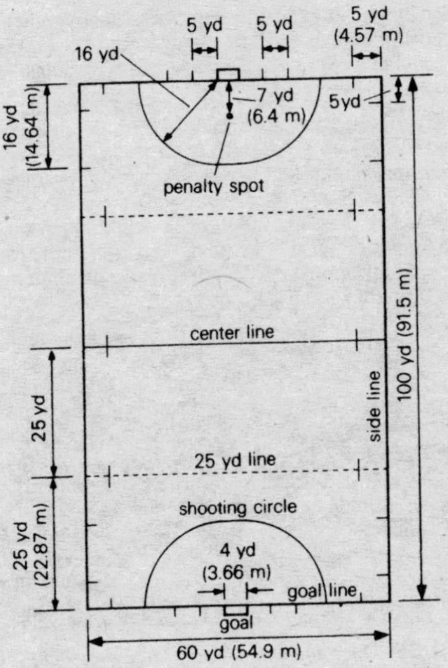

FIELD HOCKEY *The dimensions of the field.*

Fielding, Henry (1707–54) British novelist and dramatist. He wrote about 25 plays, mostly satirical and topical comedies, between 1728 and 1737, when Walpole's Licensing Act effectively banned his vigorous satire; he then turned to journalism and law studies. *Shamela* (1741), a parody of Samuel Richardson's novel *Pamela* (1740), is almost certainly by Fielding. His major novels include *Joseph Andrews* (1742), the ironical *Jonathan Wild* (1743), and *Tom Jones* (1749).

fieldmouse A small nocturnal long-tailed *mouse. *Apodemus sylvaticus*, of Europe, Asia, and N Africa, also called woodmouse. About 3.3 in (9 cm) long, with a 3.1-in (8-cm) tail, it has a rich brown coat and white underparts. Fieldmice feed on seeds and grain and can become a pest.

Field of the Cloth of Gold (1520) The meeting near Calais of Henry VIII of England and Francis I of France. Francis hoped for English support against Emperor Charles V, with whom, however, Henry subsequently formed an alliance.

Fields, W. C. (William Claude Dukenfield; 1880–1946) US film actor. After working as a vaudeville juggler and comedian he began making films in the 1920s. He frequently portrayed an alcoholic misanthrope. In *It's a Gift* (1934), *You Can't Cheat an Honest Man* (1939), *The Bank Dick* (1940), *My Little Chickadee* (1940), and other films, he exploited his genuine eccentricity and intolerance of sentimentality with comic genius.

Fieschi A leading family of Genoa (Italy) during the 13th, 14th, and 15th centuries. The Fieschi, who were *Guelfs, wielded much influence in Genoese and papal politics as ambassadors, admirals, generals, cardinals, and even popes—*Innocent IV and Adrian V (d. 1276; reigned 1276) were Fieschi.

FIELDMOUSE *This mouse tends to prefer succulent foods (peas, fruits, leaves, etc.) to dry grain and is sometimes found in houses, as well as gardens.*

Fiesole 43 48N 11 17E A city in Italy, in Tuscany situated on a hill near Florence overlooking the Arno River. It has Etruscan and Roman remains and a romanesque cathedral. It is mainly residential. Population: 114,111.

fife A small transverse *flute, pitched in B-flat and used in military fife-and-drum bands.

Fife, Duncan. *See* Phyfe, Duncan.

Fifteen Years' War (1591–1606) A struggle between the Austrain Hapsburgs and the Ottoman Turks for the possession of Hungary that followed 50 years of intermittent skirmishing. Neither side gained an ascendency but the stalemate was ended when István Bocksay (1557–1606) of Transylvania rebelled against the Hapsburgs, made a treaty with the Turks, conquered Hapsburg Hungary, and established Transylvania as an effective buffer state between the two belligerents.

fifth column A body of enemy sympathizers working within a country. The term originated in the Spanish Civil War when the Nationalist General Emilio Mola (1887–1937) is supposed to have said "I have four columns operating against Madrid and a fifth inside composed of my sympathizers."

Fifty-Four Forty or Fight (1844) Slogan taken up by those in the US who were in favor of exclusive US rights to the Oregon Territory. The territory between California and Alaska had been occupied jointly by the US and Britain. US expansionists felt the US was entitled to all lands north to latitude 54°40". A compromise was finally reached in 1846 when the Oregon Treaty set the US boundary at the 49th parallel.

fig A spreading tree or shrub, *Ficus carica*, 40in–40ft (1–12 m) high, probably native to W Asia but widely cultivated in warm temperate and subtropical regions. The dark-green leathery leaves are large (up to 12 × 10 in [30 × 25 cm]) and usually deeply lobed. The tiny flowers are borne inside a fleshy pear-shaped structure, up to 3 in (8 cm) long, which develops into the edible fig after fertilization of the flowers. Figs—eaten fresh, dried, or preserved—are rich in sugar and iron and have laxative properties. Family: *Moraceae* (mulberry family).

fighting fish One of several *labyrinth fishes, especially of the genus *Betta,* found in SE Asia and the Malay Archipelago and named for the aggression shown by the males toward each other and to immature females. Some males brood eggs in their mouths. The Siamese fighting fish (*B. splendens*) is about 2.5 in (6.5 cm) long and greenish or brown in color. Long-finned and brightly colored varieties are bred for use in fighting contests.

fig marigold A plant of the genus *Mesembryanthemum* (about 200 species), found in warm regions, especially South Africa, and widely cultivated as ornamentals. Fig marigolds are spreading herbs or shrubs, often succulent, with large brilliantly colored daisylike flowers and figlike fruits. Family: *Aizoaceae.*

figwort A square-stemmed herbaceous plant of the genus *Scrophularia* (120 species), of N temperate regions; 12–40 in (30–100 cm) tall, they have toothed leaves. The brown, yellow, or green flowers are almost spherical, with five small spreading lobes around the opening, and are borne on a branching flower stalk. A common Eurasian species is *S. nodosa*. Family: *Scrophulariaceae*.

Fiji, State of A country in the S Pacific Ocean. It consists of over 800 islands, only 106 of which are inhabited; the largest are Viti Levu and Vanua Levu. Most of the population are Indians and Fijians with some Europeans, Chinese, and other Pacific islanders. *Economy*: chiefly agricultural, sugar cane being the main cash crop; others include copra and ginger. Some gold is mined on Viti Levu and the chief exports are sugar, copra, coconut oil, and gold. Tourism is being developed and is now the second most important industry. Fiji is an important staging post on the air routes between North America and Australia and New Zealand. *History*: discovered by the Dutch explorer Tasman in 1643, the islands were visited by Captain Cook in 1774. During the 19th century the search for sandalwood brought many ships and tribal warfare was widespread until Fiji was ceded to Britain in 1874. It became independent within the Commonwealth of Nations in 1970. Tensions between Fijian and Indian groups led in 1987 to a change in government structure after Sitiveni Rabuka took power. A republic was established, and Fiji withdrew from the Commonwealth. Official language: English. Official currency: Fiji dollar of 100 cents. Area: 7055 sq mi (18,272 sq km). Population (1992 est): 750,000. Capital and main port: Suva.

Filarete (Antonio Averlino; c. 1400–c. 1469) Italian Renaissance architect. Originally a sculptor, he moved in 1451 to Milan where he designed his masterpiece, the Ospedale Maggiore. He wrote a treatise on architecture (1461–64) and, although he built little, was influential in promoting Italian classicism.

filaria A parasitic *nematode worm, mainly of central Africa, Asia, and the SW Pacific. The species *Wuchereria bancrofti* and *Brugia malayi* cause the disease **filariasis**. The tiny larval worm, measuring about 0.06 in (1.4 mm), enters the body in the saliva of a biting mosquito or mite. It then grows up to 3 in (8 cm) long in lymph and blood vessels, causing swelling and pain (*see* elephantiasis).

filbert A Eurasian shrub, *Corylus maxima,* closely related and similar to the *hazel. It is sometimes planted for its nuts, which are larger than hazelnuts and are partly hidden by long bracts.

filefish A *bony fish belonging to a family (*Monacanthidae*) found in warm coastal waters. It has a laterally flattened body, 5–10 in (13–26 cm) long, covered with small filelike or velvety scales, two dorsal fin spines, and a very small mouth. Order: *Tetraodontiformes.*

Filioque (Latin: and the Son) An article of Christian faith in the Western Church, added to the *Nicene Creed and referring to the *Holy Spirit, "Who proceedeth from the Father *and the Son*" (rather than from the Father alone). It had appeared in Spain as early as 447 but was not adopted at Rome until the 11th century. The Orthodox Church did not accept it and attacked it as an unwarranted addition made to the Creed by Rome. *Photius denounced it in the 9th century and it was one of the central issues—together with disagreement over the nature of the primacy of the *papacy—that culminated in the schism between East and West in 1054.

Fillmore, Millard (1800–74) US political leader; 13th president of the United States (1850–53). Born in Locke, N.Y., Fillmore began his political career as leader of the Anti-Masonic party in the state legislature. In 1832 he was elected to the US House of Representatives, where he later joined the *Whig Party and became the influential chairman of the Ways and Means Committee. Fillmore returned to New York in 1844 to run for governor, but was defeated. In 1848 he accepted the vice presidential nomination of the Whig Party and was elected to that office as the running-mate of Zachary *Taylor. With Taylor's death in 1850, Fillmore succeeded to the presidency. The most pressing issue faced by the nation during the Fillmore administration was the question of *slavery. In an attempt to resolve the growing bitterness over the issue, Fillmore supported the *Compromise of 1850, but his attempts to enforce the *Fugitive Slave Law aroused considerable opposition within his own party and from the *Abolition movement. He failed to gain renomination by the Whig Party in 1852. Fillmore's last attempt at elective office was his unsuccessful campaign for president as the nominee of the American (*Know-Nothing) party in 1856.

film A thin flexible strip of cellulose acetate, or similar transparent plastic, coated with a light-sensitive emulsion. A black-and-white photographic emulsion usually consists of gelatin containing tiny suspended crystals of silver halide (usually bromide or chloride). After exposure to light in a *camera these crystals are easily reduced to metallic silver when treated with the chemicals in the developer. This produces black deposits of fine particles of metallic silver on the parts of the film upon which the light has fallen, giving a reversed (or negative) image. Fixing of the film consists of bathing it in sodium thiosulfate (hypo) or other fixers to render the unchanged silver halides soluble, enabling them to be washed away with water. The sensitivity (speed) of film is usually quoted as an *ASA rating, which determines the amount of light required to form a given amount of metallic silver. *See also* color photography.

films. *See* motion pictures.

filter A device that allows one substance to pass through it but not others. For example, a filter is used to remove solid particles from a liquid or gas by passing the mixture through a porous substance, such as paper or *fiberglass, the holes in which are fine enough to prevent the passage of the particles. Such filters are used in some air-conditioning units, for water purification, etc. In optics, colored glass filters are used to select light with a certain range of wavelengths. In electronics, filters are circuits used to allow alternating currents of a certain frequency range to pass, while currents with frequencies outside the range are stopped.

finch A songbird belonging to a family (*Fringillidae*; 176 species) occurring in most regions of the world except Australia. Finches have hard conical bills used to crack open seeds, although they also feed on buds and fruit. They range in size from 4–11 in (10–27 cm) and the plumage varies in color with the species. There are two subfamilies: the *Fringillinae*, including the finer-billed *chaffinch and *brambling of the Old World, and the *Carduelinae*, comprising the heavier-billed species found in both the Old World and North America. *Compare* weaverfinch.

Fine Gael (Irish: Tribe of Gaels) Irish political party, formed in 1933. It was the senior member of ruling coalitions in Ireland (1948–51, 1954–57, and 1973–77). It is rather more conservative than the rival *Fianna Fáil.

fineness of gold A measure of the purity of gold equal to the number of parts of pure gold in 1000 parts of the alloy.

finfoot A secretive semiaquatic bird belonging to a family (*Heliornithidae*; 3 species) found in dense vegetation bordering rivers and creeks of tropical and subtropical regions of America, Africa, and Asia. Up to 24 in (60 cm) long, finfoots have olive-brown plumage and large lobed feet, a long neck, and a stiff rounded tail. Order: *Gruiformes* (cranes, rails, etc.).

Fingal's Cave A spectacular cave on the Scottish island of Staffa, in the Inner Hebrides, composed of basaltic columns. Visited by Felix Mendelssohn (1829), it inspired his overture *Fingal's Cave* (1829, revised 1832). Length: 227 ft (68 m). Height: 117 ft (35 m).

Finger Lakes A series of eleven long and narrow lakes in central New York, bounded on the E by Syracuse, the S by Ithaca, and the W by Geneseo. The two largest, Cayuga and Seneca, are approximately 40 mi (65 km) long and 2.5 mi (4 km) wide. The smaller lakes are Otisco, Scaneateles, Owasco, Keuka, Canandaigua, Honeoye, Canadice, Hemlock, and Conesus.

fingerprint The impression made by the pattern of ridges on the palmar side of the end joint of the fingers and thumbs. The taking of a person's fingerprints, which are virtually unique, for the purpose of identifying habitual criminals was begun in the early 20th century. The print is taken by rolling the fingers and thumbs, one by one or simultaneously, in ink and then rolling them on paper. Fingerprints left at the scene of a crime may be taken by photography. The FBI has more than 70 million fingerprint records on file. Classification relies on a numerical value given to a print, which identifies the finger and the pattern of ridges (of which there are 1024 primary groups).

FINGERPRINT *Loops are the commonest form of pattern (c. 65%), followed by whorls (c. 30%), and then arches (c. 5%).*

Finisterre, Cape 42 52N 9 16W The most westerly point in Spain, on the Atlantic coast.

Finland, Gulf of An arm of the Baltic Sea, extending between Finland (N) and Russia and Estonia (E and S). The ports of Helsinki and Saint Petersburg lie on the Gulf, which is frozen for 3–5 months of the year. Length: about 249 mi (400 km).

Finland, Republic of (Finnish name: Suomi) A country in N Europe, with S and W coastlines on the Baltic Sea. It includes the *Åland Islands, situated at the mouth of the Gulf of Bothnia. The land is generally low lying, apart from some small hills in the NW. Over 10% of the area consists of lakes, which, together with rivers and canals, provide an extensive network of inland waterways. The majority of the population are Finns, with minorities of Swedes, Lapps, and Russians. *Economy*: agriculture is highly mechanized and, together with cereals, dairy produce is of particular importance. Over 70% of the land is under forest, providing ample resources for the timber and pulp and paper industries. Other industries include food processing and textiles. Hydroelectricity provides the main source of power and the principal mineral resources are copper and iron ore. Tourism is an important source of revenue. The main exports are timber, pulp and paper, and machinery. *History*: prehistorically the Finnic peoples migrated into Finland, gradually driving the Lapps northward. Conquered by Sweden in the 12th century AD, Finland continued to enjoy a considerable degree of independence, becoming a grand duchy in the 16th century. The country suffered considerable hardships, however, in the recurring wars between Sweden and Russia. In the 18th century the SE was occupied by Russia and in 1809 the rest of the country was ceded to Russia, becoming an autonomous grand duchy. During this period Finnish nationalism flourished and in 1863 the Finnish language was officially recognized. It became independent in 1917, following the Russian Revolution, and a republic two years later. In 1939 it was invaded by Soviet forces and in 1940, and again in 1944, was forced to cede certain territories to the Soviet Union. A treaty of friendship between the two countries, first signed in 1948, continued until the dissolution of the Soviet Union in 1991; it was replaced by a similar treaty with Russia in 1992. Dr. Urho Kaleva Kekkonen, who had been president since 1956, resigned in 1981 and was succeeded by Dr. Mauno Henrik Koivisto. He was reelected in 1988. US president George Bush and Soviet president Mikhail Gorbachev met in Helsinki for a summit meeting in 1990. Official languages: Finnish and Swedish. Official currency: markka of 100 pennia. Area: 117,913 sq mi (305,475 sq km). Population (1992 est): 5,000,000. Capital and main port: Helsinki.

Finlay, Carlos Juan (1833–1915) Cuban physician, who discovered that yellow fever was transmitted by mosquitoes. By 1900, Finlay had persuaded the authorities to control mosquito populations and so eradicate the disease. *See also* Reed, Walter.

Finney, Albert (1936–) British actor. Following his early successful performances in plays by modern dramatists he made several films, notably *Saturday Night and Sunday Morning* (1960). He then returned to the theater to act classic roles, such as Tamburlaine and Hamlet, but occasionally made films, such as *Murder on the Orient Express* (1974) and *The Dresser* (1984).

Finnic A group of languages of the *Finno-Ugric branch of the Uralic family, which includes Finnish, Estonian, Lapp, Mari, Permic, and a number of other languages, most of which are dwindling in significance. The Finnic peoples, ancestors of the modern Finns and Estonians, migrated in prehistoric times from central Russia to the area of the E Baltic, Finland, and Karelia, bringing grain cultivation with them. Estonia became an important trading area and established a sense of national identity while the Finns inhabited more remote regions and remained fragmented until recent times. The *Lapps in the far N of the region retain their separate identity and language but other groups have mainly lost theirs. All these peoples adopted Christianity during the 11th and 12th centuries.

Finn MacCool A legendary Irish hero, leader of the Fianna (*see* Fenian cycle). The son of Cumhaill (Cool) and the father of the poet Oisin (*see* Ossian), he killed Goll MacMorna, his father's murderer, and became leader of the company.

Finno-Ugric languages A large group of languages of the *Uralic family, spoken by more than 20 million people in dispersed communities in Scandinavia, E Europe, and W Asia. Thought to have diverged about five millennia ago, the Finnic and Ugric languages can be further divided into the following major groups: Ugric (*Hungarian and Ob-Ugric) and *Finnic (Finnish, Estonian, Mari, Permic, and a number of other languages mostly spoken in the Baltic and in the region of the Volga). Periodically and to varying degrees, neighboring languages have exercised an influence on the vocabularies of the Finno-Ugric languages. Many Turkic forms, for example, have been absorbed into the Hungarian language. Although phonological processes may be shared by the majority of Finno-Ugric languages no single defining characteristic is common to all members.

fins Organs of locomotion and balance in fish and some other aquatic animals. The fins of fish are supported by bony or cartilaginous fin rays and are either median or paired. The median fins include the tail (or caudal) fin, typically used for propulsion (in conjunction with the muscular body) and the dorsal and anal fins, used for balancing. The paired pectoral fins, just behind the gills, and pelvic fins, further back, are used for steering (although in rays the large pectorals provide motive force).

Finsen, Niels Ryberg (1860–1904) Danish physician, who developed the use of light for treating certain bacterial skin disease. Although now superseded, his work stimulated research into modern radiation therapy. He founded the Medical Light Institute (now the Finsen Institute), Copenhagen, in 1896 and was awarded a Nobel Prize (1903).

Finsteraarhorn 46 32N 8 08E A mountain in S central Switzerland, the highest in the Bernese Oberland. It was first climbed in either 1812 (disputed) or 1829. Height: 14,022 ft (4274 m).

Fiordland The largest national park of New Zealand, in SW South Island. It is a mountainous region with glacial lakes and fjords, including Lakes Manapouri and Te Anau (famous for its glowworm caves), and Milford Sound. Area: about 4400 sq mi (11,400 sq km).

fir A coniferous □tree of the genus *Abies* (about 50 species). Mostly native to N temperate regions, these trees are also called silver firs, as many species have leaves with a silvery undersurface. Firs have blunt-tipped needles and erect stout woody cones; they are important softwood trees (*see* timber). The European silver fir (*A. alba*), which forms pure forests in the mountains of central Europe, is widely grown for its timber: it reaches a height of 165 ft (50 m) and its cones are up to 6 in (15 cm) long. Another widely planted timber tree is the grand, or giant, fir (*A. grandis*), which grows up to 295 ft (90 m) in its native W North America. Family: *Pinaceae.*

Firdausi (Abul Qasim Mansur; c. 935–c. 1020) The first major Persian poet, famous as the author of the epic poem *Shah-nama* (*The Book of Kings*; 1010), which recounts the history of Iran and its rulers from legendary beginnings to the conquest of the country by Arabs in 641 AD. It includes the tragic legend of Sohrab and Rustum, familiar to English readers in Matthew *Arnold's version. The *Shah-nama* was written in some 60,000 rhyming couplets (*mathnawi*), which are a distinctive feature of Persian poetry.

fire ant An *ant, *Solenopsis saevissima* (or *S. geminata*), that occurs in South America and S North America. Fire ants are serious pests because of their irritant painful sting. Subfamily: *Myrmicinae.*

firearms Any weapon that uses an explosive to discharge a missile. The two main categories are *artillery, with barrels having an internal diameter of more than 20 mm, and *small arms with calibers below 20 mm (this classification is no longer rigidly adopted).

Although gunpowder was invented in China many centuries before its description by Roger Bacon in the 13th century, a practical *cannon was not invented until the 14th century (by a German monk, Berthold Schwarz). *Guns, *mortars, and *howitzers have all evolved from the early cannon. Small-arms development began in the 15th century with the early form of the *musket, called a harquebus. They have evolved into the *pistol, *rifle, and *machine gun. *Guided missiles constitute a separate class of weapons, but can be considered as firearms in some contexts.

firebrat A primitive wingless insect, *Thermobia domestica*: a three-pronged *bristletail that is abundant in buildings all over the world. It prefers warm moist places, such as around stoves, furnaces, and bakery ovens, where it feeds on starchy or sugary materials.

fireclay A soft unbedded clay often occurring beneath coal seams. It is believed that they are fossil soils or earths in which swamp plants grew. Fireclays consist mainly of aluminum oxide and silica, being deficient in iron and alkalis; kaolin is the principal clay mineral. They are used as refractory materials, and poorer quality fireclay is used in the manufacture of sanitary earthenware.

firecrest A tiny European songbird, *Regulus ignicapillus*. It is about 3.5 in (9 cm) long and differs from its close relative, the *goldcrest, only in its black-and-white eyestripe. It uses its fine sharp bill to seek out small insects and larvae.

firefly A nocturnal beetle, also called a lightning beetle, belonging to a family (*Lampyridae*; 2000 species) common in tropical and temperate regions. Fireflies emit a greenish light—often as short rhythmic flashes—from organs on the abdomen (*see* bioluminescence). They are 0.2–1 in (5–25 mm) long and many have conspicuous orange or yellow markings. Most adults never eat (although a few feed on pollen and nectar); the larvae are carnivorous. The wingless females and larvae are called glowworms. *Lampyris noctiluca* is one of the best-known species.

Some *click beetles are also called fireflies.

Firenze. *See* Florence.

fire prevention Fire prevention and control depend on: elimination of the causes (about 25% of fires are caused by electrical faults; smoking, overheating of machinery, furnace and flue defects, and burner flames are also important causes); fire-safe design using fire-retardant coatings and compartmentalized structures to reduce the spread of fire; the provision of such protective equipment as portable fire extinguishers and automatic sprinklers; and the existence of an efficient fire-fighting service.

Class A fires (paper, wood, furnishings, and other common solid combustibles) are extinguished by cooling with water, carbon dioxide, foam, etc. A common type of extinguisher, the soda-acid device, uses carbon dioxide produced by the reaction of sulfuric acid on sodium hydrogen carbonate to force water out of a container. Class B fires (flammable liquids, such as oil, gasoline, etc.) are extinguished by smothering with chemical foam, dry powder, or carbon dioxide, or by extinguishing with halogenated hydrocarbons (e.g., BCF, bromochlorodifluoromethane). Class C fires involve electrical equipment and require nonconducting extinguishers, such as carbon dioxide, dry chemicals, and halogenated hydrocarbons. Class D fires involve burning metals, such as magnesium, sodium, etc., and require special techniques.

Automatic sprinklers are used in factories, offices, and warehouses and are usually controlled by thermostats, which turn on the sprinklers at a specified temperature. Smoke detectors are used in homes, apartments, and where materials are expected to produce smoke before bursting into flame.

fire salamander A mainly terrestrial *salamander, *Salamandra salamandra*, ranging from S Europe to SW Asia. It is 7 in (18 cm) long and glossy black with yellow or orange stripes and red patches. If molested it secretes a salamandrin (venom), which can be fatal to small mammals, from pores behind its eyes.

Fireside Chats Radio broadcasts, beginning in 1933, made by US president Franklin D. *Roosevelt to update and reassure the nation during the Great Depression and its aftermath.

Firestone, Harvey S(amuel) (1868–1938) US industrialist. After working for a carriage manufacturer and organizing his own rubber company (1896), he formed Firestone Tire and Rubber Company (1900) in Akron, Ohio. He manufactured pneumatic tires for Henry Ford's Model T and was the first to use the balloon tire. Ignoring Britain's plan to increase crude rubber prices, he started his own rubber plantation in Liberia in 1924.

firethorn. *See* Pyracantha.

fireworks Combustible devices, used for signals, flares, and displays. Gunpowder rockets and firecrackers were first used in ancient China for military purposes and celebrations and in Europe from the Middle Ages. The basic explosive, usually gunpowder, is colored by the addition of metallic salts: sodium salts for yellow, barium for green, strontium for red, and copper for blue. Metal filings are added for sparks and aniline dyes provide colored smokes. Despite safety precautions by firework manufacturers and restrictions on sales to children, fireworks still cause casualties.

firn (*or* névé) A stage in the transformation of fresh snow to glacier ice. Compaction and recrystallization of the snow increases its density and it becomes firm at a relative density of 0.5. Under further compaction firn may be transformed to glacier ice, this occurring at a relative density of 0.89–0.90.

first aid Procedures that can be carried out by a medically unqualified person on someone immediately after injury in order to save life or facilitate specialist treatment given later. The types of injury requiring first aid include bleeding, burns, choking, drowning, electric shock, fracture, and poisoning. The patient should be removed from the cause of injury unless this would worsen his or her condition. The patient's breathing should be checked and constricting clothing loosened. In the absence of breathing *artificial respiration should be attempted. Once the patient is breathing he or she is put in the recovery position (lying on the stomach with the head to one side and the leg bent at the hip and the knee). In external bleeding the injury is covered and firm pressure applied. Lifting a wounded limb, provided no fractures are suspected, often reduces bleeding. If severe fractures are suspected the patient should not be moved without specialist supervision.

First Amendment First article amending the US Constitution, first part of the Bill of Rights. It guarantees the basic fundamental rights—freedom of religion, freedom of speech, the right to assemble peaceably, and the right to petition the government in the case of grievances.

first cause In the philosophy of Aristotle, and later more generally, the beginning of all the chains of cause and effect that are supposed to explain events in the world on a deterministic basis. The first cause does not itself require a cause. The necessity of a first cause (*or* prime mover) has been used as an argument for God's existence.

fiscal policy Government economic policy in which changes in taxation, social-benefit rates, and government expenditure are used to influence the economy. It has been widely used since World War II, following the widespread acceptance of *Keynesianism. According to *monetarism, however, such "fine tuning" of the economy may actually destabilize it.

Fischer, Bobby (Robert James F.; 1943–) US chess player, who became an International Grandmaster at 15 and world champion in 1972. The championship match, against *Spassky at Reykjavík, was greatly publicized and caused a chess boom around the world. He resigned his title in 1975.

Fischer, Emil Hermann (1852–1919) German chemist, who discovered a method of separating different *sugars from each other. He then determined their structure and showed that their *optical activity depended on the three-dimensional arrangement of the atoms in their molecules, thus founding the subject of stereochemistry. For this work he was awarded the Nobel Prize in 1902. In later life, Fischer showed that proteins consist of amino acids; in 1907 he synthesized the first protein molecule from amino acids.

Fischer-Dieskau, Dietrich (1925–) German baritone. He is renowned for his performances of lieder and of a wide range of operatic roles. He has recorded all the songs of Schubert.

Fischer-Tropsch reaction The formation of a variety of organic compounds, chiefly light liquid *hydrocarbons, upon passing a mixture of hydrogen and carbon monoxide over catalysts at around 143°F (200°C). The reaction is important in the production of synthetic liquid fuels from coal. It was invented by F. Fischer (d. 1948) and H. Tropsch (d. 1935) in 1925 and was extensively used in Germany during World War II.

Fischer von Erlach, Johann Bernhard (1656–1723) Austrian architect, a genius of German baroque. Fischer trained in Rome under *Bernini. Soon after moving to Vienna he became architect to the Hapsburg court (1687). The Karlskirche (1716) and Hofbibliotek (1723) in Vienna are probably his finest achievements. He also built numerous palaces and wrote a wide-ranging history of architecture.

Fish, Hamilton (1808–93) US politician; secretary of state (1869–77). He served his native New York state in various capacities before becoming governor (1849–50) and US senator (1851–57), during which time he transferred his allegiance from the Whigs to the Republican Party. Appointed secretary of state by President *Grant, he was instrumental in negotiating the Treaty of Washington (1871) with Britain, which settled the *Alabama Claims.

fish A cold-blooded aquatic vertebrate belonging to either of the two classes *Chondrichthyes* (*see* cartilaginous fish) or *Osteichthyes* (*see* bony fish), which together comprise over 30,000 species occurring worldwide in seas and fresh waters. Ranging in size from under 0.4 in (10 mm) to over 65 ft (20 m) long, they have streamlined bodies with a covering of bony scales, a fin-bearing tail, an anal fin, one or more dorsal fins, and paired lateral, pectoral (anterior), and pelvic (ventral) fins, which are used in swimming. Oxygen is obtained from water by means of *gills situated in the wall of the mouth cavity, although a few species can also breathe air (*see* lungfish). The majority of fish are carnivorous, feeding mainly on other fish and invertebrates, although some eat plants. Large numbers of small eggs are laid (up to several million in some cases) and are usually fertilized externally. In some species internal fertilization occurs and live young may be born. Fish are of major importance as a source of food and other products (*see* fishing industry) and for sport (*see* angling). *See also* cyclostomes.

FISH

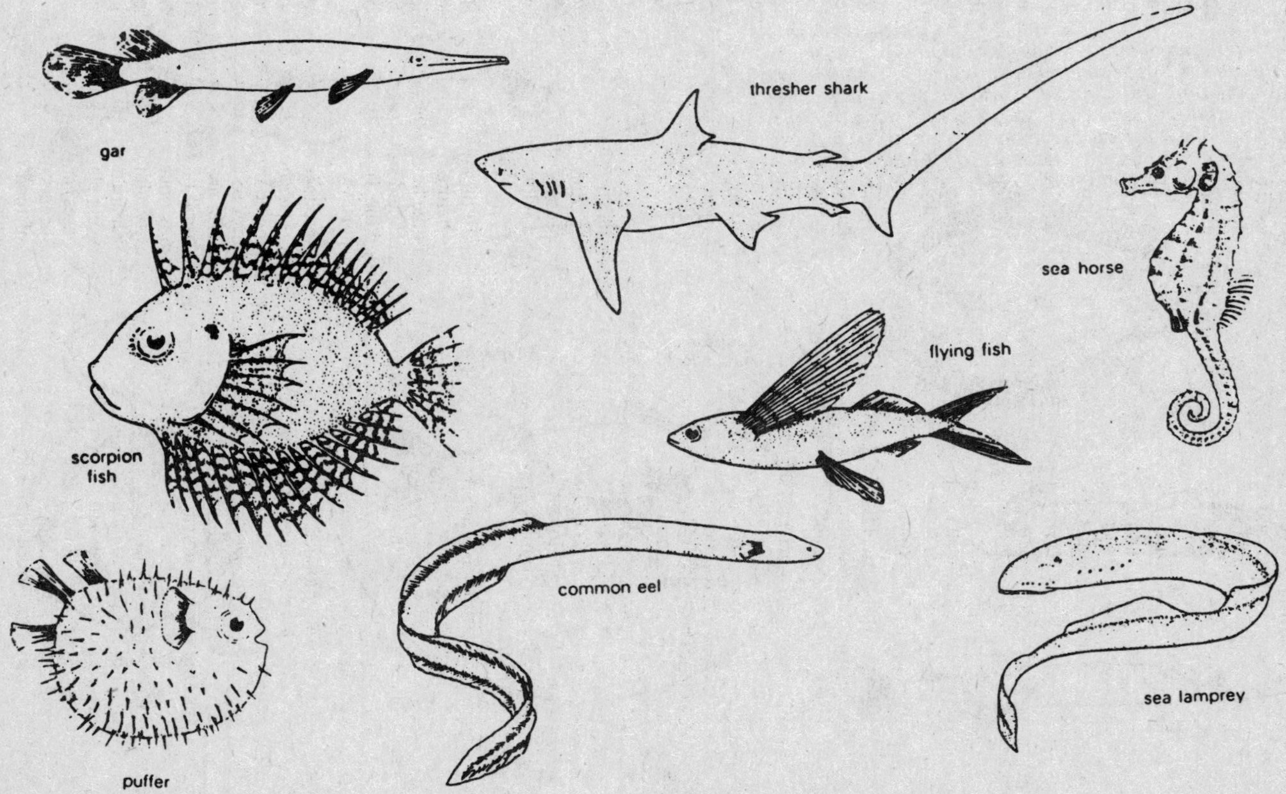
gar
thresher shark
sea horse
scorpion fish
flying fish
puffer
common eel
sea lamprey

FISH

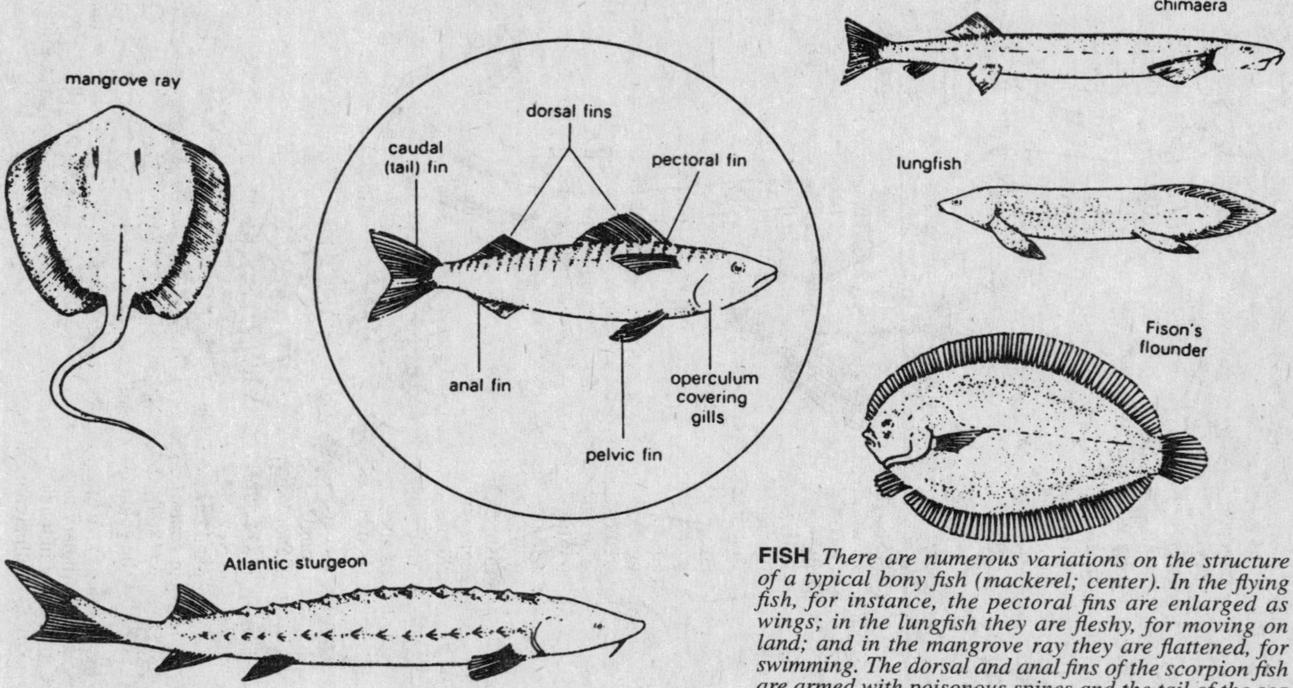

FISH *There are numerous variations on the structure of a typical bony fish (mackerel; center). In the flying fish, for instance, the pectoral fins are enlarged as wings; in the lungfish they are fleshy, for moving on land; and in the mangrove ray they are flattened, for swimming. The dorsal and anal fins of the scorpion fish are armed with poisonous spines and the tail of the sea horse is prehensile.*

fisher A rare North American mammal, *Martes pennanti* (one of the *martens), also called pekan. Fishers are brown and grow to a length of 40 in (1 m). They feed on porcupines, small animals, and fruit and are named for their habit of fishing out the contents of baited traps.

Fisher, Andrew (1862–1928) Australian statesman, born in Scotland; Labor prime minister (1908–09, 1910–13, 1914–15). He pledged Australian support for Britain in World War I.

Fisher, St John (c. 1469–1535) English prelate and humanist. The chancellor of Cambridge University and Bishop of Rochester from 1504, he opposed Henry VIII's divorce from Catherine of Aragon. He was made a cardinal a month before his execution for refusing to recognize Henry VIII as head of the Church of England. He was canonized in 1935. Feast day: July 9.

fish hawk. *See* osprey.

fishing industry The recovery and processing of fish, shellfish, etc., for human consumption and other uses. From ancient times man has fished freshwater rivers and lakes and coastal waters using lines and nets. The modern industry uses vessels with refrigerated holds, echo sounding to locate shoals, and efficient nets and recovery gear; the net is often towed behind the vessel (trawling) or left to drift in the ocean. Fish are also dredged up or sucked up, using powerful pumps. The total world catch of about 75 million tons is made up of many species, including cod, haddock, whiting, herring, lobsters, crabs, shrimps, oysters, mussels, octopus, and squid.

Fish are consumed as human food but provide many other by-products, including fish meal, fish oils, glues, pharmaceuticals, shells, pearls, etc. Overfishing of natural populations has led to a decline in many species and smaller catches, sometimes causing friction between fishing nations, such as Iceland and the UK. International agreement is required to regulate fishing and conserve stocks so that yields can be sustained indefinitely. One alternative is an increased dependence on **fish farming**, the maintenance and management of fish under controlled conditions to provide food. A long-established practice in China and the Far East, fish farming is now of major importance in many other countries, where trout, catfish, carp, eels, shrimps, and oysters are commonly reared. Hatching of the eggs and rearing take place under optimum conditions in artificial ponds or enclosures situated in lakes and coastal waters. *See also* whaling.

fish louse A tiny parasitic *crustacean of the subclass *Branchiura* (75 species) that uses sucking mouthparts to attach itself to fresh- and salt-water fish. Its flattened body has a large disklike carapace covering the head and thorax.

fish owl An *owl specialized for feeding on fish and frogs. Fish owls have naked legs and rough scaly feet to grip their slippery prey. Genera: *Ketupa* (Asia; 4 species), *Scotopelia* (Africa; 3 species).

Fisk, James (1834–72) US stockbroker. He established a successful stockbrokerage firm in New York City in 1866. He was notorious for his stock manipulation schemes and caused, with Jay *Gould, the "Erie War" (1868) in which they tried to gain control of the Erie Railroad. He and Gould were responsible for Black Friday (1869) when they caused the inflation of gold prices in an attempt to corner the gold market.

fission (biology) A form of asexual *reproduction in which an individual splits into two (binary fission) or more (multiple fission) equal parts, each part becoming a new individual. It occurs in a variety of plants, bacteria, protozoa, and some multicellular animals (e.g. corals).

fission (physics). *See* nuclear energy.

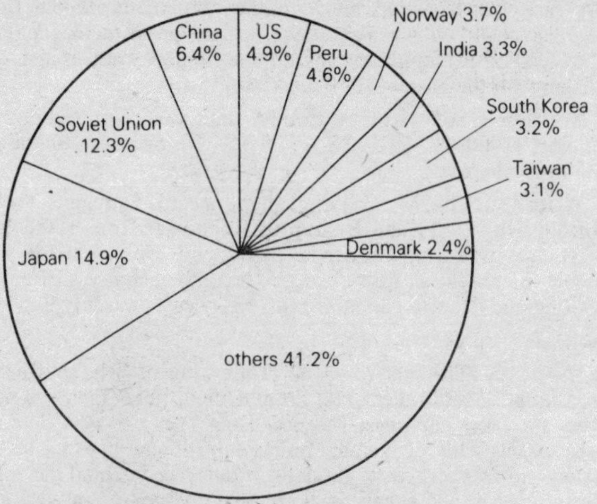

FISHING INDUSTRY *World fish catches in the 1980s.*

fission-track dating A method of dating based on the spontaneous nuclear fission of uranium 238 in the sample. The fissions are recorded as tracks, which are then compared to the tracks formed by inducing fission in the uranium 235 present. A comparison of the numbers of tracks is used as a measure of the age of the sample.

Fitch, John (1743–98) US inventor; builder of the first steamboat. During 1786–87 he built a side-paddled steamboat that he demonstrated to delegates to the Constitutional Convention. By 1790 he had built a faster and larger stern paddle steamboat that regularly ferried between Philadelphia and a port in New Jersey on the Delaware River. He was never able to make his transportation and freight business a success.

Fittipaldi, Emerson (1946–) Brazilian automobile racer, who won his first world championship aged 25 (1972). He won 14 Grand Prix races and was world champion again in 1974. In 1989 and 1993 he won the Indianapolis 500.

Fitzgerald, Edward (1809–83) British poet. He lived quietly as a country gentleman with literary tastes. His famous *Rubaiyat of Omar Khayyam* (1859) was a free adaptation of the 12th-century Persian original into his own meter and imagery.

Fitzgerald, Ella (1918–) US jazz singer, known as the "First Lady of Song." Discovered in Harlem by Chick Webb (1902–39), she toured with his band. Later she became famous with the song "A-tisket, A-tasket" (1938), performed with such musicians as Duke Ellington and Oscar Peterson, and made many albums, including *Hello Love, Duke Ellington's Song Book*, and the *Gershwin Song Books*.

Fitzgerald, F(rancis) Scott (Key) (1896–1940) US novelist. The success of his autobiographical first novel, *This Side of Paradise* (1920), enabled him to marry Zelda Sayre (1900–47) and to live out his self-created role as representative of the hedonistic Jazz Age. After 1924 Fitzgerald lived chiefly on the French Riviera, where he wrote his masterpiece *The Great Gatsby* (1925). Zelda suffered increasingly from schizophrenia and after 1930 was confined to an asylum. Fitzgerald, plagued by guilt, declined into alcoholism. His other novels include *The Beautiful and the Damned* (1922) and *Tender is the Night* (1934). *The Last Tycoon*, about Hollywood, where he spent his last years as a screenwriter, was unfinished at his death.

ELLA FITZGERALD

Fitzgerald, George Francis (1851–1901) Irish physicist, who (independently of *Lorentz) suggested that objects become shorter as their velocity increases, as an explanation of the negative results of the *Michelson-Morley experiment. The phenomenon, now known as the Lorentz-Fitzgerald contraction, was later incorporated by Einstein into his special theory of *relativity, although Fitzgerald did not live to see it.

Fitzsimmons, Bob (1862–1917) New Zealand boxer, born in England. Of legendary courage and strength, he was world middleweight champion (1891–97), heavyweight champion (1897–99), and light-heavyweight champion (1903–05). He beat many much heavier and bigger men.

Fiume. *See* Rijeka.

Five, the A group of 19th-century Russian composers dedicated to the formation of a nationalist musical tradition based on folk music. Led by *Balakirev, the other members were *Borodin, César Cui (1835–1918), *Mussorgski, and *Rimsky-Korsakov. The original name of the group was *mogutchaya kutchka* (Russian: the mighty handful).

Five Civilized Tribes Those US Indian tribes that seemed to be more advanced and more amenable to adopting European ways. All from SE US, the Cherokee, Chickasaw, Choctaw, Creek, and Seminole tribes were later forced to move to reservations in Oklahoma (1832–39). There they also patterned their lifestyle after that of the white settlers.

Five Pecks of Rice Band A 2nd-century AD religious cult of the later *Han dynasty, so called because its followers paid an annual tribute of five pecks of rice to the sect leader. Together with a sect called the Yellow Turbans, the Five Pecks of Rice Band took part in two mass Taoist rebellions, which lasted over 30 years and played a significant part in overthrowing the Han dynasty (220 AD).

Five Power Constitution The government constitution drawn up for China by *Sun Yat-sen and put into practice by the *Guomindang (Nationalists) in

1928. The government exercised five powers—executive, legislative, and judicial and those of examination (of candidates for the bureaucracy) and control (of government efficiency). The Constitution is still used by the Guomindang government of the Republic of China (Taiwan).

five-year plans Economic plans formulated by *developing countries as part of the process of industrialization; they usually include targets for construction, investment, and output to be achieved in the following five years. They were first adopted in the Soviet Union. Capitalist countries (*see* capitalism) committed to economies based on market forces tend to avoid the direction implied in five-year plans, but in a *mixed economy plans based on exhortation rather than direction are sometimes used.

fjord (*or* fiord) A long narrow sea inlet lying between steep mountain slopes, especially in Norway. Usually U-shaped, fjords are glaciated valleys that have been flooded by the sea. Many are extremely deep, some in excess of 3280 ft (1000 m), but near their mouths they usually have a considerably shallower bar or threshold.

flag A Eurasian iris, *Iris pseudacorus* (yellow or water flag), growing in marshes and ditches. Up to 50 in (1.2 m) high, it has yellow flowers and long bladelike leaves.

The sweet flag (*Acorus calamus*) is a perennial herbaceous plant native to Asia and North America and naturalized in Britain, growing at the margins of ponds, rivers, etc. About 40 in (1 m) high, it has wavy-edged leaves, which smell of tangerines when crushed, and the small yellow flowers are tightly packed on a tapering spikelike spadix, 3 in (8 cm) long. Family: *Araceae*.

flagella Long threadlike structures that project from the surface of a cell and produce lashing or undulating movements, used for locomotion or the production of water currents. Flagella occur in protozoa, motile gametes (usually sperms), lower plants, sponges, and also in bacteria (in a simpler form).

Flagellata (*or* Mastigophora) A class of microscopic single-celled animals (*see* Protozoa) having one or more long whiplike flagella, used for swimming and collecting bacteria, protozoans, and other food particles from water. Some species (subclass *Phytomastigophora*) possess chlorophyll and other pigments and can manufacture food by photosynthesis (*see* Euglena). They may also be classed as algae. Animal-like flagellates (subclass *Zoomastigophora*) include the parasites causing *trypanosomiasis and *leishmaniasis as well as free-living forms.

flageolet A musical instrument similar to the *recorder but with two thumb holes on the underside and a more complex head fitted with a slender ivory mouthpiece containing a sponge to absorb condensation. The diarist Pepys was a keen player.

Flagg, James Montgomery (1877–1960) US artist and illustrator. Most famous for his World War I "I Want You" poster of Uncle Sam, he had been a regular supplier of illustrations to magazines since the age of 12. His caricatures of the famous were collected in *The Well-Knowns as Seen by James Montgomery Flagg* (1914).

Flagler, Henry Morrison (1830–1913) US businessman. After several successful business ventures, he joined John D. Rockefeller, Sr., in the oil business in 1867. By 1870 the business had become the Standard Oil Company. He was instrumental in the development of Florida as a resort state. He organized the Florida East Coast Railway (1886) to Miami and built large luxury tourist hotels. By 1912 he had engineered the connection of the Florida Keys by bridges.

Flagstad, Kirsten Malfrid (1895–1962) Norwegian soprano, famous for her singing of Wagner roles, such as Brünnhilde in *Der Ring des Nibelungen* and Kundry in *Parsifal*. She also sang the role of Dido in Purcell's *Dido and Aeneas* and championed the songs of Sibelius.

Flagstaff 35 12N 111 39W A city in N central Arizona in the foothills of the San Francisco Peaks. Chiefly a health and recreation resort, tourism is the main industry. Lumbering and livestock raising are carried on, and Northern Arizona University and Lowell Observatory are here. Population (1990): 45,857.

Flaherty, Robert (Joseph) (1884–1951) US film director. His *Nanook of the North* (1922), filmed during a two-year stay with the Canadian Eskimos, and *Moana* (1926), filmed in the Samoan Islands, were the earliest major documentary films. His later films include *Louisiana Story* (1948).

Flamboyant In French *gothic architecture, the predominant style during the 15th century. Similar to the earlier English *Decorated style, Flamboyant takes its name from its characteristic slender and elaborate curves that wind into flamelike patterns, especially in window tracery. St Maclou, Rouen (begun 1432), is a fine Flamboyant church.

flamboyant tree An attractive tree, *Delonix regia*, also called royal poinciana, flame tree, and peacock flower. It grows to a height of 20–40 ft (6–12 m) and has showy flame-colored flowers with long protruding stamens. Native to Madagascar, it is widely planted in the tropics for shade and ornament. Family: **Leguminosae*.

flamenco A type of Spanish music originating in Andalusia, typically consisting of a song (*cante*) accompanied by dancing, in which the men perform intricate toe and heel tapping steps (*zapateados*) and the women rely on graceful hand and body movements. It was developed by gypsies and shows signs of Moorish influence; the predominant styles are *grande* (anguished) and *chico* (gay and amorous), with a variety of intermediate moods. Flamenco guitar playing has become well known outside Spain; it employs a different technique from that of the "classical" guitar, including a percussive effect obtained by tapping the body of the guitar with the fingers.

flame tree One of several unrelated trees with flame-colored showy flowers. The name is most commonly applied to *Brachychiton acerifolium* (or *Sterculia acerifolia*), a deciduous Australian tree that bears masses of small scarlet bell-like flowers on leafless branches. Family: *Sterculiaceae*. It may also refer to the *flamboyant tree.

flamingo A wading bird belonging to a family (*Phoenicopteridae*; 4 species) occurring in large flocks on saltwater lakes in warm regions of the world; 3–5 ft (90–150 cm) tall, flamingos have a long neck, a short tail, a broad wingspan, and white plumage, tinged with pink. They separate algae, diatoms, small mollusks, etc., from mud using their bills, which are lined with sievelike filters. Order: *Ciconiiformes* (herons, storks, etc.).

Flaminian Way A major Roman road that extended from Rome to Ariminum (now Rimini) on the Adriatic coast. It was named for Gaius *Flaminius, who completed it in 220 BC.

Flamininus, Titus Quinctius (c. 230–c. 174 BC) Roman general, who defeated Philip V (237–179; reigned 220–179) of Macedon at Cynoscephalae (198). In 196, at the Isthmian Games, Flamininus proclaimed the independence of the Greek states from Macedonian hegemony.

Flaminius, Gaius (d. 217 BC) Roman popular leader. An advocate of the plebeians' rights, he often challenged or disregarded senatorial authority. In 220, as consul, he built the *Flaminian Way, Rome's road to N Italy. Popular dissatisfaction with senatorial war policy inspired his election in 217 as leader against *Hannibal, who defeated and killed Flaminius at Trasimene.

Flanders (Flemish name: Vlaanderen; French name: Flandre) A historic region in Europe, in the SW of the Low Countries. It now comprises the provinces of East Flanders and West Flanders in Belgium and parts of N France and the Netherlands. *History*: in the Middle Ages Flanders formed an autonomous region ruled by the Counts of Flanders and after the 12th century it became a major industrial and commercial center, its cloth being especially important. The scene of many battles during its history, there was heavy fighting here in both World Wars. During World War II the Battle of Flanders (May 10–June 2, 1940) saw the German attack on Holland, Belgium, and France, which resulted in the Allied withdrawal from *Dunkirk.

flash point The lowest temperature at which an inflammable liquid (generally a hydrocarbon or mixture of hydrocarbons) produces enough vapor to ignite on the application of a small flame under specified conditions. Flash points are useful for setting safety standards, especially for the storage of volatile hydrocarbons and for monitoring refinery operations.

flatfish Any carnivorous *bony fish of the order *Pleuronectiformes* (about 600 species), including many important food fishes, such as *halibut, *plaice, *sole, and *turbot. They have a laterally flattened body, 4–80 in (10–200 cm) long, fringed with dorsal and anal fins. Both eyes occur on the same side of the head and they lie on their "blind" side, usually on sandy or muddy bottoms of coastal waters; the upper surface is colored to blend with their surroundings. In the larval stage one eye migrates over the head to lie near the other.

flatfoot Obliteration of the longitudinal arch of the foot, so that the entire sole is in contact with the ground on standing. It is common in young children and they usually grow out of it. Rigid flatfoot is more serious and the result of a congenital abnormality.

Flathead North American Salishan-speaking Indian tribe found in SW Montana. They were called Flatheads by white settlers who had seen deformed heads, probably of slaves, among them, but they never practiced the custom of head flattening. Basically farmers, hunters, and eventually traders, they fought against the Bannock, Shoshoni, and Blackfeet. Missionaries (1841) converted the tribe to Christianity; today, fewer than 3000 live on the Flathead Reservation in Montana.

flathead A bottom-dwelling carnivorous *bony fish of the family *Platycephalidae*, found in tropical Indian, Pacific, and E Atlantic waters. It has a tapering body, up to 55 in (1.3 m) long, and a large flat head covered with ridges and spines. It is an important food fish. Order: *Scorpaeniformes* (or *Scleroparei*).

flat racing A form of horse racing in which the horses are not required to jump obstacles. Flat races are usually run over distances between 0.5 mi (0.8 km) and 1.5 mi (2.4 km). *Thoroughbred horses are used, mainly as two- and three-year-olds. Weight handicaps are allotted in most races. The most prestigious US races are the *Triple Crown.

flatworm A flat-bodied wormlike animal of the invertebrate phylum *Platyhelminthes* (9000 species). Some flatworms are free-living (*see* planarian) but the majority are parasitic (*see* fluke; tapeworm). They have a simple body, with sense organs and a primitive brain at the front end, and range in size from 0.04 in–49 ft (1 mm–15 m). Many are hermaphrodite, i.e. each individual contains both male and female reproductive organs.

Flaubert, Gustave (1821–80) French novelist. The son of a Rouen surgeon he gave up his law studies in 1843 to dedicate himself wholly to literature. He traveled in the Near East (1849–51) and Tunisia (1857) and was a lover of the poet Louise Colet (1808–76). He worked for five years on his first novel, *Madame Bovary* (1856), a controversially explicit study of an overromantic bourgeois wife. His other major works include the exotic romance *Salammbô* (1862), *L'Éducation sentimentale* (1870), *La Tentation de Saint Antoine* (1874), and the brilliant short stories in *Trois contes* (1877).

flax A herbaceous plant of the genus *Linum* (230 species), mostly of the N hemisphere. Cultivated flax (*L. usitatissimum*) is an annual, up to 40 in (100 cm) high, with narrow leaves and blue five-petaled flowers. Its stem fibers are used to make linen, fine writing paper, and cigarette paper. The seeds contain *linseed oil. Flax is cultivated throughout Western Europe, the main producing countries being Belgium, Holland, and Northern Ireland. Family: *Linaceae.*

flea A small wingless □insect belonging to the widely distributed order *Siphonaptera* (about 1600 species). Fleas are bloodsucking parasites of birds and mammals. A flea's body, which is generally brown, is 0.04–0.40 in (1–10 mm) long and laterally flattened and its legs are modified for jumping. Fleas have irritating bites and change hosts frequently, acting as carriers of some serious diseases. The wormlike larvae use biting mouthparts to feed on dirt, excrement, and dried blood. Two important and widely distributed species are the human flea (*Pulex irritans*) and the oriental rat flea (*Xenopsylla cheopis*), which transmits bubonic plague and typhus to man.

fleabane A perennial herb of the genus *Erigeron* (about 180 species), from America and Europe; 3–16 in (8–40 cm) tall, fleabanes have strap-shaped leaves and small daisylike flower heads with purple or white ray florets and yellow centers. Herbs of the Old World genus *Pulicaria* are also called fleabane. They have daisylike yellow flowers, 0.4–1.2 in (1–3 cm) across. Family: **Compositae.*

fleawort One of several herbs of the genus *Senecio*, especially *S. integrifolius, S. palustris*, and *S. spathulifolius*, from central and N Europe. The plants are 10–40 in (25–100 cm) high, with yellow daisylike flowers, 0.8–1.2 in (2–3 cm) across. Family: **Compositae.*

Fleet Street The center of English journalism, a street in London between the Strand and the City in which most of the major newspapers have offices. It is named for the River Fleet (now a covered sewer).

Flémalle, Master of (c. 1378–1444) One of the founders (with the *van Eyck brothers) of the Flemish school of painting (*see* Flemish art). He is usually identified as Robert Campin, an artist active in Tournai from 1406. His name derives from three panels (Frankfurt-am-Main) attributed to him and mistakenly thought to have been commissioned by the abbey of Flémalle near Liège. Other works include the *Mérode Altarpiece* (the Cloisters, New York), the *Annunciation* and *Marriage of the Virgin* (Madrid), and the *Madonna of Humility* (London). His works display the careful realistic rendering of details from everyday life that characterizes the Flemish school as a whole.

Fleming, Sir Alexander (1881–1955) British microbiologist, who discovered the antibiotic *penicillin. In 1928 Fleming noticed that a mold contaminating a bacterial culture had destroyed the bacteria in its vicinity. He identified the mold as *Pencillium notatum* and named the antibacterial substance it produced penicillin. Although he found that penicillin was harmless to human cells, Fleming could not isolate or identify the antibiotic. This was later achieved by Lord *Florey and Sir Ernest *Chain, with whom Fleming shared the 1945 Nobel

Prize. Fleming also discovered lysozyme, an antibacterial enzyme found in tears and saliva.

Fleming, Ian (Lancaster) (1908–64) British author and journalist, famous for his creation of the archetypal secret agent, James Bond, in 12 novels and 7 short stories, most of them filmed. Originally a stockbroker, Fleming served as a foreign correspondent in Moscow, and in World War II became a senior naval intelligence officer.

Fleming, Sir John Ambrose (1849–1945) British electrical engineer, who constructed the first rectifying *diode in 1904. His invention greatly stimulated the development of radio and led to the invention of the triode two years later by Lee *De Forest. He also took part in the development of the electric lamp and carried out research into resistance at low temperatures. He was knighted in 1929. *See also* Fleming's rules.

Fleming, Paul (1609–40) German poet. A disciple of Martin *Opitz, his posthumously published love lyrics and religious hymns were distinguished by their sincerity and directness. Many of his poems were inspired by his thwarted love for Elsàbe Niehus, whom he met on a trading journey to Russia and Persia.

Flemings Inhabitants of N and W Belgium who speak Flemish, a dialect of *Dutch known by them as Vlaams. They number approximately 5,500,000. Like the Dutch they are descended from the Salic Franks, a Germanic people, who settled the area during the 3rd and 4th centuries AD. They retain a cultural identity distinct from that of French-speaking Belgians (*see* Walloons).

Fleming's rules A mnemonic, invented by Sir John Ambrose Fleming, for the relationship between the directions of motion, magnetic field, and electric current in *electric motors and generators. The thu*m*b represents *m*otion; the *f*irst (index) *f*inger represents the *f*ield; and the se*c*ond finger represents the *c*urrent. If the right hand is held with the thumb and first two fingers straight and mutually at right angles, the directions in a generator are indicated. The left hand indicates the directions in a motor.

Flemish art A tradition of painting that flourished in Flanders, now Belgium, from the 14th to the 18th centuries. The early dominance of manuscript illuminators was replaced in the 15 century by a major school of painters, which included the Master of *Flémalle, the *van Eycks, van der *Weyden, van der *Goes, *Bouts, *Memling, and Gerard *David. In the 16th century Flemish art was Italianized by such painters as *Gossaert and Frans *Floris, although *Bosch and *Brueghel remained largely within the Flemish tradition. Major 17th-century figures were *Rubens, *Van Dyck, *Jordaens, and *Teniers. Flemish art declined in international importance after the 17th century.

Flensburg 54 47N 9 27E A city in NW Germany, in Schleswig-Holstein on the Baltic Sea. Between 1848 and 1867 it was under Danish rule, and in 1945 at the end of World War II the German government capitulated near here. A port and naval base, its industries include shipbuilding and fishing. Population (1984 est): 86,700.

Fletcher, John (1579–1625) English dramatist. He collaborated with Francis *Beaumont on *Philaster* (1610), *The Maid's Tragedy* (1611), and many other plays, and probably with *Shakespeare on *The Two Noble Kinsmen* and *Henry VIII* (1612).

fleur-de-lys A heraldic device, which has three everted petals, resembling the bearded iris. It was the coat of arms of the French monarchy from the Middle Ages.

Fleury, André Hercule de, Cardinal (1653–1743) French statesman; chief minister (1726–43) of Louis XV. Fleury carried out important reforms, reorganizing finances, building roads, and encouraging commerce. A successful diplomat, he worked to maintain peace in Europe but involved France in the War of the *Polish Succession (1733–38) on the side of Stanisław I Leszczyński.

Flinders Island. *See* Furneaux Islands.

Flinders Range A mountain range in E South Australia. It extends N from Gulf St Vincent between Lake Torrens and Lake Frome, reaching 3904 ft (1190 m) at St Mary Peak.

flint A variety of *chalcedony. It is gray to black, is dense and tough, and breaks with a conchoidal (curved) fracture, leaving sharp edges (hence its use by Stone Age man for tools and weapons). It occurs in nodules in chalk along the bedding planes and as pebbles in river gravels and beach material.

Flint 43 03N 83 40W A city in the US, in Michigan on the Flint River. One of the several cities that surround *Detroit, its main industry is motor vehicles. Population (1990): 140,761.

flint glass A durable, brilliant, and highly refractive glass. It is used in high-quality glassware and also in lenses and prisms since it absorbs very little light. It is also known as lead glass and crystal glass.

FLN. *See* Front de Libération nationale.

Flodden, Battle of (Sept 9, 1513) The battle in which the English under Thomas Howard, Earl of Surrey (1443–1524), defeated the Scots under *James IV at Flodden Edge, Northumberland. The Scots had invaded England after allying with France against Henry VIII.

flood The overflowing of a river onto the surrounding land (**flood plain**) or the surging of sea water at high tide onto the coastal land. Disastrous floods have occurred throughout history. The flood described in Genesis 6.9 (*see* Noah) is probably apocryphal, although Sir Leonard *Woolley identified at Ur a layer of clay that he believed was deposited during a flood in about 4000 BC. More recent flood disasters include those in Lisbon (1775), Warsaw (1861 and 1964), Paris (1910), Florence (1966), Bangladesh (1974), and the central US (1993). However, floods are not always disastrous; the annual floods of the *Nile River have provided a fertile flood plain, the site of one of the earliest civilizations.

The prevention of disasters by flooding involves the accurate prediction of the behavior of rivers and tides and the provision of flood-relief channels and barrages.

Flood, Henry (1732–91) Irish politician. An impressive orator, Flood rapidly became the leader of the patriot party in the Irish Parliament. In 1775, however, he accepted a government post and the patriots henceforth branded him as an apostate. In 1781 Flood again espoused the patriot cause but quarreled with its new leader, *Grattan, and declined into political obscurity.

floodgate A movable barrier set up on spillways to control the height of water at *dams. Closure of some of the floodgates at a spillway in times of water shortage may conserve valuable amounts of water, without reducing the full spillway capacity. Vertical-lift gates are raised to permit flow beneath them, while drum gates (solid circular quadrants) rotate downward to allow water to flow over them.

Flora The Roman goddess of flowers and spring. Her spring festival, the Floralia, instituted in 283 BC, was the occasion for riotous uninhibited behavior.

Florence (Italian name: Firenze) 43 47N 11 15E A city in Italy, the capital of Tuscany on the Arno River. Florence is a major market town as well as an administrative and educational center. The manufacture of luxury goods is important but the principal industry is tourism. Its many famous buildings include the 13th-century cathedral of Sta Maria del Fiore, the campanile of Giotto, the baptistery, and many churches (including Sta Maria Novella and Sta Croce). The Ponte Vecchio (1345) across the Arno River connects the *Uffizi gallery (containing Italy's most important collection of paintings) to the Palazzo Pitti (now an art gallery). Art treasures in Florence include works by Michelangelo, Donatello, Masaccio, Giotto, Fra Angelico, Botticelli, Raphael, Titian, and Rubens. The Italian National Library (Biblioteca Nazionale) is situated here and its university was established in 1321. *History*: an early Roman colony, it had developed into an important center of trade and industry by the 12th century. It was torn by the struggles between the *Guelfs and Ghibellines (13th and 14th centuries) but flourished financially and culturally (14th–16th centuries). The rule of the *Medici family began in 1434 and this continued almost uninterrupted (*see* Savonarola, Girolamo) for three centuries. Following a period of Austrian rule, Florence became part of the new kingdom of Italy in 1861 and was the provisional capital (1865–71). Florence has suffered considerable damage in war (including World War II) and from floods, especially in November 1966. Population (1991 est): 408,500.

Flores An Indonesian island in the Nusa Tenggara group. Mountainous and volcanic, it is largely unexplored. Agriculture is shifting cultivation producing chiefly maize; sandalwood and copra are exported. Area: 6622 sq mi (17,150 sq km). Chief town: Ende.

Florey, Howard Walter, Baron (1898–1968) Australian pathologist, who, working with Sir Ernst *Chain, isolated and purified the antibiotic *penicillin, first discovered by Sir Alexander *Fleming in 1928. Florey and Chain developed techniques for producing the pure drug in large quantities. In 1941 they conducted the first clinical trials, in which penicillin proved very effective in combating bacterial infections. Florey shared the 1945 Nobel Prize with Chain and Fleming.

Florianópolis (former name: Desterro) 27 35S 48 31W A city and port in Brazil, the capital of Santa Catarina state on Santa Catarina island. It is linked to the mainland by a steel suspension bridge, the longest in Brazil. It exports sugar, tobacco, and fruit and has a university (1960). Population (1980): 153,547.

floribunda. *See* rose.

Florida A state in the extreme SE, forming a long (400 mi; 645 km) peninsula, with the Atlantic Ocean to the E and the Gulf of Mexico to the W; it borders Alabama and Georgia on the N and NE. The Florida Straits, dotted with small chains of islands, including the Florida Keys and the Dry Tortugas, separate the state from Cuba, which has figured prominently in its more recent history. It is predominantly a low-lying peninsula with many lakes and rivers, Lake Okeechobee being the largest lake. In the diversified economy manufacturing is important, especially food processing and the chemical industry. The state's mines produce phosphate, titanium, zircon, and other heavy minerals. Tourism, based on its subtropical climate, is the most important industry, with many popular resorts, such as Miami Beach and Palm Beach. The Everglades, a low-lying subtropical wilderness area of marshlands that extends over a large portion of the S tip of the state, abounds with unique wildlife. Disney World entertainment park near Orlando is the state's most popular tourist attraction. Most recently the state has become a center for space exploration with the John F. Kennedy Space Center at Cape Canaveral. Florida is known for its citrus fruits (producing 75% of the US total), especially oranges, of which it is the nation's leading producer. It also produces large quantities of vegetables. It is also a major region for breeding thoroughbred horses. *History*: following its discovery by Ponce de Leon in his famous search for the Fountain of Youth, Florida was explored by the Spanish, who founded St Augustine, now the oldest permanent white settlement in America. It was ceded to the British in 1763 and remained loyal to it during the American Revolution. Florida was returned to Spain at the end of the war, but the Spanish hold was tenuous and in 1819 it passed to the US. Wars with the Seminoles culminated with the expulsion of most of the Indians from the state. Small Indian populations continue to live in Florida, principally around Lake Okeechobee. It became a state in 1845. It was a supporter of the Confederate cause during the US Civil War. The arrival of the railroads in the 1880s brought access to the agricultural markets of the N and subsequent economic growth. Drainage of the Everglades brought increased settlement as Florida became one of the fastest-growing states. Development accelerated from the 1970s through the early 1990s, with new residents attracted by the climate and economic prosperity. Area: 58,560 sq mi (151,670 sq km). Population (1990): 12,937,926. Capital: Tallahassee.

FLORIDA *An aerial view of Miami Beach, one of the state's most famous resorts.*

Florida Keys A chain of small islands separated from the S coast of Florida by Florida Bay. It includes the islands of Key West and Key Largo and extends for over 100 mi (160 km). The islands are linked by the Overseas Highway, a complex of roads and 42 bridges.

Florio, John (c. 1553–1625) English writer, of Italian descent. While teaching at Oxford he published his important Italian-English dictionary (1598). He later held appointments at James I's court. His main work was an English translation of Montaigne's *Essays* (1603).

Floris Two Flemish artists. **Cornelis Floris** (1514–75) was an architect and sculptor, best known for designing Antwerp town hall (1561–65). His brother **Frans Floris** (c. 1516–70) was a painter. Both studied in Italy and contributed to the spread of the Italian Renaissance style in the Netherlands.

Flotow, Friedrich von (1812–83) German operatic composer. He had much success in his lifetime but his works, with the exception of the opera *Martha* (1847), have not survived.

flotsam, jetsam, and lagan Goods cast into the sea that respectively remain afloat, sink, or would sink but have attached to them a buoy, which keeps them afloat.

flounder A common name for any *flatfish or for certain species. An example is *Platichthys flesus*, which is up to 20 in (50 cm) long and lives in European coastal and fresh waters. It has a greenish or brownish mottled upper surface and is an important food and game □fish.

flour The powdered grain of wheat or other cereals, used in baking. The chief use of flour is in making bread. When the two proteins in wheat, glutenin and gliadin, are mixed with water they form gluten, which permits the dough to expand and retain the carbon dioxide resulting from fermentation of the yeast in bread dough. Different types of flour are made by varying the percentage of flour separated from the wheat. The principal commercial flours are whole wheat (100%), whole meal and stone-ground (92%), wheat meal (80–90%), and white flours (70–72%). Many nutritionists consider it important to eat food made from whole wheat and whole meal flour, rather than white flour. The former retain more of the bran (the outer skin of the wheat grain) and have more iron and calcium than white flour. They are also a good daily source of dietary *fiber. Flour with a high gluten content (strong flour) is best when yeast is called for, as in dough for bread. On the other hand a softer flour with a lower gluten content (fine flour) is used for cakes, shortbread, etc. Plain flour is all-purpose, with a moderate gluten content. Self-rising flour is plain flour with the addition of rising agents.

flower The reproductive organ of flowering □plants (angiosperms), which is essential for the production of seeds and fruits. It is made up of the perianth (petals and sepals) and the sexual organs—the *stamens producing pollen (male gametes) and the *carpels containing the female gametes. The petals and sepals serve to protect the sexual organs and, in flowers pollinated by animals, are brightly colored, scented, and secrete *nectar to attract insects and birds. Wind-pollinated flowers are typically small and inconspicuous and may lack a perianth.

flowering currant An ornamental garden shrub, *Ribes sanguineum*, native to North America. Up to 8 ft (2.5 m) tall, it has drooping spikes of pink tubular flowers that appear before the maple-shaped leaves. The fruit is a blue-black berry. The shrub has an odor of blackcurrants. Family: *Grossulariaceae* (*see* currant).

flowering quince. *See* japonica.

flowering rush A perennial freshwater plant, *Butomus umbellatus*, native to Eurasia but common throughout N temperate regions: it is a popular garden plant. It has tapering leaves, up to 40 in (1 m) long, and an umbrella-shaped cluster of pinkish flowers at the tip of a long stalk. Family: *Butomaceae*.

flowerpecker A songbird belonging to a family (*Dicaeidae*; 55 species) occurring in S Asia and Australasia. Ranging in size from 3–8 in (8–20 cm), they have stumpy tails, short bills, and variable plumage. Flowerpeckers feed on berries and nectar, thereby dispersing seeds and pollinating flowers.

fluidics The use of jets of fluid in a circuit to carry out electronic functions. Fluidic circuits can resist much higher temperatures than electronic circuits and are also unaffected by ionizing radiation and magnetic fields. They therefore have uses in nuclear reactors and spacecraft. They are also used as delay lines since they respond much more slowly than electronic circuits.

fluidization The process of supporting very fine solid particles in a stream of gas so that the combination of solid and fluid behaves like a liquid. The process is used in transporting coal dust and in the cleaning of the catalyst in *catalytic cracking in oil refining.

fluid mechanics The study of the mechanical properties of fluids. *Hydrostatics is concerned with the study of fluids at rest and hydrodynamics (*or* fluid dynamics) with fluids that are flowing. Hydraulics deals with the practical applications of these sciences. Two important aspects of hydrodynamics are the conservation of energy in fluid flow (*see* Bernoulli's theorem) and the distinction between streamline and turbulent flow. *See also* aerodynamics; Reynolds number.

fluke A parasitic *flatworm of the class *Trematoda* (over 6000 species). Typically leaf-shaped, some are elongated to fit the body cavities they inhabit. The monogenetic flukes have a single host and are generally external parasites of fishes; the digenetic flukes have life cycles involving up to four different hosts and are mainly internal parasites of vertebrates, passing early larval stages in various invertebrates.

fluorescence. *See* luminescence.

fluorescent lamp A lamp that uses fluorescence (*see* luminescence) as its source of light. It consists of a glass tube containing a low-pressure gas, such as mercury vapor. As a current passes through the gas, collisions between the electrons and atoms of the gas excite the atoms, which emit *ultraviolet radiation when they return to the ground state. The radiation strikes a phosphor coating on the inner surface of the tube, causing the phosphor to fluoresce and emit visible light.

fluoridation The addition of fluoride (usually sodium fluoride) to drinking water to reduce dental *caries (tooth decay), especially in children. The fluoride combines with apatite—the chief constituent of tooth enamel—to form fluoroapatite, which has a greater resistance to bacterial decay. The recommended level is one part of fluoride per million and if the natural concentration is below this level it is often the policy of local governments to add fluoride to the water. Controversy sometimes arises on the grounds that "medication" is being forced on people who may not wish to accept it. This measure has been shown to be effective, however, and quite safe in low concentrations (many natural water supplies contain up to four or five parts per million).

fluorine (F) A highly reactive pale-yellow halogen gas, the most electronegative element known. It was first isolated by H. Moissan in 1886 and occurs naturally in volcanic gases and as *fluorite (CaF_2) and *cryolite (Na_2AlF_6). It is prepared by electrolysis of potassium hydrogen fluoride (KHF_2) solution in dry hydrofluoric acid (HF). Fluorine became industrially important with the introduction of nuclear power. The gas uranium hexafluoride (UF_6) allows separation of the fissile ^{235}U isotope from ^{238}U by gaseous diffusion. Hydrofluoric acid is used to etch glass and can cause very painful burns to the skin. *Fluorocarbons (for example CF_2Cl_2) are chemically unreactive and have many important uses. Trace amounts of fluoride in drinking water are thought to be important in helping to prevent dental decay (*see* fluoridation). At no 9; at wt 18.9984; mp −363°F (−219.62°C); bp −306.6°F (−188.14°C).

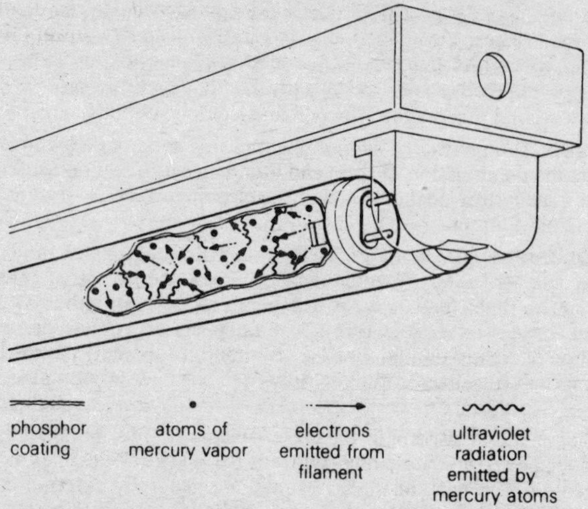

FLUORESCENT LAMP *Electrons from the filament collide with atoms of mercury vapor in the tube, producing ultraviolet radiation. This is converted to visible light by the fluorescent coating on the tube.*

fluorite (*or* fluorspar) A mineral consisting of calcium fluoride, white, green, or yellow in color. It occurs in hydrothermal veins, often as a gangue material in ore deposits, and in some igneous rocks. Most fluorite is used as a flux in iron and steel making; it is also used as a source of fluorine for manufacturing hydrofluoric acid and in the ceramic- and optical-glass industries. Blue John is a deep blue or purple variety used for ornamental purposes.

fluorocarbons Synthetic compounds of carbon and fluorine (sometimes also containing atoms of other halogens). They are extremely resistant to chemical attack, even at very high temperatures, and are nontoxic and nonflammable. They are used as refrigerants, anesthetics, heat-transfer agents, and high-temperature lubricants. The fluoroanalogue of polyethylene, polytetrafluoroethylene (Teflon), is a useful plastic in corrosive environments and has a very low coefficient of friction. Its stability at high temperatures enables it to be used for nonstick coatings on cooking utensils. Fluorocarbons have also been used in enormous quantities as propellants for aerosols, although they have been opposed on environmental grounds, as photochemical reactions in the upper atmosphere may lead to depletion of the ozone layer, thereby removing protection against harmful ultraviolet radiation.

fluorspar. *See* fluorite.

flute A woodwind instrument of ancient origin, existing in many different cultures. The modern side-blown flute (in which a column of air is made to vibrate by blowing across an elliptical mouth hole) and the *recorder are members of the same family. The flute came into prominence in the 16th century, when it was made of wood; today most flutes are metal. The modern orchestral flute (perfected by Theobald *Boehm) is about 2 ft (0.6 m) long and has a range of three octaves above middle C. □musical instruments.

flux (brazing and soldering) A substance applied to pieces to be soldered to aid the formation of the joint. Soft solder, used in electrical joints, commonly contains a core of flux, often tallow or a similar substance. For hard soldering, at higher temperatures, zinc chloride is often used. The flux lowers the melting point of the solder and also reacts with or removes surface oxides from the metals, thus keeping their surfaces clean and allowing the liquid solder to adhere to the surfaces.

flux (physics) The net amount of a directional quantity passing through a surface area at right angles to the surface. The concept of flux is used to describe phenomena that involve forces or the flow of energy, such as electric flux, magnetic flux, and luminous flux.

fly An insect belonging to the order *Diptera* (over 85,000 species)—the so-called true, or two-winged, flies—of great importance in transmitting disease. The adults have only two wings (the front pair), the hind pair being reduced to balancing organs (called halteres). The mouthparts are adapted for piercing or sucking, and most species feed on plant juices or suck the blood of mammals. The larvae—often called maggots—are typically scavengers on plant and animal refuse or parasites of pest status. Bloodsucking species, such as *mosquitoes and *tsetse flies, may transmit such diseases as malaria, sleeping sickness, and yellow fever. The order also includes the *houseflies, *blowflies, *craneflies, and *horse flies.

The name fly is also used for various flying insects of other orders: the alderfly, caddis fly, damselfly, firefly, and mayfly are examples of nondipterous flies.

fly agaric A poisonous mushroom, **Amanita muscaria*, found in woodlands, especially of birch and conifers. Its cap, 2–8 in (6–20 cm) in diameter, is scarlet or orange-red with white scales and the white stalk has a membranous collar beneath the cap. Fly agaric is seldom fatal. It was formerly used as a fly killer, hence its name.

flycatcher A small active songbird belonging to an Old World family (*Muscicapidae*; 378 species) and feeding on insects, typically caught in flight. They have small bills surrounded by stiff bristles and delicate legs used only for perching. The typical flycatchers are dull colored and include the gray-and-brown European spotted flycatcher (*Muscicapa striata*) and the black-and-white pied flycatcher (*Ficedula hypoleuca*). The tropical blue flycatchers and paradise flycatchers are beautifully colored and ornamented. *Compare* tyrant flycatcher.

Flying Dutchman In sailors' lore, a ghost ship haunting the sea around the Cape of Good Hope. Its captain, driven back from the Cape by a storm, is supposed to have sworn a blasphemous oath to round it or be forever damned. The story became popular in 19th-century literature and inspired Wagner's opera (1843) of the same name.

flying fish A □fish of the family *Exocoetidae* (about 40 species). Up to 18 in (45 cm) long, flying fish swim just below the surface in warm oceanic waters. If disturbed they launch themselves from the water by rapidly beating the tail and glide through the air using large winglike pectoral fins.

flying fox A fruit *bat belonging to the genus *Pteropus* (51 species), ranging from Africa to Australia. Flying foxes have foxlike heads and a wingspan of up to 5 ft (1.5 m).

flying lemur. *See* colugo.

flying lizard A lizard belonging to the genus *Draco* (15 species) of SE Asia, having large folds of skin between the legs supported by ribs that are spread out when the lizard jumps from a tree. They have greenish bodies and brightly colored "wings." Family: *Agamidae* (agamas). □reptile.

flying phalanger A squirrel-like *marsupial mammal, also called marsupial glider. Flying phalangers, found in E Australia and Tasmania, range from 6–40 in (14–100 cm) in length. They all have soft fur and long bushy tails and a flap of skin between the fore and hind legs enables them to glide from tree to tree. Genera: *Acrobates, Petaurus, Schoinobates*; family: *Phalangeridae*.

flying saucer. *See* unidentified flying object.

flying snake A slender arboreal snake belonging to the genus *Chrysopelea* (3 species), occurring in S Asia and the East Indies. They are diurnal, feed on small rodents, bats, birds, and lizards, and can glide short distances by launching themselves in the air and flattening their belly scales. Family: *Colubridae*.

flying squirrel A nocturnal *squirrel of the subfamily *Petauristinae* (37 species), occurring in SE Asia, North America, and Eurasia. Flying squirrels have a flap of loose skin from elbow to knee that is stretched tight by extending the legs, enabling them to glide from branch to branch. □mammal.

Flynn, Errol (1909–59) US actor, born in Tasmania. After trying a number of odd jobs, he became an actor in Hollywood, playing the handsome adventurous hero in such films as *Captain Blood* (1935), *Gentleman Jim* (1942), and (as John Barrymore) *Too Much Too Soon* (1958). His private life, which was scarcely less eventful than his film roles, was candidly recounted in two autobiographies, *Beam Ends* (1934) and *My Wicked Wicked Ways* (1959).

Fly River A river in New Guinea, rising in W Papua New Guinea and flowing generally S, forming part of the border between Papua New Guinea and West Irian, before entering the Gulf of Papua. Length: 800 mi (1300 km).

flytrap. *See* Venus' flytrap.

flywheel A large heavy wheel attached to the driving shaft of a motor to act as an energy store and to iron out fluctuations in the speed of the machine. The energy stored depends on the speed of rotation and the weight distribution of the wheel. They are used in *internal-combustion engines, power presses, etc.

f-number The ratio of the focal length of a camera lens to the diameter of the shutter opening (aperture). For example, f-8 means that the focal length is eight times the aperture. The smaller the f-number, the greater the illumination of the film. **Relative aperture** is the reciprocal of f-number.

Foch, Ferdinand (1851–1929) French marshal. At the outbreak of World War I he commanded the Ninth Army and was largely responsible for halting the German advance at the Marne and for the Allied victory at Ypres (1915). After the Somme offensive (1916), he became chief of the general staff (1917). He returned to action in 1918 and as Allied commander in chief forced the Germans back to the Rhine, effecting their defeat.

foetus. *See* fetus.

fog A cloud near the ground surface, within which visibility is reduced to less than 0.6 mi (1 km). Fog is the result of the condensation of water vapor in the lower layers of air, usually through the cooling of air to below its *dew point; it is most likely to occur with light wind conditions and a clear sky at night. It often contains dust and smoke particles and in industrial areas the increased supply of these particles causes a greater incidence of fog; in areas in which smoke occurs *smog can develop.

Foggia 41 28N 15 33E A city in Italy, in Apulia. It has a castle dating from the time of the Holy Roman Emperor Frederick II. Olives, grapes, wheat, and tobacco are grown in the surrounding region and its industries include flour milling, cheese and paper making, and engineering. Population (1989 est): 159,000.

föhn A warm dry wind that descends down the leeward side of mountains. It is a frequent occurrence in the Alps (where the name originated), the Rocky Mountains (where it is known as the **chinook**), and the Andes. In winter it can cause extremely rapid thaws of lying snow, resulting in avalanches.

Fokine, Michel (Mikhail F.; 1880–1942) Russian ballet dancer and choreographer. From 1909 he worked with Diaghilev's Ballets Russes in Paris, for which he choreographed such revolutionary ballets as *The Firebird* (1910) and *Petrushka* (1911). He went to New York in 1923 and became a naturalized US citizen in 1932.

Fokker, Anthony Hermann Gerard (1890–1939) Dutch aircraft manufacturer. Fokker opened an aircraft factory in Germany in 1912. During World War I he supplied Germany with aircraft and invented a method of firing a machine gun through the propeller of an aircraft. He later became a US citizen.

fold A buckling of sedimentary rock strata produced by compressional forces acting on it. Large-scale folding produces mountain ranges; this occurs where two continental plates collide (*see* plate tectonics) and the sediment along their margins is compressed and folded. A simple upfold is called an *anticline and a downfold, a *syncline; however, most folds are much more complex.

Foley, Thomas Stephen (1929–) US politician, Speaker of the House of Representatives (1989–). A lawyer from Washington state, he entered the House as a Democrat in 1965 and held House leadership posts from 1974. Known as a behind-the-scenes reformer who avoided antagonizing powerful interests while accomplishing his aims, Foley became majority whip in 1981 and succeeded Jim Wright as Speaker of the House in 1989. His lack of forceful leadership during the House banking scandal beginning in 1991 was widely criticized within his own party.

folic acid. *See* vitamin B complex.

Folies-Bergère A Parisian variety theater opened in 1869 and celebrated chiefly for its elaborate revues featuring dancing girls and striptease acts. Maurice *Chevalier and many other leading French entertainers have appeared there.

folk dance A form of dance developed by country people, usually for their own amusement. Folk dances derive from ancient ritual dances used in religious worship and to invoke the fertility of the land (the original purpose of the *maypole dance). They have greatly influenced other forms of dances, notably court dancing, 18th- and 19th-century ballroom dances (such as the *waltz and *polka), and *ballet. Many countries have their own traditional dances. The revived interest in folk dancing in the 20th century is reflected in the popularity of professional folk-dance companies and folk-dance societies.

folklore The social, material, and oral culture of primitive societies. The social culture comprises such forms as festivals, dances, and religious rites; the material culture comprises architecture and arts and crafts; the oral culture includes songs, tales, legends, proverbs, and riddles. The study of folklore, spurred by early collections of folk literature, such as Percy's *Reliques of Ancient English Poetry* (1765) and the *Fairy Tales* (1812–14) of the brothers *Grimm, has played an important role in the work of anthropologists, such as Franz *Boas and J. G. *Frazer.

folk music Song or dance music developed from a communal aural tradition and not composed by an individual, e.g. Irish ballads and cowboy songs. The melody and words of folk songs are often changed by a succession of performances. Folk music is characterized by modal melody and simple forms, such as dances, lullabies, work songs, and love ballads. Traditional English folk songs include "Black Is the Colour of My True Love's Hair" and "Greensleeves." During the revival of folk songs in the US in the 1960s, new music by such composers as Woody Guthrie, Joan Baez, and Bob Dylan was termed folk song or "folk," owing to its similarity to authentic folk music.

follicle-stimulating hormone. *See* gonadotrophin.

Folsom point A fluted lanceolate (leaf-shaped) stone spearhead made between 9000 and 8000 BC in the western grasslands of the US. The name derives from Folsom, N.Mex., where one was discovered (1926), with the remains of an extinct form of bison. *Compare* Clovis point.

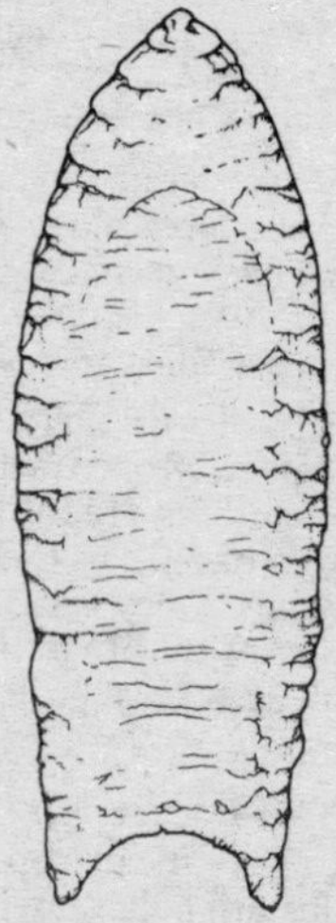

FOLSOM POINT *One of the most developed types of Stone Age weapon heads.*

Fomalhaut A conspicuous star, apparent magnitude 1.15 and 23 light years distant, that is the only bright star in the S constellation Piscis Austrinus.

Fon The predominant people of S Benin (formerly Dahomey), who speak a dialect of *Ewe. They grow maize, manioc, and yams and palm oil as a cash crop. Their villages are headed by the oldest male. A hereditary headman has general authority to arbitrate in disputes. During the 18th and 19th centuries the Fon formed the kingdom of Dahomey. The powerful king and his chiefs conducted war ceremonies, received tribute, and presided over courts. An ancestor cult involved the sacrifice of prisoners of war in return for supernatural aid.

Fonda, Henry (1905–82) US film actor and director, associated particularly with the portrayal of men of solid integrity, notably in *The Grapes of Wrath* (1940). Other films include *War and Peace* (1956), *12 Angry Men* (1957), and *On Golden Pond* (1981), which earned him his first Oscar and also starred his daughter **Jane Fonda** (1937–), a film actress. Her other films include *Barbarella* (1968), an extravaganza of sexual fantasy, and subsequent more serious roles in such films as *Klute* (1971), *Julia* (1977), *Coming Home* (1978), for which she won an Oscar, *The Electric Horseman* (1979), *The China Syndrome*

(1979), *Morning After* (1986), *Old Gringo* (1989), and *Stanley and Iris* (1990). In the 1980s, she developed a second career as a fitness advocate. She married flamboyant businessman Ted Turner in 1991. His son **Peter Fonda** (1939–) made his name as an actor and director with *Easy Rider* (1969).

Fontainebleau 48 24N 2 42E A city in N central France, in the Seine-et-Marne department. The surrounding forest inspired the Barbizon school of painters. The Royal Palace, largely built by Francis I, was the scene of Napoleon I's abdication in 1814. Fontainebleau was the headquarters of NATO from 1954 to 1966. Population (1975): 19,595.

Fontainebleau, school of The painters who decorated the Royal Palace of Fontainebleau (France) between about 1530 and 1560. The Italians Giovanni Battista Rosso (1494–1540), Francesco Primaticcio (c. 1504–70), and Niccolò dell' Abbate (c. 1512–71) were chiefly responsible for developing the particularly sensuous and elegant form of *mannerism that characterizes the school.

Fontana, Domenico (1543–1607) Italian architect and engineer. In the employ of the pope in Rome, Fontana designed the Sistine Library (1587–90) and helped complete the dome of St Peter's Basilica. He was also responsible for reerecting the Egyptian obelisk on its present site in front of St Peter's.

Fontane, Theodor (1819–98) German novelist. He began writing novels at the age of 56 after varied experience as a journalist and war correspondent. *Vor dem Sturm* (1878) is a realistic historical novel dealing with the Prussian nobility. Of several novels dealing with the place of women in society the best known is *Effi Briest* (1898).

Fontanne, Lyn. *See* Lunt, Alfred.

Fontenelle, Bernard le Bovier de (1657–1757) French philosopher and writer, who joined his uncle, Pierre *Corneille, in Paris in 1680, becoming a leading light of the contemporary salons. Renowned for his wit and his learning, he popularized the new scientific theories of Descartes and Newton in such works as *Digressions sur les anciens et les modernes* (1688) and *Éléments de la géométrie de l'infini* (1727). Pouring scorn on ancient myths and beliefs, he was a confirmed "modern," writing his *Théorie des tourbillons cartésiens* when he was 95.

Fontenoy, Battle of (May 11, 1745) The battle in the War of the *Austrian Succession in which France defeated Austria. Fought near Tournai, SE of Brussels, the battle was the French commander de *Saxe's most notable victory, leading to the conquest of Flanders. His artillery and cavalry carried the day against the Austrians, and their Dutch and English allies, who retreated toward Brussels.

Fonteyn, Dame Margot (Margaret Hookham; 1919–91) British ballet dancer. She was a member of the Sadler's Wells company and the Royal Ballet from 1934 to 1959 and also performed with most leading US and European companies, often in partnership with Rudolf *Nureyev. Her most famous performances were in classical ballets such as *Giselle, Swan Lake*, and *The Sleeping Beauty*.

Foochow. *See* Fuzhou.

Food and Agriculture Organization (FAO) A specialized agency of the *United Nations constituted in 1945 to coordinate international efforts to raise levels of nutrition and food production and to improve the management of forests. The agency, with headquarters in Rome, conducts research, makes recommendations, organizes educational programs, and encourages the export of agricultural products.

food chain A series of living organisms associated in a feeding relationship: each animal feeds on the one below it in the series. Most commonly, green plants are at the base of a food chain. They are eaten by herbivores, which in turn may be consumed by carnivores. Any animal or plant parasites are also part of the chain, and different food chains are often interconnected to form a **food web**. Other food chains are based on decomposers—organisms that feed on dead organic remains of plants and animals.

food poisoning An acute illness arising from eating contaminated food. Vomiting and diarrhea are the usual symptoms. **Salmonella* is the bacterium that most commonly causes food poisoning (salmonellosis), and symptoms begin 12–24 hours after eating the food. Patients usually recover within a few days. Another kind of food poisoning is due to a toxin (poison) produced by staphylococci: symptoms occur within one to three hours of taking the food. **Clostridium* bacteria may also cause food poisoning, the most severe form of which is *botulism.

food preservation The treatment of food to prevent its deterioration and to maintain its eating quality and nutritional value. Breakdown of food tissues is caused by enzymes, either contained within the food or produced by microorganisms—bacteria, yeasts, and fungi—growing in the food. These organisms also produce unpleasant and sometimes harmful substances. Oxidation and dehydration also contribute to spoilage. The principle of food preservation is therefore to alter the condition of food so that the activities of microorganisms are stopped. One of the oldest methods is drying or dehydration—used for meat, vegetables, cereals, milk products, etc. *Freezing is now widely used for both industrial and domestic food preservation. *Freeze drying involves freezing followed by dehydration. Heating kills microorganisms and is the principle of *pasteurization, *sterilization, etc. Further growth is prevented if food is sealed in airtight containers, such as cans (*see* canning) or bottles. A wide range of chemicals is added to food to inhibit microbial activity. Boiling with sugar (e.g. in jam) and pickling with salt or vinegar (e.g. onions, cucumbers) are traditional methods. Smoking has also been used to preserve meat and fish. Sodium benzoate, propionates, nitrates, nitrites, sulfur dioxide, and sulfites are all used by the modern food industry as well as many other compounds that enhance color, flavor, and texture for the consumer.

Fools, Feast of A festival held in medieval Europe (especially in France) on, or near, Holy Innocents' Day (Dec 28). It was organized by lower clergy. A mock pope or bishop (sometimes a boy) was elected and presided over burlesque church services. There were also processions and carnival plays as well as festive dancing and drinking.

fool's gold. *See* pyrite.

foot The lowermost part of the leg. The human foot contains 14 bones. There are seven tarsal bones, of which one (the talus) forms a hinge joint with the bones of the lower *leg and another (the calcaneus) forms the projection of the heel. The five metatarsal bones form the body of the foot and articulate with the phalanges, the bones of the toes. The first (big) toe is the most important as it provides a springboard for walking and running.

Foot, Michael (Mackintosh) (1913–) British Labour politician and historian. He worked as a journalist until elected to Parliament in 1945. He was editor (1948–52, 1955–60) of the left-wing Labour weekly the *Tribune*. He was leader of the House of Commons (1976–79) and leader of the Labour Party (1980–83). His many publications include a biography of Aneurin Bevan (2 vols. 1962–73).

foot-and-mouth disease An infectious virus disease affecting cattle, sheep, goats, pigs, and many wild animals. Symptoms, which appear 1–15 days after

FOOD CHAIN *The feeding relationships between some plants and animals of a meadow habitat are simplified in this food web; in practice many more links and various other organisms are involved.*

infection, include fever and the development of blisters in the mouth and on the foot with consequent excessive salivation and lameness. Recovery occurs in 95% of cases but production of offspring and milk yield in females is adversely affected. The disease must be notified to the authorities in many countries. Infected animals and contacts are usually slaughtered and movement of animals restricted. Vaccination is routine where the disease is endemic.

football A field game played throughout the world, the object of which is to score goals with an inflated ball. Team games using a football were played in China around 200 BC, in ancient Greece and Rome, and from the 12th century in England, where the violence and lawlessness of the game resulted in considerable injury. The modern games evolved during the 19th century as rules were formalized; in this the English preparatory schools played a large role.

American football is similar to rugby football and developed in US colleges in the 1870s; it is played with an oval ball on a field marked out as a gridiron. There are 11 players on the field at any one time, but groups of specialized players are used in different phases of the game. The teams toss to decide which is to kick first. The game progresses in downs, or periods when the team in possession of the ball (offensive team) is advancing the ball toward the goal by passing or running with it. A down ends when a play is completed. The offensive team has four downs in which to advance the ball 10 yd (9 m). If this distance is not covered in the first three downs, the offensive team usually kicks the ball to the opponent. The other team then has the chance to substitute offensive for defensive players. If the 10 yd is covered, the offensive team maintains possession of the ball. A touchdown, in which the ball is taken across the opponents' goal line, scores six points; a conversion after a touchdown, in which the ball is taken over the goal line again from scrimmage or is kicked between the goalposts scores respectively two points or one point; a field goal (kicked from anywhere on the field) scores three points; a safety, in which a team scores a touchdown against itself, scores two points for its opponents.

Soccer (*or* association football) dates back to the founding in England of the Football Association (1863). It is an 11-a-side game played with a spherical ball weighing 14–16 oz (396–453 g) and having a circumference of 27–28 in (69–71 cm). The traditional positions of the players are: goalkeeper; right and left back; right, center, and left halfback; outside right, inside right, center forward, inside left, and outside left. These positions, established early in the 20th century, have now become very flexible, and a modern line-up consists more generally simply of strikers, midfield players, and defenders. The teams toss for the first kick (the kick-off), following which the teams compete for the ball, trying to kick or head it into the opponents' goal. Only the goalkeeper may use his hands, and then only in his penalty area. Played all over the world, the game is governed internationally by the *Fédération internationale de Football association.

Australian Rules is an 18-a-side game that originated in the Australian goldfields in the 1850s and is extensively played in some states, especially Victoria. It is a fast open game played with an oval ball measuring 22.75 × 29.5 in (57.2 × 73.6 cm), with which players may run as long as they bounce it every 10 yd (9 m). The ball must be punched instead of thrown (as it is in rugby football). There are four goalposts without crossbars at each end. A goal, kicked between the two inner posts, scores six points; a behind, kicked between an inner and an outer post, scores one point.

Canadian football is similar to American football but is played with 12-a-side teams on a larger field and has slightly different scoring and rules.

FOOTBALL

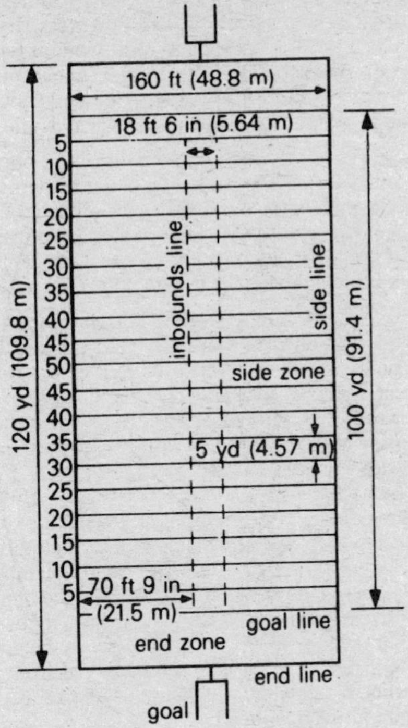
160 ft (48.8 m)
18 ft 6 in (5.64 m)
120 yd (109.8 m)
100 yd (91.4 m)
5
10
15
20
25
30
35
40
45
50
45
40
35
30
25
20
15
10
5
inbounds line
side line
side zone
5 yd (4.57 m)
70 ft 9 in
(21.5 m)
goal line
end zone
end line
goal

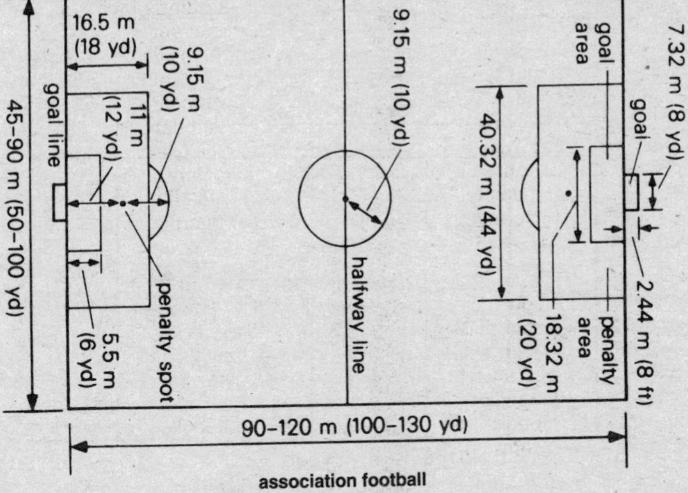
touch line
45–90 m (50–100 yd)
16.5 m
(18 yd)
goal line
11 m
(12 yd)
9.15 m
(10 yd)
5.5 m
(6 yd)
penalty spot
9.15 m (10 yd)
halfway line
40.32 m (44 yd)
goal area
goal
7.32 m (8 yd)
2.44 m (8 ft)
penalty
area
18.32 m
(20 yd)
90–120 m (100–130 yd)

association football

FOOTBALL

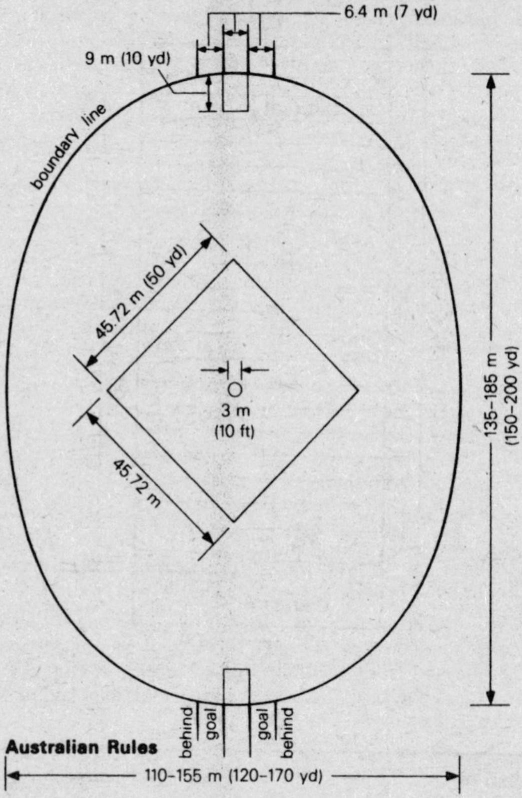

Australian Rules

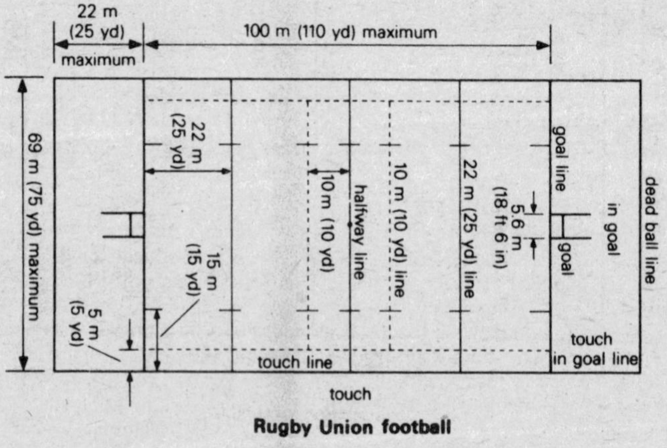

Rugby Union football

Rugby football uses an oval ball that is kicked or passed by hand. The game was first played at Rugby School, England, according to tradition in 1823. In 1871 the Rugby Football Union was formed, but its ban on professionalism led in 1893 to the secession of the Rugby League (then called the Northern Union); there are therefore two types of rugby. Rugby Union football (*or* rugger) is a 15-a-side amateur game played throughout the world. The ball is 11–11.25 in (27.9–28.6 cm) long. A try, in which the ball is touched down behind the opponents' goal line, is worth four points; a goal (a try "converted" by kicking the ball over the crossbar of the goalposts), a further two points; a penalty goal, resulting from a kick awarded as a penalty against the opposing team, three points; and a drop goal, from the field, three points. A scrum, in which the forwards of both teams battle for the ball in a tight mass, is used to restart the game after minor infringements. For more serious infringements a penalty kick is given to the opposing side. Rugby League football is a 13-a-side game with slightly different rules and scoring in which professionalism is allowed; it is played mainly in N England.

Foraminifera An order of small single-celled animals (□*Protozoa*) found on the sea bed or as part of the *plankton. They form calcareous often multichambered shells, ranging in size from under 0.02–0.20 in (0.5–5 mm), from which they extend fine branching pseudopodia to trap small protozoans and algae. Class: **Sarcodina*. *See also* Globigerina; Nummulites.

Forbes, George William (1869–1947) New Zealand statesman; prime minister (1930–35). Leader of the United (formerly Liberal Party), he was forced by economic difficulties into a coalition (1931) with the Reform Party but their combined efforts failed to solve the problems of the Depression.

Forbidden City The central part of *Beijing, so called because entry was forbidden to all but the emperor's family and servants. It was surrounded by a wall 2.5 mi (4 km) long and from the 15th century onward it contained the royal palace and residences and offices of the emperor's servants and ministers. It is now a complex of museums.

force The agency that changes either the speed or the direction of motion of a body (symbol: *F*). It is a *vector quantity defined as the product of the mass of the body and the acceleration produced on it. Force is measured in newtons. *See also* centripetal force; Coriolis force.

Ford, Ford Madox (F. Hermann Hueffer; 1873–1939) British novelist, grandson of the Pre-Raphaelite artist Ford Madox Brown. Among his 80 or more novels and books of criticism and memoirs are the novels *The Good Soldier* (1915) and *Parade's End* (1924–28), a tetralogy. He founded and edited the *English Review* (1908) and, in Paris, the *Transatlantic Review* (1924), in which he published the early works of *Pound, *Joyce, *Hemingway, and many other writers.

Ford, Gerald R(udolph) (1913–) US political leader; 38th president of the United States (1974–77). Born in Omaha, Nebr. and given the name Leslie King, Ford was later renamed for his stepfather. He was educated at the University of Michigan and at Yale Law School and began his political career with election to the US House of Representatives in 1948. Ford gradually distinguished himself as one of the most loyal Republicans in Congress, and in 1964 he was elected House minority leader. With the resignation of Vice Pres. Spiro *Agnew in 1973, Ford was appointed to succeed him by Pres. Richard *Nixon, according to the procedure established by the 25th Amendment to the *Constitution. Following Nixon's resignation as a result of the *Watergate Affair, Ford became the first US president to succeed to that office without having been elected. One of Ford's most controversial actions as president was his pardon of Nixon for any crimes he might have committed while in office. For the most part, Ford continued the foreign policy of the Nixon administration, aimed at achieving *détente with the Soviet Union. In 1976, Ford was defeated for re-election by Democratic candidate Jimmy *Carter.

GERALD R. FORD *President (1974–77) who worked to heal the nation in the aftermath of Watergate and Nixon's resignation.*

Ford, Henry (1863–1947) US industrialist. He left school at age 15 and worked as a machinist in Detroit for several years. In 1887 he became the chief engineer of the Detroit Edison Illuminating Co., working in his spare time on a new type of gasoline engine, which he perfected in 1892. The prototype proved so successful that Ford began to devote all of his time to automobile production, organizing the Ford Motor Co. in 1903. The most popular of Ford's vehicles, the "Model T" was first manufactured in 1908, and through the introduction of the assembly-line method of production in 1913, millions of Model T Fords were made available to the American public at economical prices. Although Ford was strongly opposed to the unionization of workers at his plants, he voluntarily instituted hour and wage standards. Later in life, he established the Ford Foundation to support his many philanthropic endeavors.

Ford, John (1586–c. 1640) English dramatist, the last major figure of Elizabethan and Jacobean drama. He collaborated with *Dekker and others at first, writing his own major plays between 1627 and 1638. Those most frequently performed are the revenge tragedies *The Broken Heart* (c. 1630) and *'Tis Pity She's a Whore* (c. 1632).

Ford, John (Sean O'Feeney; 1895–1975) US film director. He received much critical acclaim for *The Informer* (1935), *The Grapes of Wrath* (1940), and other films on social themes, but is best known as a director of popular westerns. These include *Stagecoach* (1939), *Rio Grande* (1950), and *How the West Was Won* (1962).

foreign aid Help given to poor countries by richer ones. Foreign aid can take several forms, including gratis payments, low interest loans, gifts in kind, etc. Foreign aid is usually given to the *developing countries to relieve natural disasters, to assist them in their efforts to industrialize, or for political reasons, such as to bolster up a friendly regime. One of the most ambitious programs of foreign aid was the *Marshall Plan in which the US provided funds to assist the recovery of Europe after World War II.

foreign exchange. *See* exchange rates.

Foreign Legion A French military force, the Légion étrangère, formed in 1831 to serve in France's African colonies. Its recruits are international but its officers are usually French. One of its regiments formed the *Organisation de l'Armée secrète (OAS) in Algeria (1961) and was subsequently disbanded. The Legion's headquarters are at Aubagne, near Marseilles, with units in Corsica and Djibouti.

forest An area of land covered largely with trees and undergrowth. Over 20% of world land area is forest, both natural and artificially planted, making forests a vital part of the global ecosystem as major suppliers of oxygen as well as timber. They also provide habitats for wildlife and are widely used for recreation.

The species of trees growing depends mainly on climate. Northern coniferous forests consist largely of pine, spruce, and firs and provide softwood for paper pulp, furniture, construction, etc. In more temperate regions forests consist primarily of mixed deciduous trees, especially oak, ash, elm, beech, sycamore, and other hardwoods, used mainly in furniture. In Mediterranean climates, the trees are adapted to hot dry summers and include the evergreen oaks. Broad-leaved evergreen trees are also found in New Zealand and South America, together with southern conifers. Tropical forests are characterized by a great diversity of species, usually of tall evergreen trees, with many climbing vines and epiphytes. The major tropical rain forests are in the Amazon and Orinoco river basins, with others in Africa and SE Asia. In neighboring regions of lower and more seasonal rainfall, an open savanna forest predominates, consisting of scattered deciduous trees.

Forestry, the cultivation and management of forests, is of major economic importance. Much research and development has been invested in improving varieties of trees for commercial use and in better methods of planting, pest control, thinning, felling, and extraction and of processing the timber into usable products.

Forester, C(ecil) S(cott) (1899–1966) British historical novelist, famous as the creator of Horatio Hornblower, a heroic but self-doubting British naval officer of Napoleonic times whose career he chronicled in a series of novels, beginning with *The Happy Return* (1937). Forester abandoned his medical studies for writing after the success of his first novel, *Payment Deferred* (1926).

forget-me-not An annual or perennial herb of the genus *Myosotis* (50 species), of temperate regions; 2–24 in (5–60 cm) tall, it has oblong hairy leaves and long spikes of small flowers, usually blue with white centers (young flowers are often pink). The fruits are small nutlets. Several species are grown as garden flowers. Family: *Boraginaceae*.

Forlì 44 13N 12 02E A city in Italy, in Emilia-Romagna. It has some ancient buildings, including a 15th-century citadel. Its various manufactures include furniture, textiles, felt, household appliances, and footwear. Population (1980 est): 110,755.

formaldehyde (*or* methanal; HCHO) A colorless toxic gaseous aldehyde. It dissolves in water to produce a solution known as formalin, which is used as a preservative. Formaldehyde is made by the catalytic oxidation of *methanol or petroleum gases and is used to make synthetic resins.

Forman, Miloš (1932–) Czech film director. His films, which include *The Fireman's Ball* (1967), are noted for their blend of humor and social criticism. In 1968 he went to the US, where he made *Taking Off* (1970) and *One Flew over the Cuckoo's Nest* (1976), for which he won an Academy Award.

formic acid (HCOOH) A colorless corrosive liquid *fatty acid with a pungent smell. It is made industrially by treating sodium formate (HCOONa) with sulfuric acid and is used in textile finishing and chemical manufacture. Formic acid occurs naturally in nettles and insects. Its name comes from the Latin *formica*, ant, whose sting is due to the secretion of formic acid.

Formigny, Battle of (Apr 15, 1450) The battle during the last period of the *Hundred Years' War in which the French forces routed the English army near Caen. The victory led directly to the fall of Caen, and then of Normandy, to the French.

Formosa. *See* Taiwan.

Forrest, Nathan Bedford (1821–77) US Confederate general. He joined the Confederate army as a private in 1861 and quickly rose in the ranks, becoming a general in 1862. With no formal military education, he organized his own cavalry and used them as a base in daring raids and battles at Fort Donelson (1862), Shiloh (1862), Rome, Ga. (1863), Chickamauga (1863), and Nashville (1864). Although he personally was exonerated, his career was marred when African American soldiers were massacred at Fort Pillow (1864). He was active in the Ku Klux Klan after the war.

Forrestal, James Vincent (1892–1949) US statesman; secretary of defense (1947–49). A banker, who had risen to president of a Wall Street firm by 1938, he was appointed under-secretary of the Navy in 1940 and became secretary in 1944. When the president's cabinet was reorganized to include a secretary of defense he served in that capacity. He was known for his strong stand against the Soviet Union.

Forster, E(dward) M(organ) (1879–1970) British novelist. Educated at King's College, Cambridge, where he returned as a fellow in 1946, his fiction and social criticism stress the importance of human affection and the need to cultivate both the intellect and the imagination. His novels include *Where Angels Fear to Tread* (1905), *The Longest Journey* (1907), *A Room with a View* (1908), *Howard's End* (1910), and *A Passage to India* (1924). *Maurice*, a novel portraying a homosexual relationship, was published posthumously in 1971.

Forsythia A genus of shrubs (about 7 species), sometimes called golden bell, native to E Europe and Asia and widely grown as garden ornamentals. The masses of four-petaled yellow flowers appear before the leaves, which are toothed and oval. The slender stems make the plants suitable for wall shrubs and hedges. The most common garden forsythia is the hybrid *F. intermedia*. Family: *Oleaceae* (olive family).

Fortaleza (*or* Ceará) 3 45S 38 35W A city and port in E Brazil, the capital of Ceará state on the Atlantic Ocean. Exports include cotton, rice, coffee, and sugar. Its university was established in 1955. Population (1991): 1,748,334.

Fortas, Abe (1910–82) US lawyer and associate justice of the Supreme Court (1965–69). After holding offices in several government departments, he opened his own law firm in Washington, DC. Appointed a Supreme Court justice by President *Johnson in 1965, he was nominated to fill the chief justice position in 1968. His failure to be approved by the Senate and accusations of bribery and conflict of interest led to his resignation from the court in 1969.

Fort-de-France (former name: Fort Royal) 14 36N 61 05W The capital and main port of Martinique since 1680, on the W coast. It was almost destroyed by an earthquake in 1839 and by fire in 1890. It is an important tourist resort and the site of a French naval base. Exports include sugar, cocoa, and rum. Population (1982 est): 100,000.

Forth, River A river in SE Scotland, rising on the NE slopes of Ben Lomond and flowing 65 mi (104 km) E through Stirling to Alloa. The river then expands into the **Firth of Forth** (an inlet of the North Sea) extending 51 mi (82 km) in length and 19 mi (31 km) wide at its mouth. It is spanned by the cantilever iron Forth Rail Bridge (designed in the 1880s by Benjamin Baker) and a road bridge (1964). **The Forth and Clyde Canal**, 37 mi (60 km) long, links the Rivers Forth and Clyde.

Fortin barometer A type of mercury *barometer, invented in 1810 by the French instrument maker Nicolas Fortin (1750–1831). The reservoir of mercury is contained in a leather bag attached to an evacuated glass tube marked with a fixed scale. The level of the mercury in the reservoir is set at zero by adjusting the leather bag.

Fort Knox 37 54N 85 59W A military base in N Kentucky. Established in 1917, it is the site of the US Depository, which contains US gold reserves.

Fort Lamy. *See* N'djamena.

Fort Lauderdale 26 08N 80 08W A city and resort in SE Florida, on the Atlantic Ocean. It is the site of one of the largest marinas in the world. Population (1990): 149,377.

Fort Myers 26 37N 81 54W A resort city in SW Florida, on the Caloosahatchee River. Known for its palm-tree-lined streets, it is a popular retirement center. Thomas Alva Edison's winter home (1885) is here. Population (1990): 45,266.

FORTRAN (*for*mula *tran*slation) A computer-programming language. It is a high-level language (*see* program) used for representing mathematical formulae in a form that can be processed by a computer. Widely used among scientists and engineers, it has also found applications in the business community.

Fort Stanwix, Treaties of (1768, 1784) Agreements between the British and the Iroquois Indians, in which the British gained present-day W Pennsylvania, West Virginia, New York, and Kentucky for gifts worth $10,000. The fort, located at the site of Rome, N.Y., was built for defense against the Indians and was renamed Fort Schuyler in 1776.

Fort Sumter. *See* Charleston.

Fort Ticonderoga A fort in NE New York, in the city of Ticonderoga, between lakes George and Champlain. The French built the fort in 1755 to protect the waterways between New York and Canada. It was captured by the British in 1759 (French and Indian War) and by the Americans under Ethan Allen in 1775 (American Revolution). In 1777 it was briefly recaptured by the British. Originally called Fort Carillon, it was renamed Fort Ticonderoga in 1775 by the Americans and restored as a museum in 1909.

Fortuna The Roman goddess of fortune and good luck. She was usually portrayed standing on a ball or wheel, indicating her mutability, and holding a cornucopia from which she distributes her favors. She is identical to her Greek counterpart, *Tyche.

Fort Wayne 41 05N 85 08W A city in NE Indiana, on the Maumee River. Founded by the French in 1680, the fort was built in 1794. An important communications center, its main manufactures are electrical equipment and motor vehicles. Population (1990): 173,072.

Fort William (Canada). *See* Thunder Bay.

Fort Worth 32 45N 97 20W A city in NE Texas near Dallas. The center of the N Texas industrial area, its manufactures include aircraft, refined oil, and food products. Population (1990): 447,619.

forty-niners. *See* Gold Rush.

forum A Roman marketplace, similar to the Greek *agora. The forum was the civic center of the town, containing all the main temples and public buildings. The most famous forum is in Rome; it was laid out in the 1st century BC, but later frequently modified.

fossa A catlike mammal, *Cryptoprocta ferox*, found only in Madagascar. It is about 60 in (150 cm) long including the tail (28 in [70 cm]) and has short legs and short orange-brown fur. It feeds almost entirely on lemurs. Family: **Viverridae*; order: *Carnivora*.

fossil The remains or traces of a plant or animal that lived in the past, usually preserved in sedimentary rock. It may be the whole or part of the organism itself that is preserved, usually chemically altered; alternatively it may have dissolved away leaving an impression (mold), which preserves its exact shape, or a cast, when it has been replaced exactly by mineral matter. Examples of fossils are whole mammoths preserved in ice, insects preserved in amber, and coal (the carbonized remains of extinct swamp plants). Trace fossils include excrement, burrows, or fossil tracks. A derived fossil is found in a more recent sediment than the one in which it was originally preserved, because of erosion and redeposition. A zone fossil is used in biostratigraphy to delimit a stratigraphic zone; such fossils must be widely distributed and have a limited vertical range in successive rock strata to be useful for this purpose. The study of fossils is called *paleontology.

fossil fuels The mineral fuels *coal, *oil, and *natural gas that occur in rock formations. They were formed by the deposition millions of years ago of the remains of vegetation (coal) and living organisms (oil and gas), which were buried under subsequent deposition and later subjected to heat and pressure.

Fossil fuels supply a large proportion of our current *energy needs, but the reserves are finite. Gas and oil in particular are rapidly being exhausted. *Alternative energy sources are therefore now being investigated and *nuclear energy is being developed to take their place.

FOSSIL *Some extinct animals and plants from past geological ages.*

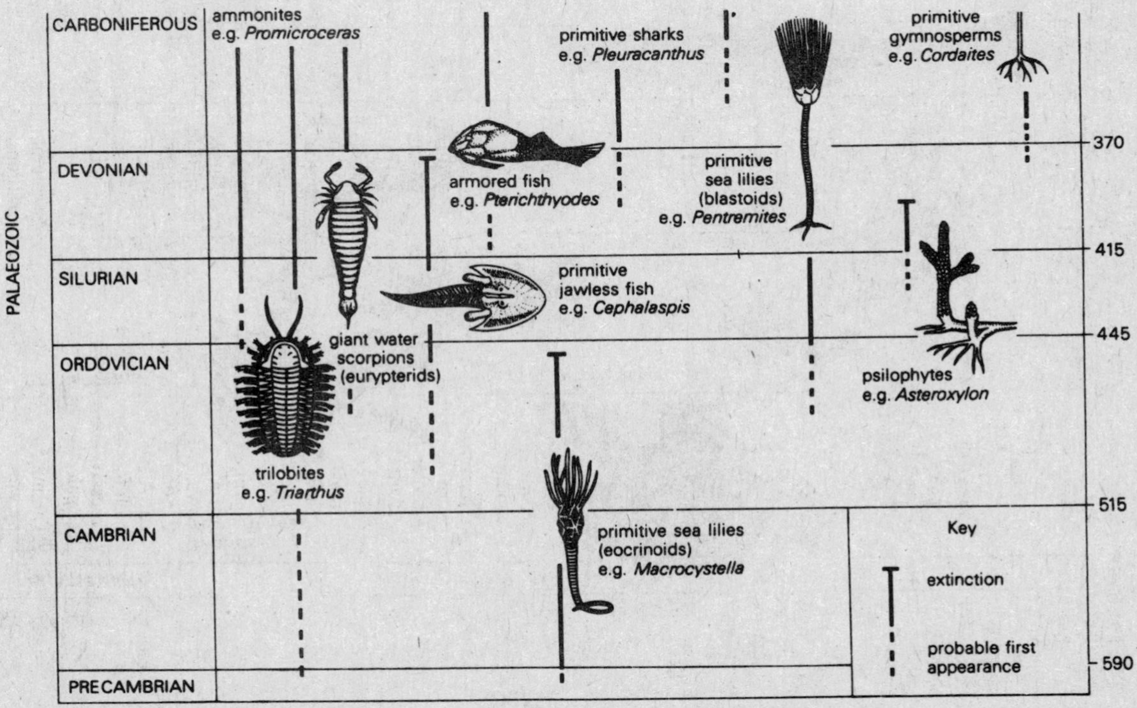

FOSSIL

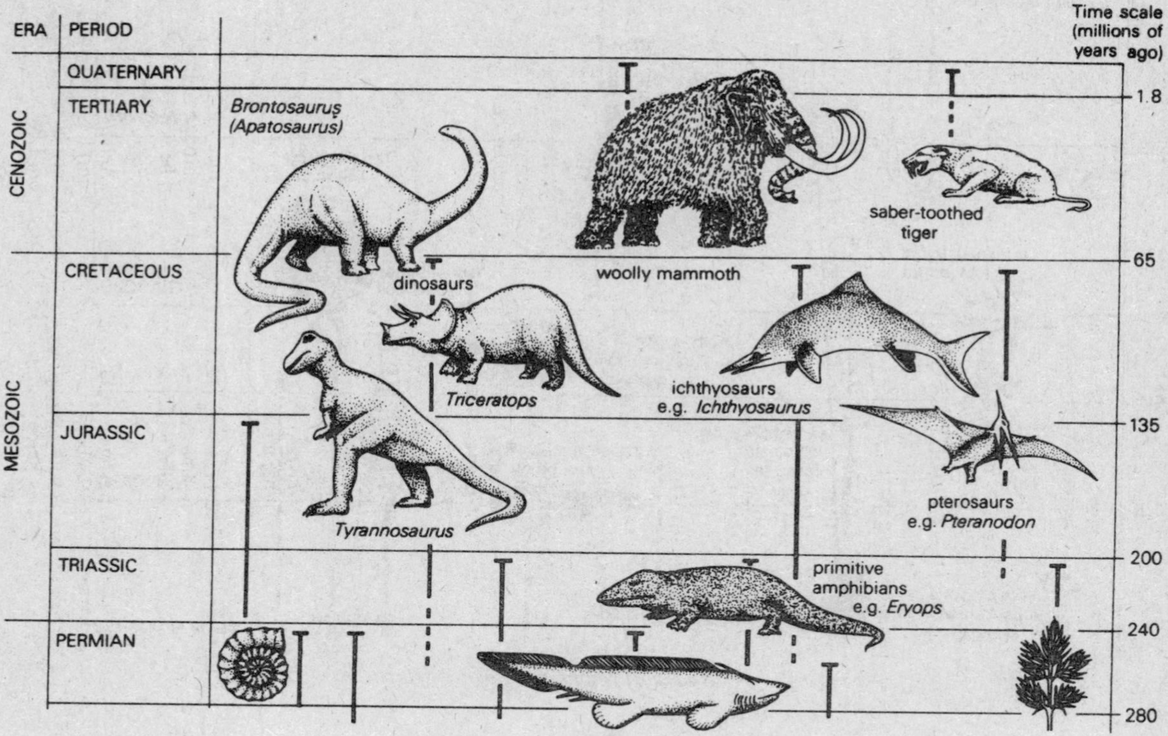
ERA
PERIOD
CENOZOIC
MESOZOIC
QUATERNARY
TERTIARY
CRETACEOUS
JURASSIC
TRIASSIC
PERMIAN
Time scale (millions of years ago)
1.8
65
135
200
240
280
Brontosaurus (Apatosaurus)
dinosaurs
Triceratops
Tyrannosaurus
woolly mammoth
saber-toothed tiger
ichthyosaurs e.g. Ichthyosaurus
pterosaurs e.g. Pteranodon
primitive amphibians e.g. Eryops

Foster, Stephen Collins (1826–64) US composer of such songs as "Swanee River" (1851) and "Beautiful Dreamer" (1864). Foster was self-taught and turned to African-American plantation songs for melodic inspiration. Although popular and successful during his lifetime, he died in poverty. Other works include "Oh! Susannah" (1848), "Camptown Races" (1850), "My Old Kentucky Home" (1853), "Jeanie With the Light Brown Hair" (1854), and "Old Black Joe" (1860).

Fotheringhay 52 32N 0 25W A village in England, in Northamptonshire on the River Nene. Fotheringhay Castle (of which little remains) was the scene of Richard III's birth (1452) and the execution of Mary, Queen of Scots (1587).

Foucault, Jean Bernard Léon (1819–68) French physicist, after whom the *Foucault pendulum (1851) is named. He also worked on light, measuring its speed and showing that its speed decreased in water (1850). He also invented the gyroscope (1852).

Foucault pendulum A very long pendulum with a heavy bob, capable of oscillating for a long period. It demonstrates the earth's rotation since, as it swings, its plane of oscillation slowly rotates. At the poles it would rotate through 360° in 24 hours; at a latitude λ, the number of hours for a complete rotation is given by $24/\sin \lambda$. It was invented by Jean *Foucault and first demonstrated in 1851 in Paris using a 62-lb (28-kg) lead ball suspended from a wire 220 ft (67 m) long.

Fouché, Joseph, Duc d'Otrante (1759–1820) French politician. A priest and teacher, he became politically active in the French Revolution, being elected a deputy in the National Convention in 1792. He participated in the overthrow of Robespierre (1794) and became minister of police under Napoleon but was forced into exile in 1816 after the restoration of the monarchy.

Fouqué, Friedrich Heinrich Karl, Baron de la Motte (1777–1843) German novelist and dramatist. Of French aristocratic descent, he was a prolific writer of chivalric romances and dramas, many of them adapted from Scandinavian sagas. His best-known work is the romance *Undine* (1811), the story of a watersprite who marries a human.

Fouquet, Jean (c. 1420–81) French painter and manuscript illuminator, born in Tours. After visiting Italy, he worked for Charles VII and later for Louis XI, whose tomb he helped design. For the royal treasurer, Étienne Chevalier, he painted *The Virgin and Child* (Antwerp) and *Chevalier with His Patron St Stephen* (Berlin), which were formerly joined as the *Mehun Diptych*. A manuscript of Josephus's *Jewish Antiquities* (Bibliothèque National, Paris) contains his finest illuminations, noteworthy for their depiction of French towns and countryside.

Fouquet, Nicolas (1615–80) French politician; finance minister (1653–61) under Louis XIV. He amassed a large fortune, partly through fraudulent dealings, which were revealed to the king by *Colbert, and he was arrested and imprisoned for life.

four-eyed fish A freshwater *bony fish of the family *Anablepidae* (2 species), found in Central and South America. Up to 12 in (30 cm) long, they have horizontally divided eyes with separate retinas for cruising just below the water surface, the upper halves being modified for aerial vision. Live young are born. Order: *Atheriniformes*.

Fourier, (François Marie) Charles (1772–1837) French socialist. Fourier advocated the organization of society on cooperative principles. He sought the abolition of all constrictions, including marriage, and set out his plan of an ideal society in *Le Nouveau Monde industriel* (1829–30).

Fourier, Jean Baptiste Joseph, Baron (1768–1830) French mathematician and physicist. After a career in the army, during which he served in Egypt under Napoleon, Fourier turned to science, his prime interest. While investigating heat, he discovered a method of expanding a periodic function in terms of sine and cosine waves, now known as **Fourier analysis** (*see* harmonic analysis). The discovery attracted widespread interest and Fourier was subsequently made a baron by Napoleon (1808).

Fourneyron, Benoît (1802–67) French engineer, who invented the modern water *turbine, producing the first large-scale model in 1832. It was quickly adopted by industry but was not used for generating hydroelectric power until 1895.

Four Noble Truths The fundamental doctrine of Buddhism, set forth by Gautama in the first discourse at Benares. The Truths are: existence is characterized by suffering; the cause of suffering is craving; to end craving is to end suffering; the way to achieve this is the *Eightfold Path.

four o'clock plant A bushy perennial herb, *Mirabilis jalapa*, also called marvel of Peru, native to tropical America but widely grown as an ornamental; 16–30 in (40–75 cm) high, it bears clusters of red, pink, white, yellow, or streaked flowers, which are tubular with a wide flared mouth and open in the late afternoon. Family: *Nyctaginaceae*.

Fourteen Points (1918) Terms for a peace settlement proposed by the US president Woodrow Wilson, in World War I. They called for recognition of national aspirations, free trade, and an international league of nations and inspired the subsequent Treaty of *Versailles.

Fouta Djallon (*or* Futa Jallon) A mountainous plateau area in NW Guinea. The Niger, Senegal, and Gambia Rivers rise in the range. The area is covered chiefly by savanna and cattle raising is the main activity.

fowl, domestic. *See* poultry, domestic.

Fowler, H(enry) W(atson) (1858–1933) British lexicographer and prescriptive stylist. With his brother **Francis Fowler** (1870–1918) he wrote *The King's English* (1906) and edited the *Concise Oxford Dictionary* (1911). His most famous work, *Modern English Usage* (1926), has been described as "a collection of prejudices erected into a system."

Fowles, John (1926–) British novelist, whose works treat philosophical, psychological, and social themes in a rich and often fantastic manner. His novels include *The Collector* (1963), *The Magus* (1966), and *The French Lieutenant's Woman* (1969), which have been filmed, *Daniel Martin* (1977), *Mantissa* (1982), and *A Maggot* (1985). Other books include the short stories in *The Ebony Tower* (1974).

Fox North American Algonquian-speaking Indian tribe; also known as Mesquakie, or "red earth people." They were found in Wisconsin, where they warred against the French and Sioux, and in the Great Lakes area during the early 18th century. Eventually allied with the Sauk, they were relegated to a Kansas reservation (1842). In 1859 they settled in Tama, Iowa, where the majority reside today.

fox A carnivorous mammal belonging to the *dog family (*Canidae*). Foxes have pointed ears, short legs with hairy pads on their feet, and large bushy tails. Generally nocturnal, they are solitary stealthy hunters, feeding on small mammals, birds, insects, and some fruit. The most familiar is the *red fox (*Vulpes vulpes*), found in forest and woodland and now venturing into suburban gardens. Some species are specialized for life in difficult habitats, such as the *Arctic fox and the *fennec. The unusual South African bat-eared fox (*Otocyon megalotis*) feeds mainly on termites and has teeth resembling those of an insect-eating mammal. Chief genera: *Vulpes* (9 species), *Dusicyon* (South American foxes; 8 species).

Fox, Charles James (1749–1806) British Whig politician; the first British foreign secretary (1782). He entered Parliament (1768) as a supporter of Lord *North but joined the *Rockingham Whigs in opposing North's American policy. Fox resigned and joined North in a coalition that briefly took office in 1783. Fox supported the French Revolution, over which issue many Whigs joined the Tories, and in 1798 he was dismissed from the privy council for opposing war with Revolutionary France. He was foreign secretary again briefly before his death in 1806.

Fox, George (1624–91) English religious leader, founder of the *Quakers. A Puritan by upbringing and originally a shoemaker's apprentice, Fox became dissatisfied with the formalism of established Christianity and the state's control of the church. In 1646 he had a personal revelation and thereafter preached a gospel of love, stressing the immediate guidance of the Holy Spirit. He was frequently imprisoned for his beliefs and he made several missionary journeys abroad, notably to North America in 1671. His best-known work is his *Journal* (1674).

Foxe, John (1516–87) English religious writer. He fled to the Continent during the reign of Mary I and on his return wrote a history of the English Protestant martyrs from the 14th century to his own time. Usually known as *The Book of Martyrs* (1563), it fed the growing Catholic persecution of the time, to which Foxe himself was outspokenly opposed.

foxglove A herbaceous plant of the genus *Digitalis*, especially *D. purpurea*, a biennial herb, 18–60 in (45–150 cm) tall, native to W Europe but naturalized elsewhere. Foxgloves have large gray-green oblong leaves and tall one-sided spikes of drooping bell-shaped flowers, up to 3 in (6.5 cm) long, purple, yellow, or white in color, often with purple spots in the center. The dried leaves contain *digitalis. Family: *Scrophulariaceae*.

foxhound A dog belonging to one of two breeds used for foxhunting. The English foxhound is strongly built with a deep chest and long neck. The American foxhound is descended from the English breed but is of lighter build. In both, the short coat is a combination of black, tan, and white. Height: 23–25 in (56–63 cm).

foxhunting A sport in which huntsmen on horseback pursue a fox with a pack of 20 to 30 *foxhounds, which hunt their quarry by scent. Fully organized in Britain since the 18th century, hunting achieved the status of a national pastime and has influenced many aspects of rural life. Foxhunting is also popular in the E US, and jackalhunting and draghunting (in which hounds follow a prepared trail) are found as substitutes in other parts of the world.

fox terrier A breed of □dog developed in England for hunting foxes and badgers. It is sturdy with a short tail, a broad tapering muzzle, and small ears that are folded forward over the face. There are two coat varieties—smooth-haired and wire-haired—and coloring is mainly white with black and tan markings. Height: 14–16 in (37–39 cm).

foxtrot A ballroom dance in 4/4 time with a syncopated rhythm in which couples combine slow walking steps with quick running steps. It was developed in the US about 1914 from the two-step, a dance in 2/4 time with even rhythms.

Foyle, Lough An inlet of the Atlantic Ocean, in N Ireland. Fed by the Foyle River, it lies between NE Co Donegal in the Republic of Ireland and NW Co Londonderry in Northern Ireland.

fracture The breaking of a bone. This usually occurs as a result of injury but it may happen very easily in bones diseased with cancer or *osteoporosis (pathological fracture). In a simple fracture the ends of the broken bone are not displaced; in a compound fracture the broken bone pierces the skin. A stress fracture is a crack arising in a bone exposed to repeated small injuries, for example in the feet of soldiers marching long distances. The bones of children are relatively soft and flexible; such bones are more likely to be bent than completely broken—this is called a greenstick fracture. Fractures are treated by aligning the ends of the broken bone and immobilizing them. Healing will result quickly. Sometimes, however, it is necessary to pin fractures surgically.

JEAN HONORÉ FRAGONARD The Swing *(1768–69) was commissioned by the Baron de Saint-Julien, who is seen in the bottom left of the painting eyeing his mistress on the swing. The baron had originally specified that the older man pushing the swing should be a Roman Catholic bishop.*

Fragonard, Jean Honoré (1732–1806) French *rococo painter, born in Grasse. He trained with *Chardin and *Boucher in Paris and studied in Italy (1756–61), concentrating on the work of *Tiepolo. He established his reputation with a history painting, *Coresus Sacrificing Himself to Save Callirhoë* (1765; Louvre), but soon turned to more lighthearted and delicately erotic subjects, e.g. *The Swing* (Wallace Collection, London) and *The Progress of Love* (Frick Collection, New York). His interest in Dutch painters, whose influence can be seen in a number of his landscapes and portraits, was strengthened by a visit to Holland in the 1770s. He suffered financial ruin during the Revolution. His subject matter and style of painting no longer found popular favor and he died in obscurity.

France, Anatole (Jacques Anatole François Thibault; 1844–1924) French novelist, son of a Parisian bookseller. His novels are noted for their erudition, skepticism, and elegance. His intervention in the *Dreyfus case (1897) marked the beginning of his commitment to socialism and, during his final years, communism. In such novels as *L'Île des pingouins* (1909) and *Les Dieux ont soif* (1913) his view of mankind is deeply pessimistic. He was awarded the Nobel Prize in 1921.

France, Republic of A country in W Europe, bordering on the English Channel in the N, the Atlantic Ocean in the W, and the Mediterranean Sea in the S. It includes the island of Corsica and several overseas regions (Martinique, Guadeloupe, and French Guiana). Overseas territories include French Polynesia, New Caledonia, and St Pierre and Miquelon. Fertile lowlands cover most of the N and W of France, rising to the Pyrenees in the S, the Massif Central in the SE, and the Vosges, Jura, and Alps in the E. The principal rivers are the Seine, the Loire, and the Rhône. *Economy*: compared with other industrial countries in W Europe, agriculture remains important although the number of people employed in this sector has decreased owing to the reorganization of many of the numerous small peasant holdings into larger units. Animal products and the production of cereals are important; the wine industry is a major source of revenue. There have been large-scale developments in the industrial sector since World War II, especially in iron and steel, motor vehicles, aircraft, mechanical and electrical engineering, textiles, chemicals, and food processing. Its mineral wealth includes iron ore, potash, bauxite, coal, and sulfur. Natural gas is being developed in the foothills of the Pyrenees, but a considerable proportion of power still comes from hydroelectric sources. Exports have risen dramatically in the postwar period, especially textiles, iron and steel, motor vehicles, machinery, and arms. Economic growth has slowed down in recent years, however, and the economic strategies of recent prime ministers have failed to deal with the increasing problems of inflation, trade deficits, and unemployment. *History*: present-day France approximates the ancient region of *Gaul, which was conquered by Julius Caesar in the 1st century BC. It became part of the Roman Empire and in the 1st century AD Christianity was introduced to the provinces into which Gaul was divided. From the 3rd to the 5th centuries, it was overrun by German tribes, including the Goths, Vandals, and *Franks (from whom the name France is derived). The Frankish kingdom reached its peak under Charlemagne (reigned 768–814) and his *Carolingian dynasty continued to rule in France until 987, when Hugh Capet became the first *Capetian king. During the 10th century Norsemen (Vikings) established themselves in what became Normandy and in 1066 invaded England. The claims of English kings to French territory were realized on a large scale by the *Angevins and consequent conflict between France and England culminated in the *Hundred Years' War (1337–1453), as a result of which the English were expelled from all of France, except Calais. The Capetians were succeeded by the *Valois dynasty (1328–1589), a period that saw the beginning of France's long rivalry with Spain for hegemony in Europe. During the *Wars of Religion the last Valois king, Henry III, was succeeded (1589) by the first *Bourbon, Henry IV. The first half of the 17th century was dominated by Cardinal de *Richelieu and his successor as chief minister, Cardinal *Mazarin. They were responsible for France replacing Spain, after the Thirty Years' War, as the supreme European power (1659). During the reign (1643–1715) of *Louis XIV France reached the zenith of its power and brilliance. Decline, however, began before his death and gathered speed in the following decades. The disastrous *Seven Years' War forced France to recognize British supremacy in North America and India and the political reaction and economic incompetence of the later Bourbon kings precipitated the *French Revolution in 1789. The First Republic was proclaimed (1792) and Louis XVI was guillotined (1793) in spite of the military opposition of the major European powers (*see* Revolutionary and Napoleonic Wars). In 1799 *Napoleon Bonaparte overthrew the Directory, becoming first consul and, in 1804, emperor. By 1808 he had brought most of continental Europe under his sway but in 1815 he was finally defeated at Waterloo and exiled. The Bourbons were restored until 1830, when the July Revolution raised Louis Philippe to the throne. Overthrown in the *Revolution of 1848, the monarchy was replaced by the Second Republic of which Louis Napoleon became president; in 1852 he proclaimed himself emperor as *Napoleon III. During the Second Empire France underwent the beginnings of industrialization but its prosperity was not sufficient to achieve victory in the *Franco-Prussian War, in which Napoleon's ignominious leadership led to his overthrow (1870). The subsequent Third Republic lasted until 1940, in spite of scandal (e.g. the *Dreyfus and *Stavisky affairs), *World War I, and political dissension (there were 44 successive governments between 1918 and 1940). After the outbreak of World War II France fell to Germany and a pro-German government was established at Vichy, while *de Gaulle led the Free French resistance in London. In 1944 France was liberated by the Allies and de Gaulle established a provisional government that gave way (1946) to the Fourth Republic. The immediate postwar period was overshadowed by war in Indochina and by the crisis in Algeria that precipitated the fall of the Fourth Republic (1958). De Gaulle was recalled from retirement and, as president of the Fifth Republic, instituted a period of firm government. In May 1968, however, the Republic was shaken by serious revolts among students and a wave of strikes and in 1969 he resigned. Gaullist principles nevertheless continued to influence government under his successors Pompidou and Giscard d'Estaing. Mitterrand's election (1981) made him the first socialist to hold the office of president in 35 years but his power was diminished after rightist Jacques Chirac became premier in 1986. After Mitterrand was reelected in 1988, prime ministers were generally more conservative than the socialist president but cooperated with him. France actively sought a peaceful settlement to the Iraq-Kuwait conflict in 1990; when all efforts failed, Mitterrand sent troops as part of the UN allied forces during the Persian Gulf War in 1991. In 1992, France barely approved the Maastricht Treaty for a closer European union, which went into effect in 1993. Official language: French. Official currency: franc of 100 centimes. Area: 209,912 sq mi (543,814 sq km). Population (1992 est): 56,900,000. Capital: Paris. Main port: Marseilles.

Franche-Comté A planning region and former province in E France, bordering on Switzerland. Part of Burgundy until 843 AD, it was overrun successively by many powers before being finally annexed to France in 1678. The main occupations are farming, especially dairy farming and cattle rearing, and forestry. Area: 6014 sq mi (15,579 sq km). Population (1981 est): 1,090,800.

Francis I (1494–1547) King of France (1515–47). His reign was dominated by rivalry with the Holy Roman Emperor *Charles V. In the course of the conflict, which continued intermittently until 1544, Francis was taken prisoner at *Pavia (1525). At home, he won control over the French church through the Concordat of Bologna (1516), suppressed French Protestantism, and ordered an attack on the *Waldenses in S France (1545).

Francis I (1708–65) Duke of Lorraine (1729–37), Grand duke of Tuscany (1737–65), and Holy Roman Emperor (1745–65). He married (1736) *Maria

Theresa, who succeeded to the Austrian dominions in 1740 in the face of much opposition. He was elected emperor during the consequent War of the *Austrian Succession (1740–48).

Francis I (Emperor of Austria). *See* Francis II (Holy Roman Emperor).

Francis II (1544–60) King of France (1559–60); the son of *Henry II and *Catherine de' Medici and husband (1558–60) of *Mary, Queen of Scots. He was dominated by the *Guise family, which used him in its struggle against the Protestant *Condé in the early phase of the *Wars of Religion.

Francis II (1768–1835) The last Holy Roman Emperor (1792–1806) and, as Francis I, the first Emperor of Austria (1804–35). Following three defeats by the French in the Napoleonic Wars, he allied with *Napoleon until 1813. After the Congress of *Vienna (1815), he was guided by his conservative chief minister *Metternich.

Francis Ferdinand (1863–1914) Archduke of Austria and heir apparent to his uncle, Emperor *Franz Josef. His assassination (June 28, 1914) by a Serbian nationalist at Sarajevo precipitated *World War I.

Francis of Assisi, St (Giovanni di Bernardone; c. 1182–1226) Italian friar and founder of the *Franciscans, born in Assisi. The son of a merchant, he renounced his worldly life in 1205 to live in poverty and devote himself to prayer and charitable works. By 1209 he had a band of followers with whom he went to Rome (1210), where he obtained papal approval of his new order. He traveled throughout Spain, the Holy Land, and Egypt, later retiring to Assisi and giving up the leadership of his order. A profoundly humble man, in paintings he is often portrayed in the countryside among animals and birds, which he called his sisters and brothers. His love of nature is also reflected in his famous hymn, *Canticle of the Sun*. He received the *stigmata in 1224, was canonized in 1228. Feast day: Oct 4.

Francis of Sales, St (1567–1622) French Roman Catholic prelate and devotional writer, born in Savoy. He played a leading part in the Counter-Reformation by reconverting the people of Chablais from Calvinism to Roman Catholicism. As Bishop of Geneva from 1602 he cofounded the Order of the Visitation, an order of nuns. Feast day: Jan 29.

Francis Xavier, St (1506–52) Spanish *Jesuit missionary, known as the Apostle of the Indies. While studying in Paris (1523–34) he met St *Ignatius of Loyola and helped him found the Jesuit order. From 1541 he worked in the Indies, India, and Japan, establishing missions and making many converts. Feast day: Dec 3.

Franciscans An order of friars founded in 1209 by St *Francis of Assisi. His rule was devised to impose both personal and corporate poverty on the order's members. The rule was revised in 1221 and again in 1223, when it was confirmed by the pope. Within Francis's lifetime the expanding order found complete poverty practically difficult, and a schism ensued in the early 14th century regarding how strictly the rule should be followed. Despite a resulting decline, the order survived and has remained an important missionary and charitable branch of the Roman Catholic Church.

francium (Fr) The heaviest alkali metal, a very unstable radioactive element discovered in 1939 by Perey. The longest-lived isotope ^{223}Fr has a half-life of 22 minutes; traces of the element exist in nature, as decay products of ^{227}Ac. At no 87; at wt 223.

Franck, César Auguste (1822–90) Belgian composer, organist, and teacher, who settled in Paris in 1834. He became organist of Ste Clotilde in 1858, a post he held until his death. His pupils included D'Indy and Chausson. Franck was influenced by Bach and evolved a highly chromatic form of harmony. He also developed "cyclic form," the use of the same theme in more than one movement of a work. His compositions include *Symphonic Variations* (for piano and orchestra; 1885), a symphony (1886–88), a violin sonata (1886), and a string quartet (1889).

Franck, James (1882–1964) US physicist, born in Germany, whose experiments in collaboration with Gustav Hertz on the excitation of gases when bombarded with electrons won them the Nobel Prize in 1925. Their experiments provided evidence that the energy levels inside atoms were quantized. He also made valuable contributions to photochemistry. During World War II Franck worked on the development of the atom bomb but opposed its use on populated areas.

Franco, Francisco (1892–1975) Spanish general and statesman; dictator from 1939 until his death. He entered the Infantry Academy in 1907, aged 14, was posted to Spanish Morocco in 1912, and became the youngest captain in the Spanish army in 1915. By 1935 he was chief of the General Staff and in the following year, on July 18, staged a military uprising against the Republican Government of *Azaña that precipitated the *Spanish Civil War. In October 1936, he became head of state in the Nationalist Zone and commander in chief of the rebel forces. By 1939, with help from Hitler and Mussolini, he had defeated the Republican forces and become the absolute leader of all Spain. Franco's fascist government, in which the National Movement (*see* Falange Española) was the only political party, remained sympathetic to Hitler but maintained an officially neutral position throughout World War II. Spain was excluded from the newly formed UN in 1945 but its international isolation was broken during the Cold War, when Franco's anticommunism made him a more attractive ally. In 1953 he signed a military-assistance agreement with the US. Although his government achieved considerable economic advance for Spain, especially in the 1960s, he operated a ruthless dictatorship that tolerated no opposition. However, during his last years he permitted a perceptible liberalization, which foreshadowed the country's move to democracy under his named successor, King *Juan Carlos.

francolin A *partridge belonging to a genus (*Francolinus*; 41 species) occurring in Africa and Asia; 27–46 cm long, francolins are usually a dull brownish color with black, white, or chestnut markings and are popular gamebirds.

Franconia A duchy of early medieval Germany, now in Rhineland-Palatinate, Baden-Württemberg, Hessen, and Bavaria. Its duke, Conrad, was the first elected king of Germany (911–18) but the duchy was subsequently comparatively unimportant and by the 13th century had been fragmented into small principalities.

Franco-Prussian War (1870–71) A war between France and Prussia. Fearing Bismarck's proposals to make a relative of William I of Prussia the king of Spain (*see* Ems telegram), France declared war. Within two months Napoleon III and his army were defeated at the battle of *Sedan but French resistance continued. Napoleon was deposed and the Third Republic was established but the Prussians besieged Paris, which eventually capitulated. The Treaty of Frankfurt imposed a huge indemnity on France, which ceded Alsace and Lorraine to the newly established German Empire; France was left economically weakened and politically divided.

frangipani A tropical American tree, *Plumeria rubra*, cultivated throughout the tropics and known in Asia as pagoda tree or temple flower. Up to 20 ft (6 m) tall, it has tapering long-stalked leaves with parallel veins and round clusters, up to 10 in (25 cm) across, of pink, reddish-purple, white, or yellow flowers, which are very fragrant and used to make perfume. Family: *Apocynaceae*.

Frank, Anne (1929–45) German–Dutch Jewish girl, who died in a German concentration camp. Her diary became a symbol of Jewish resistance and courage following its publication in 1947. She wrote it while hiding from the Nazis in Amsterdam in 1942–43.

Frankfort 38 11N 84 53W The capital city of Kentucky on the Kentucky River. Its major industry is whiskey distilling. Population (1990): 25,968.

Frankfurt am Main 50 06N 8 41E A city in central Germany, in Hessen, on the Main River. A major banking and commercial center, it is famed for its trade fairs, especially the annual book fair. Its gothic cathedral is 13th century and the university was established in 1914. It is the birthplace of Goethe and the original home of the Rothschilds. Its industries include the manufacture of chemicals, pharmaceuticals, and machinery. *History*: it was the seat of the imperial elections (9th to 18th centuries) and coronations (1562–1792) of the Holy Roman emperors. The first German national assembly met here (1848–49). Population (1988): 592,000.

Frankfurt an der Oder 52 20N 14 32E A city in eastern Germany, on the Oder River. Severely damaged in World War II, the part of the city on the E bank of the river was incorporated into Poland in 1945. A trading center since medieval times, its manufactures include machinery and furniture. Population (1990): 87,000.

Frankfurter, Felix (1882–1965) US jurist. Born in Vienna and educated in the US, Frankfurter served as assistant US attorney and as counsel to the War Department before accepting an appointment as professor at Harvard Law School in 1914. After World War I, he was a legal adviser to Pres. Woodrow *Wilson at the *Paris Peace Conference, and in 1920 he helped to found the American Civil Liberties Union. As a strong political supporter of the *New Deal programs, Frankfurter was often consulted on legal matters by Pres. Franklin *Roosevelt. In 1939, Roosevelt nominated him to be an associate justice of the US Supreme Court. Considered a liberal when appointed, he was soon labeled a conservative for his continued belief that judges should practice restraint rather than follow an activist policy. He sat on the court until poor health forced his retirement in 1962.

frankincense (*or* olibanum) An aromatic gum resin obtained chiefly from trees of the genus *Boswellia*, especially *B. carteri*, which grows in the Middle East. It is usually supplied commercially in yellowish blocks covered with white dust, smells of balsam when heated, and burns brightly giving off a fragrant odor. Frankincense has been known since ancient Egyptian times and is still used as an *incense, in fumigants, and in perfumes.

Franklin The northernmost district of Canada, in the *Northwest Territories, consisting of Canada's Arctic archipelago and some northerly peninsulas. Covered by tundra and ice cap, it has large oil reserves. The inhabitants are mostly Eskimo hunters and fishermen. Area: 549,253 sq mi (1,422,565 sq km). Population (1976): 7180.

Franklin, Benjamin (1706–90) US diplomat, scientist, and author. He established a printing business in Philadelphia and became well known for his *Poor Richard's Almanac* (1732–57), which contained many maxims on the virtues of thrift and hard work. His experiments with static electricity, especially the famous episode in which he flew a kite during a thunderstorm (and was lucky not to be killed), established the electrical nature of thunderstorms and led him to invent the lightning conductor. His political prominence began in 1737, when he became deputy postmaster of Philadelphia, where he promoted street lighting and the establishment of a city police force. In the disputes that led to the American Revolution he represented Pennsylvania's case to Britain (1757–62, 1766–75) and as a member of the *Continental Congress helped frame the Declaration of Independence (1775). Famous as a diplomat in Paris (1776–85), he enlisted French help for the colonies and later negotiated peace with Britain (1783). Franklin is also well known as the founder of a club that became (1743) the American Philosophical Society. His *Autobiography* was first published in complete form in 1868.

BENJAMIN FRANKLIN *Statesman, diplomat, and inventor, a leading force in colonial America and the American Revolution.*

Franklin, Sir John (1786–1847) British explorer. After service in the Royal Navy, during which he fought at Trafalgar (1805), he was subsequently governor (1836–43) of Van Dieman's Land (now Tasmania). In 1845 he sailed with two ships, never to return, to look for the *Northwest Passage. Successive search expeditions failed to find the men until 1859, when their skeletons and records were found on King William Island. Franklin had virtually discovered the passage but had become ice-bound and he and his companions died of scurvy or starvation.

Franks A Germanic people, who invaded Roman *Gaul from the Rhineland between the 3rd and 5th centuries AD. One of the Frankish tribes, the Salian Franks, gained control of most of Gaul under their ruler *Clovis (d. 511) and were converted to Christianity. The Frankish state was ruled by the *Merovingian dynasty (named for Clovis's grandfather, Merovech) until its replacement by the *Carolingians (named for *Charlemagne) in 751. The Carolingian empire lasted until its division in 843. The western Frankish kingdom was the nucleus of modern France.

Franz Josef (1830–1916) Emperor of Austria (1848–1916) and king of Hungary (1867–1916). His long reign saw the rise of national tensions in the Empire, which led to the establishment of the Dual Monarchy of *Austria-Hungary, under which Austria and Hungary coexisted as equal partners under the Austrian crown. He was defeated by the Prussians in the Austro-Prussian War of 1866 but in 1879 he allied with the recently formed German Empire and in 1882 with Italy, forming the *Triple Alliance. His ultimatum to Serbia, following the assassination by a Serbian nationalist of his nephew, Archduke *Francis Ferdinand (1914), led to *World War I.

Franz Josef Land (Russian name: Zemlya Frantsa Iosifa) An archipelago of about 85 islands in Russia, in the N Barents Sea, the largest being Aleksandra Land, George Land, Graham Bell Island, Salisbury Island, and Wilczek Land. They were discovered in 1873 by Austrians and annexed by the Soviet Union in 1926. They are 90% icebound and have no permanent population. Total area: about 79,905 sq mi (20,700 sq km).

Fraser, (John) Malcolm (1930–) Australian statesman; Liberal prime minister (1975–83). He served in several cabinet posts (1966–72) before becoming Liberal Party Leader. Appointed caretaker prime minister on the dismissal of *Whitlam, he remained in office until the Liberals were defeated in the 1983 elections, when he also resigned as leader of the Liberal Party.

MALCOLM FRASER

Fraser, Peter (1884–1950) New Zealand statesman; Labour prime minister (1940–49). Born in Britain, he helped form the Democratic Party (1913; the Labour Party from 1916) and entered Parliament in 1918. He influenced Allied strategy in the Pacific during World War II and helped to establish the UN (1945).

Fraser, Simon (1776–1862) Canadian explorer and fur trader, born in the US. He started working for the Northwest Company in 1792 and by 1801 had become a partner. He was responsible for the establishment of new trading posts W to the Pacific Ocean and explored the river later named for him. During his leadership (1811–18) of the Red River department of the Northwest Company he was accused of attacking and massacring the competition's settlers in that area. Although acquitted, he retired in 1818.

Fraser River A river in W Canada, the chief river of British Columbia. Rising near Mount *Robson, it flows rapidly through mountain gorges until it reaches flat farmland in the SW, where it empties into the Strait of Georgia near Vancouver. Length: 850 mi (1370 km).

fraud In law, making a false representation, by words or conduct or by withholding facts where there is a duty to disclose them, in order to obtain a material advantage. To prove fraud it is necessary to show that a false representation was made (1) knowingly, (2) without belief in its truth, or (3) recklessly, without concern whether it was true or not. To obtain damages it must be shown that the defendant intended the injured party to act on the fraudulent representation and that he did so to his detriment. A contract based on fraud may be declared void at the option of the injured party.

Fraunhofer, Joseph von (1787–1826) German physicist, who greatly improved the quality of lenses and prisms and made improvements to the design of optical instruments. His superior equipment enabled him to detect numerous dark lines in the sun's spectrum (1814), now known as **Fraunhofer lines**. The eight most prominent lines are still known by the letters he gave them.

Frazer, Sir James George (1854–1941) British anthropologist, mythologist, and writer. Frazer's major work *The Golden Bough* (first edition 1890) was a description of "the long evolution by which the thoughts and efforts of man have passed through the successive stages of magic, religion, and science." Although his interpretation of his observations was sometimes unsound, the results of his work were far reaching, influencing people outside the anthropological field, including T. S. Eliot.

Frazier, Joe (1944–) US boxer, who was Olympic heavyweight champion (1964), world heavyweight champion (1971–73), and the first man to defeat Muhammad *Ali professionally. He was defeated by George Foreman.

Frederick (I) Barbarossa (c. 1123–90) Holy Roman Emperor (1152–90; crowned 1155), who was engaged in a long struggle with the papacy. He made six expeditions to Italy and was ultimately unsuccessful against the Lombard cities, which regained their independence in 1183. Papal opposition to his ambitions was exacerbated when he set up an antipope to *Alexander III, who excommunicated Frederick in 1160. He finally made peace with the pope in 1177. He failed to subdue his powerful cousin, *Henry the Lion, but he established his authority in Poland, Hungary, Bohemia, and Burgundy. In 1189, he set out on the third *Crusade during which he died.

Frederick I (1657–1713) The first king of Prussia (1701–1713) and, as Frederick III, Elector of Brandenburg (1688–1701). Austria conceded his royal status in return for military aid in the War of the *Spanish Succession (1701–14). He encouraged Prussian industry and agriculture and also fostered the arts and learning; he was a patron of *Leibniz.

Frederick I (King of Sicily). *See* Frederick II (Holy Roman Emperor).

Frederick II (1194–1250) Holy Roman Emperor (1220–50), the last emperor of the *Hohenstaufen dynasty and, as Frederick I, king of Sicily (1198–1250). As leader of the fifth Crusade (1228–29) he captured Jerusalem but remained an opponent of papal policy and was excommunicated three times (1227, 1239,

1245). A man of wide learning, he was a noted patron of the arts and sciences but neglected the government of his possessions, which consequently declined.

Frederick (II) the Great (1712–86) King of Prussia (1740–86), who made Prussia a major European power. He succeeded to the throne after an extraordinarily severe childhood at the hands of his father *Frederick William I. An exponent of enlightened despotism (*see* Enlightenment), he liberalized the Prussian legal code and introduced economic and social reforms that reinvigorated Prussian society and institutions. His conquest of Silesia (1740) gave rise to the War of the *Austrian Succession (1740–48), after which his possession of the region was confirmed. His victory in the *Seven Years' War (1756–63) confirmed the military supremacy of Prussia, both in Germany and in Europe. At his palace of Sans Souci, near Potsdam, a distinguished circle of artists and writers, including *Voltaire, gathered around Frederick, who was himself a writer and composer.

Frederick III (1415–93) The last Holy Roman Emperor to be crowned by the pope in Rome (1452) and, as Frederick IV, German king (1440–93). As archduke of Austria from 1424, Frederick unified the major Hapsburg domains, but failed to win the Bohemian and Hungarian crowns and to resist the Turks. In 1485 *Matthias Corvinus of Hungary conquered Austria, which was recovered in 1490 by Frederick's son *Maximilian I.

Frederick (III) the Wise (1463–1525) Elector of Saxony (1486–1525), whose possession of silver mines made him Germany's richest ruler. A devout Catholic, he nevertheless protected *Luther at the castle of Wartburg after the papal ban of 1521.

Frederick III (Elector of Bradenburg). *See* Frederick I (king of Prussia).

Frederick (V) the Winter King (1596–1632) Elector of the Palatinate (1610–23). Frederick, who was the son-in-law of James I of England, accepted the Bohemian crown in 1619 and led the Protestant revolt against Emperor Ferdinand II (*see* Thirty Years' War). He was defeated at the battle of White Mountain (1620) and died a throneless exile.

Frederick IX (1899–1972) King of Denmark (1947–72), who as regent (1942–47) had encouraged Danish resistance to the Germans in *World War II.

Frederick Henry (1584–1647) Prince of Orange and Count of Nassau. The younger son of *William the Silent, he became stadtholder and captain general of the United Provinces in 1625. He successfully waged war against Spanish rule but his autocratic outlook was unpopular. His attempts to make peace were fulfilled at *Westphalia (1648), shortly after his death.

Fredericksburg 38 18N 77 29W A city in E Virginia, SW of Alexandria. Here, the Confederates defeated the Union Army in the Battle of *Fredericksburg in 1862. Mary Washington College (1908) is here, as are many historic buildings. Population (1990): 19,027.

Fredericksburg, Battle of (1862) US Civil War battle, a Confederate victory. Union Gen. Ambrose Burnside planned to cross the Rappahannock River in the hope of taking Richmond in the wake of Lee's retreating army. Because of Burnside's hesitancy and delays in constructing pontoon bridges across the river, Lee's troops had a chance to regroup and, behind stone walls, constantly repelled Burnside's attacks—14 times in all—leaving behind more than two Union casualties for every Confederate casualty.

Frederick William (1620–88) Elector of Brandenburg (1640–88), known as the Great Elector. He inherited Germany's weakest electorate. By furthering dynastic claims in Prussia, Pomerania, and the lower Rhineland, he created for his

Hohenzollern family the strongest territorial state in N Germany. His fiscal and administrative reforms established the base upon which the great power of *Prussia was created in the 18th century.

Frederick William I (1688–1740) The second King of Prussia (1713–40), who made his country strong and prosperous. He strengthened the army, passed financial reforms, resettled the east, freed the serfs on his own domain (1719), and instituted compulsory primary education (1717); he also centralized administration and in 1720 acquired most of Swedish Pomerania.

Frederick William II (1744–97) King of Prussia (1786–97), who pursued a policy of territorial aggrandizement. He profited from the second and third partitions of Poland in 1793 and 1795 and from 1792 until 1795 he joined Austria against Revolutionary France. At home his Religious Edict (1788) granted religious toleration, but was limited in effect, and the law code of 1794 included some liberal statutes.

Frederick William III (1770–1840) King of Prussia (1797–1840). His neutral attitude toward Napoleon damaged the prestige of Prussia, which was subjected to France by the Treaty of *Tilsit (1807) following defeat at *Jena and Auerstädt. After Prussia's liberation (1813), Frederick William introduced some reforms but became more repressive in the face of liberal attacks.

Frederick William IV (1795–1861) King of Prussia (1840–61) in a period of social unrest and nationalism. His conservatism triggered off the *Revolution of 1848, which forced him to grant a constitution (1850). This failed to prevent a resumption of reactionary government, which, owing to Frederick William's insanity, was in the hands of his brother, later *William I, from 1858.

Fredericton 45 57N 66 40W A city in E Canada, the capital of New Brunswick. Its industries include the manufacture of wood and plastic products. Tourism, military administration, and distribution are important. The University of New Brunswick was established here in 1785. Population (1986 est): 44,000.

Freedman's Bureau (1865–74) US government agency established to ensure the welfare of newly freed slaves. Officially the US Bureau of Refugees, Freedmen, and Abandoned Lands, it provided medical aid, food, some jobs, and schools for the former slaves. Its land program for the restoration and redistribution of war-damaged lands in the South failed, as did its programs concerning civil rights.

Freedom of Information Act (1967) US legislation that provided for more public access to government records. It limits the release of information to the public only when that information involves national defense, confidential financial information, or law enforcement and when its release would be harmful to the national interest.

free enterprise. *See* capitalism.

free-form jazz A style of US *jazz developed by Ornett Coleman (1930–), John Coltrane (1926–), and others in the 1960s. Free-form jazz is based on a single theme that is subject to any form of melodic, harmonic, or rhythmic improvisation; it espouses highly complex musical relationships that often result in *atonality.

Free French French forces organized in London by General *de Gaulle in defiance of Marshal Pétain's surrender to Germany in World War II.

freemasonry A secret society for men, which declares itself to be based on brotherly love, faith, and charity. Its origins are uncertain but it probably developed from the medieval stonemasons' guilds. In its modern form freemasonry dates from the establishment (1717) in England of the Grand Lodge, to which over 8000 private lodges are now affiliated. During the 18th century, masonry spread to America and the colonies as well as to continental Europe. Its ceremonies, which are allegorical and illustrated by symbols (many of which are the tools of a working mason), demand a vow of secrecy as well as a belief in God (the great architect of the universe) and are based on Old Testament anecdotes and moralities.

Opposition to masonry originated with a papal bull (1738) excommunicating masons; Roman Catholics have never since accepted its principles or its secrecy. In France and some other European countries it assumed a political character and was condemned by governments. Mussolini and Hitler both outlawed masonry and it is banned in E Europe.

free port A port (such as Hong Kong or Singapore) forming a free-trade area, where goods may be landed, handled, processed, and reexported without incurring *customs duties. Such duties become payable when the goods are moved into adjacent territory. The Hanseatic towns were early examples of free ports.

Freesia A genus of ornamental South African plants (20 species), cultivated commercially, especially as a source of cut flowers. Growing from corms to a height of 30 in (75 cm), they have sword-shaped leaves and funnel-shaped lemon-scented flowers, white, orange, yellow, blue, purple, or pink in color, growing in one-sided clusters. Most cultivated varieties are hybrids derived from *F. refracta* (with yellowish flowers) and *F. armstrongii* (rose-purple flowers). Family: *Iridaceae.*

Free Silver A popular campaign of the late 1800s that unlimited silver be coined in the US. Because the coining of silver had been discontinued in 1873 and because the gold supply was dominated by Eastern businessmen, groups made up of less influential persons outside the East and particularly in the West campaigned for a return to bimetalism. Free silver became a symbol of regeneration of the economy and was an issue of the presidential campaign of 1896 between William McKinley and William Jennings Bryan.

Free Soil Party (1848–54) US political party that advocated barring slavery in territory newly acquired by the Mexican War. Antislavery factions joined together in 1848, after the *Wilmot Proviso had failed to pass in Congress, and chose former Pres. Martin Van Buren as their presidential candidate. Although he failed to win the election his party did manage to elect enough candidates to upset the balance in Congress. By 1854 the party had been absorbed into the Republican Party, which made the Free-Soil antislavery idea part of its platform.

freestyle wrestling. *See* wrestling.

Freetown 8 20N 13 05W The capital and main port of Sierra Leone, on the Atlantic coast. It was founded in the late 18th century as a refuge for freed slaves and was capital of British West Africa (1808–74), becoming the capital of Sierra Leone in 1961. The University of Sierra Leone was founded here in 1967. It has trade in ginger, diamonds, and gold; industries include fish processing. Population (1974 est): 214,443.

free trade International trade that takes place without tariffs or quotas. World production is maximized by free trade, but the distribution of a particular product may be inequitable and countries may encounter domestic pressures from their own producers to apply *tariffs. Conditions in international trade came closest to free trade in the mid-19th century following the demise of *mercantilism, but since then tariff barriers have been erected again. A group of countries may agree between themselves to lower tariffs and achieve a measure of free trade (*see* General Agreement on Tariffs and Trade) or they may form a free-trade area (e.g. the *European Economic Community) surrounded by a tariff barrier.

free verse Poetry without regular meter or form and depending on the rhythms and patterns of natural speech. The original French term, *vers libre*, was coined during the 1880s by poets who wished to emphasize rhythm as the essential principle of poetic form. Major exponents of this form include Ezra Pound, D. H. Lawrence, and William Carlos Williams.

free will In philosophy and theology, the ability of man to choose his own destiny, as opposed to the idea that everything that happens to him is inevitable. Philosophers are concerned to discover what the presuppositions and implications of free will are, compared to those of *determinism. They are also concerned to discover to what extent free will and determinism can be compatible. The problem has confronted philosophers since man began to think about abstract matters and is one to which there is no easy solution. In a theistic context, determinism is replaced by *predestination, the view that all events, including human choice, are fixed by the will of God. In the Christian Church, controversy arose in the 5th century between followers of Pelagius, who taught that man is able to choose salvation or damnation, and St *Augustine, who held that man could only be saved by divine grace. The controversy again became a live issue at the Reformation, the Calvinists rejecting free will and claiming that men were consigned for eternity to salvation or damnation, irrespective of merit.

freeze drying A method of drying foods for preservation in which the food is rapidly frozen under very low pressure. Any water present freezes and then sublimes under the low pressure.

freezing The preservation of food by keeping it frozen. The basic principle in all food preservation is to arrest the development of the microorganisms responsible for the decay of the food. Home freezers achieve this by keeping food at a temperature of about −0.4°F (−18°C). On thawing, the deterioration process restarts. Most foods are well preserved by freezing, with little loss in nutritional value, but some with a high water content within the cells of the food, such as strawberries and cucumbers, become soggy after freezing as a result of damage to the cell structure by ice formation. Most vegetables are blanched (boiled for 2–4 minutes) before freezing to arrest the action of enzymes. It is the residual enzymic action that determines the recommended storage time.

Frege, Gottlob (1848–1925) German mathematician and logician, who extended *Boole's work on symbolic logic by using logical symbols not already used in mathematics (symbols for *or, if-then*, etc.). This is now standard practice in logic. Frege published a massive work in which he applied symbolic logic to arithmetic. This, however, was invalidated by a paradox presented by Bertrand *Russell. In Frege's system, some sets, or classes, of things are not members of themselves; for example, the set (all cats) is not itself a cat. Others are; for example, the set (all things that are not animals) is itself not an animal. Russell's paradox is: is the set (all sets that are not members of themselves) a member of itself?

Frei (Montalva), Eduardo (1911–82) Chilean statesman, who defeated Salvador *Allende in 1964 to become the first Christian Democratic president of Chile. His promises of radical reform were not enough to win him reelection and he was defeated by Allende in 1970.

Freiburg. *See* Fribourg.

Freiburg im Breisgau 48 00N 7 52E A city in SW Germany, in Baden-Württemberg in the Black Forest. It has a university (1457) and a notable gothic cathedral, built of red sandstone. A major tourist center, its manufactures include precision instruments and pharmaceutical products. Population (1988): 186,000.

Fremantle 32 07S 115 44E A seaport in Western Australia, SW of Perth at the mouth of the Swan River. Kwinana, an important industrial complex with oil and nickel refineries and bulk-grain facilities, is nearby. Population (1991): 22,709.

Frémont, John C(harles) (1813–90) US explorer, cartographer, and political leader. He joined the Topographical Corps of the US Army in 1838. During the 1840s, he explored and mapped large areas of the American Far West. His most important expeditions were along the route of the Oregon Trail in 1842, to the Great Basin west of the Rockies in 1843–44, and through the Sierra Nevada Range in 1846. During this last expedition, which took place at the outbreak of the *Mexican War, Frémont ignored the orders of Gen. Stephen *Kearny and took part in the conquest of California for the US. Frémont was later court-martialed for this action and resigned from the army. After he was granted a pardon by Pres. James *Polk, Frémont began a political career. In 1853–54 he served as US senator from California and in 1856 he waged an unsuccessful campaign for the presidency as the first candidate of the *Republican Party. Frémont returned to the army as a major general during the *Civil War, serving in the Far West and in W. Virginia. Later in life he became involved in the construction of western railroads and served as governor of the Territory of Arizona (1873–83).

French A Romance language spoken by 45 million people in France, and extensively in Canada, Belgium, Switzerland, and elsewhere. It is the official language of 21 countries. Standard French, based upon the Parisian dialect known as Francien, has been France's official administrative language since 1539. It has replaced most northern dialects, known collectively as *langue d'oïl*, and has superseded the Occitan dialects of S France, known as *langue d'oc* (*see* Provençal). During the 17th century the *Académie Française and the publication of a standard dictionary (1680) quickly stabilized the language. French grammar has been simplified from Latin and the phonology has greatly altered. There are no noun case declensions and the verb is conjugated for three persons. Pronunciation does not, however, distinguish as many grammatical differences as the written form.

French, Daniel Chester (1850–1931) US sculptor. As a young man in his native Massachusetts, he sculpted *The Minute Man* (1875) for the town of Concord. It has remained an important symbol of the American spirit. He finished the *Lincoln*, seated in the Lincoln Memorial in Washington, D.C., in 1922. Other works include *Europe, Asia, Africa, and America* (1907; in the New York City Custom House) and *Alma Mater* (1915; Columbia University).

French and Indian War (1754–63) The conflict for empire in North America between France on one side and Britain and the American colonists on the other. It constituted the American front of the *Seven Years' War. France and its Indian allies had the initial advantage of superior land forces but British sea blockades eventually defeated the French. The war's climax was reached in the battle for Quebec in which the commanders of each side, *Montcalm and *Wolfe, were mortally wounded. In the concluding Treaty of *Paris (1763) Britain gained Canada and all lands E of the Mississippi.

French art and architecture The styles of art and architecture in France from the early Middle Ages. Until the *Renaissance, architecture dominated French artistic expression. Many French cathedrals and churches date from the Merovingian or Carolingian periods, which evolved features that anticipated the *romanesque architecture of the 11th and 12th centuries. The *gothic style is celebrated in the cathedrals of Notre-Dame and at Chartres, Rheims, and Amiens. The 13th century also produced some outstanding miniature painting, especially in Paris, a school that reached its height in the 1320s with the work of Jean *Pucelle. The Renaissance in France found expression chiefly in domestic architecture and decoration, notable examples including the chateaux at Amboise and Chambord. The school of *Fontainebleau, founded by Francis I, was profoundly influenced by Italian *mannerism; the 16th century also saw the work of the *Clouet family, who were portraitists, and of the sculptor Jean *Goujon. The great exponents of classicism—*Poussin, *Claude, and *La Tour—dominated French art in the first half of the 17th century, and the influence of *Versailles was felt throughout Europe. The *rococo style of the 18th century was exemplified by the work of *Watteau, *Fragonard, and *Boucher and contrasted the contemporaneous naturalism of *Chardin. The outstanding exponent of late 18th-century *neoclassicism was *David. The latter's followers, *Géricault and *Delacroix, were notable among the Romantics of the 19th century, which also saw the work of *Ingres, *Courbet, and the *Barbizon school. French art in the late 19th century is associated with *impressionism, but the period also witnessed the work of *Gauguin, *Van Gogh, and *Cézanne, an important influence on the development of *modern art (*see also* cubism). *See also* Louis XIV; Louis XV; Louis XVI.

French bean An annual herb, *Phaseolus vulgaris*, also called kidney bean, probably native to South America but widely cultivated. It has large heart-shaped leaves and white pealike flowers. Both dwarf and twining varieties are grown for their *beans, usually eaten in the pod. Family: **Leguminosae*. *See also* haricot bean.

French Canadians French-speaking citizens of Canada descended from immigrants who settled, mainly in Quebec, as farmers during the 17th and 18th centuries. They comprise approximately 30% of the Canadian population, are mainly Roman Catholic, and have a distinct culture. The desire to preserve their identity has promoted a strong separatist movement.

French Community An association of states, comprising France and its former colonies, established by the new Fifth Republic after a constitutional referendum (1958). It succeeded the French Union, which in turn replaced the empire. In addition to France it includes Guadeloupe, Guiana, Martinique, Mayotte, La Réunion, St Pierre and Miquelon, Southern and Antarctic Territories, French Polynesia, New Caledonia, and Wallis and Futuna.

French Equatorial Africa (French name: Afrique Équatoriale Française) A former federation of French territories in W central Africa comprising (1910–59) the present-day independent states of the Central African Republic, Chad, Congo (Republic of), and Gabon.

French Guiana A French overseas region on the NE coast of South America. A narrow fertile coastal belt rises to a mountainous interior, which is covered in dense forest rich in valuable timber. *Economy*: timber is the principal export and sugar is the main commercial crop, although the large reserves of minerals, land, timber, and fish have as yet been little developed. *History*: Europeans in search of *Eldorado explored the region from the early 16th century, but it was not settled until the 17th century, when the French, Dutch, Portuguese, and English competed for possession. In 1817 it was finally obtained by the French, who established penal colonies, including the notorious one on Devil's Island, in the territory. The French Guianese have had full French citizenship since 1848 and have been represented in the National Assembly since 1870. Area: about 34,740 sq mi (91,000 sq km). Population (1981 est): 66,400. Capital: Cayenne.

French horn An orchestral brass instrument, which evolved from the hunting horn. It consists of a long narrow coiled tube with a wide bell and a cup-shaped mouthpiece. In its original form the horn could only play its own natural harmonic series of notes; in the 18th century, crooks of tubing of different length were inserted to enable it to play in a variety of keys. In the 19th century valves were fitted giving the horn in F a complete range of about three octaves above B below the bass stave. It is a transposing instrument, its music being written a fifth higher than it sounds.

French India A former French overseas territory in India, comprising Chandernagor (an enclave in Bengal) and the coastal settlements of Pondicherry, Karikal, Yanam, and Mahé. It was restored to India (1949–54).

French literature Writings in Old French, the *langue d'oïl*, date from the 10th century AD; major works appeared only in the 12th century. The *chansons de geste* celebrated the military exploits of the French nobility in the Crusades and other wars. From classical and Arthurian romances by Chrétien de Troyes and others developed such allegorical romances as *Le Roman de la rose* (c. 1230) of Guillaume de Lorris. The lyric poetry of courtly love of the southern *troubadours and the northern *trouvères was followed in the 15th century by the more personal poetry of Charles d'Orléans and François Villon.

During the 16th century Pierre de Ronsard and the other members of the *Pléiade rivaled the poets of Renaissance Italy, while the major prose works were the comic masterpieces of Rabelais and the *Essais* of Montaigne. The influence of classicism during the 17th century, the golden age of French literature, is seen in the tragic dramas of Corneille and Racine, the comedies of Molière, and the prose of Descartes and Pascal. During the 18th century the greatest writing was that of Rousseau, Voltaire, and Montesquieu, in the field of social philosophy.

Among the leading figures of the Romantic movement during the early 19th century were Chateaubriand and Victor Hugo. Reacting against Romanticism, such novelists as Stendhal, Balzac, Flaubert, and Zola favored realism and naturalism. Baudelaire, reacting against the Romantic poets de Vigny and de Musset and the Parnassian Gautier, was one of the first symbolist poets; he was succeeded by Verlaine, Mallarmé, Rimbaud, and, in the 20th century, by Valéry, a contemporary of the surrealist poet Apollinaire.

Major French novelists of the 20th century include Proust, Gide, and Montherlant as well as the existentialists Sartre and Camus. French drama flourished with plays by Anouilh, Jean Cocteau, and the absurdist writers Ionesco and Beckett. Such novelists as Alain Robbe-Grillet and Nathalie Sarraute pioneered the **nouveau roman.*

French Polynesia (former name: French Settlements in Oceania) A French overseas territory in the S Pacific Ocean consisting of several island groups. The most important of these are the Gambier Islands, the Society Islands, the Tuamotu Archipelago, the Tubuai Islands, and the Marquesas Islands. The islands produce copra and phosphates. Area: about 1500 sq mi (4000 sq km). Population (1980): 155,000. Capital: Papeete.

French Republican calendar The calendar adopted (1793) in France during the French Revolution and retained until 1806, when the Gregorian *calendar was reintroduced. The revolutionaries' purpose was to design a calendar without ecclesiastical associations. The year began on Sept 22 (the date in 1792 when the Republic came into being) and had 365 days divided into 12 months of 30 days each. The remaining 5 days (Sept 17–22) were festivals, an extra one being added in a leap year. Each month was divided into 3 periods of 10 days (a *décade*) and was renamed: Vendémaire (French: vintage; Sept 22–Oct 21),

Brumaire (mist), Frimaire (frost), Nivôse (snow), Pluviôse (rain), Ventôse (wind), Germinal (seedtime), Floréal (blossom), Prairial (meadow), Messidor (harvest), Thermidor (heat), Fructidor (fruits).

French Revolution The overthrow of the French monarchy as a reaction to the corrupt, feudal, and incompetent government of the Bourbon kings. In 1789 Louis XVI was forced to summon the *States General but its Third Estate, opposing aristocratic attempts to dominate proceedings, formed its own National Assembly. Riots followed, the *Bastille was stormed, the king was mobbed at Versailles, and the Assembly (from July the Constituent Assembly) promulgated the Declaration of the *Rights of Man. Feudalism was abolished and in September 1791, a new constitution was accepted by the king following his thwarted attempt to flee France (the flight to Varennes). However, his continuing uncooperativeness fostered the growing republicanism of what became the Legislative Assembly (October 1791) and then the National Convention (September 1792). The Convention proclaimed a republic and in January 1793, Louis was executed. The moderate *Girondins, discredited by France's war reverses (*see* Revolutionary and Napoleonic Wars), were now ousted by the *Jacobins and power passed to the Committee of *Public Safety. Under *Robespierre the Committee conducted a *Reign of Terror in which thousands of suspected antirevolutionaries were executed but his extremism brought (1794) his downfall on 9 Thermidor (July 27; *see* French Republican calendar). The so-called Thermidorean reaction led to the establishment of the *Directory (1795), which struggled for four years with economic crises until Napoleon's coup d'état of 18 Brumaire (1799) brought the Revolution to an end.

French Somalia. *See* Djibouti, Republic of.

French Southern and Antarctic Territories A French territory (since 1955) comprising *Adélie Land in Antarctica with the islands of Amsterdam and St Paul and the Kerguelen and Crozet archipelagos in the Indian Ocean.

French Sudan. *See* Mali, Republic of.

French West Africa (French name: Afrique Occidentale Française) The former French territories in West Africa comprising (1895–1958) the present-day independent countries of Benin, Guinea, Ivory Coast, Niger, and Senegal.

Freneau, Philip (1752–1832) US poet. He described his experience as a prisoner during the American Revolution in *The British Prison Ship* (1781). After independence he became a sea captain and later edited the popular *National Gazette* (1791–93). He then went back to sea for a period before retiring to his farm, where he wrote philosophical nature poetry. An important early American poet, he wrote "The Wild Honeysuckle," "Eutaw Springs," and "To a Caty-Did."

frequency The number of cycles completed by a vibrating system in unit time, usually one second (symbol: ν or f). The unit of frequency is the *hertz. The angular frequency, ω, is related to the frequency by the equation $\omega = 2\pi\nu$ and is measured in radians per second.

frequency modulation. *See* modulation.

fresco A classical and Renaissance method of wall decoration in which pure pigments dissolved in water were applied to the wet lime-plastered surface of a wall, producing a chemical reaction that made the colors a permanent part of the wall. Up to about 1500 the design was sketched freehand onto the rough plaster surface (the *arricciato*). Separate areas of the sketch were then filled in with fine smooth plaster (the *intonaco*) and detailed color was applied in layers of different pigments. Subsequently the *cartoon, as used by *Michelangelo, *Raphael, *Holbein, and others, allowed for more complicated premeditated design. The composition was drawn on sheets of paper, later applied to the wall, and the design pricked through with a stylus or with charcoal dust forced through the stylus piercings. Fresco painting was revived in the 20th century by the Mexican muralists *Orozco and *Rivera.

Frescobaldi A family of bankers, which dominated the mercantile and political life of Florence until it was divided in the dispute between the *Guelfs and Ghibellines at the end of the 13th century. The Frescobaldi opened a bank in London in the 1270s and financed the wars of Edward I and II. Receiving considerable privileges as reward, they were increasingly unpopular, fleeing the country in 1310 to escape prosecution.

Fresnel, Augustin Jean (1788–1827) French physicist, who (with Thomas *Young) used his work on interference to formulate the wave theory of light. *See also* Fresnel lens.

Fresnel lens A convex optical lens used principally in spotlights. It is thinner and therefore absorbs less light and heat than a normal convex lens with an equally short focal length. This is achieved by making the surface a series of stepped concentric rings, each with the same curvature as the equivalent normal convex surface at that radius. Named for A. *Fresnel.

Fresno 36 45N 119 45W A city in central California, in the San Joaquin River valley. Most of its industries are related to agriculture: grape and wine processing, citrus fruit processing, the manufacturing of containers, and the production of machinery. Population (1990): 354,202.

Freud, Sigmund (1856–1939) Austrian psychiatrist and pioneer of psychoanalysis. Freud studied medicine and, in 1882, joined the staff of a psychiatric clinic in Vienna. An interest in hypnosis developed through his collaboration with Josef *Breuer and his meeting, in 1885, with Jean-Martin *Charcot. Following the publication with Breuer of *Studies in Hysteria* (1895), Freud evolved his theory that neuroses were rooted in suppressed sexual desires and sexual experiences of childhood, either real or imagined. In *The Interpretation of Dreams* (1899), he analyzed the content of dreams in terms of unconscious desires and experiences, often dating from childhood. His emphasis on the sexual origin of mental disorders aroused great controversy, particularly his view that the sexual desires of children dated from birth, not puberty. In 1902 Freud established a circle of his colleagues in Vienna, which later (1910) became the International Psycho-Analytical Society. However, many of its members, including Carl *Jung and Alfred *Adler, resigned over disagreements with its founder. Freud left Vienna in 1938, following the Nazi invasion, joining his son in London, where he remained until his death.

Although subsequently modified, Freud's theories shed light on the workings of the unconscious mind and the motives, desires, and conflicts involved in human behavior. His other books include *The Psychopathology of Everyday Life* (1904), *Totem and Taboo* (1913), *Beyond the Pleasure Principle* (1920), and *Moses and Monotheism* (1939). His daughter **Anna Freud** (1895–1982) was a founder of child psychoanalysis. Coming to London with her father in 1938 she established the Hampstead Child Therapy Clinic. Her writings include *Introduction to the Technique of Child Psychoanalysis* (1927) and *Normality and Pathology in Childhood* (1965).

Freyja (*or* Freya) The Norse goddess of love and fertility, the sister of Frey, the god of sunshine, rain, and fertility. She is the Norse counterpart of Venus and is the leader of the *Valkyries. In some sources she is identified with *Frigga.

friarbird A noisy chattering *honeyeater of the genus *Philemon* (16 species), also called leatherhead. Friarbirds resemble jackdaws but have naked patches on the head and horny outgrowths on the bill.

SIGMUND FREUD *With his grandson Stephan (child of his youngest son Ernst) in Berlin (1922).*

Fribourg (German name: Freiburg) 46 50N 7 10E A city in W Switzerland. Its many medieval buildings include the Cathedral of St Nicholas (13th–15th centuries) and it has a university (1889). Industries include the production of beer, chocolate, and machinery. Population: 39,695.

Frick, Henry Clay (1849–1919) US industrialist. After forming and running his own coke-oven manufacturing business in Pennsylvania, by the age of 40 he headed Carnegie Brothers and Company (later Carnegie Steel Company). Although often at odds with Andrew Carnegie, Frick ran the company efficiently and was responsible for its expansion and purchase of the Mesabi ore holdings so that the company would no longer be dependent on others for its raw materials.

friction A force exerted at the boundary between two solids or fluids that retards motion between them. In solid friction a distinction is drawn between sliding friction and rolling friction. Sliding friction is further divided into dynamic friction, defined as the minimum force needed to keep a body sliding, and static friction, defined as the minimum force needed to move a stationary body. The latter is slightly greater than the former. In rolling friction the force of resistance is less than in sliding friction as the rolling body moves up the side of a depression made in the stationary body. This accounts for the effectiveness of wheels and ball bearings.

The coefficient of friction is defined as the ratio of the frictional force to the perpendicular reaction between the surfaces. Friction is caused primarily by the two surfaces interlocking at the microscopic level. It is reduced by the use of lubricants, such as grease or graphite (*see* tribology). It is sometimes desirable to increase friction between surfaces, as in brake linings, clutch plates, and shoe soles. For this purpose rough hard-wearing materials are used.

Friedan, Betty (1921–) US feminist; president of the *National Organization for Women (NOW) (1966–70). Her book *The Feminine Mystique* (1963) began the contemporary feminist movement, and by 1966 she had helped to found NOW. Other works include *It Changed My Life* (1976), in which she recounted her life in the feminist movement; and *The Second Stage* (1981), a call for a change of direction in the movement.

Friedland, Battle of (June 14, 1807) A battle in the Napoleonic Wars fought near Friedland, East Prussia (now Pravdinsk, Lithuania). The French under Napoleon defeated the Russians, under Gen. Levin Bennigsen (1745–1826). The victory enabled the French to occupy Königsberg and led to the Treaty of *Tilsit between Napoleon and Alexander I of Russia.

Friedman, Milton (1912–) US economist. A conservative economist, Friedman is known for his theories on monetary supply, which contradict those of *Keynes. His published work, which argues for the free market economy, includes *A Theory of the Consumption Function* (1957) and *Capitalism and Freedom* (1962). He won the 1976 Nobel Prize. He collaborated with his wife Rose on *Free to Choose* (1980), criticizing government involvement in the economy.

Friedrich, Caspar David (1774–1840) German Romantic landscape painter, who studied at the Copenhagen Academy (1794–98). From 1798 he lived in Dresden, where he became friendly with *Goethe and other writers. His first major painting, an altarpiece painted in 1808, initiated a controversy over the use of landscape in religious subjects; successive works such as *Wreck of the Hope* (1822; Kunsthalle, Hamburg) are notable for their symbolism of despair and man's insignificance in relation to nature.

Friendly Islands. *See* Tonga, Kingdom of.

Friesian cattle A breed of large black-and-white dairy cattle originating from the province of Friesland in the Netherlands. They were exported to North America by early settlers and there developed as Holstein-Friesians. They are very popular high-yielding milk producers and crosses, especially with a Charolais or Hereford bull, are good beef animals.

Friesland A province in the N Netherlands, bordering on the IJsselmeer. Much of the land is below sea level and there are strong dikes and an extensive canal system. Agriculture is important, especially cattle raising and dairy farming; the famous *Friesian breed of cattle came from here. Area: 1468 sq mi (3803 sq km). Population (1981 est): 589,252. Capital: Leeuwarden.

frigate A naval vessel, smaller than a *destroyer, used mainly for carrying guided missiles and displacing about 2400 tons. Earlier sailing frigates included the *Constitution* ("Old Ironsides"), a US vessel that acquired fame in the Revolutionary War.

frigate bird A seabird belonging to the genus *Fregata* and family *Fregatidae* (5 species), occurring in tropical and subtropical oceanic regions, also called man-of-war bird because it often steals food from other birds in midair; 31–45 in (80–115 cm) long, frigate birds have narrow wings spanning up to 7.5 ft (2.3 m), a long hooked bill, and a forked tail. Males are glossy black and develop an inflatable red throat sac in the breeding season; females are brownish black with white underparts. Order: *Pelecaniformes* (gannets, pelicans, etc.).

Frigga (*or* Frigg) The Norse goddess of married love and the hearth, the wife of *Odin. In some legends she is identified with *Freyja; her name is preserved in *Friday*.

frilled lizard A slender pale-brown arboreal lizard, *Chlamydosaurus kingi*, occurring in dry regions of Australia and feeding chiefly on ants. Up to 40 in (1 m) long, it has a scaly membrane around its neck that forms a large frill, thereby deterring likely enemies. Family: *Agamidae*.

Friml, Rudolph (1879–1972) Czech-born composer and pianist, who settled in the US in 1906. He is remembered for his operettas, such as *Rose Marie* (1916) and *The Vagabond King* (1925). He also wrote a piano concerto and light pieces for the piano.

Frisch, Karl von (1886–1982) Austrian zoologist, best known for his work on animal behavior, especially of bees. He found that bees communicate with each other by means of a circling "dance" or by wagging movements to indicate the location of a source of food from the hive. Von Frisch also worked on the sensory abilities of fish. He shared a Nobel Prize (1973) with *Lorenz and Niko *Tinbergen.

Frisch, Ragnar (1895–1973) Norwegian economist. As professor of economics at Oslo University and editor of *Econometrica*, Frisch was concerned with the application of statistics to economics. He received, with Jan *Tinbergen, the first Nobel Prize for Economics (1969).

Frisches Haff. *See* Vistula Lagoon.

Frisian A Germanic language formerly spoken along the North Sea coastal region of Holland as far as Schleswig in Germany. It is now principally confined to Friesland province in Holland and certain offshore islands including Heligoland. It is the language most closely related to English. The Frisians were traditionally a seafaring and commercial people. More recently they have become known for dairy and beef farming.

Frisian Islands A chain of islands in the North Sea extending along the coast of, and politically divided between, the Netherlands, Germany, and SW Denmark. The chain comprises three main groups: the West, North, and East Frisian Islands. The chief occupations are fishing, sheep and cattle raising, and tourism.

fritillary (botany) A bulbous perennial plant of the genus *Fritillaria* (80 species), mostly native to N temperate regions. The leaves are narrow and the bell-shaped flowers droop from slender stalks. The European snake's head (*F. meleagris*), also called leopard lily and toad lily, has reddish-purple chequered flowers. The crown imperial (*F. imperialis*), native to N India, has a cluster of pendant red flowers at the top of a tall (48 in [120 cm]) stem, topped by a tuft of leaves. Both species are popular garden plants. Family: *Liliaceae*.

fritillary (zoology) A *nymphalid butterfly, usually brown or orange marked with black. The caterpillars feed at night—violets are the commonest food plant—but many species hibernate soon after hatching. Chief genera: *Boloria, Melitaea*.

Friuli-Venezia Giulia A region in the extreme NE of Italy. It was formed in 1947, incorporating Trieste in 1954, and is semiautonomous. It consists of mountains along the N border with Austria and a coastal plain in the S. The economy is largely based on agriculture, the region's farmers producing cereals and maize in the lowlands, fruit and vines in the foothills, and livestock in the mountains. Manufacturing industries include textiles, food processing, chemicals, and ship building. Area: 3031 sq mi (7850 sq km). Population (1991): 1,216,398. Capital: Trieste.

Frobisher, Sir Martin (c. 1535–94) English navigator. He made three attempts (1576, 1577, 1578) to discover the *Northwest Passage, giving his name to a bay on Baffin Island and bringing back "black earth," which was mistakenly thought to contain gold. He later served against the Spanish *Armada and raided Spanish treasure ships.

Froebel, Friedrich Wilhelm August (1782–1852) German pioneer of nursery education. Throughout his life, Froebel was fascinated by the underlying unity of all things. His view of man was one of harmonious growth, and he applied this concept to the development of children in *The Education of Man* (1826). Although influenced by *Pestalozzi, Froebel disagreed with his theory that young children should remain only with their mothers. His view that children should spend time together in creative play led him to found the first kindergarten (1837) at Blankenburg.

frog A tailless amphibian of the family *Ranidae*, which includes bullfrogs, hairy frogs, and leopard frogs. Many other so-called frogs, such as *tree frogs, are actually toads. The European frog (*Rana temporaria*) grows to 4 in (10 cm). Greenish-brown with black markings, it spends most of its life on land, feeding on insects, and only returns to water to breed. Other species, such as the edible frog (*R. esculenta*), may spend most of their lives in water. Order: **Anura.*

frog-bit A Eurasian perennial water plant, *Hydrocharis morsus-ranae*, found in ponds, ditches, etc. It has floating stems arising from submerged roots, rounded leaves, and white flowers, 0.8 in (2 cm) in diameter. Family: *Hydrocharitaceae*.

frogfish A slow-moving carnivorous fish belonging to a family (*Antennariidae*, about 60 species) occurring on the bottom, usually in shallow tropical waters. Frogfish have a robust body, up to 12 in (30 cm) long, with camouflaging patterned fleshy flaps and warty skin, limblike pectoral fins, and often a wirelike projection from the snout, which lures prey. Order: *Lophiiformes*.

froghopper A small jumping insect belonging to the family *Cercopidae* (about 2000 species). Froghoppers feed on plant juices, sometimes becoming pests. Eggs are laid on stems or roots and the *nymphs remain stationary until adult. They often protect themselves against predators and desiccation with a cover of white froth ("cuckoo spit"), produced by blowing air mixed with fluid from the anus through a valve in the abdomen. For this reason they are often known as cuckoo-spit insects and spittlebugs. Order: **Hemiptera.*

frogmouth A nocturnal bird belonging to a family (*Podargidae*; 12 species), occurring in forests of SE Asia and Australasia; 10–22 in (25–55 cm) long, frogmouths are well camouflaged with a mottled gray and brown plumage. They have a wide-gaping bill and prey chiefly on beetles, frogs, mice, and small birds. Order: *Caprimulgiformes* (nightjars, etc.).

Froissart, Jean (1337–c. 1400) French chronicler and poet. He traveled widely in Europe and served at the court of Edward III of England. His *Chronicles*, covering the years from 1325 to 1400, are a detailed and colorful record of the Hundred Years' War. He also wrote a verse romance, *Méliador*, and many ballades.

Fromm, Erich (1900–80) US psychologist and philosopher, born in Germany. Fromm left Germany for the US in 1934 and became well known for his controversial analyses of social ills in modern industrial society. In *The Sane Society* (1955), he charged the consumer society with being responsible for isolation, loneliness, and doubt among individuals. His other works include *The Art of Loving* (1956) and *The Revolution of Hope* (1968).

Fronde (French: sling) French uprising between 1648 and 1653, so called because the combatants employed slingshots. The first Fronde, a protest against excessive tax demands and the administration of *Mazarin, was led by the Paris parlement. It was quickly suppressed (1649) by the royal army led by *Condé. In 1650 Condé himself led a second, aristocratic, revolt against Mazarin's authority. Contention among its leaders and an upsurge of support for the monarchy led to its collapse.

front In □meteorology, the interface between two air masses of different thermal characteristics and origins. Where the air masses converge the warm air, being lighter, rises and slopes over the cold air. Distinctive weather phenomena are associated with fronts, particularly the development of depressions, and they are very important in short-term weather forecasting.

Front de Libération nationale (FLN) An Algerian nationalist group that organized the war of independence against France (1954-62). Formed in 1954, the FLN began a campaign of terrorism and sabotage. In 1956 it organized itself like a government, sending diplomatic missions abroad, and in 1958 set up a provisional government in Tunis under Ferhat *Abbas. In 1962 the French under Gen. de Gaulle agreed to Algerian independence and when *Ben Bella became president in 1963 the FLN became Algeria's sole political party.

Frontenac, Louis de Buade, Comte de Palluau et de (1620–98) French soldier; governor of New France (1672–82, 1689–98), who promoted French expansion in North America. His fur-trading activities, challenged by the Iroquois Indian confederacy, and his policy of expansion, caused dissension that led to his recall. When war broke out with England in 1689 he was reinstated. He attacked New England settlements with the help of Indian allies, defended Quebec, and eventually subdued the Iroquois.

frost A weather condition that occurs when the temperature falls below 32°F (0°C). It is recognized by the icy deposit that forms but if the air is very dry this will not occur. In weather forecasting grades of severity of frost are distinguished as slight (32–26°F [−0.1–−3.5°C]), moderate (26–20°F [−3.6–−6.4°C]), severe (20–11°F [−6.5–−11.5°C]), and very severe (below 11°F [−11.5°C]). A distinction is made between ground frost, measured at grass level, and air frost, measured at a height of 4 ft (1.4 m).

Frost, Robert Lee (1874–1963) US poet. In 1885 his family moved to New England, where he spent most of his life and worked as a teacher and farmer. The poetry collections *A Boy's Will* (1913) and *North of Boston* (1914), published during a stay in England, brought him fame. The books *New Hampshire* (1923), *Collected Poems* (1930), *A Further Range* (1936), and *A Witness Tree* (1942) were awarded Pulitzer Prizes. His work, often pastoral and lyrical, has a dark undercurrent of fear and suffering relieved only by stoical acceptance.

frostbite Damage to part of the body, usually a hand or foot, resulting from exposure to extreme cold. The blood vessels to the affected limb constrict so that little blood (and therefore essential oxygen) reaches the skin, nerves, and muscles. This may lead to loss of sensation, ulcers, and eventually gangrene, necessitating amputation. Initial treatment is to gently warm the affected part.

froth flotation A method of separating mineral ore from waste or one ore from another. The unpurified pulverized ore is agitated with water and a reagent that binds preferentially with the desired ore and alters its surface properties. Air is then passed through the mixture and the ore is carried to the surface by the bubbles to form a froth, which can then be removed.

frottola (Italian: untruth, silly story) A popular Italian song form of the early 16th century. It was a setting of fashionable verse in four parts, the voice being accompanied by three instrumental parts and the music being repeated for each stanza.

fructose A simple sugar (monosaccharide) that is sweeter than sucrose and present in green leaves, fruits, and honey. Its phosphate derivatives are important in the carbohydrate metabolism of living organisms.

fruit The fertilized ovary of a flower, which contains the seed (or seeds) and may incorporate other parts of the flower (e.g. the receptacle in strawberries, the bracts in pineapples). The variation in the structure of fruits reflects the different means they have evolved to ensure dispersal of the seeds, which is essential to prevent overcrowding and enable the plant to spread and colonize new habitats. Fleshy fruits, for example, are usually eaten by animals, the seeds passing out with their feces. Animals can also carry hooked or sticky fruits on their bodies. Seeds dispersed by wind are usually very light: they are either forcibly ejected from their fruits, for example from the *capsule of poppy and the pods of leguminous plants, or they remain attached to the fruit, which can itself remain airborne for considerable distances, for example the winged fruits of sycamores and ash trees. Some fruits are distributed by water: coconut fruits can be transported several hundred miles by sea. The word fruit is popularly restricted to the fleshy edible fruits, many of which are of economic importance to man: **fruit farming** constitutes an important branch of commercial *horticulture. In terms of world production the most important fruit crops are: apples, pears, and cherries (in cool temperate regions); grapes, peaches, and figs (warm temperate); citrus fruits and dates (subtropical); bananas and pineapples (tropical).

fruit bat A vegetarian *bat belonging to the family *Pteropidae* and suborder *Megachiroptera* (150 species). Fruit bats occur in tropical and subtropical regions of the Old World. With a body length of up to 16 in (40 cm), they are typically larger than insect-eating bats and have better vision; only one genus (*Rousettus*, 13 species) uses *echolocation. Most eat fruit although some feed on flowers or nectar. Certain tropical trees are adapted for pollination by fruit bats. *See also* flying fox. ☐mammal.

fruit fly A fly belonging to the family *Trypetidae* (1200 species)—the true fruit flies. (Insects of the family *Drosophilidae* are known as small fruit flies: *see* Drosophila.) True fruit flies have spotted or banded wings and the larvae of many species feed on fruit, often causing serious damage. For example, the Mediterranean fruit fly (*Ceratitis capitata*) is a pest of almost all succulent fruits, while the North American apple maggot (*Rhagoletis pomonella*) tunnels into apples.

Frunze. *See* Bishkek.

Fry, Christopher (C. Harris; 1907–) British dramatist. The verbal excitement of his earliest verse plays, *A Phoenix Too Frequent* (1946) and *The Lady's Not for Burning* (1948), seemed to presage a revival of poetic drama, but the popularity of his work declined after the early 1950s. His other plays include *Venus Observed* (1950), *The Light Is Dark Enough* (1954), and *Curtmantle* (1962).

Fu'ad I (1868–1936) King of Egypt (1922–36). He became sultan in 1917 under the British protectorate and king when Britain granted limited independence in 1922. He tried to curb the nationalist Wafd Party and in 1931 suspended the 1923 constitution. Popular pressure forced him to restore it in 1935.

Fuchs, Sir Vivian (Ernest) (1908–) British explorer. He was director of the Falkland Islands Dependencies Survey Scientific Bureau (1947–50). Later he led the Commonwealth Trans-Antarctic Expedition and with help from Sir Edmund *Hillary he covered and surveyed 2173 mi (3500 km) in 1957–58, during the International Geophysical Year. He was again director of the Falkland Islands Survey (1960–73).

FRUITS

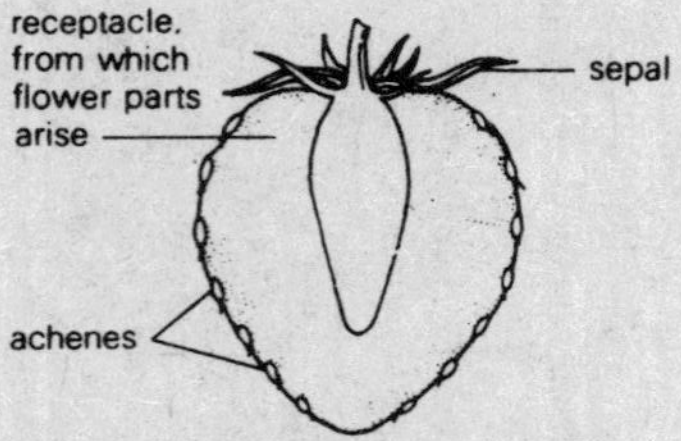

strawberry *The true fruits, which are formed from the ovary and contain the seeds, are the achenes on the surface of the fleshy receptacle.*

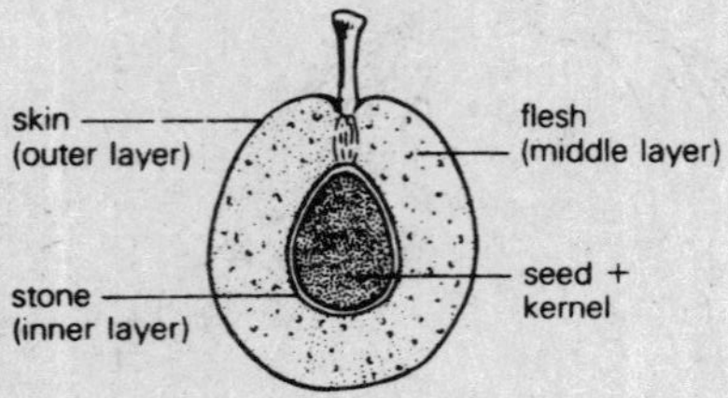

plum *This fruit, like all drupes (stone fruits), is made up of three layers.*

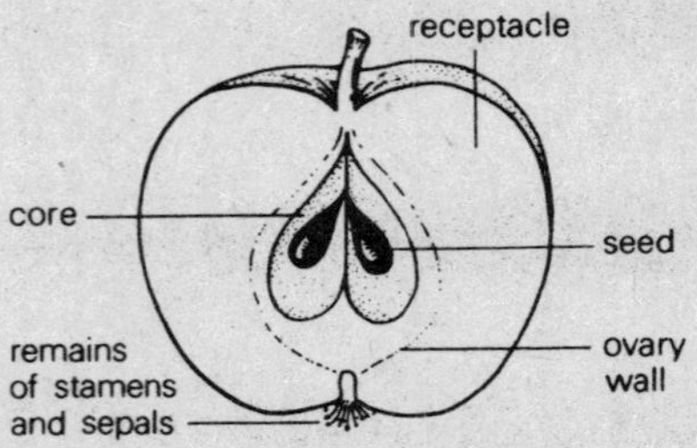

apple *The flesh of the apple is the receptacle; the core develops from the ovary and contains the seeds.*

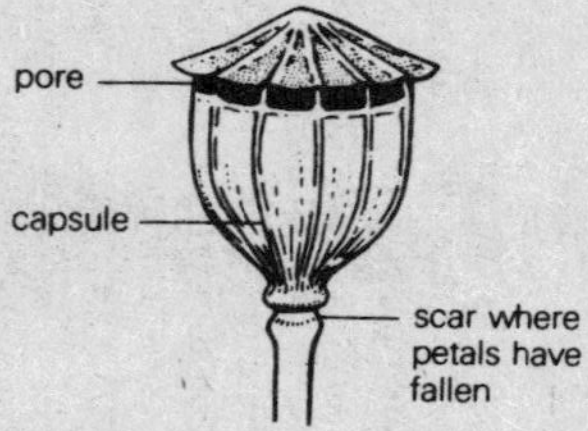

poppy *The seeds within the capsule are shaken out through the pores.*

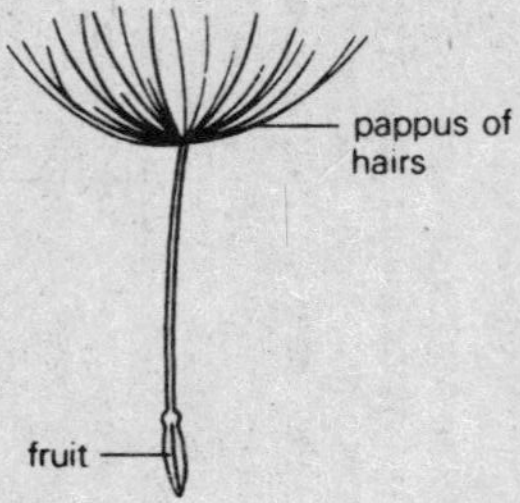

dandelion *The pappus acts as a parachute.*

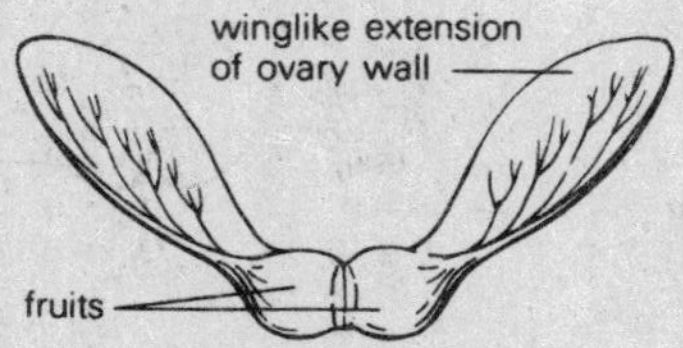

sycamore *The two winged fruits separate and are carried away by the wind.*

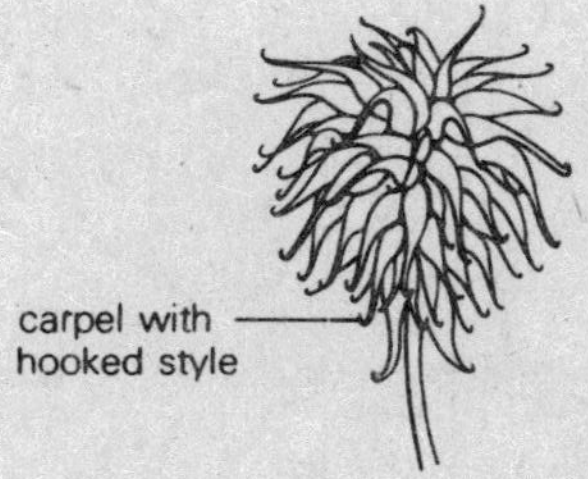

herb bennet *The hooks cling to the fur of animals, which thus disperse the seeds.*

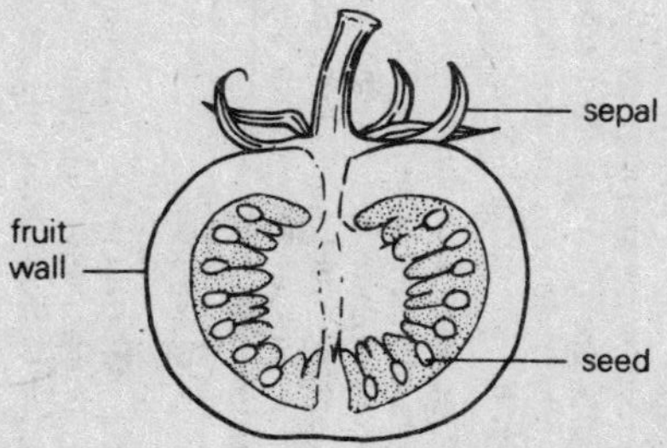

tomato *The flesh of the tomato (a berry) is formed from the ovary.*

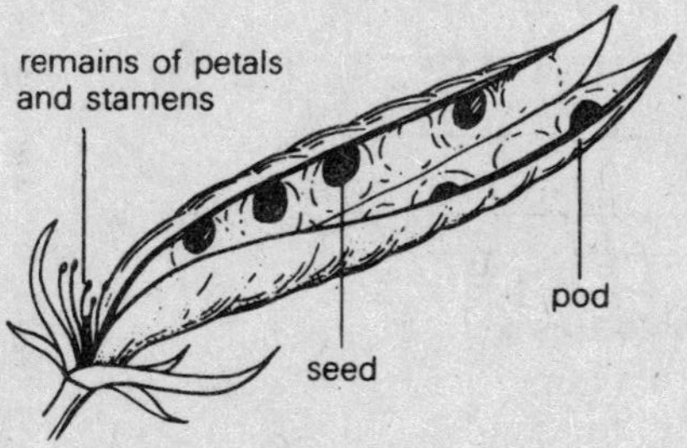

lupin *When ripe, the pod splits open and curls back, ejecting the seeds.*

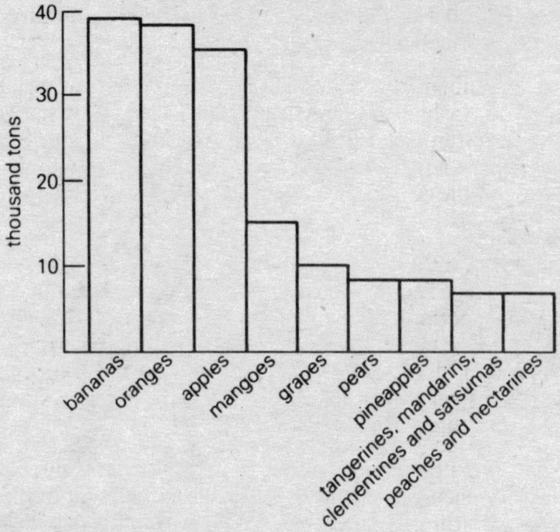

FRUIT *World production of fruit.*

Fuchsia A genus of shrubs and herbs (100 species) mostly native to tropical America and widely cultivated as ornamentals. The plants range from creeping forms, bushes, and small trees to epiphytes. They have deep-pink, red, or purple drooping flowers all along the branches; each flower has four long flaring colored sepals surrounding the shorter petals, below which the stamens and stigma protrude. Most cultivated forms are varieties of *F. magellanica*, *F. coccinea*, and *F. arborescens* or hybrids between them. Family: *Onagraceae* (willowherb family).

Fucus. *See* wrack.

fuel cell A device that converts the energy of a chemical reaction directly into an electric current. In the simplest type oxygen and hydrogen are fed through two separate porous nickel plates into an electrolytic solution. The gases combine to form water and thus set up a potential difference between the two plates. Fuel cells are distinguished from *batteries in that the latter need to be recharged and do not consume their chemicals. Fuel cells provide a clean source of power but are rather bulky.

fuel injection The pumping of fuel in the form of a spray directly into the cylinders of an *internal-combustion engine. This is necessary in the case of continuous-combustion engines, such as rocket motors and *gas turbines. In Diesel engines fuel injection is also used and in some gasoline engines it replaces the normal *carburetor as it gives a more even fuel distribution in the combustion chamber.

fuels. *See* fossil fuels.

Fugard, Athol (1932–) South African dramatist, educated at Cape Town University. His plays, which include *Blood Knot* (1969) and *Boesma and Lena* (1969), treat the plight of outcast individuals in an uncaring society with humor and humanity.

Fugger, Hans (1348–1409) German weaver, who founded a family business that dominated European finance in the 15th and 16th centuries. Through diligence and advantageous marriage the family weaving business expanded under his grandson **Jakob Fugger** (1459–1525) to include mining interests and to handle papal financial business.

Fugitives An influential group of US poets and critics associated with Vanderbilt University in Nashville, Tenn., during the 1920s. They included Allen *Tate, Robert Penn *Warren, John Crowe *Ransom, and Cleanth Brooks (1906–). The themes of their writing derived from their concern with the history and traditional culture of the American South. They published the poetry magazine *The Fugitive* (1922–25).

Fugitive Slave Laws US legislation that protected slave owners and penalized runaway slaves. The two most important were passed in 1793 and 1850. In 1793 Congress sanctioned the rights of slave owners to reclaim their fugitive slaves. Northerners countered with "personal liberty" laws and the Underground Railroad, a system of secretly transporting slaves north to freedom. The 1850 law imposed stronger penalties on those aiding fugitive slaves, precipitating even stronger opposition from the North.

fugue A piece of polyphonic music, generally having three or four parts (*or* voices), in which each part enters in turn with a statement of the main theme (*or* subject). After stating the subject each voice continues with the secondary theme (*or* counter-subject). Fugues are not composed to strict patterns; episodes in different tonalities are often interspersed with subsequent groups of entries of the voices. At the climax the voices are overlapped in close succession (*stretto*).

Fujian (Fu-chien *or* Fukien) A province in SE China, on Taiwan Strait, famous for its beauty. Over a hundred dialects have arisen among its mountain population. Since the 17th century food shortages resulting from insufficient agricultural land have prompted much emigration. It is opposite Taiwan and its military strength has been considerably increased since 1950. Chief products are sugar, rice, tea, timber, and fish. There is some light industry. Area: 47,970 sq mi (123,000 sq km). Population (1990 est): 30,050,000. Capital: Fuzhou.

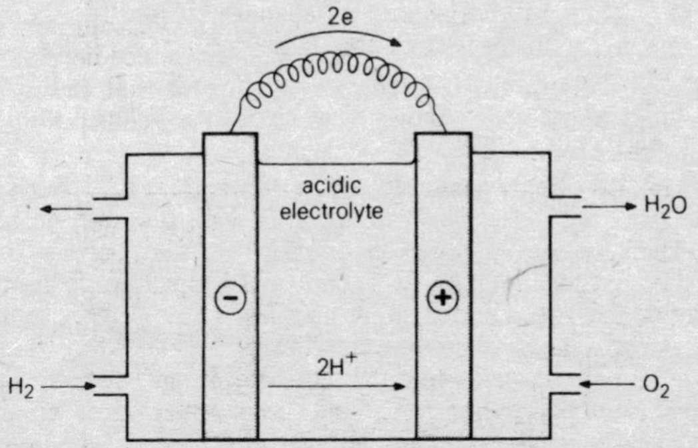

FUEL CELL *Hydrogen gas (H_2) is passed over a negative electrode containing a catalyst, which ionizes the gas into ions (H^+) and electrons (e). In an acidic electrolyte the ions migrate to the positive electrode over which oxygen is bubbled. The electrons flow through an external circuit as a current. At the positive electrode water is formed according to the equation* $2H^+ + \frac{1}{2}O_2 + 2e \rightarrow H_2O$.

Fujimori, Alberto (1958–) University professor and president of Peru (1990–). Of Japanese ancestry, he entered the 1990 presidential campaign as an outsider opposing the traditional rule by Peru's entrenched upper classes. After his upset victory in the election, he tried to improve Peru's economy by complying with terms set by international lenders and by helping the peasants, but he still faced determined opposition from revolutionary movements such as the Maoist Shining Path. Frustrated by his lack of success and disintegrating political and economic conditions Fujimori suspended the constitution and dissolved the nation's legislature in April 1992. These decisions led to widespread international criticism. He supported a new constitution, which was adopted in 1993.

Fujiwara The most illustrious of Japan's noble families. Fujiwara greatness reached a peak between the 9th and 12th centuries. From 858 the office of regent became a Fujiwara monopoly and government was mainly conducted through the Fujiwara family council. Intermarriage with the imperial family became so common that most emperors were partly of Fujiwara blood. The other base of Fujiwara power was their proprietorship of numerous private estates. From the late 11th century, however, their predominance was challenged by the reinvigorated imperial family and in the 12th century they were forced to yield most of their authority to new provincial warrior leaders.

Fujiwara style A sophisticated and refined sculptural style, also called the Heian style, prevailing in Japan from the 9th to the 12th centuries, when the Fujiwara clan was politically dominant.

Fujiyama (English name: Mount Fuji) 35 23N 138 42E The highest mountain in Japan, it is a dormant volcano in S central Honshu. Long regarded as a symbol of Japan, it has a symmetrical snow-capped (Oct–May) cone and a Shinto shrine. Height: 12,388 ft (3776 m).

Fukien. *See* Fujian.

Fukuoka 33 39N 130 21E A port in Japan in N Kyushu on Hakata Bay. An ancient commercial center, *Kublai Khan was twice defeated here (1274, 1281). Kyushu University was established in 1910. Industries include textiles and shipbuilding. Population (1990): 1,237,062.

Fukushima 37 44N 140 28E A city in Japan, in N Honshu. A major commercial center, its chief industry is silks. Population (1990): 237,528.

Fukuyama 34 29N 133 21E A city in Japan, in SW Honshu. It developed around a 17th-century castle and is now a commercial and industrial center. Population (1990): 365,612.

Fulani A Muslim people scattered over a large area of W Africa from Lake Chad to the Atlantic coast. They are a mixed Negroid and, probably, Berber racial type. Their language, known as Fulfulde (*or* Fula), belongs to the Atlantic division of the Niger-Congo family. Their social and cultural patterns are varied, reflecting influences from surrounding peoples. They were originally nomadic herdsmen but many have adopted agriculture and a sedentary way of life. The herdsmen remain egalitarian while the latter are organized more hierarchically. They are generally polygynous and favor cousin marriage, which reflects Islamic influence. In N Nigeria many adopted the *Hausa language and culture and, as a result of religious wars (1804–10), established a Muslim empire in which they were the ruling elite.

Fulbright, J(ames) William (1905–) US political leader. He was president of the University of Arkansas (1939–41) before serving in the US House of Representatives (1943–45) and US Senate (1945–75) as a Democrat. Sponsor of the Fulbright Act (1946), he was responsible for a US government international student exchange program. While chairman of the Senate Committee on Foreign

Relations (1959–75), he advocated accommodation with the communists backed by strong deterrents and opposed US involvement in Vietnam.

Fulbright Exchange program An international exchange scholarship program, devised by Senator J. W. *Fulbright after World War II. The program is ultimately the responsibility of the US Department of State, which, in association with other governments, has made more than 100,000 awards to students and teachers.

Fuliang (former name: Ching-te-chen *or* Jingdezhen) 29 17N 117 12E A town in E China, in Jiangxi province on the Chang River. It has been known for its porcelain since the 6th century AD. Population (1987 est): 309,000.

Fuller, Melville Weston (1833–1910) US jurist, lawyer, and Chief Justice of the US Supreme Court (1888–1910). He began to practice law in Chicago in 1856 and, while building up his practice, served in the Illinois state legislature as a Democrat. Appointed chief justice by Pres. Grover Cleveland, he ruled that the US income tax law of 1894 was unconstitutional (*Pollock* v. *Farmers Loan and Trust Co.,* 1895) and that the "separate but equal" segregation laws would be upheld (*Plessey* v. *Ferguson,* 1896). From 1897 to 1899 he arbitrated the Venezuelan-British boundary dispute and from 1900 to 1910 was part of the Hague Court of International Arbitration.

Fuller, (Richard) Buckminster (1895–1983) US architect and inventor. He briefly attended Harvard and embarked on an unorthodox career in which he sought to maximize energy resources through improved technology. His Dymaxion house (1928) and Dymaxion car (1933) were designed to reduce waste and environmental pollution. In 1948 he experimented with the prototype for the Wichita house, a form of inexpensive, mass-produced housing that could be easily dismanted and rebuilt. His most widely accepted architectural innovation was the *geodesic dome, a lightweight and economical structure built of mutually supporting interlocking rods. In 1958 he supervised the construction of the world's largest geodesic dome in Baton Rouge, La. Among Fuller's published works are *Operating Manual for Spaceship Earth* (1969) and *Earth Inc.* (1973).

fuller's earth A nonplastic *clay rich in montmorillonite, with the property of absorbing and decolorizing oil and grease. It was formerly used for whitening and removing the grease from fleeces (fulling). It is still used in the textile industry and in refining fats and oils. It is believed to have been formed by extremely fine-grained volcanic ash settling in water.

Fullerton 33 52N 117 55W A city in SW California, SE of Los Angeles. Machinery, paper products, and processed foods are made. Population (1990): 114,144.

fulmar A maritime North Atlantic bird, *Fulmarus glacialis.* It is about 18 in (46 cm) long and dark gray above with white underparts. Its range and numbers have increased, as a result of food in the form of offal from trawlers and whalers. Family: *Procellariidae* (petrels).

Fulton, Robert (1765–1815) US engineer and inventor. Trained as a gunsmith and draftsman, he left America in 1786 and lived in Europe for the next 20 years, eventually being recognized as a gifted inventor. Among his most famous inventions in this period were a movable ramp for canal boats, a steam-powered excavator, and an improved process for the construction of cast-iron aqueducts. Fulton also became deeply interested in naval technology, and with the support of the French government he developed (1801) the first submarine, which he called the *Nautilus.* Fulton returned to the US in 1805 and concentrated on the improvement of steam-powered navigation. He designed and constructed the *Clermont,* a side paddlewheeler, which proved its speed and reliability in a trial run from New York City to Albany in 1807. Fulton devoted the rest of his life to the establishment and maintenance of steamboat lines along the Hudson.

fumaric acid. *See* maleic acid.

fumitory A branching annual herb of the genus *Fumaria* (about 60 species), native to Eurasia and also found in North America. It has much divided compound leaves (feathery in some species) and dense spikes of pink, white, or reddish-purple flattened tubular flowers. The fruit is a nutlet. A common species is *F. officinalis.* Family: *Fumariaceae.*

Funchal 32 40N 15 55W The capital of the Madeira Islands, Portugal on the S coast of Madeira. Its mild climate and picturesque setting make it a popular tourist resort and it has a cathedral (1485–1514). The islands' chief commercial center, it exports Madeira wines, embroidery, and wickerwork. Population (1980 est): 100,000.

functionalism (architecture) A doctrine principally associated with the *international style. Its main tenet is that the more fitted to its purpose a building is, the more beautiful it will be. The doctrine was developed under Louis *Sullivan in the 1890s, but found its most vocal advocate in *Le Corbusier, who defined a house as a machine for living in. Functionalism led to a very severe style, lacking in all ornamentation and idiosyncracy. Although still influential, its dominance faded after 1930, and function is no longer accepted as the sole attribute of beauty in architecture.

functionalism (sociology) A perspective, based on an analogy with the workings of a biological organism, which emphasizes the contribution constituent parts of a society (groups and institutions) make to the continuity or change of the whole society. Also known as structural-functionalism, the approach was used by *Durkheim and was a major influence in sociology in the US and the UK after World War II as a result of the work of Talcott *Parsons.

fundamental constants Any of several constants that frequently appear in physical equations. The term is often reserved for five constants: the velocity of *light (c), *Planck's constant (h), the charge (e) and mass (m_e) of the *electron, and the fine structure constant (α). The latter is defined as $e^2/2hc\epsilon_0$, where ϵ_0 is the electric constant; its value is approximately 1/137 and it is a measure of the strength of the *electromagnetic interaction. These constants may be regarded as fundamental in that their values determine the magnitude of many physical effects. Other constants sometimes taken as fundamental include the electric constant, the magnetic constant, Avogadro's number, the Boltzmann constant, and the gravitational constant.

fundamentalism A religious movement among some US Protestants arising after World War I. It insisted on the completely literal truth of the Bible, of the New Testament miracles, and of such traditional teachings as the Virgin Birth and bodily resurrection of Christ. It rejected any scientific knowledge, such as the theory of evolution, which conflicted with a literal reading of the Bible. Interest in fundamentalism increased dramatically in the late 1970s and early 1980s.

Fundy, Bay of An inlet of the Atlantic Ocean in SE Canada, between Nova Scotia and New Brunswick. Long and narrow, it has tides up to 66 ft (20 m) high, from which electricity is generated.

Fünen. *See* Fyn.

Fünfkirchen. *See* Pécs.

fungi Unicellular or multicellular organisms belonging to the group *Mycota* (about 50,000 known species), usually regarded as plants and including mushrooms, mildews, molds, yeasts, etc. All fungi lack chlorophyll and therefore (unlike green plants) cannot manufacture their own food by photosynthesis. Some are saprophytes, feeding on dead organic matter by means of digestive enzymes; others are parasites of plants or animals. The body of most fungi consists of a network of branching threadlike structures (hyphae), forming a mycelium. Sexual reproduction results in the formation of spores, which may be produced in a specialized structure called a fruiting body: this is the visible part of mushrooms, puffballs, etc. Other fungi consist of single cells, which can reproduce asexually by simple division into two daughter cells. Fungi are distributed worldwide in terrestrial, freshwater, and marine habitats. Some live in the soil and play a vital role in bringing about *decomposition of dead organic matter. Other fungi (e.g. *Penicillium* and *Streptomyces*) are of great importance as a source of *antibiotics. Many parasitic fungi cause disease in animals and man (*see* infection) or in plants (e.g. the smuts and rusts), while some saprophytes are destructive to timber (*see* dry rot). Some fungi form associations with other plants, most notably with algae to form *lichens.

funnel weaver A *spider, also called funnel web spider, belonging to a worldwide family (*Agelenidae*). It builds funnel-shaped webs in grass, among debris, and under rocks and floorboards. The grass spider (*Agelena naevia*), 0.75 in (18–19 mm) long, is a common North American species.

fur The skin of certain mammals including its covering of hair. The hair is usually short and soft next to the skin for insulation with longer guard hairs forming an outer protective layer. The untreated skins (pelts) of such animals as sheep, mink, rabbits, chinchilla, etc., are cleaned and stretched before undergoing tanning to make the skin into *leather. Many wild fur-bearing species are now protected to prevent them from becoming extinct and "furs" made from synthetic fibers have replaced many natural fashion furs.

Furies. *See* Erinyes.

furlong A unit of length traditionally based on the length of a furrow. It is equal to 220 yards (⅛ mile; 200 m) and is still used in horseracing.

Furneaux Islands 40 0S 148 0E An Australian group of islands, in Bass Strait off the NE coast of Tasmania. The chief islands are Flinders (the largest), Cape Barren, and Clarke. Sheep farming is the principal activity.

furniture Movable domestic artifacts, which are indispensable for civilized life. Examples exist from as early as 3000 BC in Egypt. In Europe medieval furniture was gothic in style and consisted principally of *chests, beds, seats, and tables, but Renaissance designers and craftsmen, working exclusively for the noble and rich, produced work in which function was subordinated to art, such as cabinets richly ornamented with jewels and precious metals. During the 17th and 18th centuries architects, such as Robert *Adam, were increasingly concerned with the design of furniture for the interiors of their buildings. Such furniture ranked with paintings and other arts, both socially and economically.

In the 19th century, factory production led to debased design against which a few progressive designers, notably William *Morris, struggled. The 20th century has seen the introduction of simplified design and new materials, such as steel and plastic, reflecting modern functional needs.

Fürstenbund A league of German princes founded in 1785 and led by Frederick the Great of Prussia. Intended as a temporary expedient against Hapsburg ambitions in Germany, the league was Prussia's first attempt to unite the other German states under its leadership, finally achieved in 1871.

Fürth 49 28N 11 00E A city in S Germany, near Nuremberg in Bavaria on the Regnitz River. The Fürth-Nuremberg railroad line (1835) was the first in Germany. Toys and mirrors are manufactured. Population (1984): 98,500.

furze. *See* gorse.

fuse, electrical A length of wire designed to melt when the electric current passing through it exceeds a specified safe level, thus breaking the circuit. It is used to protect electrical equipment and low-voltage wiring, *circuit breakers being used for higher voltages. Domestic fuses commonly consisted of a length of fuse wire (usually tin or copper alloys) mounted in a glass screw plug.

Fuseli, Henry (Johann Heinrich Füssli; 1741–1825) British painter of Swiss birth. He first worked as a translator of foreign books in London before studying art in Rome (1770–78). On his return his paintings, notably *Nightmare* (1782) and his illustrations of Shakespeare and Milton, showed his taste for horror and drama. He became professor of painting at the Royal Academy in 1799 and Keeper in 1804.

fusel oil A liquid mixture of organic substances including butanol and isoamyl alcohol. It has an unpleasant smell and taste and is a by-product of the distillation of alcohol produced by fermentation.

Fushun 41 51N 123 53E A city in NE China, in Liaoning province. Its oil, steel, and chemical industries are based on its oil-shale and vast coal deposits. Aluminum production is also important. Population: (1990): 1,202,388.

fusion (physics). *See* nuclear energy.

Fust, Johann (1400–66) German printer, who financed *Gutenberg's development of the printing press. Fust sued Gutenberg for the repayment of his loan and, when Gutenberg was unable to repay it, took possession of his equipment and set up the first successful printing firm.

Futa Jallon. *See* Fouta Djallon.

Futuna Islands. *See* Wallis and Futuna.

futurism **1.** In Italy, an early 20th-century movement in the arts. It was founded in 1909, when the poet *Marinetti published a literary manifesto demanding the obliteration of past Italian culture and the establishment of a new society, literature, and art glorifying the speed and mechanization of modern life. A second manifesto (1910) was published by artists led by *Boccioni, *Balla, and *Severini. Using a cubist style and such subjects as cars, trains, moving animals, etc., they aimed to represent multiple phases of motion in one painting. Italian futurism died during World War I but its influence was sustained in subsequent art movements, notably *vorticism. **2.** In Russia, a movement that rejected traditional Russian literature. *Mayakovskii and *Khlebnikov were among the writers and artists who signed a manifesto called "A Slap in the Face for Public Taste" (1912) and adopted an experimental and innovative attitude toward language. The Russian futurists supported the Revolution but were curbed in the 1930s by the Soviet government.

Fuzhou (Fu-chou *or* Foochow) 26 10N 119 20E A port in SE China, the capital of Fujian province on the Min delta. An ancient capital, it was the center of foreign trade from the 10th–19th centuries. It is the site of Fujian Medical University. It has varied industries and its exports include timber and sugar cane. Population (1990): 874,809.

Fylingdales The site of an early-warning radar station in NE England, in North Yorkshire, built to give warning of nuclear attack.

Fyn (German name: Fünen) The second largest Danish island, situated between the Little Belt and the Great Belt. Fishing is important and its fertile soil supports cereal growing, dairy farming, and cattle rearing. Area: 1344 sq mi (3481 sq km).

G

gabbro A dark-colored coarse-grained basic igneous rock formed by the crystallization at depth of basalt magma. It is the plutonic equivalent of basalt. Calcic plagioclase feldspar (usually labradorite), clinopyroxene (usually augite), and frequently olivine are the main constitutents. Gabbro usually occurs in layered complexes or igneous intrusions.

Gaberones. *See* Gaborone.

Gabin, Jean (Jean-Alexis Moncorgé; 1904–76) French film actor. He is best known for his portrayals of brave but vulnerable heroes in films during the 1930s, notably *La Grande Illusion* (1937) and *Le Jour se lève* (1939). His later films include *L'Affaire Dominici* (1973).

Gable, (William) Clark (1901–60) US film actor. He established his popularity as a leading man during the early 1930s, when he played many tough masculine roles. His films include *A Free Soul* (1931), *It Happened One Night* (1934), which earned him an Academy Award, *Gone with the Wind* (1939), and *The Misfits* (1961).

Gabo, Naum (Naum Neemia Pevsner; 1890–1977) Russian sculptor. A pioneer of *constructivism, he and his brother Antoine *Pevsner formulated its main ideals in their *Realist Manifesto* published in Russia in 1920. Working later in Berlin (1923–33), England (1936–45), and the US after 1946, he made numerous constructions of glass, plastic, metals, etc., a favorite device being nylon threads stretched over a plastic framework.

Gabon, Republic of An equatorial country in West Africa, on the Gulf of Guinea. Coastal plains rise to plateaus on either side of the Ogooué basin. The population is mainly Fang. *Economy*: almost three-quarters of the land is forested and timber was formerly the most important resource, especially okoumé, a soft wood used for plywood. Now, however, the exploitation of its vast mineral wealth forms the basis of the economy. Oil production is by far the chief revenue producer, giving Gabon the highest per-capita income in sub-Saharan Africa; however, by the 1990s, oil supplies were nearly depleted. Production of natural gas is rapidly increasing; other minerals include iron ore, uranium, and manganese, of which Gabon has one of the richest deposits. Mining and forestry are both hindered by transport difficulties but this is now being improved by the construction of the trans-Gabon railroad. Agriculture consists chiefly of subsistence farming. The main exports are oil, timber, manganese, and uranium. *History*: trading posts were set up by the Portuguese in the late 15th century and the area later became a center of the slave trade. Settled by the French in the mid-19th century, it became one of the four territories of French Equatorial Africa in 1910. It gained internal self-government as a member of the French Community in 1958 and became independent in 1960. Gabon instituted a one-party political system in 1967 but in 1980 permitted independent candidates to run in legislative elections. Nonetheless, the ruling party captured all the seats. Student protest movements and opposition from the underground antigovernment group known as *morena* characterized Gabon's social and political climate in the 1980s. Anti-French sentiments and pro-*morena* support in some French circles created a strain in relations between the two countries. Prodemocracy demonstrations in 1990 were marked by violence, and France sent troops to keep order. The first multiparty elections were held later that year amid speculation that they were rigged in favor of President Bongo. In 1993, Gabon hosted the second African/African-American Summit. President: Omar Bongo. Official language: French; Bantu languages are widely spoken. Official currency: CFA (Communauté financière africaine) franc of 100 centimes. Area: 103,089 sq mi (267,000 sq km). Population (1988): 1,222,000. Capital and main port: Libreville.

gaboon viper A highly venomous *puff adder, *Bitis gabonica,* occurring in African rain forests. Up to 7 ft (2 m) long, it has a thick body and a broad head with hornlike projections on its snout and is patterned with buff, brown, and purple rectangles and triangles. It feeds on small mammals, gamebirds, lizards, and frogs.

Gabor, Dennis (1900–79) British electrical engineer, born in Hungary. He won the 1971 Nobel Prize for physics for his invention of *holography.

Gaborone (former name: Gaberones) 24 45S 25 55E The capital of Botswana. The seat of government was transferred here from Mafeking in 1965. It contains part of the University of Botswana and Swaziland. Population (1988): 110,000.

Gabriel (c. 1776–1800) The leader of the first significant US slave uprising. He planned to attack Richmond, Va., with a thousand slaves, seize the arsenal, and establish an independent African-American state. An informer warned the governor and Gabriel was captured and hanged with other rebels.

Gabrieli, Andrea (c. 1520–86) Italian composer and organist. He became chief organist of St Mark's, Venice, in 1585; he composed madrigals, motets, and instrumental and organ music. His nephew **Giovanni Gabrieli** (c. 1557–1612) became second organist of St Mark's in 1585. He was one of the first composers to incorporate instrumental parts into vocal works and to write antiphonal music for several choirs or orchestras.

Gad, tribe of One of the 12 *tribes of Israel. It claimed descent from Gad, the son of Jacob and his concubine Zilpah. Its territory was in Transjordan, NE of the Dead Sea.

Gaddafi, Moammar al- (*or* Qaddafi; 1942–) Libyan colonel and statesman. In 1969 he led a revolt that overthrew the Libyan monarchy and in 1970 became chairman of the Revolutionary Command Council. His Arab nationalist and Islamic socialist policies have led to a reorganization of Libyan society and an active foreign policy. He favored territorial acquisition and often supported terrorism. However, during the Persian Gulf crisis of 1990–91, he urged a diplomatic settlement rather than war.

Gaddi, Taddeo (c. 1300–66?) Florentine painter, who was the pupil and assistant of *Giotto. His independent works include the frescoes of the *Life of the Virgin* (Baroncelli Chapel, Sta Croce, Florence). His son **Agnolo Gaddi** (c. 1350–96), also influenced by Giotto, painted frescoes of the *Story of the True Cross* in the choir of Sta Croce and the *Life of the Virgin* (Duomo, Prato).

gadfly A *botfly or *warble fly whose parasitic larvae irritate animals, arousing them to bursts of frantic running.

gadolinium (Gd) A *lanthanide element named for the Finnish chemist J. Gadolin (1760–1852). It is used in television-tube phosphors. At no 64; at wt 157.25; mp 2398°F (1313°C); bp 5857°F (3233°C).

Gadsden Purchase (1853–54) A treaty between the US and Mexico providing for the transfer of approx. 30,000 sq mi (78,000 sq km) of territory S of the Gila River. Since the Treaty of Guadalupe Hidalgo, which ended the *Mexican War, did not clearly define the boundary between the two countries, Pres. Franklin *Pierce authorized his minister to Mexico, James Gadsden, to negotiate for the purchase of a strip of land that would consolidate American claims in the area. The purchase price eventually agreed upon was $10 million. The territory within the Gadsden Purchase later became part of the states of Arizona and New Mexico.

gadwall A *dabbling duck, *Anas strepera,* that breeds in sheltered inland fresh waters of North America and Eurasia and winters in S Europe, Africa, and the S United States. It is 19–20 in (48–51 cm) long and has a gray barred plumage, a brown head and rump, and white and reddish wing markings.

Gaea (*or* Gaia) A Greek goddess personifying the earth. The wife and mother of Uranus (Heaven), by whom she bore the *Titans, the *Cyclops, and the *Gigantes, she incited the revolt of the Titans against him. From the blood of the wounded Uranus were born the *Erinyes.

Gaelic A language of the Goidelic group of *Celtic languages. Irish Gaelic is spoken in Ireland as a first language by approximately 100,000 people and as a second language by around 700,000. It is an official language of the Republic of Ireland. Scottish Gaelic (*or* Erse), which is spoken in the NW coastal region of Scotland and in the Hebrides, is an offshoot of Irish Gaelic that became a distinct dialect around the 13th century.

Gagarin, Yuri Alekseevich (1934–68) Soviet cosmonaut, who on Apr 12, 1961, became the first person to orbit the earth. He remained in orbit for 89 minutes, reaching a height of about 187 mi (301 km). He died when a plane he was testing crashed.

Gage, Thomas (1721–87) British soldier; commander in chief of British forces in North America (1763–74). His hostility to the grievances of the colonists contributed to the outbreak of the *American Revolution. He helped to draft the *Intolerable Acts in response to the *Boston Tea Party. He was replaced by William *Howe after military failures at the start of the Revolution.

Gaia. *See* Gaea.

Gaillardia A genus of herbaceous plants (about 20 species), native to North America. Several species are cultivated in gardens, especially the blanket flowers *G. aristata* and *G. grandiflora* (perennials) and *G. pulchella* (an annual). The single or double daisylike flowers have purple centers and yellow, orange, or white fringed ray florets. Family: **Compositae.*

Gainsborough, Thomas (1727–88) British portrait and landscape painter. His training with the French engraver Gravelot, introduced him to *rococo portraiture. He also studied the art of *Van Dyck, whose elegant style is reflected in Gainsborough's *Countess Howe* and the *Blue Boy*. His landscapes were at first influenced by *Ruisdael and *Hobbema and later by *Rubens, particularly in the *Harvest Wagon*. In his later years he painted idyllic rustic scenes. He was a founding member of the Royal Academy.

Gainesville 29 40N 82 20W A city in N central Florida, SW of Jacksonsville. The University of Florida, established in 1853, is here. Important industries are lumber and concrete products and food processing. Population (1990): 84,770.

Gaitskell, Hugh (Todd Naylor) (1906–63) British politician; leader of the Labour Party (1955–63). He was elected to Parliament in 1945 and became chancellor of the exchequer (1950–51). After the defeat of the Labour Party in the 1959 general election, Gaitskell unsuccessfully attempted to change the constitution. After the divisive 1960 party conference, Gaitskell engineered (1961) the reversal of the party's controversial disarmament policy and reunited the party.

galactic cluster. *See* star cluster.

GAINSBOROUGH The Painter's Daughters with a Cat. *This unfinished picture was painted soon after 1759, when the painter began seeking fashionable clients.*

galago. *See* bushbaby.

Galahad In *Arthurian legend, the son of *Lancelot and Elaine. As the most perfect exemplar of knighthood, he was (in many romances) the only knight to succeed in the quest of the *Holy Grail.

galangal A flavoring obtained from the rhizomes of a Chinese perennial herb, *Alpinia officinarum,* that may be used in place of ginger. The plant grows to a height of 20 ft (6 m), with long bladed leathery leaves and pink, yellow, or white fragrant flowers borne in long dense clusters. Family: *Zingiberaceae.*

Galápagos finches. *See* Darwin's finches.

Galápagos giant tortoise A large rare *tortoise, *Testudo elephantopus,* found on the Galápagos Islands, where they were formerly slaughtered for meat. Up to 5 ft (1.5 m) long and weighing up to 331 lb (150 kg), there are numerous subspecies, some now extinct, distinguishable by their different shell shapes. The only other surviving species of giant tortoise is *T. gigantica* of the Seychelles.

Galápagos Islands (Spanish name: Archipiélago de Colón) An archipelago of Equador in the Pacific Ocean, W of the mainland. It consists of 12 main islands and several smaller ones, all of volcanic origin. They became well known following Charles *Darwin's visit in 1835, during which he collected evidence that influenced his theories on natural selection. The islands contain a large number of endemic species, including the giant tortoise; many islands now form nature reserves. Area: 2868 sq mi (7428 sq km).

Galatea **1.** In Greek legend, a nymph who loved the shepherd Acis and was loved by Polyphemus. When Acis was killed by his rival she turned him into a river. **2.** The name of a statue that came to life in answer to the prayers of *Pygmalion.

Galaţi 45 27N 28 02E A port in E Romania, on the Danube River. Largely rebuilt after World War II, it has a naval base, the country's largest shipyards, and iron, steel, and textile industries. Population (1992 est): 325,000.

Galatians, Epistle of Paul to the A New Testament book written by the Apostle Paul to churches in central Asia Minor in the middle of the 1st century AD. In it he defends his claim to be the apostle to the Gentiles, expounds justification by faith, and warns against those who were encouraging the converts to rely on Jewish ceremonial rites for their acceptance by God.

galaxies Huge assemblies of many millions of stars, gas, and dust, bound together by gravitational interactions. The majority are not independent systems but are members of clusters of galaxies. Almost all the matter in the universe is concentrated in galaxies and clusters of galaxies. **Spiral galaxies** are large flattened systems with spiral arms winding outward from a central nucleus. **Elliptical galaxies** are actually spheroidal, possibly sometimes even spherical, with no clear internal structure. They vary greatly in size and mass, the largest giant ellipticals exceeding 10^{12} solar masses. The third general category, **irregular galaxies**, have no definite shape or structure.

Galaxy (*or* Milky Way system) The spiral *galaxy to which the sun belongs. It contains about a hundred thousand million (10^{11}) stars. Most lie in the flattened galactic disk, comprising two spiral arms that wind out from a bulging central nucleus; the sun is about 33,000 light years from the center. The roughly spherical halo surrounds the nucleus and disk; it is only sparsely populated with stars and globular *star clusters.

Galbraith, John Kenneth (1908–) US economist and diplomat, born in Canada. He became a professor of economics at Harvard University in 1949. As a disciple of the economic philosophy established by John Maynard *Keynes, Galbraith skillfully analyzed the post-World War II US economy in his critically acclaimed works *American Capitalism: The Concept of Countervailing Power* (1952) and *The Affluent Society* (1958). During the administration of Pres. John F. Kennedy, Galbraith served as US ambassador to India (1961–63). Returning to Harvard, Galbraith became increasingly involved in current affairs. Among his later books are *The New Industrial State* (1967), *Economics and the Public Purpose* (1973), and his autobiography, *A Life in Our Times* (1981).

Galen (129–c. 199 AD) Greek physician and scholar, whose ideas dominated medicine until the Renaissance. From his studies of such animals as monkeys and dogs, Galen showed the importance of the spinal cord in muscle activity, the role of the ureter in kidney and bladder function, and that arteries carry blood rather than air. However, he held mistaken views on blood circulation, including the idea that blood seeped through minute pores in the wall of the heart separating the two ventricles. Galen also wrote on philosophy, law, and mathematics and his medical writings were later translated into Arabic and Latin.

galena The principal ore of lead. It is a lead-gray dense but soft metallic mineral, found as cubic crystals of lead sulfide in hydrothermal veins and as replacement deposits in limestones. Galena ore bodies almost always contain silver, and much of the world's silver comes from these ores.

Galerius (Gaius Galerius Valerius Maximianus; c. 250–311 AD) Eastern Roman emperor (305–11) after the abdication of Diocletian. Galerius was probably responsible for continuing the persecution of the Christians begun by Diocletian in 303 but in 311 he proclaimed a limited toleration of Christianity. His authority was challenged by the emperor in the West and the ensuing conflict lasted until 308.

Galicia 1. A medieval kingdom in NW Spain, now in La Coruña, Pontevedra, Lugo, and Orense. Galicia was colonized by the *Visigoths from the 6th century and became a subkingdom of Castile in the late 11th century. It retained its own flourishing language and culture. 2. A province in E Europe, which became an independent principality in 1087 until conquered by the Mongols in the 13th century. Subsequently part of Poland (14th century) and Austria (18th century), Galicia was divided between Poland and Austria after World War I and Poland and the Soviet Union after World War II. The Soviet part is now part of Ukraine.

Galilee A district of N Israel, bordering on the Jordan River and the Sea of Galilee. It comprised the northernmost region of ancient Palestine and is famous as the scene of Jesus Christ's early ministry. Under the Romans, Galileans were noted for their religious zeal and nationalism and from the fall of Jerusalem (70 AD) to the Middle Ages Galilee was a center for rabbinic scholarship. From 1892, a number of Zionist settlements were established in Galilee, which was included in its entirety in the state of Israel (1949). *See also* Zealots.

Galilee, Sea of (Sea of Tiberias *or* Lake of Gennesaret; Hebrew name: Yam Kinneret) A lake in NE Israel. It is fed mainly by and drained by the Jordan River; its surface is 686 ft (209 m) below sea level. It was the scene of many episodes in the life of Christ. Area: 64 sq mi (166 sq km).

Galileo Galilei (1564–1642) Italian mathematician, physicist, and astronomer, whose emphasis on mathematical analysis anticipated the experimental method of scientific inquiry. Born in Pisa, legend has it that he demonstrated that the rate of fall of a body is independent of its mass by dropping weights from the Leaning Tower of Pisa. He is also reputed to have worked out that the period of a pendulum is independent of its amplitude by watching a swinging chandelier in Pisa Cathedral. In 1609 Galileo, on learning of the invention of a simple telescope, designed one himself and used it to study the sky. He soon made a number of discoveries, including sunspots and Jupiter's satellites, which convinced him of the superiority of *Copernicus's heliocentric system over the *Ptolemaic system. He wrote a witty and vigorous book, *Dialogue on Two World Systems* (1632), in which he presented these two opposite viewpoints, making Ptolemy's system look foolish. As the Roman Catholic Church had condemned Copernicus's work in 1616, Galileo was forced by the Inquisition to recant his views and placed under house arrest for the rest of his life. In a probably apocryphal story Galileo, following his recantation, is said to have murmured "Eppur si muove" ("Still it moves," referring to the earth, which the Church insisted was stationary at the center of the universe).

gall A swelling or excrescence on plants caused by abnormal proliferation of cells, which can be caused by mechanical injury but is more often the result of attack by insects, mites, fungi, bacteria, or viruses. Some galls are self-limiting, including the oak apples caused by the *gall wasp, while others are tumorous, such as the crown gall induced by the bacterium *Agrobacterium tumefaciens.*

Gall, Franz Joseph (1758–1828) German physician and founder of the practice of *phrenology. He held the view that the shape of the skull reflected the shape of the underlying brain and hence the character of the individual. Although this idea is now discredited, Gall's work did provide a stimulus for research on the brain itself.

Galla A people of Ethiopia numbering about 10 million and making up about 40% of the Ethiopian population. They were originally nomads who spread from the SE region during the 16th century to many other areas, where they largely adopted a sedentary existence and local customs, losing their own distinctiveness. Their language belongs to the *Hamito-Semitic family.

Gallatin, (Abraham Alfonse) Albert (1761–1849) US statesman, born in Switzerland. He settled in Pennsylvania as a young man and was instrumental in helping to settle the Whiskey Rebellion of 1794. He then became a US Congressman (1795–1801), establishing the House Committee on Finance. President Jefferson appointed him secretary of the treasury (1801–13); during his term he was responsible for reducing the national debt. He went to Europe to negotiate the Treaty of Ghent (1814), which ended the War of 1812, and stayed on as minister to France (1816–23). He also was minister to Britain (1826–27).

gall bladder A saclike organ 2.8–4 in (7–10 cm) long, close to the liver, that receives and stores *bile (formerly called gall) formed by the liver. The gall bladder is connected to the liver by the hepatic ducts and to the intestine by the common bile duct. Crystallization of bile components forms *gallstones, which may block the bile duct or cause gall bladder infections (cholecystitis).

Galle (former name: Point de Galle) 6 01N 80 13E A seaport in SW Sri Lanka. The country's chief port under the Portuguese and its capital under the Dutch, it declined with the growth of Colombo. It has a cement factory. Population (1981): 77,183.

Galle, Johann Gottfried (1812–1910) German astronomer, who was the first to observe *Neptune. *Leverrier predicted (1846) the existence of Neptune and asked Galle to search the area in which he expected it to be. Galle discovered it the same day.

galleon A large oceangoing sailing vessel of the 15th–19th centuries, usually having a tall stern and high sides. Galleons were typically square-rigged on the foremast and mainmast and lateen-rigged on one or two after masts. They were widely used by the Spanish in the 16th and 17th centuries as transport between Europe and the New World and were often attacked and captured by pirates. Several sunken galleons, with their treasures still aboard, have been located by divers in the Caribbean Sea.

Gallicanism A movement in France asserting the rights of the French Roman Catholic Church, clergy, and monarchy against papal interference. It was an issue as early as the 13th century but reached its zenith in 1682 with the promulgation by the French bishops, at Louis XIV's instigation, of Four Gallican Articles defending the king's authority in temporal affairs and recognizing the authority of a general council of the Church over that of the pope.

Galli-Curci, Amelita (1882–1963) Italian coloratura soprano. Largely self-taught, she made her debut in Rome in 1909 as Gilda in Verdi's *Rigoletto*. She achieved great success in the same role at her New York debut (1916). She retired, owing to illness, in 1930.

Gallic Wars (58–51 BC) The campaigns in which Julius Caesar annexed Transalpine *Gaul (France). Caesar's intervention in Gallic intertribal warfare was prompted by concern for Italian security; his ambition to conquer Gaul for the Romans developed later. NE Gaul was pacified by 57 BC and the tribes along the Atlantic coast by 56 BC. In 52 Caesar defeated the tribes of central Gaul, led by *Vercingetorix. Caesar's own account of the Gallic Wars has survived.

gallinule A bird belonging to the family *Rallidae* (rails). Gallinules are widely distributed, occurring on semistagnant water, such as ponds, edged by dense vegetation, and commonly have blue, green, or purple plumage for camouflage. They are 12–18 in (30–45 cm) long and have long slender toes enabling them to run over floating vegetation. *See also* moorhen.

Gallipoli (Turkish name: Gelibolu) 40 25N 26 41E A seaport in European Turkey, on the NE coast of the Dardanelles. Taken by Turkey in about 1356, it is strategically important for the defense of Istanbul. The town had to be largely rebuilt after the Gallipoli campaign (*see* World War I). Population (1970): 14,600.

gallium (Ga) A metallic element with a low melting point and high boiling point, discovered in 1875 by Lecoq de Boisbaudran. Gallium is found as a trace element in a number of minerals and is often concentrated in chimney soot. **Gallium arsenide** (GaAs) is a *semiconductor that is widely used in electronic devices, particularly the field-effect *transistor and the Gunn diode (*see* Gunn effect). At no 31; at wt 69.72; mp 86°F (29.78°C); bp 4362°F (2403°C).

Gällivare 67 10N 20 40E A city in N Sweden. The main industry is iron mining, based on the rich deposits discovered in the 18th century. Population: 25,417.

gall midge A small delicate fly with hairy antennae, also called a gallfly and gall gnat, belonging to the family *Cecidomyiidae.* The majority of species eat plants and lay their eggs in galls. Others are general scavengers or predators and parasites upon other insects. *See also* gall wasp.

gallstones Stones in the *gall bladder formed from *cholesterol, *bile pigments, or most usually a mixture of both. In some people they cause no symptoms; in others they may give rise to pain, indigestion, nausea, and vomiting. The usual treatment is surgical removal of the gall bladder (cholecystectomy).

Gallup, George Horace (1901–84) US public-opinion pollster. The techniques that he devised for gauging public opinion while working in advertising became a standard feature of political life. In 1935 he established the American Institute of Public Opinion and successfully predicted the US presidential election in 1936. Afterward his polling organization grew rapidly.

gall wasp A small *wasp 0.24–0.31 in (6–8 mm) long, also called gallfly, belonging to the family *Cynipidae.* Gall wasps lay their eggs in plant tissues, particularly oak trees and rose plants, which respond by producing *galls. Thus, *Biorhiza pallida* produces the oak apple gall and *Diplolepis rosae* produces the robin's pincushion gall.

Galois, Évariste (1811–32) French mathematician, who pioneered the branch of modern mathematics known as group theory. His life was dogged by ill luck; three papers that he submitted to the Académie des Sciences were rejected or lost and he was refused admission to the École Polytechnique. He turned to politics, supporting the Republican cause, and was twice arrested. He died following a duel.

Galsworthy, John (1867–1933) British novelist and dramatist. He studied law but embarked on a literary career in 1897 with a volume of short stories, published pseudonymously. *The Man of Property* (1906) began the famous novel series *The Forsyte Saga,* chronicling the decline of a rich English family. His plays, usually rather artificial expositions of moral and social issues, include *The Silver Box* (1906) and *Strife* (1909).

Galton, Sir Francis (1822–1911) British scientist, who studied methods of improving the mental and physical abilities of human populations by selective mating, a science that he called *eugenics. Galton argued that mental as well as physical attributes were inherited, an idea that his cousin Charles *Darwin later endorsed. Galton also made contributions to meteorology and pioneered the use of fingerprinting for personal identification.

Galvani, Luigi (1737–98) Italian physician, who pioneered research into the electrical properties of living things. He observed how frog muscles twitched when they were touched by metal contacts but he wrongly attributed this to innate "animal electricity" (the current was actually produced by the metal contacts). The *galvanometer was named for him.

galvanized steel Steel coated with zinc to prevent corrosion. The zinc may be deposited by electroplating the steel in molten zinc, spraying with molten zinc, or by coating it with zinc powder and heating it.

galvanometer An instrument for measuring small electric currents. The moving-coil galvanometer consists of a coil of wire suspended in a magnetic field. A current passing through the coil causes it to rotate until balanced by the opposing torsion in the suspending thread. The angle of rotation is used to measure the current. In the moving-magnet instrument the magnet is suspended in the earth's magnetic field and deflection is caused by a current passing through the surrounding coil.

Galveston 29 17N 94 48W A city in Texas, on the Gulf of Mexico. Subject to hurricanes (one of which killed 8000 people in 1900), it has had to undertake large protective schemes. Its port handles sulfur, cotton, and wheat and industries include chemicals and hardware. Population (1990): 59,070.

Galway (Irish name: Gallimh) 53 16N 9 03W A port in the Republic of Ireland, the county town of Co Galway. It has the University College (founded 1845), part of the National University of Ireland, and a Roman Catholic cathedral (begun 1957). The Galway Theatre produces Irish-language plays. Salmon and eel fishing are important. Population (1991): 50,842.

Galway, James (1939–) Irish flautist of worldwide reputation. He studied in Paris with Jean-Pierre Rampal. His silver and gold flutes were made to his own specifications. The composer Rodrigo wrote his *Concierto pastorale* (for flute and orchestra; 1978) for him.

Gama, Vasco da (c. 1469–1524) Portuguese navigator. In 1497, under the patronage of *Manuel I, he departed with three ships to continue *Dias's search for the route to India. He rounded the Cape of Good Hope and reached Mozambique and Malindi (now in Kenya). Aided by an Indian pilot he crossed to Calicut (1498). Received with hostility by the Indians, he withdrew. Following the murder of the Portuguese settlers left by Cabral's expedition to Calicut, da Gama was sent out on a punitive expedition (1502) to establish Portugal's influence in the Indian Ocean. He bombarded Calicut and returned to Portugal with considerable amounts of booty. Some 20 years later he went back to India as Portuguese viceroy and died there.

Gambetta, Léon (1838–82) French statesman. A lawyer, Gambetta, who was an opponent of *Napoleon III (1868), was elected to the Legislative Assembly in 1869. Strongly republican, he took advantage of the capture of Napoleon in 1870 in the *Franco-Prussian War to proclaim a provisional government of national defense. His spectacular escape from besieged Paris in a balloon and his courageous organization of the defenses of France from Tours earned him a wide and popular reputation. He was instrumental in founding the *Third Republic but his term as prime minister (1881–82) was unsuccessful because of opposition to his democratic policies and he was forced to resign.

Gambia, Republic of The A country in West Africa, on the Atlantic Ocean, occupying a narrow strip along the Gambia River and surrounded by Senegalese territory. Swamps along the river give way to drier savanna. The majority of the inhabitants are Mandingo. *Economy*: overwhelmingly agricultural, producing groundnuts for export and rice for the home market. Mineral resources are sparse and there is little industry. Attempts to develop the economy include plans for an oil refinery and tourism is being encouraged. *History*: in the 15th century the mouth of the Gambia River was explored by the Portuguese and, in the 16th century, by the English, who established a trading settlement on James Island in 1661. The area was administered from the British colony of Sierra Leone from 1807 until 1843, when it became a crown colony until again coming under Sierra Leone in 1866. Separated again in 1888, it achieved internal self-government in 1963 and independence in 1965 with Sir Dawda Jawara as president, becoming a republic within the British Commonwealth in 1970. An attempted coup in 1981 was subdued with military aid from Senegal; close ties between the two countries were reinforced with the formation of the Senegambia Confederation in 1982. In 1990, Gambia joined a coalition of West African troops that helped to enforce a ceasefire in Liberia. Official language: English. Official currency: dalasi of 100 butut. Area: 4125 sq mi (10,689 sq km). Population (1991 est): 875,000. Capital and main port: Banjul.

Gambia River A river in West Africa. Rising in the Fouta Djallon plateau in Guinea, it flows mainly NW through Senegal and The Gambia to enter the Atlantic Ocean. It is navigable to oceangoing vessels for 200 mi (320 km). Length: 700 mi (1125 km).

Gambier Islands 23 10S 135 00W A group of coral islands in the S Pacific Ocean, in French Polynesia forming an extension of the Tuamotu Archipelago. They have been used for French nuclear tests. Area: 11 sq mi (30 sq km). Chief settlement: Rikitea.

gamboge (*or* camboge) A hard brittle gum resin obtained from various SE Asian trees of the genus *Garcinia.* It is orange to brown in color and turns bright yellow when powdered. Artists use gamboge as a pigment and to color varnishes. In medicine and veterinary medicine it is used as a strong purgative.

gamebird A bird that is hunted for sport or for food. Birds that are frequently hunted include pheasants, grouse, partridges, turkeys, guinea fowl, ducks, snipe, and woodcock.

gamelan A type of orchestra common in Indonesia and Thailand, consisting mainly of tuned percussion instruments (particularly gongs and bells). A gamelan was heard at the Great Paris Exhibition of 1889; Debussy was influenced by its sonorities.

gamete A reproductive cell—either male or female—produced in the sex organs of plants or animals and containing half the number of *chromosomes present in a body (somatic) cell. On *fertilization the new individual therefore has a complete set of chromosomes, half from each parent. The female gamete (*see* egg) is large and immotile and contains abundant cytoplasm, while the male gamete (*see* sperm) is motile, with little cytoplasm.

game theory The branch of mathematics that seeks to analyze and solve problems arising in economic, business, or military situations on the assumption that each participant adopts strategies that will maximize gain (payoff) and minimize loss, as in playing a game. Worked out originally by John von *Neumann and Oskar Morganstern, it was successfully used in World War II in an analysis of submarine warfare.

Distinction is made between games for one player (solitaire) in which no conflict arises, games for two players or teams (chess, football) in which conflict is an essential aspect of strategy, and games in which there are more than two participants (poker, roulette) and one person's gain is not directly reflected by another person's loss. When chance is important, information is incomplete, or participants' goals are obscure, the theory is more complex.

gametophyte. *See* alternation of generations.

Gamliel The name of several important rabbis. **Gamliel the Elder** (Greek name: Gamaliel; early 1st century AD), a grandson of *Hillel, was president of the Jewish council of Jerusalem and a teacher of St *Paul. His grandson **Gamliel II** succeeded *Johanan ben Zakkai as head of the school at Jabneh (Yavneh) and is regarded as one of the founders of rabbinic Judaism.

gamma globulin. *See* globulin.

gamma radiation Highly energetic electromagnetic radiation emitted by certain radioactive substances as a result of transitions of nucleons from a higher to a lower energy level and when an elementary particle and its antiparticle annihilate each other. The wavelength of gamma radiation is between 10^{-10} and 10^{-14} m.

Ganda A Bantu people of the region W and N of Lake Victoria. They are agriculturalists, whose staple crop is bananas. The largest tribe in Uganda, they were formerly ruled by a king (Kabaka) in their own kingdom of *Buganda.

Gander 48 58N 54 34W A town in E Canada, in Newfoundland. A major World War II base, it has one of the world's largest airports, responsible for air-traffic control over the North Atlantic.

Gandhara An ancient region now in NW Pakistan. It was conquered by the Achaemenians (6th century BC) and by *Alexander the Great (327–325 BC). In the early centuries AD it became a center for a Buddhist art that combined Greco-Roman and oriental characteristics. *See also* Taxila.

Gandhi, Indira (1917–84) Indian stateswoman; prime minister (1966–77; 1980–84). Daughter of Jawaharlal *Nehru, in 1942 she married Feroz Gandhi (d. 1960), who was not a relation of Mahatma Gandhi. She was a cabinet minister under Lal Bahadur *Shastri, whom she succeeded as prime minister. She won substantial victories in the 1971 and 1972 elections. In 1975 she was accused of electoral malpractices and threatened with the loss of her seat. A state of emergency was subsequently declared and strict authoritarian government imposed. She was defeated in the elections of 1977 by Morarji Desai but returned to power in 1980. In the wake of sectarian violence with the Sikh religious sect after she had ordered the army to storm the Golden Temple in Amritsar, Indira Gandhi was assassinated by members of her personal bodyguard who were Sikhs. **Rajiv Gandhi** (1942–91), her elder son, succeeded her as prime minister. His efforts to unite the country behind him were successful, and he became prime minister in his own right, 1984–89. He was assassinated while campaigning for reelection. Her younger son **Sanjay Gandhi** (1946–80) caused controversy over alleged corruption in government office and was later killed in an air crash.

Gandhi, Mohandas Karamchand (1869–1948) Indian nationalist leader. Mahatma ("Great Soul") Gandhi was born in W India and went to England in 1888 to study law. In 1893 he moved to South Africa and became a champion of the rights of the Indian community, introducing a policy of noncooperation with the civil authorities (*see* satyagraha), which he utilized after his return to India (1914). There he took up the cause of home rule, becoming leader of the *Indian National Congress. His noncooperation policy was inaugurated in 1919 and was then extended to civil disobedience (e.g. nonpayment of taxes). Following imprisonment (1922–24), Gandhi withdrew from national politics to travel around India. He campaigned against the degradation of untouchables and encouraged the development of Indian craft industries. Returning to politics in 1927, in 1930 he made his famous walk from Ahmedabad to the sea, where he distilled salt from sea water in protest against the government's salt monopoly, and was again imprisoned. In 1932 he undertook his first "fast unto death," against the government's attitude to untouchables, and in 1933 retired to his ashram at Wardha. Returning to political life in the late 1930s, he became committed to the aim of complete independence for India. In 1942, when the Japanese were threatening India, the British Government offered India complete independence after the war in exchange for cooperation in winning it. Gandhi demanded that the British should withdraw immediately from India. The British responded by jailing Gandhi and the other Congress leaders until 1944, when they were released to discuss independence and partition.

Gandhi, with □Nehru, played a crucial part in the independence talks and although initially opposed to partition he finally accepted the establishment of Pakistan. When violence subsequently broke out in Bengal between Hindus and Muslims, Gandhi undertook a fast in an attempt to halt the conflict. His advocacy of friendship between Hindus and Muslims caused intense resentment among Hindu fanatics, one of whom (Nathuram Godse) assassinated him as he went to a prayer meeting. Gandhi was never a member of the cabinet, but for many years before his death was regarded as the supreme Indian leader.

MOHANDAS (MAHATMA) GANDHI *The architect of noncooperation in British India leaves a conference in London (1931).*

Gandzha. *See* Kirovabad.

Ganesa One of the principle Hindu deities, portrayed as having an elephant's head on a human body. His father *Shiva beheaded him, but then decided to save him and replaced his human head with that of the first creature he found. A popular god, he is the teacher of the gods and is invoked at the start of any undertaking since he is believed to remove obstacles.

Ganga Two related dynasties in medieval India. The **Western Ganga** ruled over much of Mysore in S India (present-day Karnataka) from the 2nd century until the early 11th century, when they were overthrown by the Cola. The **Eastern Ganga** ruled Kalinga from the 11th to the 15th centuries and were responsible for many glorious monuments, perhaps most notably the Jagannath temple at Puri.

Ganges River (*or* Ganga) The great river of N India. Formed by several headstreams in the Himalayas, one of which emanates from an ice cave, it flows generally E across the broad Ganges plain to join the Brahmaputra River, thereafter continuing as the Padma River, which empties into the Bay of Bengal by way of the largest delta in the world. It is used to irrigate the Ganges plain, which contains several of India's main cities (Delhi, Agra, Varanasi, and Lucknow) and which, after the Yangtze Valley (China), is the world's most populous agricultural area. It is of immense religious importance, being the Hindus' most sacred river. Length: 1557 mi (2507 km).

ganglion (anatomy) A collection of nerve cell bodies, especially one outside the central *nervous system. Sensory ganglia carry out preliminary analysis of the information coming from sense organs. Motor ganglia coordinate the discharges from a number of nerve fibers. *See also* neuron.

ganglion (cyst) A small fluid-filled swelling occurring under the skin and close to a joint, usually the wrist. They are most common in children. Treatment is needed only if the cysts are large or painful, in which case they are surgically removed. A former treatment was to hit them with the family Bible.

Gang of Four. *See* Jiang Qing.

gangrene Death of tissues, most commonly those of a limb. This usually results from narrowing of the blood vessels of the legs by *atherosclerosis or because of diabetes. If the tissues become infected the condition is called wet gangrene. Treatment is aimed at improving the blood flow to the limbs by surgery to the vessels or by rest; in advanced cases amputation may be necessary.

Gangtok 27 20N 88 39E A city in India, the capital of Sikkim. It is an agricultural trading center. Population (1981): 36,768.

gannet A seabird belonging to the family *Sulidae,* distributed worldwide. (Tropical members of the family are called *boobies.) The North Atlantic gannet (*Sula bassana*), also called solan goose, reach 35 in (90 cm) in length. It is white with black wingtips and has a long stout bill and a long wedge-shaped tail. Gannets feed on fish and nest in dense colonies on rocky islands and cliffs. Order: *Pelecaniformes* (cormorants, pelicans, etc.).

Gansu (*or* Kansu) A mountainous province in N China, prone in the E to severe earthquakes. Livestock is kept and cereals, cotton, and tobacco are grown in the river valleys. It has oil, coal, hydroelectric power, and a nuclear plant. *History*: it became part of China in the 3rd century BC, but after the introduction of Islam in the 13th century its Muslim population was continually rebellious and it only came under full Chinese influence in the 19th century. On the route to China from the Middle East, along which traveled Marco Polo, it is strategically important. Area: 137,100 sq mi (355,100 sq km). Population (1990): 22,371,141. Capital: Lanzhou.

Ganymede In Greek legend, a Trojan prince of great beauty carried off by Zeus to be his cupbearer in exchange for some immortal horses or a golden vine.

gaon (Hebrew: eminence) A Jewish scholar and communal leader. The geonim were the heads of the Jewish Babylonian academies from the 6th–11th centuries. Much of their surviving work is in the form of *responsa,* discursive replies to questions concerning the Bible, *Talmud, or *Mishnah. The most celebrated gaon was Sa'adya (892–942), Talmudic scholar, philosopher, poet, grammarian, and the translator of the Bible into Arabic.

Gaoxiong (*or* Kao-hsiung; Japanese name: Takao) 22 36N 120 17E A city in SW Taiwan, the second largest on the island and its leading port. Under Japanese occupation (1895–1945) it became an important naval base. It is a major industrial center, its industries including oil refining, fishing, and food processing. Population (1986 est): 1,310,000.

gar A freshwater *bony fish, also called garpike, belonging to a family (*Lepisosteidae*; 7 species) found in North and Central America. Gars have a slender body, up to 11 ft (3.5 m) long, covered with enameled scales, and a long alligator-like snout with sharp teeth; they feed mainly on smaller fish. Order: *Semionotiformes.* □fish.

Garbo, Greta (Greta Gustafson; 1905–90) Swedish actress. Her exceptional beauty and aloofness contributed much to her portrayal of tragic heroines in such films as *Grand Hotel* (1932), *Queen Christina* (1934), *Anna Karenina* (1935), and *Camille* (1936). As a comedienne she excelled in *Ninotchka* (1939). She retired in 1941, her private life remaining as enigmatic as it had been during her years of stardom.

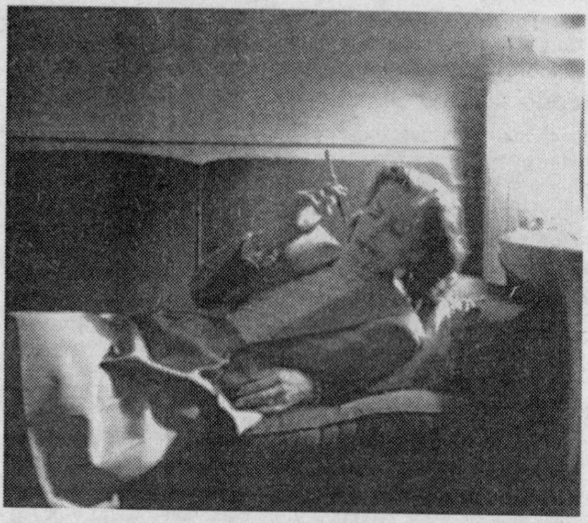

GRETA GARBO *A portrait by Sir Cecil Beaton.*

García Lorca, Federico (1898–1936) Spanish poet and dramatist. He began writing poems while a student in Granada and Madrid, winning international fame with *Gipsy Ballads* (1928), noted for their boldly original imagery. His visits to the US and Cuba (1929–30) inspired the anguished poems of *Poet in New York* (1940). His masterpiece is the trilogy of folk tragedies *Blood Wedding* (1933), *Yerma* (1934), and *The House of Bernarda Alba* (1936). He was shot by Nationalist partisans at the outset of the Spanish Civil War.

Garda, Lake (Latin name: Lacus Benacus) A lake in central N Italy. Sheltered on the N by the Alps, it has a temperate climate that attracts vacationers and tourists. Area: 143 sq mi (370 sq km).

garden cress. *See* cress.

Garden Grove 33 46N 117 57W A city in SW California, SE of Los Angeles. Industries include ceramics, plastics, aluminum products, and electronic parts. Population (1990): 143,050.

Gardenia A genus of ornamental shrubs and trees (60–100 species) native to tropical and subtropical Africa and Asia. Many are richly scented and used in perfumes and tea. The shiny evergreen leaves are oval and pointed. Single flowers have four or five strap-shaped petals, often creamy white, but many cultivated varieties have showy double flowers. The fruits are large and berrylike. *G. jasminoides* is a popular pot plant. Family: *Rubiaceae* (madder family).

Garden of the Gods An area in Colorado. It consists of remarkable formations of eroded red sandstone rocks, some of which resemble animals, gargoyles, and cathedral spires.

Gardner, John (1933–82) US author. He taught creative writing at the State University of New York at Binghamton. His works, noted for their unusual themes and experimental style, include *Grendel* (1971), *The Sunlight Dialogues* (1972), *Nickel Mountain* (1973), *October Light* (1976), *On Moral Fiction* (1978), *Freddy's Book* (1980), *The Art of Living* (1981), and *Mickelsson's Ghosts* (1982).

Garfield, James A(bram) (1831–81) US statesman; Republican president (1881). A teacher, state legislator, and soldier in the Civil War, he served in the US Congress as a Republican representative from Ohio (1863–80) where he was chairman of the Committee on Appropriations and Republican chairman. He was elected to the Senate in 1880 but failed to serve because he was nominated to run as president and elected to that position that same year. Four months after his inauguration in 1881, he was shot by a disgruntled voter, Charles J. Guiteau; he lived for two and one-half months, thus precipitating the question of succession to the presidency in cases of disablement.

garfish. *See* needlefish.

garganey A small *dabbling duck, *Anas querquedula,* that breeds in shallow fresh waters of N Eurasia and winters along African and Asian coasts; 14–16 in (36–40 cm) long, the male is brown with pale underparts, gray wings, green and white wing bars, and a broad white eye stripe; females are mottled brown.

gargoyle A water spout, in the shape of a grotesque person or animal, that appears chiefly in gothic architecture. Gargoyles project from parapet gutters to carry water draining from the roof clear of the walls.

Garibaldi, Giuseppe (1807–82) Italian soldier, a hero of the movement for Italian unification (*see* Risorgimento). Influenced by Mazzini, he joined an attempted republican revolution in Sardinia-Piedmont (1834) and was forced to flee to South America, where he spent 10 years fighting in a series of wars of liberation. He returned to Italy to join the *Revolution of 1848, fighting the Austrians and, after the flight of Pope Pius IX, playing a leading part in the heroic but unsuccessful defense of Rome against the French. Following another period of exile, he gave his support to the unification movement led by Cavour and Victor Emmanuel II of Sardinia-Piedmont. In 1860 he set out from Genoa on the Expedition of a *Thousand, which was to achieve the conquest of Sicily and Naples and their incorporation in the new kingdom of Italy. He continued to serve Victor Emmanuel in the 1860s and also fought for the French in the Franco-Prussian War (1870–71).

Garland, Judy (Frances Gumm; 1922–69) US singer and film actress. She began her career at the age of five as a singer in vaudeville. Her films included *The Wizard of Oz* (1939), in which she sang "Over the Rainbow" and established herself as a star, *Meet Me in St Louis* (1944), *A Star is Born* (1954), and *Judgment at Nuremberg* (1961). She married five times; although an unhappy private life interfered with her career, she maintained her reputation as an enormously popular singer. Her daughter **Liza Minnelli** (1946–) is also a singer and actress. She is best known for her starring roles in the musical film *Cabaret* (1972) and *Arthur* (1981).

garlic A widely cultivated perennial herb, **Allium sativum,* native to Asia and naturalized in S Europe and North America. Its leafless flower stem grows to a height of 24 in (60 cm). The garlic bulb has a membraneous skin enclosing up to 20 bulblets, called cloves. The bulb has a pungent aroma and taste and is a classic flavoring agent in cooking.

garlic mustard A biennial or perennial Eurasian herb, *Alliaria petiolata* (*A. officinalis, Sisymbrium alliaria*), up to 40 in (100 cm) high, also called Jack-by-the-hedge and hedge garlic. The heart-shaped toothed leaves smell of garlic when crushed. Small white four-petaled flowers are borne in a terminal cluster. Family: **Cruciferae.*

Garner, John Nance (1868–1967) US politician and lawyer; vice president (1933–41). After serving in the Texas legislature (1898–1902), he was elected as a Democrat to the US House of Representatives and served 1903–33. He was responsible for the presidential nomination of Franklin D. Roosevelt in 1932 and then was chosen as his running mate. As vice president he expedited New Deal legislation, a program he did not entirely favor. He retired in 1941.

garnet A group of minerals with compositions varying within the series pyralspite (pyrope, $Mg_3Al_2Si_3O_{12}$; almandine, $Fe_3{}^{2+}Al_2Si_3O_{12}$; and spessartite, $Mn_3Al_2Si_3O_{12}$) or ugrandite (grossular, $Ca_3Al_2Si_3O_{12}$; andradite, $Ca_3(Fe^{3+},Ti)_2Si_3O_{12}$; and uvarovite, $Ca_3Cr_2Si_3O_{12}$). Garnets occur chiefly in metamorphic rocks. They are used as abrasives, almandine being the most important, and flawless crystals are semiprecious stones. Birthstone for January.

Garonne River A river in SW France. Rising in the central Pyrenees, it flows N through Toulouse and joins the Dordogne River near Bordeaux, entering the Atlantic Ocean by the Gironde estuary. It is linked to the Mediterranean Sea by the Canal du Midi. Length: 360 mi (580 km).

garpike. *See* gar.

Garrick, David (1717–79) English actor. He went to London with Samuel *Johnson in 1737 and began his long theatrical career with a highly acclaimed performance as Richard III in 1741. His natural style of acting contrasted with the prevailing formal conventions. As manager of the Drury Lane Theatre from 1747–76, he introduced innovations in production, lighting, and scenery.

Garrison, William Lloyd (1805–79) US abolitionist and journalist. In the antislavery movement in Boston from the age of 25, he started a newspaper, *The Liberator* (1831–61), and cofounded the American Anti-Slavery Society (1833) serving as its president from 1841. A pacifist, he believed in changing public opinion and exerting moral pressure, unlike those who believed in immediate change, achieved by violence if necessary. When Pres. Abraham Lincoln issued the Emancipation Proclamation (1863) and the 13th Amendment was passed (1865), Garrison turned his attention to women's suffrage, prohibition, and American Indian rights.

Garter, Order of the A British order of knighthood, traditionally founded by Edward III in 1348 and comprising chiefly the sovereign and 25 knights companion. Its motto is *Honi soit qui mal y pense* (The shame be his who thinks badly of it), supposedly the words of Edward III on tying to his leg a garter dropped by a lady at a party. The motto is inscribed on the dark blue garter worn by the knights of the order on the left leg below the knee.

Garvey, Marcus (Mosiah) (1887–1940) US African-American nationalist leader; born in Jamaica. He promoted African-American pride and an independent African-American economy and advocated African-American separatism and a Back to Africa movement. In 1914, in Jamaica, he established the Universal Negro Improvement Association (UNIA) and by 1916 had started branches in the US. He established a shipping company, Black Star Line, in 1919 and decreed himself the leader of the African Republic, a would-be nation in Africa. By 1923, however, his businesses had gone into bankruptcy and he was on trial for mail fraud. He served two years in prison before Pres. Calvin Coolidge commuted his sentence and deported him to Jamaica.

Gary 41 34N 87 20W A city in Indiana, on Lake Michigan. Founded by the US Steel Corporation (1905), it is one of the world's major steel producers. Population (1990): 116,646.

gas constant (R) The constant that occurs in the ideal *gas law: $pV = RT$. Its value is 8.314 joules per kelvin per mole.

Gascony A former duchy of SW France. After Roman rule Gascony was conquered by the Visigoths and then by the Franks. By the end of the 10th century its dukes had achieved autonomy from the French crown but in 1052 it fell to Aquitaine and came under English control in the 12th century. It formed the nucleus of English possessions in France until regained by the French at the end of the Hundred Years' War (1453).

gases Substances that distribute themselves evenly throughout a closed container. The behavior of a gas under variations of temperature, pressure, and volume are fairly accurately described by the *gas laws and the *kinetic theory of gases. When gases are cooled or compressed they become *liquids. However, there is a temperature (the critical temperature) above which a gas cannot be liquefied by pressure alone.

Gaskell, Elizabeth Cleghorn (1810–65) British novelist. In 1832 she settled in Manchester, the industrial setting of her first novel, *Mary Barton* (1848). Her other novels include *Cranford* (1853), and *North and South* (1855). She also wrote the first biography of her friend Charlotte Brontë (1857).

gas laws Relationships between the absolute temperature (T), pressure (p), and volume (V) of a gas. The simplest laws are *Boyle's law ($p \propto 1/V$) and *Charles's law ($V \propto T$), which are combined in the ideal gas equation: $pV = RT$, where R is the *gas constant. However, no real gas obeys this equation exactly. Most later gas laws are modifications of this equation, taking into account the volume occupied by the molecules themselves and the attractive forces between the molecules. The best known of these is *Van der Waals equation.

Gaspé Peninsula A peninsula in SE Quebec province in SE Canada. Bounded on the NW by the St Lawrence River, on the E by the Gulf of St Lawrence, and on the S by Chaleur Bay and New Brunswick province, it is well known for its hunting, fishing, and scenery. The Shickshock Mountains run W to E in N Gaspé; the highest point is Mt Jacques Cartier (4,160 ft; 1,268 m) in the NE. First visited by Jacques Cartier in 1534, it was settled by the French Acadians in the 1600s and, during the American Revolution, by refugee British sympathizers from the US. Farming and fishing in the summer and lumbering in the winter are the chief economic activities. Area: 11,390 sq mi (29,500 sq km).

Gassendi, Pierre (1592–1655) French physicist and philosopher, an ardent believer in the experimental approach to science. He advocated the atomic theory of matter (*see* atomism) and in this influenced the ideas of Robert *Boyle. His astronomical works supported Galileo's ideas. In philosophy he wrote extensively on *Epicureanism and formulated objections to *Descartes' *Meditations.*

Gasser, Herbert Spencer (1888–1963) US physiologist, who shared a Nobel Prize (1944) with Joseph *Erlanger for their work on the function of nerve fibers.

gastric ulcer. *See* peptic ulcer.

gastrin A hormone released by cells of the stomach wall in the presence of food. Gastrin stimulates secretion of gastric juice by the gastric glands.

gastritis Inflammation of the lining of the stomach. Acute gastritis usually results from such irritants as alcohol or aspirin. If the patient stops taking the irritant, the condition usually resolves quickly. Chronic gastritis is common in old people and often symptomless, but it may be associated with pernicious *anemia.

gastroenteritis Infection of the stomach and intestines. Food poisoning is one cause of gastroenteritis, but usually it cannot be related to a meal and no particular bacteria can be incriminated. Gastroenteritis is characterized by diarrhea and vomiting and usually occurs in areas where hygiene is poor. It is particularly dangerous in babies.

gastropod A single-shelled *mollusk belonging to the class *Gastropoda* (about 40,000 species), including *snails and *slugs, *limpets, and *sea hares. Measuring 0.3–8 in (0.1–20 cm) in length, gastropods occupy terrestrial, freshwater, and marine habitats. They move by undulating the muscular foot and have two pairs of retractable sensory head tentacles, one pair bearing simple eyes. They feed by scraping plant or animal matter with a rasping tongue (radula). Most gastropods have internal fertilization: the mating individuals may be of separate sexes or hermaphrodite.

Gastrotricha A phylum of minute wormlike animals (1800 species) found in salt and fresh waters; 0.004–0.06 in (0.1–1.5 mm) long, gastrotrichs have a scaly often spiny cuticle and a ciliated underside; they creep over decaying vegetation, on which they feed. Many are *hermaphrodites and one group exhibits *parthenogenesis, i.e. unfertilized eggs give rise exclusively to females.

gastrula A stage in the embryonic development of an animal in which the cells of the *blastula (the preceding stage) undergo complex movements, resulting in the formation of three distinct germ layers. These layers—the ectoderm, mesoderm, and endoderm—will later differentiate into the tissues and organs of the body. A central cavity (archenteron) is the primitive gut.

gas turbine A form of *internal-combustion engine consisting of a *turbine in which the power to drive the blades is provided by hot gas. The gas turbine is a flexible engine with many applications, the most useful being in aviation (*see* jet engine). It consists of a *compressor, a combustion chamber, and the turbine. Atmospheric air is fed under pressure from the compressor to the combustion chambers, where a fuel, such as natural gas, gasoline, or oil is burned; the hot gases then drive the turbine, which in turn drives the compressor. Power is supplied either in the form of thrust from a jet or rotation of the turbine shaft. □heat engine.

Gates, Horatio (?1728–1806) American general. British-born, he saw action in America in the French and Indian War and returned to settle there in 1772.

During the American Revolution, his army defeated the British under *Burgoyne at *Saratoga (1777). Defeated by Cornwallis at *Camden (1780), he retired until 1782, when he joined Washington's staff.

Gates, William Henry, III (1955–) US businessman, cofounder of Microsoft Corporation. Involved with computer businesses from high school, in 1975 he founded Microsoft, which grew rapidly as the MS-DOS (Microsoft Disk Operating System) and a variety of software became widely used in the 1980s. Microsoft's dominance in software made Gates one of the richest men in the US as the company expanded its software applications.

GATT. *See* General Agreement on Tariffs and Trade.

Gatun, Lake (Spanish name: Lago Gatún) An artificial lake in the Panama Canal Zone. It was created in 1912 to maintain the water level in the Gaillard Cut. Area: 166 sq mi (430 sq km).

gaucho A nomadic cattleherder of the Argentine, Uruguayan, and Paraguayan pampas in the 18th and 19th centuries. Often a mestizo (of mixed European and Indian ancestry), gauchos were at first independent herders but, like the US *cowboys, became employees of ranchers. They disappeared following the plowing of the pampas and the introduction of pure-breed stock raising. Gauchos were the source of a rich folk tradition.

Gaudí y Cornet, Antonio (1852–1926) Spanish architect with a highly individual approach. Gaudí's work had strong affiliations to *Art Nouveau, but also drew inspiration from gothic and *Mudéjar sources. He also made use of the style of the *gothic revival in the incomplete Sagrada Familia in Barcelona (1880s). He worked exclusively in Barcelona, beginning with the Casa Vicens (1878) and a house for his patron, Count Güell. In the 1890s his style changed radically, and certain later buildings, for example the Casa Battló (1905), tended to resemble natural growths more than architecture.

Gauguin, Paul (1848–1903) French postimpressionist painter, born in Paris. After five years at sea he became a stockbroker (1871), painting only as a hobby. His early works were influenced by the impressionists with whom he exhibited (1881–86). He became a full-time painter in 1883 and moved to Brittany in 1886, where he developed a style called *synthetism in such paintings as *Vision after the Sermon*. He visited Martinique in 1887 and stayed with Van *Gogh in Arles in 1888. Seeking the inspiration of a primitive civilization, he moved to Tahiti (1891), where the symbolism in such paintings as *Nevermore* was influenced by native superstitions. He is noted also for reviving the art of woodcutting.

Gauhati 26 10N 91 45E A city in India, in Assam. The former center of British administration in Assam, Gauhati is an important trading center and has an oil refinery. Its many temple ruins make it a Hindu pilgrimage center. Its university was established in 1948. Population (1991): 577,591.

Gaul An ancient region of Europe. It was divided by the Romans into Transalpine Gaul (the area bound by the Rhine, Alps, and Pyrenees) and Cisalpine Gaul (N Italy). Transalpine Gaul was settled from about 1500 BC by Celtic tribes, who inhabited Cisalpine Gaul after around 500 BC. Subsequent Gallic expansion southward brought conflict with Rome, which the Gauls sacked in 390, and the Roman conquest of Cisalpine Gaul was not completed until the mid-2nd century. In 121 the Romans annexed S Transalpine Gaul, which they called Gallia Narbonensis, and between 58 and 50 Caesar subdued the rest of Gaul, finally crushing the Gallic tribal leader *Vercingetorix at Alesia. Augustus organized Transalpine Gaul into four provinces—Narbonensis, Belgica, Lugdunensis, and Aquitania. During the 1st century AD Gaul, especially Narbonensis, was extensively romanized and prospered until the barbarian invasions in the 5th century.

PAUL GAUGUIN Self-portrait *(1889). Another of the artist's paintings,* The Yellow Christ *(1889), can be seen in the background.*

Gaullists The supporters of the policies of General *de Gaulle, especially his independent foreign policy and drive toward industrial expansion, which were motivated by a wish to reestablish France as a world power. De Gaulle's Rassemblement du Peuple français (1947–53) was succeeded by the Union de Démocrates pour la République, which was reorganized by Jacques *Chirac as the Rassemblement pour la République.

gaur the largest of the wild cattle, *Bos gaurus,* of hilly forests in S Asia. Up to 6 ft (2 m) high at the shoulder, bulls can weigh up to 1 ton. Gaurs are dark brown with white socks and both sexes have horns, the tips pointing upward in bulls and inward in cows.

gauss (G) The unit of magnetic flux density in the *c.g.s. system equal to a flux density of one maxwell per square centimeter. Named for Karl Friedrich *Gauss.

Gauss, Karl Friedrich (1777–1855) German mathematician, regarded (with *Newton and *Archimedes) as one of the greatest mathematicians of all time. He influenced all aspects of mathematics and much of physics. His greatest contributions were in the fields of probability theory, number theory, complex numbers, algebra, and electricity and magnetism.

Gautier, Théophile (1811–72) French Romantic poet and critic. Influenced by Victor *Hugo, his early writings include *Poésies* (1830) and *Les Jeunes-France* (1833). The brief lyrical poems in *Émaux et camées* (1852) embody his belief in the value of art for its own sake. He wrote much influential art, ballet, and dramatic criticism and traveled widely in Europe, the Middle East, and Russia.

gavial (*or* gharial) A long-snouted □reptile, *Gavialis gangeticus,* occurring in N Indian rivers and sacred to Hindus; 13–16 ft (4–5 m) long, it has long slender sharp-toothed jaws, which it sweeps from side to side to catch fish. It is the only member of its family (*Gavialidae*). Order: *Crocodilia* (*see* crocodile).

Gävle 60 41N 17 10E A seaport in E Sweden, on an inlet of the Gulf of Bothnia. Ice-free for nine months of the year, it exports timber, wood pulp, and paper. Its industries include ship building. Population (1978 est): 87,378.

Gawain In Arthurian legend, a knight of the Round Table, the nephew of King Arthur and the son of King Lot of Norway and the Orkneys. He was known for his purity and courage.

Gay, John (1685–1732) British poet and dramatist. A friend of Pope and Swift, his *Fables* (1727, 1738) were the most successful of his several satirical poems. His best-known work is the ballad opera *The Beggar's Opera* (1728), a comic blend of social satire and parody of fashionable Italian opera, using traditional tunes.

Gaya 24 48N 85 00E A city in NE India, in Bihar. A center of Hindu pilgrimage, it is situated 6 mi (10 km) S of Buddh Gaya, which is sacred to Buddhists. Population (1991): 291,220.

gayal A species of domestic cattle, *Bos frontalis,* of Burma. Gayals are similar to the wild *gaur, but are smaller, measuring about 60 in (150 cm) at the shoulder, and have a wider spread of horns. Gayals may be a domesticated form of gaur.

Gay Liberation. *See* homosexuality.

Gay-Lussac, Joseph Louis (1778–1850) French chemist and physicist. He discovered the element boron (1808) and the law that gases combine in a simple ratio by volume (**Gay-Lussac's law**). He also discovered *Charles' law independently of Charles and published his results first.

Gaza (Arabic name: Ghazzah) 31 30N 34 28E The largest town in the *Gaza Strip. Gaza has been inhabited continuously for over 3000 years; in biblical times it was a Philistine center, where Samson was killed (Judges 16). Its products now include pottery and textiles. Population (1980 est): 120,000.

Gaza Strip A strip of coastal territory, 30 mi (50 km) long, on the SE corner of the Mediterranean Sea. Following the Arab-Israeli War of 1948–49, the only part of Palestine held by Egypt was a strip of land on the coast that became known as the Gaza Strip. Egypt did not integrate the Strip into its own state, but established a military governorship here. Held by the Israelis for a short time in 1956–57, it was taken by them again in 1967, and is now under Israeli military administration. Under the Camp David agreement (1979) between Israel and Egypt, eventual self-government for the area was planned. The Gaza Strip suffers from extreme overpopulation, many Palestine refugees being housed in squalid camps. Agriculture is the chief pursuit, especially the growing of citrus fruit. Clashes between Palestinians and Israelis continued in the strip after a 1993 agreement outlined self-government for the area.

gazelle A slender antelope of the genus *Gazella* (about 12 species), of Africa and Asia; 20–35 in (50–90 cm) high at the shoulder, gazelles are distinguished from other antelopes by light and dark horizontal stripes on the face. Brown to gray in color, gazelles may also have a dark band along the sides above the lighter belly. In most species both sexes have horns, which are generally lyre-shaped, ridged, and backward-curving with a forward-pointing tip.

Gaziantep 37 04N 37 21E A city in S Turkey, near the Syrian border. Known for its Hittite remains, Gaziantep is situated near ancient trade routes and has changed hands frequently. It is an important market town. Population (1990): 603,434.

Gdańsk (German name: Danzig) 54 22N 18 41E A port in N Poland, on the Baltic Sea. It is an industrial center with shipbuilding, metallurgy, chemicals, and food processing; exports include coal, grain, and timber. Its university was founded in 1970. *History*: it developed as an important trade center during the Renaissance. It was under Prussian control (1793–1807 and 1814–1919), becoming a free city under the League of Nations in 1919. In 1939 it was annexed by Germany, an act that precipitated World War II; the city was returned to Poland in 1945. From the early 1980s the city was a center of opposition to Poland's communist regime. Population (1992 est): 465,000.

Gdynia 54 31N 18 30E A port in N Poland, on the Baltic Sea. Originally a fishing village, it was developed (1924–39) to replace Danzig (*see* Gdańsk) as Poland's port, becoming Poland's main shipbuilding center and naval base. Population (1992 est): 252,000.

Ge A group of South American Indian peoples of Brazil and N Paraguay who speak languages of the Macro-Ge group. Its numerous different tribes are very diverse in their range of cultural patterns. They are largely hunters and gatherers but some have adopted cultivation. Their social organization tends to be complex. Besides clan divisions, there is a variety of associations based on age, sex, occupation, etc., each autonomous in its respective sphere.

gean. *See* cherry.

Geber (14th century) Spanish alchemist, whose suggestion that different metals consist of mercury and sulfur in different proportions laid the foundation for the belief in the *philosopher's stone. He was also an experimental chemist, preparing nitric and acetic acids and white lead. He assumed the name Geber, which is the Latin form of Jabir, in honor of the 8th-century Arab alchemist Jabir ibn Hayyan.

gecko A slender long-tailed nocturnal lizard belonging to the widely distributed family *Gekkonidae* (650 species), found in a wide range of habitats including deserts and rain forests; 1.2–14 in (3–35 cm) long, many geckos have fleshy toe pads covered with microscopic hooks enabling them to cling to smooth surfaces, such as ceilings. They feed on insects and have well-developed vocal cords producing a variety of chirps and barks. The tokay (*Gekko gecko*) of E Asia is a large arboreal gecko and lays its eggs in crevices. □reptile.

Gediminas (c. 1275–1341) Grand Duke of Lithuania (1316–41). One of Lithuania's greatest rulers, he founded the state by unifying the Lithuanian tribes. He extended his dominions, which he defended against the *Teutonic Knights. He was converted to Christianity in 1323. Gediminas made Vilnius the capital of Lithuania.

Geelong 38 10S 144 26E A city and major port in Australia, in S Victoria on Corio Bay. Wool, wheat, and oil are the principal exports. Population (1991 est): 152,800.

gegenschein (German: counterglow) A very faint glow in the night sky that can sometimes be seen on the *ecliptic in a direction directly opposite the sun's position. It is part of the *zodiacal light.

Gehenna In the Bible, the Valley of Hinnom, outside Jerusalem. At one time it was apparently the site of human sacrifices and was therefore considered an unclean place. In Jewish thought it came to represent a place where sinners are punished and in the New Testament it is a name for hell.

Gehrig, Lou (1903–41) US baseball player. He joined the New York Yankees in 1923 and played for them until illness forced his retirement in 1939. During his career as a first baseman he played in a record 2,130 consecutive games, had a lifetime batting average of .340, hit 493 home runs, held many individual records, and was nicknamed the "Iron Horse." He was voted a member of the Baseball Hall of Fame in 1939.

Geiger, Hans (1882–1945) German physicist, who in 1913 invented the *Geiger counter for detecting ionizing radiation in connection with his work on cosmic rays. During World War II he participated in Germany's unsuccessful attempt to build an atomic bomb.

Geiger counter A device that detects and counts ionizing radiation and particles. Essentially it consists of a metal cylinder containing low-pressure gas and a wire anode running along its central axis. The anode is held at a potential difference just less than that required to produce a discharge in the gas. Ionizing particles passing into the tube through a window at one end induce discharges, which can be counted by a suitable circuit. Named for Hans *Geiger.

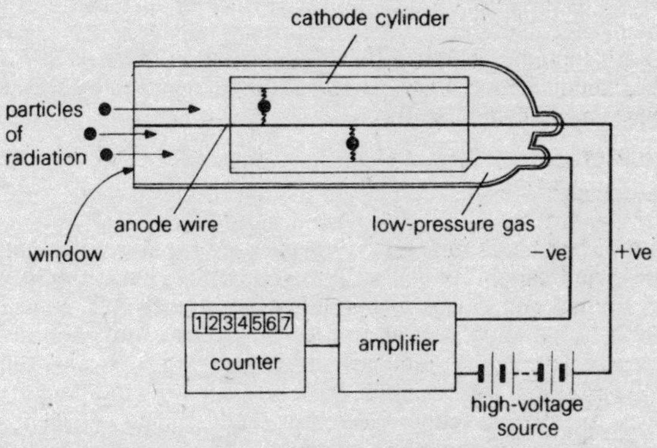

GEIGER COUNTER *The radiation entering the tube causes an electrical discharge through the gas between the anode and cathode, sending an electrical pulse to the counter.*

geisha A Japanese woman whose profession is to entertain men in a restaurant. Geishas, who are not prostitutes, sing and dance or engage their clients in conversation. In modern Japan geishas are employed primarily for the benefit of the tourist trade.

gel. *See* colloid.

Gela 37 04N 14 15E A city in Italy, in Sicily. Founded by Greek colonists in 689 BC, it fluorished under the rule of Hippocrates in the 5th century BC. Abandoned in 281 BC, it was refounded in 1233. Its industries include fishing and petrochemicals. Population (1990 est): 90,000.

gelada A large *Old World monkey, *Theropithecus gelada,* of Ethiopian mountains; 47–59 in (120–150 cm) long including the tufted tail (28–31 in; 70–80 cm), it has a cape of dark-brown hair with two bare patches on the chest and lives in large groups, feeding on roots, leaves, and fruit.

gelatin A protein derived from bones and skins. In solution it forms a reversible gel that becomes fluid as the temperature rises and solidifies on cooling. Because of this property it is widely used in the food industry as a stabilizer in jellies and confectionery, in drug preparations, and in photographic emulsions.

Gelderland A province in the E Netherlands, bordering on Germany. Predominantly rolling upland, the fertile soils of the Rhine Valley produce vegetables, fruit, and dairy products while the poorer soils in the N produce fodder crops. The NW is also an important tourist area. Manufactured products include cotton and paper. Area: 1981 sq mi (5131 sq km). Population (1988 est): 1,785,000. Capital: Arnhem.

Gell-Mann, Murray (1929–) US physicist, who won the 1969 Nobel Prize for his theoretical work on elementary particles. In 1953 he introduced the concept of *strangeness to account for the absence of certain expected interactions. He also formulated the theory of *unitary symmetry and introduced the concept of quarks (*see also* particle physics).

Gelsenkirchen 51 30N 7 05E A city in NW Germany, in North Rhine-Westphalia. A *Ruhr coal mining center and port on the Rhine-Herne Canal, it has a moated palace (16th–18th centuries). Its manufactures include steel, chemicals, and glass. Population (1988): 284,000.

Gemini (Latin: Twins) A conspicuous constellation in the N sky near Orion, lying on the *zodiac between Cancer and Taurus. The brightest stars are *Pollux and the somewhat fainter *Castor.

Gemistus Pletho. *See* Pletho, Georgius Gemistus.

gemsbok. *See* oryx.

gemstones Minerals or mineral fragments used for decorative purposes, particularly jewelry. Desirability is usually based on the gem's beauty (in terms of color, transparency, and luster), its durability (gemstones must be hard), and rarity. Diamond, ruby, sapphire, and emerald are precious stones, the others (amethyst, agate, jasper, onyx, aquamarine, topaz, garnet, etc.) are semiprecious. Not all are crystalline; for example, opal and jade are amorphous. Gemstones are usually artificially cut (either faceted or rounded) and polished; some, such as onyx, are suitable for engraving, as cameos for instance. Many can be synthetically produced.

gene A unit of the hereditary material of an organism that provides the genetic information necessary to fulfill a single function. The term was first coined by W. L. *Johannsen in 1909.

Genes were initially conceived as a string of beads comprising the *chromosome; they were later defined as lengths of the chromosome that were physically indivisible during the exchange of chromosomal material that occurs during *meiosis. Alternatively, a gene was defined as the shortest length of the chromosome that could undergo *mutation. However, with the discovery of the structure of *DNA and the molecular basis of heredity, a gene is now regarded as being a functional unit (cistron) corresponding to a specific sequence of the *genetic code. Structural genes code for individual polypeptides (*see* peptides), while regulator genes control the activity of the structural genes.

General Agreement on Tariffs and Trade (GATT) A set of trade agreements, in operation from January 1948, establishing procedures and tariffs for international trading. Signatories agree to favorable tariffs between members and the reduction of trade restrictions, on condition that home producers do not suffer losses as a result. During the negotiations of 1964–67 the principle of a single tariff for all industrial manufactures was agreed upon, with a resulting reduction in trade costs. There are more than 115 member countries, which are responsible for more than 80% of world trade. The secretariat of GATT, which is a specialized agency of the *United Nations, is in Geneva.

General Services Administration (GSA) US government agency that establishes policy and provides for management of the government's property and records. It is responsible for the construction and operation of buildings; the procurement and distribution of supplies; utilization and disposal of property; transportation, traffic, and communications management; stockpiling of strategic materials; and the management of automatic data processing resources programs. Established in 1949, the GSA headquarters are in Washington, D.C.

General Strike (1926) A national stoppage of work by members of Britain's major industries, May 3–12. The General Strike began when the Trades Union Council (TUC) called out its members in support of miners. The strike extended to all forms of transport, the iron and steel industries, and many other trades. However, the government was able to keep essential services going. Nothing was gained and labor unions in general found themselves worse off after the retaliatory Trade Union Act was passed in 1927.

Genesis The first book of the Bible, traditionally ascribed to Moses. It recounts the creation of the universe and of man (Adam), the fall of Adam through disobedience and his exclusion from the Garden of Eden, the events of the Flood and the deliverance of Noah and his family, and the scattering of the nations at *Babel. The remainder of the book gives particular attention to the lives of Abraham, Isaac, Jacob, and Joseph. It also introduces the fundamental Old Testament theme of the *covenant between God and Israel.

Genesee River A river that flows from N central Pennsylvania NW and then NE through New York to Rochester, where it empties into Lake Ontario. Running through the Allegheny Plateau, its valleys yield farm products; hydroelectric projects along the river produce power. Length: 144 mi (232 km).

genet A carnivorous mammal of the genus *Genetta* (9 species) of Africa and Europe. Genets range in size from the 20-in (50-cm) Abyssinian genet (*G. abyssinica*) to the 40-in (100-cm) African giant genet (*G. victoriae*). They have retractile claws, long tails (up to 20 in [50 cm]), foxlike heads, and pale fur with dark spots or stripes. Genets are stealthy nocturnal hunters, preying on roosting birds and small mammals. Family: **Viverridae.*

Genet, Jean (1910–86) French novelist and dramatist. His autobiographical *A Thief's Journal* (1948) tells of his life in reformatories and prisons and among the criminals and prostitutes of various European cities. In his novels, which include *Our Lady of the Flowers* (1944) and *Miracle of the Rose* (1946), he describes this underworld with poetic intensity. His plays, in which elements of ritual and fantasy are emphasized, are *Deathwatch* (1947), *The Maids* (1947), *The Balcony* (1956), *The Blacks* (1958), and *The Screens* (1961).

genetic code The means by which information for the organization and function of living cells is carried by *DNA and *RNA molecules. Evidence for the nature of the genetic code was provided in the 1960s by the work of *Crick, M. W. Nirenberg (1927–), *Khorana, and many others. They found that the basic symbol of the code was a sequence of three consecutive bases of the DNA molecule. Therefore, according to the combination of the four possible bases—adenine, guanine, cytosine, and thymine (DNA) or uracil (RNA)—the different triplet sequences (or codons) could specify the 20 or so amino acids commonly used by cells for protein synthesis and give start and stop signals for the process. Investigations in many species have shown that the code seems to apply universally.

genetics The study of heredity and variation in living organisms. The science of genetics is founded on the work of Gregor *Mendel, who, in 1865, established the basic laws of inheritance. In the early 20th century *chromosomes and their *genes were established as the carriers of information determining inheritable characteristics, and with the discovery of the structure of *DNA in 1953, the molecular basis of genetics was revealed.

Genetics is important in plant and animal breeding, in understanding inherited diseases and abnormalities, especially in man, and in obtaining strains of microorganisms beneficial to man, such as yeasts used in brewing and fungi for the production of antibiotics. By means of genetic engineering, genes can now be transferred between species.

Geneva (French name: Genève; German name: Genf) 46 13N 6 09E A city in SW Switzerland, on the SW corner of Lake Geneva. It is a cultural and commercial center with over two-thirds of the population employed in the service sector, banking and international finance being particularly important. Industries include the production of watches, precision instruments, and chemicals. It is the base of many international organizations including the International Red Cross, the World Health Organization, and the International Labor Organization. The European headquarters of the UN is also here, occupying the buildings that formerly housed the League of Nations. It has a cathedral (12th–13th centuries) and a university (1559). *History*: originating as a prehistoric lake dwelling, it was later a Roman city. It became the center of the Calvinist Reformation and a refuge for persecuted Protestants. Population (1991 est): 167,000.

Geneva, Lake (French name: Lac Léman; German name: Genfersee) A lake on the Rhône River lying partly in Switzerland and partly in France. Geneva (at its W end) and Lausanne and Montreux are on the Swiss N shore, while the French resort of Evian lies on its S shore. Its scenic beauty is dominated by the Alps to the S. Area: 223 sq mi (577 sq km).

Geneva Bible An English translation of the Bible published in 1560 by Puritan exiles in Geneva. It is also called the Breeches Bible because of the use of the word in the translation of Genesis 3.7.

Geneva Conferences **1.** (1932–34) An international conference on *disarmament. Representatives of 59 states attended the opening meeting, but the major powers were unable to come to an agreement and in 1933 Hitler withdrew Germany from both the conference and the *League of Nations. Continuing deadlock led to the postponement of the conference, which did not reassemble. **2.** (1954) A conference convened following the conclusion of the *Korean War. Discussions on the settlement of Korea, attended by representatives of the US, Soviet Union, the UK, France, North Korea, South Korea, and the People's Republic of China ended without agreement. The war in *Indochina was also discussed by representatives of the US, the Soviet Union, the UK, France, China, Vietnam, Cambodia, Laos, and the *Viet Minh; a ceasefire line was settled along the *seventeenth parallel.

Geneva Conventions International agreements covering the care and protection of noncombatants and wounded troops in wartime. Inspired by the establishment of the International *Red Cross, the first conference, attended by representatives from 16 countries, met in Geneva in 1864 to formulate a code of practice for the treatment of wounded soldiers. Later conventions (1906, 1929) ratified further agreements, covering assistance for forces at sea and treatment of *prisoners of war. In 1949 a fourth convention concerning the protection of civilians was incorporated and the others revised. Most states accept the conventions as morally binding. Neutral countries and the International Red Cross have a supervisory role in wartime but enforcement is difficult as violation cannot be punished.

Genghis Khan (c. 1162–1227) The founder of the Mongol empire. Originally called Tamujin, he adopted the title Genghis Khan (Emperor of All) in 1206 after uniting under his command the nomadic Mongol tribes of the Siberian steppes and destroying Tatar power. Organizing his horsemen into highly mobile and disciplined squadrons called *ordus* (hence "hordes"), he attacked China's frontiers. Although his armies breached the Great Wall and captured Peking, they failed to conquer China completely. Advancing westward, Genghis, by ruthless massacres and pillage, crushed all resistance in Afghanistan, Persia, and S Russia. After his death, his son Ogadai (1185–1241) executed Genghis's plans for the empire's organization.

genipap The fruit of *Genipa americana,* a small West Indian tree. The genipap resembles a brown orange and is used in preserves and beverages. Family: *Rubiaceae* (madder family).

Genk 50 58N 5 30E A city in Belgium. The center of an important coal-mining region, its manufactures include mining machinery. Population (1981 est): 61,399.

Gennesaret, Lake of. *See* Galilee, Sea of.

Genoa (Italian name: Genova) 44 24N 8 56E A port in NW Italy, the capital of Liguria on the Gulf of Genoa. A major maritime city during the Middle Ages, it possesses many notable buildings dating from then. These include the cathedral of San Lorenzo (1118) and a university (1471). Genoa is Italy's chief port and also a major industrial center with ship building, heavy engineering, steel processing, and oil refining. Population (1991): 701,032.

genotype The genetic constitution of an individual organism, which comprises its *genes and determines the physical characteristics (*see* phenotype) of that individual.

genre painting A type of painting representing some aspect of everyday life. Although earlier examples exist, genre painting first became popular in 17th-century Holland, where the political, economic, and religious structure favored its development under such painters as *Vermeer, *Steen, and de *Hooch. Notable 18th-century examples are the works of *Hogarth and *Chardin. Genre painting became particularly widespread in the 19th century, when the impressionists and Victorian painters enthusiastically adopted it. Although now overshadowed by abstract art it is still practiced.

Genseric (*or* Gaiseric; d. 477 AD) King of the *Vandals (428–77), who played a major role in bringing about the fall of the *Roman Empire. He led the Vandals from Spain to N Africa, which he conquered after seizing Carthage from the Romans in 439. In 455 he sacked Rome.

Gent. *See* Ghent.

gentian A herbaceous plant of the widely distributed genus *Gentiana* (about 400 species), which includes many alpine perennials. The leaves are opposite and unstalked. The flowers have four or five petals, usually blue, arranged to form a bell or funnel with spreading lobes. The fruit of most species is a capsule. Many gentians are cultivated in rock gardens. Family: *Gentianaceae.*

gentian violet A purple dye derived from *aniline. It is used as an antiseptic, a chemical indicator, and as a dye.

Gentile, Giovanni (1875–1944) Italian philosopher. Gentile held to Hegelian theories about the dominance of the will; a thinking person had a spiritual unity that was realized in the *pure act*—hence his doctrine of "actualism." As Mussolini's minister of public education he was instructed to reform the educational system, which for him meant purging it of teachers suspected of democratic or

single-factor inheritance

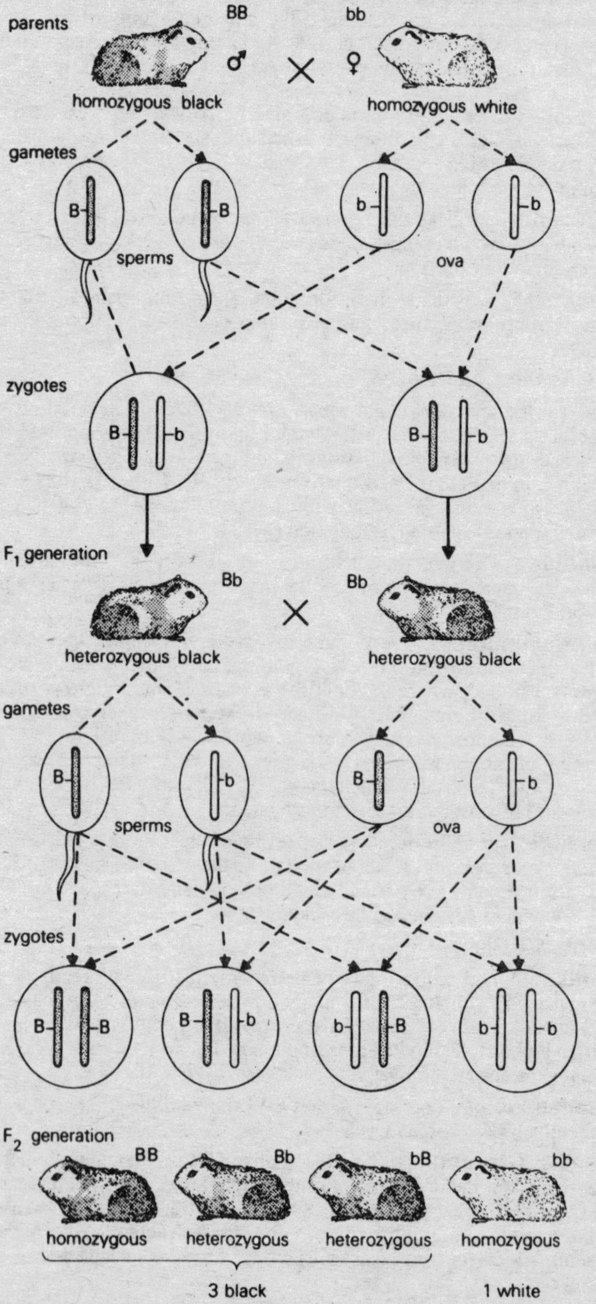
parents
BB
bb
♂
×
♀
homozygous black
homozygous white
gametes
B
B
b
b
sperms
ova
zygotes
B
b
B
b
F1 generation
Bb
Bb
×
heterozygous black
heterozygous black
gametes
B
b
B
b
sperms
ova
zygotes
B
B
B
b
b
B
b
b
F2 generation
BB
Bb
bB
bb
homozygous
heterozygous
heterozygous
homozygous
3 black
1 white

1031

GENETICS

two-factor inheritance

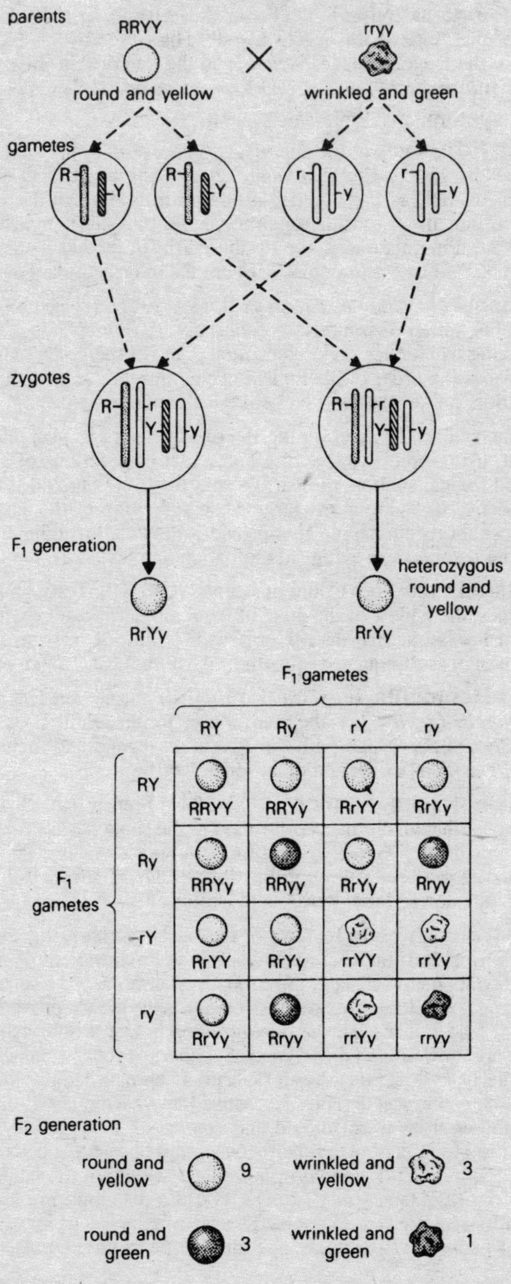

liberal tendencies. His former collaborator *Croce protested in vain against this process.

Gentile da Fabriano (Niccolò di Giovanni di Massio; c. 1370–1427) Florentine painter of the *international gothic style. His fresco cycles (completed by *Pisanello) for the Doge's Palace, Venice, and the Lateran Basilica, Rome, have perished. The *Adoration of the Magi* (Uffizi) shows his richly decorated style.

geocentric system. *See* Ptolemaic system.

geochemistry The study of the chemical composition of the earth. It involves estimating the absolute and relative abundance of the constituent elements and their isotopes, as well as their distribution and migration in the various geochemical environments (lithosphere, atmosphere, biosphere, hydrosphere) and in the rocks and minerals that make up the earth. In the earth's crust, oxygen (47%), silicon (28%), and aluminum (8%) are the most abundant elements.

geochronology The study of dating geological events, rocks, sediments, and organic remains, either absolutely or relatively. Absolute dating involves radioactive *dating techniques giving an actual date BP (before present). Relative dating establishes the order of geological events in relation to each other, using fossil correlation, pollen analysis, archeological evidence, etc.

geodesy The science of determining the exact shape and size of the earth or portions of it, using precise surveying and exact calculations of gravitational force. Related topics, such as the earth's rotational effects and tides, are also studied. Geodetic surveying is the large-scale surveying of the earth's surface, taking into account its curvature. This provides the data for fixing exact control points for more detailed surveying (triangulation and leveling).

Geoffrey Martel (1006–60) Count of Anjou (1040–60). Through his marriage (1032) to Agnes, the widow of the duke of Aquitaine, he unsuccessfully claimed Aquitaine for his heirs. However, Geoffrey's policy of territorial expansion found fruition in his subsequent acquisition of Touraine and much of Maine.

Geoffrey of Monmouth (c. 1100–54) English chronicler. His major work, *Historia Regum Britanniae,* was the main source for the whole body of medieval European literature concerned with the Arthurian legend and included the stories of King Lear, Cymbeline, and other legendary figures.

Geoffroy Saint-Hilaire, Étienne (1772–1844) French naturalist, who originated the concept that all animals conformed to the same basic structural plan or "unity of composition." Geoffroy saw modern species as unchanging but derived from ancestral species through the appearance of successful "monstrosities." This foreshadowed later concepts of evolution.

geography The study of the features of the earth's surface, together with their spatial distribution and interrelationships, as the environment of man. During the earliest development of geography the Greeks, notably Herodotus, Eratosthenes of Cyrene, and Ptolemy, were concerned with the shape of the earth and the location of land and sea. Through exploration in later centuries more knowledge of the earth was amassed and modern geography was founded as a discipline in the early 19th century by the German scholars Humboldt and Ritter. During the 20th century geography has moved away from a regional approach, in which different areas were studied and compared, to a more systematic approach. The discipline is now divided between the physical and social sciences. Physical geography includes geomorphology (the study of the landforms of the earth), biogeography (the study of soils and the distribution of animals and plants), and climatology (*see* climate). The main branches of human geography are historical geography (studying spatial change in an area over a period of time or reconstructing past landscapes), economic geography, urban geography, and political geography.

geological time scale A time scale covering the whole of the earth's history from its origin about 4600 million years ago to the present. The largest divisions are eras (Paleozoic, Mesozoic, and Cenozoic); these are subdivided into periods and the Tertiary and Quaternary periods are further subdivided into epochs; epochs consist of several ages, and ages can be divided into chrons. A number of eras together is an eon. This is known as the chronomeric standard scale of chronostratigraphic classification. The stratomeric standard scale refers to the bodies of rocks formed in these time intervals; the corresponding terms are group (era), system (period), series (epoch), stage (age), and chronozone (chron). The divisions are not uniform time intervals but are based mainly on major evolutionary changes. For example, at the beginning of the Cambrian, about 570 million years ago, marine organisms suddenly became abundant and varied. □geology.

geology The study of the earth: its origin, history, structure, composition, and the natural processes acting on it. The branches of geology are historical (including geochronology, stratigraphy, and paleontology); physical (including geomorphology, geophysics, petrology, mineralogy, crystallography, and geochemistry); and economic, involving the distribution and occurrence of the economically important rocks and minerals, such as petroleum.

geomagnetic field The earth's magnetic field, causing a compass needle to align N–S. It is believed to be caused by the liquid-iron core acting as a dynamo resulting from the convection currents moving in it. The magnetic poles do not coincide with the geographic poles, and their positions vary with time. Complete reversals of the earth's magnetic field have occurred in the past; relic magnetism in rocks, which coincides with the magnetic alignment adopted at the time of their formation, provides strong evidence for the theory of sea-floor spreading and continental drift (*see* plate tectonics). The three **magnetic elements** of the earth's field are the *magnetic dip, the *magnetic declination, and the horizontal field strength, which together completely define the earth's field at any point on its surface.

geometrid moth A moth of the family *Geometridae,* occurring in Europe, Asia, and North America. The name is derived from the looping method of locomotion of the caterpillars, which are known as inchworms, loopers, or measuring worms. The adults, known as pugs, umbers, carpet moths, etc., have slender bodies, a weak flight, and camouflaging coloration, often resembling dead leaves.

geometry A branch of mathematics concerned with the properties of space and shapes. In *Euclidean geometry the space corresponds to common notions of physical space and the shapes are idealizations of the common shapes that occur in real life. Other branches of geometry include *non-Euclidean geometry, such as the geometry of the surface of a sphere; *Riemannian geometry, which is used in *relativity theory; and *analytic geometry, in which algebra is used to solve geometrical problems. *See also* topology.

geophysics The study of the physical forces acting on, and particularly within, the earth. Sophisticated equipment is used to study the properties, structure, composition, and evolution of the earth. Important branches of geophysics are seismology, geomagnetism, vulcanology, natural radioactivity, and the earth's rotation and gravitational field. Much geophysical data has been collected in recent years as a result of geophysical prospecting, particularly for petroleum.

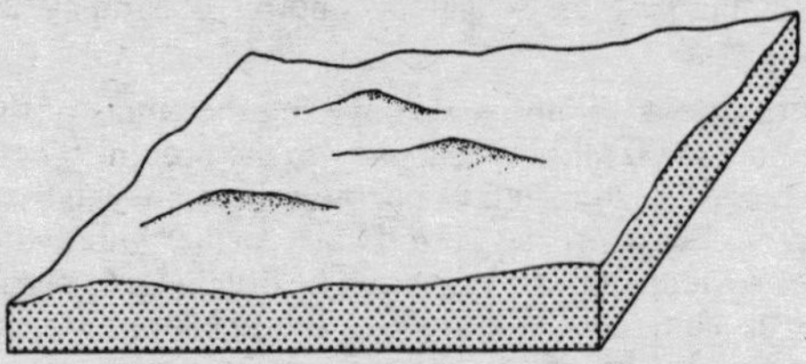

1 *Desert conditions resulted in the lowest rock layer being sandstone.*

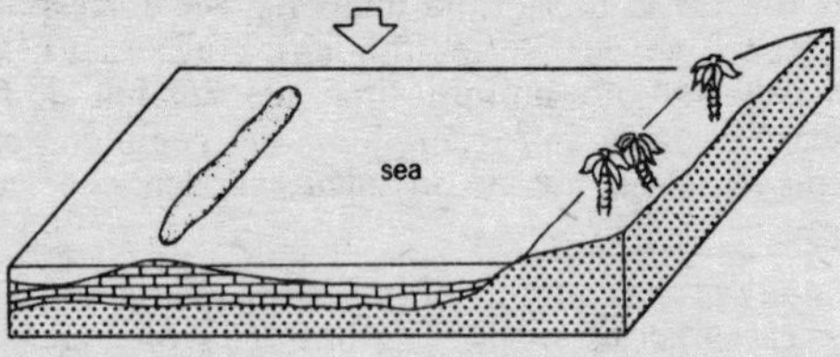

2 *The advance of a warm sea over much of the area saw the deposition of chalk.*

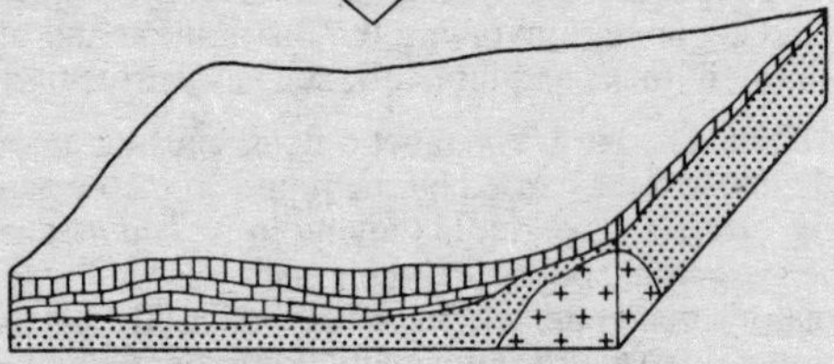

3 *Following the retreat of the sea the area was covered with a fine sediment eventually forming clay and an igneous intrusion of granite was forced up by volcanic activity into the overlying strata.*

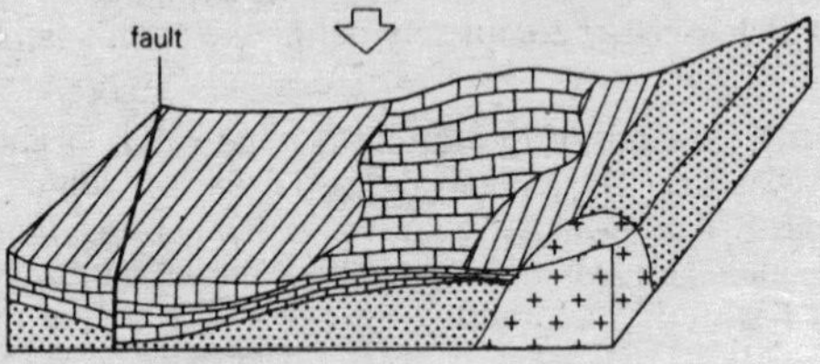

4 *The area was then subjected to folding, faulting, and erosion to form the present day landscape.*

geological map

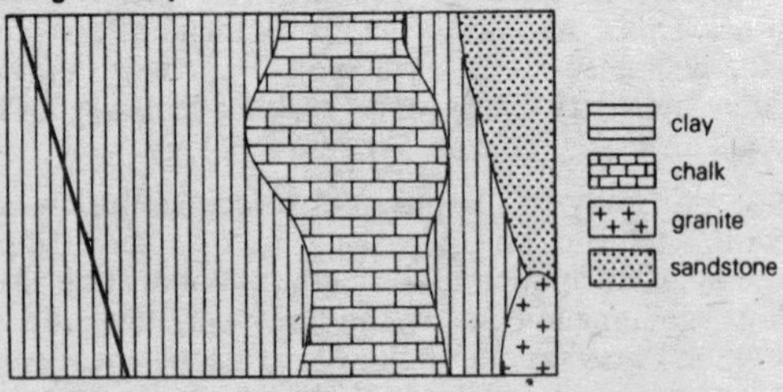

The map of the same area shows the rock types that would be exposed if the overlying soil and vegetation were stripped away.

stages in the evolution of the geological strata of a small area

GEOLOGY

Era	Period	Epoch	millions of years ago
Cenozoic	Quaternary	Holocene	
		Pleistocene	1·8
	Tertiary	Pliocene	
		Miocene	
		Oligocene	
		Eocene	
		Palaeocene	65
Mesozoic	Cretaceous		135
	Jurassic		200
	Triassic		240
Palaeozoic	Permian		280
	Carboniferous		370
	Devonian		415
	Silurian		445
	Ordovician		515
	Cambrian		590
Precambrian	Precambrian		4500

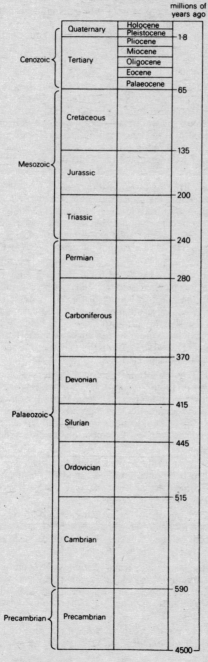

geological time scale

geopolitics The study of the influence of geographical factors upon international politics. It suggests that a state's foreign policy is influenced by its desire to obtain, for example, sufficient agricultural land. The term was coined by the Swedish political scientist Rudolf Kjellen (1864–1922) and was used by the Nazis, who justified their expansionist ambitions as the seeking of *Lebensraum* (living space). As a result geopolitics was discredited and has become outdated by technological developments.

George I (1660–1727) The first Hanoverian king of Great Britain and Ireland (1714–27) and Elector of Hanover (1698–1727). He divorced his wife, Sophia Dorothea, for infidelity (1694) and imprisoned her for 32 years. A successful soldier and a shrewd diplomat, he was nonetheless unpopular in Britain because he seemed to subordinate British to Hanoverian interests. He never learned English and left government to his Whig ministers, particularly after they saved George and his mistresses from disgrace in connection with the *South Sea Bubble.

George II (1683–1760) King of Great Britain and Ireland and Elector of Hanover (1727–69), succeeding his father George I. He married *Caroline of Ansbach in 1705. His reliance on his ministers, especially Sir Robert *Walpole, influenced the development of constitutional monarchy. He was an ardent soldier and in the War of Austrian Succession fought at Dettingen (1743), the last British monarch to appear in battle. He was a patron of musicians, notably Handel.

George III (1738–1820) King of Great Britain and Ireland (1760–1820) and Elector (1760–1815) and king (1815–20) of Hanover, succeeding his grandfather George II. He married Charlotte Sophia of Mecklenburg-Strelitz (1744–1818) in 1761. The political instability of the 1760s was blamed by the Whigs unjustly on George's alleged attempts to influence Parliament through corrupt "king's friends." He shared with Lord *North the blame for the loss of the American colonies but was more astute in backing William *Pitt the Younger as prime minister (1783–1801). From the 1780s he suffered periods of madness and was permanently insane by 1811.

George IV (1762–1830) King of the United Kingdom and of Hanover (1820–30), succeeding his father George III, for whom he was regent (1811–20). He secretly married a Roman Catholic, Maria Fitzherbert, in 1785 but the marriage was invalid and in 1795 he married *Caroline of Brunswick. They were separated in 1796. Although intelligent and artistic, George's dissipation and extravagance and his heartless treatment of Caroline undermined the prestige of the monarchy.

George V (1865–1936) King of the United Kingdom (1910–36), second son of Edward VII, whose heir he became on the death (1892) of his elder brother Albert Victor. In 1893 George married *Mary of Teck. He gave valuable political advice during the many crises of his reign.

George VI (1895–1952) King of the United Kingdom (1936–52) Second son of George V, he succeeded to the throne when Edward VIII abdicated. He married (1923) Lady Elizabeth Bowes-Lyon (*see* Elizabeth the Queen Mother). His example inspired Britain during World War II.

George, St The patron saint of England and of soldiers. His cult was brought to England by Crusaders returning from Palestine, where he was believed to have been martyred during Emperor Diocletian's rule. In art he is usually portrayed slaying a dragon to rescue a maiden, a legend that probably derives from the *Pegasus myth. Feast day: Apr 23.

George, Lake A lake in E New York, N of Albany, that runs NE from the village of Lake George to Ticonderoga near the Vermont border, where it joins an outlet to Lake Champlain. Strategically located, Lake George was important during the French and Indian Wars and the American Revolution. It is a popular resort area. Area: 33 mi (54 km) long; 1–3 mi (1.6–5 km) wide.

Georgetown (*or* Penang) 5 26N 100 16E A city in NW Peninsular Malaysia, the capital of Penang state. The first British Malayan settlement, it is now Malaysia's chief port, exporting tin, rubber, and copra. Population (1980): 250,578.

Georgetown 6 46N 58 10W The capital and main port of Guyana, on the Atlantic Ocean at the mouth of the Demerara River. Founded by the British in 1781, it was later occupied by the French and the Dutch. It has twice in recent years (1945, 1951) been badly damaged by fire. Exports include sugar, rice, and bauxite. Its university was founded in 1963. Population (1985 est): 170,000.

Georgia A state on the SE coast. It is bordered by Florida on the S, Alabama on the W, Tennessee and North Carolina on the N, and South Carolina on the NE, where the Savannah River forms the boundary between the two states. In the SE Georgia fronts the Atlantic Ocean. The state can be divided into three physiographic regions: the higher elevations of the Appalachian Mountains in the N; a rolling coastal plain with forests and swamps in the S; and the Piedmont Plateau separating the two. Manufacturing is important and widely dispersed. Georgia is the nation's major textile producer; other industries include motor vehicles and aircraft assembly, chemicals, and food processing. The state is also a major source of building stone and is noted for its fine marble. Agriculture is important; poultry has replaced cotton as the major item and Georgia is a leading US producer of peanuts. Other products include tobacco, watermelons, and other fruits (especially peaches), with some cattle and pig raising. Forest products are produced throughout the state. Its capital, Atlanta, is the cultural and economic center of the SE and the state has a rich traditional folk culture. *History*: first visited by De Soto in 1540, the state was originally inhabited by Creek and Cherokee Indians. Subsequently, both Spain and England claimed the area. The first British settlers arrived in 1733, led by James Oglethorpe, who intended the colony to be a refuge for debtors. Named for George II, it became the 13th of the original colonies. Oglethorpe succeeded in routing Spanish troops in 1743, thus safeguarding the colony's future. A large part of the state fell to the British during the American Revolution. With the development of agriculture after the war, settlement grew. Georgia was the first southern state to ratify the Constitution (1788). A proslavery state with a cotton-based economy, Georgia seceded from the Union and joined the Confederate cause in the Civil War. It suffered considerable damage, most notably the burning of Atlanta (1864) and later in that year General Sherman's March to the Sea. It was the only southern state to integrate its public schools in the 1950s without incident. In 1976, Jimmy Carter, originally a Georgia peanut farmer and former governor, was the state's first native son to be elected to the US presidency. In 1983 the state passed desegregation legislation governing its institutions of higher learning. Area: 58,876 sq mi (152,488 sq km). Population (1990): 6,448,216. Capital: Atlanta.

Georgia, Republic of (*or* Georgia) A republic in SE Europe, a former republic of the Soviet Union. It is a mountainous region with many holiday resorts on the Black Sea coast. The population is predominantly Georgian. Georgia is rich in minerals, especially manganese and coal, and a gold field was discovered in 1941. The region also has vast hydroelectric resources. The main crop is tea; citrus fruits, grapes, and tobacco are also important to agriculture. *History*: Christianity was introduced in the 4th century AD. An independent kingdom for most of the Middle Ages, Georgia was divided between Persia and Turkey in 1555, passing to Russia in the 19th century. It became independent in 1918 but subsequently formed part of the Transcaucasian Soviet Federated Republic (*see* Transcaucasia). It became a constituent republic in 1936. As communism collapsed in the Soviet Union in 1991, Georgia claimed independence. Area: c. 26,900 sq mi (c. 69,700 sq km). Population (1987): 5,266,000. Capital: Tbilisi.

Georgian The language spoken by the Georgian peoples of Georgia, Azerbaijan, NE Turkey, and Isfahan province in Iran. It belongs to the Kartvelian or *South Caucasian group and is written in a script derived from Aramaic with Greek influences and has a literature dating from the 5th century AD. It is the official language of Georgia.

Georgian Bay A large bay in central Canada, in NE Lake Huron in Ontario. Its many islands and irregular coastline make it a popular recreational area.

Georgian style A style of British architecture prevalent during the reigns of George I to George IV (1714–1830). The period was subject to several different influences but was dominated by *Palladianism and *neoclassicism. Well-proportioned elegance was the keynote of Georgian architecture, characterized by the symmetrical use of 12-paned sash windows in domestic architecture and the restrained use of classical features in public buildings.

geostationary orbit. *See* communications satellite.

geothermal energy Heat produced in the earth's interior, which may provide a source of usable energy. Volcanoes, geysers, and hot springs are all sources of geothermal energy, although only the latter two provide convenient energy sources. Countries that make use of geothermal energy include Iceland (where it is an important source of power), Italy, New Zealand, and the US. Although geothermal energy is being actively explored as an alternative energy source, it currently supplies only about 0.1% of the world's energy requirements.

Gera 50 53N 12 6E A city in S Germany, on the Weisse Elster River in Thuringia. Its manufactures include machinery, textiles, and furniture; there are uranium mines nearby. Population (1990): 130,000.

geranium A herbaceous plant of the genus *Pelargonium* (250 species), most species of which are native to South Africa and widely cultivated as house and garden plants. They have roundish leaves and rounded clusters of showy flowers, usually red or pink. Most horticultural geraniums are hybrids, of which the most important are the zonal pelargoniums, with a dark ring near the center of each leaf. Family: *Geraniaceae.*

Horticultural geraniums should be distinguished from related plants of the genus *Geranium* (*see* cranesbill).

Gérard, François (Pascal Simon), Baron (1770–1837) French painter, born in Rome. He was the pupil of *David but later rivaled him at the court of Napoleon with his elegant portraits, e.g. *Josephine Bonaparte* (Louvre), and history paintings. After Napoleon's fall, he became painter to Louis XVIII, who ennobled him in 1819.

gerbil A small *rodent belonging to the subfamily *Gerbillinae* (over 100 species) of Africa and Asia, also called jird and sand rat. Ranging in size from 2–8 in (5–20 cm), gerbils have long hind legs. They inhabit dry open country and spend the day in underground burrows, feeding at night on seeds and roots. Chief genera: *Gerbillus, Tatera*; family: *Cricetidae.*

gerenuk A long-necked antelope, *Litocranius walleri,* of E African bush country. About 40 in (100 cm) tall at the shoulder, gerenuks are bright chestnut with white underparts; only males have the curved backward-pointing horns.

They feed by rearing up on their hind legs and cropping leaves from thorny shrubs.

GERENUK *A male on the lookout for approaching predators; the animal has a good view because of its long neck.*

geriatrics The medical specialty that deals with the diseases and problems of old age. With improved standards of living and medical care, the number of people surviving to old age has increased and the suitable care of elderly patients is of great importance. In the past little active treatment was given, the patients being virtually bedridden in hospitals, almshouses, etc. Now, however, the aim is to restore as much function and activity as possible, by encouraging patients to engage in suitable activities with the aid of physiotherapy and occupational therapy.

Géricault, (Jean Louis André) Théodore (1791–1824) French painter, born in Rouen. His famous *Raft of the Medusa* (1819; Louvre), for which he used corpses in the morgue as models, was based on a contemporary shipwreck, which had become a political issue. While visiting England (1820–22), he produced a number of lithographs depicting poor people. He also painted his favorite subject—horses (e.g. *Derby at Epsom*; Louvre). His last works, inspired by a psychiatrist friend, were five portraits of the insane. Despite his early death after a riding accident, he greatly influenced French Romantic painters, especially *Delacroix.

German A language of the West *Germanic language group. It is the official language of Germany and Austria and one of the four official languages of Switzerland. High German, the official and written form, developed from dialects of the highland areas of Germany and Austria. Old High German was spoken before 1100 AD when Middle High German, based on Upper German dialects, became the standard form. Modern High German developed from the 16th-century dialect of Luther, whose biblical translations spread this form. Low German exists only in a spoken form in the lowland areas of N Germany and is derived from Old Saxon and Middle Low German speech. The main difference between Low and High German is the sound system, especially the consonants.

germander A herbaceous plant of the worldwide genus *Teucrium* (300 species), with square stems and simple toothed leaves. The small tubular two-lipped flowers, borne in groups in the axils of leaflike bracts, are usually pinkish-purple. The perennial water germander (*T. scordium*) is a Eurasian species. Family: **Labiatae.*

Germanic languages A subgroup of the *Indo-European language group. Its member languages are spoken in Britain, Scandinavia, Germany, the Netherlands, and Iceland. There are three recognized subgroups: East Germanic, North Germanic, and West Germanic. The first of these is now extinct but it included Gothic, one of the earliest Germanic languages. North Germanic covers the *Scandinavian languages. West Germanic includes modern English and German among its descendants as well as *Dutch (Netherlandic) and *Frisian. These developed from their earlier forms, High and Low German, Anglo-Saxon, Middle English, and Old Saxon. Also developed from Germanic origins are *Yiddish and Afrikaans (*see* Afrikaner). All three branches can be traced back to an unrecorded Proto-Germanic language, which has been reconstructed by philologists by comparing and tracing back similar modern languages using such generalizations as those stated in Grimm's Law (*see* Grimm).

Germanicus Julius Caesar (15 BC–19 AD) Roman soldier, who was adopted by his uncle, Emperor Tiberius, in 4 AD. In 17 he was appointed to govern Rome's E provinces and died mysteriously in Antioch, perhaps as a result of poison. Germanicus married *Agrippina the Elder and was the father of Caligula.

germanium (Ge) A brittle gray-white metalloid, discovered by C. A. Winkler (1838–1904) in 1886. Like *gallium it is present in coal and is concentrated in chimney soot as well as in the flue dusts of zinc smelters, from which it is obtained commercially. The element is a *semiconductor and its most important uses are in the electronics industry. Germanium compounds include the volatile tetrachloride ($GeCl_4$) and the dioxide (GeO_2), which has a high refractive index and is used in lenses. At no 32; at wt 72.59; mp 1721°F (937.4°C); bp 5131°F (2830°C)

German literature Little vernacular German literature earlier than the 12th century survives. The fragmentary *Hildebrandslied* (c. 800) is the only extant example of early heroic verse. The major works of medieval German literature were the epics the *Nibelungenlied* and *Gudrun,* several court epics based on French models, and the love lyrics of the wandering minnesingers, notably those of Walther von der Vogelweide. The Reformation had a great influence, especially through Luther's translation of the Bible (1522; 1534); Lutheran ideals were often expressed in the poetry of the *Meistersingers, the best known of whom was Hans Sachs. The Thirty Years' War, portrayed in Grimmelhausen's novels, resulted in cultural insecurity in the 17th and early 18th centuries and adherence to French models. An upsurge of national feeling in the 18th century resulted in a literary revival; the literature of the Enlightenment, represented most notably by Lessing, was succeeded by the **Sturm und Drang* movement and at the end of the century by romanticism.

Goethe and Schiller outgrew *Sturm und Drang* emotionalism and espoused classicism instead, although Goethe's *Faust* remains balanced by warmth of feeling. The poets Hölderlin and Heine, the novelist and dramatist Kleist, and the dramatist Büchner were not associated with particular literary movements.

The aestheticism of the late 19th and early 20th centuries, found in the poems of George and the plays of Hofmannsthal, was paralleled by the realism of Fontane's novels. The social malaise of Germany at the time of World War I was reflected in expressionism, elements of which appear in the works of various writers, influencing the mysticism in Rilke's poetry, the nightmare visions in Kafka's novels, and the search for new social and aesthetic values in the novels of Thomas Mann and Hesse and the dramas of Brecht.

The economic and political character of West Germany after World War II has been analyzed in the novels of Böll and Grass. The Swiss playwrights Max Frisch and Friedrich Dürrenmatt have written a number of influential plays. In East Germany postwar literature suffered from an official insistence on a restrictive form of socialist realism; only recently have poets and novelists emerged who show signs of being able to develop their individual talents. The reunification of Germany (1990) inspired hope that a new national literature would emerge.

German measles A common contagious disease of children and young adults caused by a virus. Known medically as rubella, it is a mild infection producing a pink rash and a sore throat. If a woman is infected in early pregnancy she may give birth to a malformed child; for this reason immunization of schoolgirls is encouraged.

German shepherd dog (*or* Alsatian) A breed of large strongly built □dog originating in Germany. It has a coarse coat that can range in color from white to black but is often black and tan. German shepherds are used as working dogs, especially for police work, as guard dogs, and as guide dogs for the blind. Height: 24–26 in (61–66 cm) (dogs); 22–24 in (56–61 cm) (bitches).

Germany A country in central Europe, comprising between the end of World War II and 1990 (*see* below) the German Democratic Republic (East Germany) and the Federal Republic of Germany (West Germany). The region was occupied by German tribes from about 500 BC and came repeatedly into conflict with the Romans from the 2nd century BC. Overrun by the Huns in the 4th and 5th centuries, the area was dominated by the *Franks from the 6th century and was christianized in the late-7th to 8th centuries. After the death of the Carolingian Louis the Pius his empire was divided (843), the E part becoming the eastern Frankish Kingdom, the nucleus of Germany. After the failure of the Frankish dynasty the German kings became nominally elective (*see* electors) but medieval Germany was in practice ruled by a series of hereditary dynasties. The first of these, the Saxons, was founded by Henry the Fowler in 919 and from the election (963) of his son as Holy Roman Emperor (*see* Otto [I] the Great), the German kings claimed the imperial title by right. The 11th–13th centuries were dominated by struggle between the emperors and popes over the *investiture controversy, which with the conflict between *Guelfs and Ghibellines gave rise to a sustained period of civil strife. In the 13th century, following the fall of the *Hohenstaufen dynasty, the first *Hapsburg emperor was elected and from the 15th century the imperial title remained almost continuously in the family. In the later Middle Ages the power of the princes was challenged by the *Hanseatic League of northern ports, which wielded political as well as commercial power. The 16th and 17th centuries were dominated by religious strife, following Luther's inception of the *Reformation at Wittenberg in 1520 and the subsequent division of Germany into a predominantly Protestant N and Roman Catholic S. The religious conflict was not resolved until the conclusion (1648) of the *Thirty Years' War. In the 17th century the Hohenzollern Electors of Brandenburg acquired Prussia, which, as a kingdom from 1701, became the dominant German state and, under *Frederick (II) the Great, a major European power. In 1806 the Holy Roman Empire was brought to an end by Napoleon, who formed the *Confederation of the Rhine in its place. The post-Napoleonic German confederation was dominated by Austria and Prussia and in 1834 the latter was the moving influence behind the formation of the *Zollverein (customs union). Prussian power increased further with victory in the *Austro-Prussian War (1866), which permanently destroyed Austrian influence in Germany, and in the *Franco-Prussian War (1870–71). In 1871 Bismarck achieved his cherished ambition of creating a German Empire. The late 19th and early 20th centuries saw rapid industrialization, an aggressive armaments program, and the rise of Germany as a colonial power, especially in Africa; its international aspirations were a major cause of *World War I. Defeated in 1918, the Empire came to an end (1919) and was replaced by the *Weimar Republic, which was plagued by the economic difficulties that facilitated *Hitler's rise to power in the early 1930s. His aggressive foreign policy, aimed at the establishment of a new German empire, led to the annexation of Austria and the Sudetenland (1938) and then of Czechoslovakia (1939). Finally, his invasion of Poland precipitated World War II. Following Germany's defeat the country was divided into British, French, Soviet, and US occupation zones before the subsequent formation of the two separate states, the German Democratic Republic and the Federal Republic of Germany. Deteriorating economic and political conditions in East Germany in 1989 led to sharp increases in the number of East Germans fleeing to the West. East German leaders were too late in preparing reforms, and the government effectively collapsed. As the Berlin Wall was torn apart by Germans anxious to reunite, plans to join the two countries accelerated. In October 1990 the two Germanies were reunited into a single country. The nation faced serious economic problems stemming from the virtual disintegration of the East's economic infrastructure. Rebuilding the economy preoccupied the government during the early 1990s, but Germany continued as a European leader, urging closer EEC relations. Chancellor: Helmut Kohl. Official language: German. Official currency: Deutsche mark of 100 pfennigs. Population (1990 est): 77,600,000. Capital: Berlin. Area: 137,746 sq mi (356,762 sq km).

German Democratic Republic (GDR; commonly called East Germany) The E part, long a separate country, of Germany. The N part of the region, which borders on the Baltic Sea and includes the island of *Rügen, is generally low lying and contains many lakes. The Harz Mountains rise in the W, the Thuringian Forest in the SW, and the Erzgebirge in the SE. The main rivers are the Elbe and the Oder. *Economy*: although traditionally strong in such areas as precision engineering (including optical instruments) and electronics, as well as heavy industries, such as shipbuilding, machinery, and chemicals, the economy faced severe problems after German reunification. Light industries, such as textiles and food products also experienced a slowdown. The main mineral resource is lignite, which supplies over half of the country's basic energy. It has two nuclear power stations. Oil and coal (all East German coal mines were largely exhausted and closed by the end of 1977) were imported. The agricultural sector gradually declined in importance although forestry remained an important source of revenue. Exports include lignite, potash, textiles, and photographic paper. *History*: formed from the Soviet-occupied zone of Germany following World War II, it was given a provisional constitution as the German Democratic Republic in 1949, becoming independent in 1954. The leading architect of the new state was Walter Ulbricht, in whose hands real power lay from its establishment, and in 1960, following the death of Pres. Wilhelm Pieck, he became chairman of the newly established Council of State. The early years of economic austerity and curbs on civil liberties led to much discontent and in 1953 serious riots, particularly in East Berlin, were suppressed by Soviet troops, but the flow of refugees to West Germany continued until 1961, when the *Berlin Wall was erected. From the early 1970s there was a marked improvement in living standards and relations with West Germany have eased slightly with a treaty calling for closer relations being ratified by both countries in 1973. Disagreement between West and East Germany over the political status of the GDR continued into the mid-1980s but then eased. Political and economic crises in 1989 triggered a flood of refugees to West Germany. Desperate to prevent the nation's collapse, East German leaders loosened their hold on the country. Eventually yielding to the demands of the people, the government agreed to join with the West in a reunified Germany, formally marked on Oct 3, 1990. The transition from a communist state to a democratic one has severely strained eastern Germany's economy, especially the job market. Area: 41,757 sq mi (108,178 sq km).

Germany, Federal Republic of (commonly called West Germany) The W part, long a separate country, of Germany. For administrative purposes, West Germany was divided into 11 *Länder* (German *Land,* state). Extensive plains in the N, which border on the North Sea, rise to a central hilly area with the peaks of the Alps in the extreme S. The chief rivers are the Rhine, Danube, Ems, Weser, and Elbe. *Economy*: rapid reconstruction, particularly of the industrial sector, followed World War II. There is a large amount of heavy industry, especially in the center and the N, including electrical engineering, iron and steel, motor vehicles, shipbuilding, and chemicals. The manufacture of photographic equipment and optical and other scientific instruments is also important. Considerable mineral resources include coal, iron ore, lead and zinc, and potash. Although the agricultural sector has declined in importance, there is a considerable amount of forestry (now mainly under state control) and an important wine industry, especially in the Rhine and Moselle Valleys. Tourism is an important source of revenue. The main exports include motor vehicles, machinery, chemicals, and electrical-engineering products. *History*: formed from the British-, French-, and US-occupied zones following World War II, it became fully independent in 1955. The capital was transferred to Bonn although West Berlin remained a part of the Federal Republic. In the postwar years it enjoyed a spectacular economic recovery making it the most prosperous country in W Europe. The import of foreign labor became increasingly essential to the continued industrial expansion, although the total number of *Gastarbeiter* (guest workers; *see* migration) has varied according to the fortunes of the economy. Christian Democratic governments under Adenauer and Ehrhard were followed in the early 1970s by the Social Democrats under Willi Brandt, and this contributed to better relations with East Germany and other E European countries. In 1982 the coalition government of Social Democrats and Free Democrats led by Helmut Schmidt collapsed, after his government received a vote of no confidence in the Bundestag. In a stunning victory, Helmut Kohl, the Bundestag choice, received close to 50% of the German vote and a large majority of the seats in parliament. Mindful of Germany's position between superpower interests, West Germany sought "cordial" relations with the Soviet Union and closer ties to East Germany. The stream of refugees from East to West grew to a torrent in 1989 as political and economic conditions in the East worsened. By the end of 1989 it was apparent that the people in both countries wanted unification, which formally took place on Oct 3, 1990. The former West Germany was clearly the dominant force in the united Germany. Area: 95,989 sq mi (248,620 sq km).

germination The process by which an embryo plant within a seed is transformed into a recognizable plant with roots, stem, and leaves. Water, warmth, and oxygen stimulate germination, which begins with the emergence of the root (radicle) and is followed by the shoot (plumule). Energy for the process is provided by the *cotyledons (seed leaves), which either remain below ground (hypogeal germination, as in the broad bean) or form the first leaves of the seedling (epigeal germination, as in the marrow squash).

Germiston 26 15S 28 10E A city in South Africa, in the S Transvaal. It contains the world's largest gold refinery and serves the Witwatersrand mines. It is an important railroad junction and has extensive railroad-engineering industries. Population (1985): 117,000.

Gerona 41 59N 2 49E A city in NE Spain, in Catalonia. It was besieged several times in the 17th–18th centuries. The fine gothic cathedral (1312–1598) has an exceptionally wide single nave. Industries include textiles, paper, and food processing. Population (1986): 68,000.

Geronimo (1829–1909) A leader of the Chiricahua *Apaches. Born in the territory that would later become Arizona, Geronimo led his people in armed resistance to the attempts of the US Army to restrict them to a reservation in the 1870s. Although *Cochise, another Apache leader, agreed to end hostilities in 1872, Geronimo continued his campaign until his surrender in 1886. The Chiricahuas were subsequently resettled near Fort Sill, Okla., and it was there that he dictated his autobiography, *Geronimo: His Own Story,* shortly before his death.

Gerry, Elbridge (1744–1814) US patriot, politician; US vice president (1813–14). A delegate from Massachusetts to the Continental Congress (1776–81) he was a signer of the Declaration of Independence. He served as a representative in Congress (1789–93) and was part of the group sent by Pres. John Adams in 1797 to negotiate a treaty with France and became involved in the *XYZ Affair. He was Massachusetts governor (1810–12) and then US vice president under Pres. James Madison. The term "gerrymander" was coined from his name and the salamander-shaped result of senatorial redistricting while he was the governor of Massachusetts.

Gershwin, George (Jacob Gershvin; 1898–1937) US composer and songwriter. He wrote many songs for musical shows and films, perhaps the best-remembered being "The Man I Love," "I Got Rhythm," and "Lady Be Good." His jazz-inspired orchestral works include *Rhapsody in Blue* (1924) and *An American in Paris* (1928); the opera *Porgy and Bess* (1935) is still widely performed. His brother **Ira Gershwin** (1896–1983) wrote the lyrics to many of his songs.

Gerson, Jean de (1363–1429) French theologian and chancellor of the University of Paris. He was one of the earliest advocates of restricting papal power (*see* Gallicanism). His efforts to end the *Great Schism of the Western Church by calling a general council were rewarded at the Council of *Constance (1415), of which he was a leading member.

Gesner, Conrad (1516–65) Swiss physician, who was a founder of modern zoology and botany. He compiled a survey of knowledge of animal life, the *Historiae animalium* (5 vols, 1551–87), and described many plant species, often in the form of woodcut illustrations. His other works include a bibliography of authors and their works, a survey of world languages, and a compendium of the recorded knowledge of the world.

Gestalt psychology A school of *psychology that originated in Germany in the early 20th century: Wolfgang *Köhler and Kurt *Koffka were its founders. It regards mental processes as wholes (gestalts) that cannot be analyzed into smaller components. According to this theory, when something is learned the individual's entire perception of the environment has been changed.

Gestapo (German: *Ge*heime *Sta*ats*po*lizei, secret state police) The Nazi secret police formed in 1933 under Goering. Administered from 1936 by the *SS, the two organizations were the chief instruments of atrocities carried out by the Nazi Party in Germany and German-occupied Europe.

gestation. *See* pregnancy.

Gesualdo, Carlo, Prince of Venosa (c. 1560–1631) Italian composer. His madrigals employ extraordinary harmonic effects. He was also famous for his lute playing and notorious for the murder of his first (unfaithful) wife.

GERONIMO *Apache Indian chief who led border raids against both US and Mexican troops before being captured in 1886.*

Getty, J(ean) Paul (1892–1976) US businessman. He made his fortune in oil, becoming a millionaire at the age of 22. He founded the J. Paul Getty Museum at Malibu, Calif.

Gettysburg 39 50N 77 14W A town in S Pennsylvania, SW of Harrisburg and York. Settled as a town in the late 1700s, it was the scene of Abraham Lincoln's Gettysburg Address and the Battle of Gettysburg in 1863. Population (1990): 7025.

Gettysburg, Battle of (July 1–3, 1863) One of the most significant battles of the *Civil War, fought in S Pennsylvania as part of the Confederacy's second invasion of the North. The battle began unexpectedly since both armies were uncertain of the other's position. The first day ended with a slight southern advantage, but a delay in the Confederate attack on the second day shifted the advantage to the Federal troops. On the third day, a large force of Confederates, under the command of Gen. George Pickett, charged the center of the Union line, advancing briefly despite massive artillery fire, but eventually withdrawing with losses of more than 60%. The battle was considered a great victory for Union Gen. George Meade, and it ended the Confederacy's hope of carrying the war to the North. The casualties suffered by both sides were enormous; the Union lost 23,000 men and the Confederates 25,000. Four months after the battle, Pres. Abraham *Lincoln traveled to Gettysburg to dedicate a military cemetery where he delivered the **Gettysburg Address** (Nov 19, 1863). It later became one of his best known and most quoted speeches.

Geulincx, Arnold (1624–69) Belgian-born philosopher. He was converted to Protestantism and settled in Holland. In response to *Descartes' mind–body relationship problem Geulincx originated the "two clock" theory, whereby body and mind are conceived of as keeping perfect time, side by side, without interaction. For Geulincx, when a mental or physical process takes place, God occasions it, hence the term "occasionalism" applied to this doctrine (*see also* Malebranche).

geysers Jets of hot water and steam issuing intermittently from holes in the earth's crust, some reaching heights of up to 230 ft (70 m). Geysers are found in volcanically active or recently active regions, for example, in Iceland. They occur when water from deep within the crust becomes superheated and suddenly boils, gushing up to the surface like a fountain. Cones of sinter (deposits of silica) frequently build up around the vents of geysers.

Gezira, El (*or* al-Jazirah) A triangular plain in the Sudan, between the Blue and White Nile Rivers. The Gezira irrigation scheme, using water from the Makwar Dam (completed 1925), makes possible the production of cotton, millet, fodder crops, and groundnuts.

Ghana, Republic of A country in West Africa, on the Gulf of Guinea. Coastal plains rise to undulating country around Accra, and, in the center, the basin of the Volta River rises to plateaus, especially in the N and W. The inhabitants are chiefly of black Sudanese stock but there are a large number of tribal units. *Economy*: chiefly agricultural. Food crops are varied, and increased production is being encouraged through such schemes as "Operation Feed Yourself" in an effort to make the country more self-sufficient. The main cash crop is cocoa, of which Ghana is the world's chief producer. There is also a concentration on such crops as rubber and cotton to provide raw material for industry, in an effort to diversify the economy. Gold and diamonds are mined, as well as manganese, bauxite, and limestone. Hydroelectricity is being developed, particularly through the Volta Dam, and oil was found offshore in 1978. Forestry is important and there are wide reforestation schemes. Fishing limits were extended from 30 mi to 200 mi (48 km to 322 km) in 1977. In spite of government efforts, economic difficulties continue, exacerbated by crop failures and also by such problems as large-scale smuggling. The main export is cocoa; others include timber and gold. *History*: from the Middle Ages several small kingdoms flourished in what is now Ghana. In 1472 the Portuguese and subsequently other Europeans set up trading posts in the region, which they called the Gold Coast. It became a center of the slave trade and the scene of rivalry between the British and Dutch. The British abolition of slavery led to prolonged wars with the

Ashanti slavetraders in the 19th century. The area became the British colony of the Gold Coast in 1874. In 1957, together with the British part of Togo, it became independent, its new name, Ghana, being that of a medieval N African empire. In 1960 it became a republic within the British Commonwealth, with Dr. Kwame Nkrumah as its first president. His government became increasingly dictatorial and in 1966 he was overthrown in a military coup. Military rule continued until 1969, when civilian government was reestablished. In 1972, however, a second military coup took place under Col. Ignatius K. Acheampong. He was forced to resign in 1978 and, with his successor, Lt. Gen. Fred Akuffo, was executed following a military coup (1979) led by Fl. Lt. Jerry Rawlings. A new civilian government was formed (1979) with Dr. Hilla Limann as president but this was overthrown in another military coup led by Rawlings in December 1981. To stem smuggling activities all borders were closed in 1982. The expulsion from Nigeria of illegal aliens caused a mass migration of Africans, among them one million Ghananians. Ghana was forced to open its borders, and the repatriation of the returning nationals created a national emergency. Abortive coups against Rawlings's government during the 1980s and early 1990s were indicative of the growing opposition to his regime. In 1991, Rawlings announced that a new constitution would be drafted that would pave the way to democracy. It was adopted in 1992, and Rawlings was elected president as a civilian. Official language: English. Official currency: cedi of 100 pesawas. Area: 92,010 sq mi (238,305 sq km). Population (1990 est): 15,310,000. Capital: Accra. Main port: Takoradi.

gharial. *See* gavial.

Ghats Two mountain ranges lying along the W and E coasts of India. The **Western Ghats**, which extend about 932 mi (1500 km) from N of Bombay to Cape Comorin, are the higher, rising to 8840 ft (2693 m). With the plentiful rain brought by the W winds, they have dense natural vegetation and are used for tea planting. The **Eastern Ghats** extend, with several breaks, about 880 mi (1400 km) from near Cuttack to the Nilgiri Hills.

Ghaznavids A Turkish dynasty that ruled in E Iran, Afghanistan, and N India (977–1186). The Ghaznavids created the first powerful Muslim state in India and prepared the way for the spread of Islam there. Founded by Sebuktigin (d. 997), a Turkish soldier, the dynasty's territories centered on Ghazna (Afghanistan) and reached its peak with *Mahmud of Ghazna. Following the battle of Dandanqan in 1040, the Ghaznavids lost their lands in Persia to the Seljuqs.

Ghazzah. *See* Gaza.

Ghegs One of the two major ethnic divisions of the Albanian people (*see also* Tosks). The Ghegs live N of the Shkumbi River and differ from the Tosks in dress and other customs.

Ghent (Flemish name: Gent; French name: Gand) 51 02N 3 42E A city in Belgium, at the confluence of the canalized Scheldt and Lys Rivers. One of Belgium's oldest cities, it has a university (1816) and a gothic cathedral. It is a major port and the textile center of the country; other economic activities include metallurgy, chemicals, and banking. Population (1988 est): 232,500.

gherkin A trailing West Indian vine, *Cucumis anguria,* with lobed leaves and small yellow flowers. It is cultivated for its prickly edible fruit, 0.98–3 in (2.5–7.5 cm) long, which is borne on a crooked stalk and used when immature for pickling. The "gherkins" sold in pickle mixtures are immature *cucumbers. Family: *Curcurbitaceae* (gourd family).

ghetto Any slum area occupied by an ethnic minority. Originally a ghetto was that quarter of a city to which Jews were restricted by law. Originating in Italy in the Middle Ages, ghettos were established during the *Counter-Reformation in many European cities. During the 19th century legal restrictions fell into disuse in W Europe and the communities became bound solely by customs and religion. However, in the 20th century ghettos were revived by the Nazis, for example in *Warsaw. In the US the term is applied to those areas of cities occupied by poor minorities.

GEYSERS *The Pohutu geyser, North Island, New Zealand.*

Ghibellines. *See* Guelfs and Ghibellines.

Ghiberti, Lorenzo (c. 1378–1455) Florentine Renaissance sculptor. Ghiberti trained as a goldsmith and painter but made his name as a sculptor in 1402, when he won the competition for the bronze relief sculptures for the north doors of the Baptistry of the Florentine Duomo. Finished in 1424, these New Testament scenes, mainly in the *international gothic style, were followed by Old Testament scenes in the Gates of Paradise (1425–52), strongly influenced by antique sculpture. Simultaneously he wrote *I commentarii,* which included histories of ancient and early Renaissance art and an autobiography. His other works include three statues of saints (1416–25) for Orsanmichele.

Ghirlandaio, Domenico (Domenico di Tommaso Bigordi; 1449–94) Florentine painter of the early *Renaissance. From 1481–82 he worked on a fresco in the Sistine Chapel but his major undertaking was the fresco cycle (1486–90) in Sta Maria Novella, Florence. These scenes from the life of the Virgin and St John the Baptist are notable for their portrayal of Florentine personalities in contemporary dress. The tenderly painted *Old Man and Boy* (Louvre) is a fine example of his portraiture.

ghost The disembodied spirit of a dead person, believed in many cultures to be capable of manifesting itself to the living. Ghosts are still venerated in tribal societies in Africa, Asia, and Polynesia (*see* ancestor worship). Certain feasts in the Roman calendar were devoted to their propitiation. The Roman Catholic doctrine of *purgatory fostered ghost beliefs by sanctioning the notion that the dead could request prayers from the living. Post-Reformation ghosts exhibited more secular interests, demanding revenge or restitution of such wrongs as misappropriated inheritances. Skepticism grew in the 18th century but the *gothic revival initiated a revival in ghost stories, now enjoyed purely for their spine-chilling qualities. In modern times, spirit communication has been the mainstay of *spirtualism and hauntings continue to be reported.

ghost shark. *See* chimaera.

Giacometti, Alberto (1901–66) Swiss sculptor and painter. Working chiefly in Paris after 1922, he was influenced initially by *cubism and primitive art and later by *surrealism, particularly in his abstract construction of sticks, glass, wire, etc., entitled *The Palace at 4 am* (New York). After breaking with surrealism in 1935, he developed a unique figure style, characterized by spindly elongated forms.

Giambologna (Giovanni da Bologna *or* Jean de Boulogne; 1529–1608) Italian mannerist sculptor of Flemish birth. Working from 1557 in Florence, where he was patronized by the Medici, he produced many fountains and religious sculptures in addition to small bronze statues. His works include *Samson and a Philistine* (1567; Victoria and Albert Museum).

Giant's Causeway 55 14N 6 32W A promontory in N Northern Ireland, in Antrim on the North Channel. It consists of several thousand closely packed basaltic columns, mainly hexagonal in shape, formed by an outpouring of lava into the sea. According to legend it was built as a bridge for the giants to cross between Ireland and Scotland.

giant star A large very luminous star lying above the main sequence on the *Hertzsprung-Russell diagram. *See also* red giant.

giant tortoise. *See* Galápagos giant tortoise.

giant water bug A large brown *water bug of the family *Belostomatidae* (up to 200 species), found in tropical and temperate regions. Giant water bugs, sometimes over 0.40 in (10 mm) long, are strong fliers and are often attracted to light. In some species, for example *Belostoma plumineum,* the female forcibly lays her eggs onto the back of the male, attaching them with a glue.

gibberellins A group of organic compounds that stimulate plant growth. First isolated from the fungus *Gibberella fujikuroi,* over 30 gibberellins are now known. When applied to plants they stimulate the growth of leaves, stems, flowers, and fruit and break the dormancy of seeds and tubers; hence their importance in horticulture and agriculture.

gibbon A small *ape belonging to the genus *Hylobates* (7 species), of S Asia; 18–26 in (45–65 cm) long, they have long arms with slender hands and hooked fingers used to swing through trees. On the ground they walk upright or run on all fours. They live in family groups, feeding chiefly on fruit and leaves, and have a loud whooping call. Family: *Hylobatidae. See also* siamang.

GIBBON *These apes are noted for their agility in trees. This individual* (Hylobates lar) *from Borneo manipulates a twig while clinging to a tree branch.*

Gibbon, Edward (1737–94) British historian. Sent to Europe by his father, he traveled in Switzerland and later (1764–65) in Italy. His ironic treatment of Christianity in his monumental *The History of the Decline and Fall of the Roman Empire* (1776–88) aroused contemporary controversy, but the work gained acceptance as successive volumes appeared. Its epic scope and dignity of style have ensured its survival.

Gibbons v. Ogden (1824) US Supreme Court decision that defined commerce as described in the Constitution. It permitted the federal judiciary to void any state law that interfered with interstate commerce. Aaron Ogden, licensed by New York state to operate steamboats in state waters, sought to prevent Thomas Gibbons from using the same waters for the same purpose. The court ruled that Gibbons had a right to use New York state waters and voided the New York commercial monopoly law.

Gibbs, Josiah Willard (1839–1903) US physicist, who was a professor at Yale University (1871–1903). Gibbs founded chemical thermodynamics, which is largely based on the function known as the Gibbs free energy. He is also known for his phase rule, relating the number of parameters that can be varied in a system of more than one phase. His papers were published between 1876 and 1878.

G. I. Bill (Servicemen's Readjustment Act of 1944). Legislation enacted to aid World War II veterans' reentry into civilian life. Job placement, educational expenses, unemployment pay, and home or business financing were made available. In 1945 and during the Korean War the benefits were expanded. The Readjustment Benefits Act of 1966 established benefits for all veterans.

Gibraltar A British crown colony occupying a tiny peninsula at the S tip of Spain. The sandy isthmus that links it to the Spanish mainland rises sharply to the 1400 ft (427 m) limestock Rock of Gibraltar, which contains numerous caverns and galleries. The population is mainly of Spanish, Genoese, and Portuguese descent. *Economy*: its strategic position makes it a naval and air base of great importance; British defense expenditure together with tourist earnings and fees for services to shipping form the basis of its economy. Tourist attractions include the colony's barbary apes, the only monkeys native to Europe. *History*: settled by the Moors in 711 AD, the Rock of Gibraltar was taken by Castile in 1462, becoming part of united Spain. It was captured in 1704 by the British to whom it was formally ceded by the Treaty of Utrecht (1713). The colony became an important British naval base. Claims to Gibraltar have long been made by Spain but a UN proposal to end British occupation was defeated in a referendum in 1967. In 1969 Spain closed its frontier with Gibraltar leading to a manpower shortage (as much of its workforce was domiciled over the border in Spain); the frontier was reopened in 1984. Official languages: English and Spanish. Official currency: Gibraltar pound of 100 pence. Area: 2.5 sq mi (6.5 sq km). Population (1980 est): 29,787.

Gibraltar, Strait of A strait between Europe (Spain and Gibraltar) and Africa (Morocco), joining the Atlantic Ocean and the Mediterranean Sea, of which it is the only outlet. It narrows to 8 mi (13 km) and is of great strategic importance.

Gibran, Khalil (1883–1931) Lebanese mystic and poet. He studied in Beirut and Paris and settled in New York in 1912. His major work in English is *The Prophet* (1923), a romantic blending of religion and philosophy.

Gibson, Althea (1927–) US tennis player. She was the first African American to play in major tennis championships (1951) and to win major titles: Wimbledon singles (1957, 1958); United States singles (1957, 1958); and the women's doubles at Wimbledon (1956–58).

Gibson, Charles Dana (1867–1944) US artist and illustrator. Working in pen and ink, he did illustrations for magazines, including *Collier's Weekly,* and was the creator of the "Gibson Girl," the ideal woman of the turn of the century. He also illustrated books, among them *The Prisoner of Zenda,* and painted portraits in oils. His sketches were collected in *The Education of Mr. Pipp* (1899), *The Americans* (1900), *The Social Ladder* (1902), and *The Gibson Book* (1906).

Gibson Desert A desert in central Western Australia. It consists of a vast arid area of active sand dunes and desert grass. Area: 85,000 sq mi (220,000 sq km).

Gide, André (1869–1951) French novelist and critic. Much of his work is semiautobiographical and deals with the conflict between desire and discipline, reflecting his homosexuality and consequent conflict with conventional morality. His visits to North Africa from 1893–96 gave him a sense of freedom, celebrated in *Fruits of the Earth* (1897). In 1895 he married his cousin Madeleine Rondeaux, the inspiration of two short works, *The Immoralist* (1902) and *Strait Is the Gate* (1909). In 1908 he was one of the founders of the important literary journal *La Nouvelle Revue française.* His longer novels are *The Vatican Cellars* (1914) and *The Counterfeiters* (1926). For a short time he was drawn to communism but soon became disillusioned. His *Journal,* which he kept from 1885 until his death, is a major work of literary autobiography. He won the Nobel Prize in 1947.

Gideon v. Wainwright (1963) US Supreme Court decision that guaranteed the right to an attorney for all persons charged with a serious crime. It instructed states to pay attorney's fees for those unable to afford the charges. Clarence Gideon had been tried and convicted by a Florida court without benefit of attorney, despite his request for a state-appointed attorney. The court overruled his conviction; he was retried and acquitted. This case imposed federal regulations on state proceedings.

Gielgud, Sir (Arthur) John (1904–) British actor. He is noted for his distinguished speaking voice and for his many fine performances in Shakespearean productions. His *Hamlet,* first performed in 1929, received especial acclaim. From the 1970s he also acted in plays by modern dramatists, such as Harold Pinter and Edward Bond, and in many films.

Gierek, Edward (1913–) Polish statesman, who succeeded *Gomulka as first secretary of the Polish United Workers' Party (1970–80). Born in Poland, he lived in France and Belgium from 1923–48. A communist from 1931, he became a member of the politburo in 1956 and came to power following the demonstrations against food prices in 1970.

Giessen 50 35N 8 42E A city in Germany, in Hessen on the Lahn River. The university (1607) contains the chemist Liebig's laboratory. Its manufactures include rubber, machine tools, leather, and tobacco. Population (1984): 71,800.

Gifu 35 27N 136 46E A city in Japan, in central Honshu. It was *Nobunaga's headquarters in the 16th century. Manufactures include paper lanterns and textiles. Population (1990): 410,324.

Gigantes In Greek mythology, the giant sons of *Uranus (Heaven) and *Gaea (Earth), whose rebellion against the Olympian gods was defeated with the help of Heracles. They were subsequently associated with earthquakes and volcanoes.

Gigli, Beniamino (1890–1957) Italian tenor. He became a world-famous opera singer and was regarded as the successor to Caruso. Toscanini brought him to La Scala, Milan, in 1920, where he made his debut as Faust in Boito's *Mefistofele.* He gave his final concert in 1955.

Gijón 43 32N 5 40W A port in NW Spain, in Asturias on the Bay of Biscay. Its many ancient buildings include Roman baths and medieval palaces. It is an important manufacturing center with metallurgical and chemical industries. Population (1991 est): 259,000.

Gila monster A rare venomous lizard, *Heloderma suspectum,* occurring in the SW US and N Mexico; 20 in (50 cm) long, it has a stout black body with pink blotches and bands and small beadlike scales and feeds at night on eggs. It has a strong bite and grooved teeth that inject a nerve poison. Family: *Helodermatidae.*

gilbert (Gb) The unit of magnetomotive force in the *c.g.s. system equal to the magnetomotive force produced by a current of 40π amperes passing through a single coil. Named for William *Gilbert.

Gilbert, Sir Humphrey (c. 1539–83) English navigator. Half-brother of Sir Walter *Raleigh, Gilbert had a notable career as a soldier in Ireland (1567–70, 1579) and the Netherlands (1572). His first attempt to reach North America was a failure (1578) but in 1583 he landed at St John's, Newfoundland, which he claimed for Elizabeth I. He was lost at sea on his return voyage.

Gilbert, William (1544–1603) English physicist and physician to Elizabeth I. One of the early adherents of the experimental method, his *De magnete* (1600) listed many experimental observations concerning magnets, including the discovery of magnetic dip. He suggested that the earth is a spherical magnet, that other magnets point toward its poles, and that the planets are held in their orbits by magnetic attraction. He was the first English scientist to accept the ideas of *Copernicus; he was also responsible for many new terms, including *electricity* and *magnetic pole.*

Gilbert, Sir William Schwenk (1836–1911) British comic dramatist. He wrote comic verses, published as *Bab Ballads* (1869), while studying law. In 1870 he met Arthur *Sullivan, the composer for whom he wrote the libretti for 14 popular operas. His plays written after Sullivan's death in 1900 were less successful.

Gilbert Islands. *See* Kiribati, Republic of.

Gilbert of Sempringham, St (c. 1083–1189) English priest, who founded the Gilbertines, the only indigenous religious order of medieval England, at Sempringham, Lincolnshire. It was composed of nuns, lay sisters and brothers, and canons. It was dissolved by Henry VIII. Feast day: Feb 4.

Gilded Age In the US, an era (1865–1900) marked by ostentatious materialism and governmental corruption. *The Gilded Age* (1873) by Mark *Twain (with Charles Dudley Warner; 1829–1900) described and named the period.

Gilgamesh An ancient Mesopotamian hero whose adventures are related in the collection of fragmentary texts known as the *Epic of Gilgamesh.* These are inscribed on 12 tablets discovered in the library of the Assyrian king Ashurbanipal (reigned 669–626 BC), at Nineveh. They relate how Gilgamesh defeats and then befriends the savage man Enkidu, rejects the love goddess *Ishtar, journeys to consult an immortal wise man, Utnapishtim, about the secret of eternal life, and gains and then loses the plant of immortality.

Gillespie, Dizzy (John Birks G.; 1917–93) US jazz trumpeter, band leader, and composer, who was one of the originators of *bop. Gillespie played with many different bands in the 1930s and 1940s before forming his own band in 1945. In later years Gillespie incorporated singing and comedy into his performances. His recordings include *Groovin' High* and *Hot vs Cool*; in 1980 he published his autobiographical *To Be or Not to Bop.*

Gillingham 51 24N 0 33E A city in SE England, in Kent on the Medway estuary. The largest of the Medway towns, it has extensive dockyards at Chatham and varous light industries. Fruit growing is important in the area. Population (1981): 93,741.

gills The respiratory organs of aquatic animals: specialized thin-walled regions of the body surface through which dissolved oxygen is taken into the blood and carbon dioxide released into the water. The gills of fish lie in gill slits on each side of the gullet. Each gill consists of many leaflike gill filaments, which provide a large surface area over which water is pumped. The gills of mollusks (such as the mussel) and fanworms are ciliated and trap food particles in the respiratory currents. The external gills of amphibian larvae (tadpoles) are feathery structures projecting from the body wall.

gillyflower (*or* gilliflower) A name given to various clove-scented flowers, originally applied to plants of the pink family (*Caryophyllaceae*), such as the carnation.

gin A *spirit distilled usually from grain flavored with juniper berries (the name is derived from the Dutch *jenever,* juniper). Gin, with little flavor, is generally drunk with tonic water, *vermouth, fruit juice, etc. Martini cocktails are a mixture of gin and dry vermouth served very cold, sometimes with ice. Dry or London Dry gin is the gin most frequently used for mixed drinks. Sloe gin takes its flavor from the fruit of the blackthorn tree, or sloe berries.

ginger A perennial herbaceous plant, *Zingiber officinale,* native to SE Asia and widely grown in the tropics for its pungent underground stems (rhizomes), used as a spice, food, and flavoring and in medicine. Its leafy stems grow about 40 in (1 m) high; the leaves are 6–12 in (15–30 cm) long and the flowers grow in dense conelike spikes. The plants are sterile, and propagation is by cuttings from the rootstocks. Family: *Zingiberaceae.*

gingivitis Inflammation of the gums. It may be caused by ill-fitting dentures or by infection in debilitated people or those taking antibiotics.

ginkgo A deciduous *gymnosperm tree, *Ginkgo biloba,* also called maidenhair tree, that is the sole living representative of a group of trees that flourished in the Carboniferous period (370–280 million years ago). Growing to a height of 98 ft (30 m), it has lobed fan-shaped leaves, 5 × 4 in (12 × 10 cm), which are pale green and turn yellow in the fall, and fleshy plumlike yellow fruits containing edible kernels. The ginkgo is native to China and widely planted for ornament. Family: *Ginkgoaceae.*

Ginsberg, Allen (1926–) US poet. His first book, *Howl* (1956), a rambling attack on contemporary America, was a popular work of the *Beat movement. In the 1960s he traveled in Asia, India, and South America. His later work, in *The Change* (1963), *The Fall of America* (1973), and other books, is fragmentary and rhapsodic.

Ginsburg, Ruth Joan Bader (1933–) US jurist, associate justice of the US Supreme Court (1993–). She graduated first in her class from Columbia Law School and later became a law professor (1963–80). During this period she became involved in women's legal issues and was noted for her arguments before the Supreme Court on gender equality. In 1980 she was appointed by President Carter to the US Court of Appeals for the District of Columbia and served there until her Supreme Court appointment by President Clinton.

ginseng An extract of the forked roots of either of two herbs, *Panax quinquefolium* or *P. schinseng,* used as a stimulant drug in the Far East and to make aromatic bitters. It is said to have aphrodisiac and life-prolonging properties. *P. quinquefolium* is grown commercially in North America; *P. schinseng* in Korea and Japan. Family: *Araliaceae* (ivy family).

Giorgione (c. 1477–1510) Italian painter of the Venetian school, born in Castelfranco. He trained under Giovanni *Bellini and worked with *Titian, whom he influenced, on frescoes for the façade of the German Exchange in Venice (1508). Most of his paintings are small-scale secular pictures of a type previously unknown. Their subject matter is often inexplicable, particularly in the *Tempest* (Accademia, Venice), notable for its atmospheric landscape. *The Sleeping Venus* (Gemäldegalerie, Dresden), completed by Titian, and *The Three Philosophers* (Kunsthistorisches Museum, Vienna) show the romantic and dreamlike mood of his paintings. His portraits, e.g. *Laura* (Vienna), influenced many Venetian painters. He probably died of the plague.

Giotto (Giotto di Bondone; c. 1266–1337) Italian painter and architect, who laid the foundation for *Renaissance painting. He was born in Vespignano, near Florence, and was probably the pupil of *Cimabue. The fresco cycle of St Francis, in the upper church of S Francesco, Assisi, is thought to be an early work. Certainly by his hand are the innovative frescoes of scenes from the lives of Joachim and Anne and the Virgin and Christ in the Arena Chapel, Padua. He also painted frescoes in Sta Croce, Florence. In 1334 he became architect of the city and surveyor of Florence Cathedral, for which he designed the campanile.

Gir A breed of *zebu cattle originating from the Gir forest of W India. They have characteristic domed foreheads with backward-curving horns and long ears and are yellowish red to black in color. Traditionally a dairy breed, they are also used for draft purposes.

giraffe A hoofed *mammal, *Giraffa camelopardalis,* of tropical African grasslands. Measuring 10 ft (3 m) at the shoulder, with a neck 8 ft (2.5 m) long, giraffes are marked with a patchwork of reddish-brown blotches on a buff-colored background. They feed on leaves, using their long necks and prehensile lips and tongues. Both sexes have permanent skin-covered horns. Giraffes live in small groups led by a mature male and can go for long periods without drinking. They usually sleep standing up. Family: *Giraffidae.*

Giraudoux, Jean (1882–1944) French dramatist, novelist, and diplomat (from 1910–40). His early literary reputation was established by a series of poetic novels, including *Elpénor* (1919) and *Suzanne et le Pacifique* (1921). His stylized plays, often blending elements of tragedy, comedy, and fantasy, include *Amphitryon 38* (1929), *Tiger at the Gates* (1935), *Ondine* (1939), and *The Madwoman of Chaillot* (1949).

Girl Scouts. *See* Scouting.

giro A low-cost system for transferring money. It originated in Austria in 1883 and the British National Giro was set up by the Post Office in 1968. All accounts are held at the Giro Center (in Bootle, Lancashire), which transfers money from one account to another on receipt of a completed form. Bank giro operates similarly, but accounts are held at bank branches.

Gironde River A wide estuary in SW France, on the Bay of Biscay. Formed by the confluence of the Garonne and Dordogne Rivers near Bordeaux, it is used by oceangoing vessels. Length: 45 mi (72 km).

Girondins A French Revolutionary political group. Named from the Gironde, where their support was strong, the Girondins were moderate republicans. They became prominent in the newly formed Legislative Assembly (1791), where, suspicious of counterrevolution and seeking to unite the Revolution's supporters, they involved France in war against Austria and Prussia. Military failure undermined their influence and, after the overthrow of the monarchy, they were themselves ousted by the more radical *Jacobins (1793). Many Girondins were subsequently executed.

Girtin, Thomas (1775–1802) British landscape painter, famous for being among the first to perfect watercolor technique. His use of broad transparent washes without the old monochrome underpainting produced heightened atmospheric effects, as in *White House at Chelsea.*

Giscard d'Estaing, Valéry (1926–) French statesman; president (1974–81). He was minister of finance and economic affairs from 1962–66, when he established the Independent Republican Party. He returned to this post (1969) under Pompidou, whom he succeeded as president. In the 1981 presidential elections he was defeated by Mitterrand. His attempts at liberal reform were thwarted by his party's dependence on Gaullist support. He served in the National Assembly (1984–89) and worked with the European Parliament.

Gish, Lillian (1899–1993) US actress, who began her career as a child actress on stage with her sister **Dorothy Gish** (1898–1968). Both acted for the director D. W. *Griffith in several early silent films, including *The Birth of a Nation* (1915) and *Intolerance* (1916), and subsequently worked in both films and the theater. The later films of Lillian Gish include *Duel in the Sun* (1946) and *The Night of the Hunter* (1955).

Gislebertus (early 12th century) French *romanesque sculptor. Probably trained in the workshop associated with the Abbey of Cluny, Gislebertus developed an original and powerfully expressive style. His best-known sculptures are those around the west doorway and on the capitals of columns at the Cathedral of St Lazarus, Autun (c. 1125–35).

VALÉRY GISCARD D'ESTAING *With the German chancellor Schmidt at the meeting of EEC heads of state in Ireland (1979).*

gittern An early type of guitar with four gut strings, played with a plectrum. It is known to have been a popular instrument for accompanying the voice at various periods between the 13th and 17th centuries but it lost favor after the Restoration.

Giulio Romano (Giulio Pippi; c. 1499–1546) Italian mannerist painter and architect, born in Rome (*see* mannerism). He was the pupil of *Raphael, whom he assisted in the decoration of the Vatican apartments and the Villa Farnesina. After Raphael's death, Giulio completed some of his works. In 1524 he settled in Mantua, where he designed and decorated the Palazzo del Tè, notable for its Room of the Giants, completely covered with illusionistic frescoes.

Giza, El (*or* al-Jizah) 30 01N 31 12E A city in N Egypt, forming a suburb of Cairo on the Nile River. Nearby are the great pyramids of *Khafre, *Khufu, and Menkaure, one of the Seven Wonders of the World, and the Sphinx. Tourism is important and it has textile and film industries. Population (1986 est): 2,156,000.

Glace Bay 46 11N 59 58W A city in E Canada, on the coast of *Cape Breton Island. Located over coal seams that have been mined since 1858, it is now chiefly a fishing center. From here Marconi sent his first wireless message (1902). Population: 21,836.

glacier A mass of ice and *firn of limited width lying chiefly, or completely, on land and moving downslope from its source. Different glacier forms exist; **cirque glaciers** are contained in depressions on mountain slopes or valley heads. **Valley glaciers** are contained within preexisting valleys and are frequently tongue-shaped in plan, originating either from cirque glaciers as an alpine type or from an icesheet as an outlet type. The longest of these is the Lambert Glacier, 250 mi (400 km) long. Where a glacier emerges from a valley onto a lowland area, a lobe-shaped **piedmont glacier** results; an example is the Malaspina Glacier in Alaska (US). **Glaciation** is the action of glacier ice on the land surface. The most recent period of extensive glaciation took place during the Pleistocene epoch, when about 30% of the world's surface area was ice covered. The main landforms resulting from glaciation are either erosional or depositional. Erosional features include the formation of U-shaped valleys and *cirques. Those of depositional origin include glacial *drift and *till. When water is also involved in the formation of glacial landforms the term fluvioglacial is used; fluvioglacial deposits include *eskers and *kames.

Glacier National Park A national park (1911) in the E Rocky Mountains in NE Montana that joins Waterton Lakes National Park in Canada to form Waterton-Glacier International Peace Park (1932). The Continental Divide runs through the park; the highest point is Mt Cleveland (10,448 ft; 3185 m). Area: 1583 sq mi (4100 sq km).

gladiators The slaves, prisoners of war, condemned criminals, or volunteers who fought in amphitheaters for the entertainment of the ancient Roman people. Gladiatorial combat began as a feature of funeral games but their popularity was soon so great that statesmen sponsored shows to enhance their political prestige. Pairs of gladiators would fight to the death unless the audience spared the loser. Several Roman writers condemned gladiatorial shows.

Gladiolus A genus of ornamental perennial herbaceous plants (300 species), native to Europe, Africa, and the Mediterranean regions and widely cultivated. Growing from a corm, the flowering stem reaches a height of 4 ft (1.2 m), with funnel-shaped flowers, usually red, yellow, orange, or white, grouped on one side. The leaves are sword-shaped. Gladioli cultivated for cut flowers have been developed mainly from South and East African species. Principal garden forms are *G. cardinalis, G. primulinus, G. psittacinus, G. purpurea-auratus,* and *G. saundersii.* Family: *Iridaceae.*

Gladstone, W(illiam) E(wart) (1809–98) British statesman; Liberal prime minister (1868–74, 1880–85, 1886, 1892–94). Elected to Parliament in 1832, he was initially a Tory. He supported the repeal of the *Corn Laws, which split the Tories, with some joining the Whigs (shortly to be termed Liberals). As chancellor of the exchequer (1852–55, 1859–66) Gladstone introduced a series of budgets that reduced tariffs and government expenditure. In 1867 he became leader of the Liberal Party. His first ministry disestablished the Irish Church (1869) and introduced the *Education Act (1870), the first Irish *Land Act (1870), and the Ballot Act (introducing secret ballots). Defeated in the 1874 election, he resigned the Liberal leadership. He again became member of Parliament and prime minister in 1880. His second ministry achieved a second Irish Land Act (1881) and further parliamentary reform (1884) but its failure to save *Gordon from Khartoum led to Gladstone's resignation. His last ministries followed his conversion to Irish *Home Rule.

An impressive speaker, Gladstone with his Conservative opponent Disraeli dominated British politics in the second half of the 19th century.

Glamis 56 37N 3 01W A village in E Scotland. Macbeth was thane of Glamis. Nearby Glamis Castle was the childhood home of Queen Elizabeth the Queen Mother and birthplace of Princess Margaret.

gland An organ or group of cells that is specialized for synthesizing a specific chemical substance (secretion) from constituents of the blood and releasing its secretion for use by the body. Man and higher animals have two kinds of glands. The *endocrine glands lack ducts and release their secretions (which are hormones) directly into the bloodstream. The exocrine glands have ducts through which their products are secreted. Exocrine glands include the salivary glands, the sweat and sebaceous glands in the skin, and the pancreatic cells that secrete digestive enzymes.

Plants also have glands, which secrete a variety of products including latex, resin, nectar, and tannin.

W. E. GLADSTONE *The British prime minister summoned all his powers of oratory to convince the House of Commons of the need for Irish Home Rule, but his bill was rejected (1886).*

glanders A highly contagious disease of horses, donkeys, and related animals caused by the bacterium *Pfeifferella mallei,* which can also infect other animals and man. Onset of symptoms can occur several months after infection and include the formation of nodules in the lungs, liver, spleen, etc., ulceration of the mucous membranes, enlarged lymph nodes, nasal discharge, and pus-filled blisters. The disease is usually chronic. There is no known cure and slaughter of infected animals is compulsory in most countries.

Glanville, Ranulf de (d. 1190) English jurist; chief minister (1180–89) under Henry II. He assisted Henry with his extensive legal reforms and reputedly wrote the *Tractatus de legibus et consuetudinibus regni Angliae,* the earliest treatise on English common law. He died at the siege of Acre during the third Crusade.

Glaser, Donald Arthur (1926–) US physicist, who was awarded the 1960 Nobel Prize for his invention of the *bubble chamber (1952), an instrument that makes visible the tracks of ionizing particles. His first bubble chamber measured only 6 in (15 cm) across and contained ether.

Glasgow 55 53N 4 15W The largest city in Scotland, the administrative center of Strathclyde Region on the River Clyde. The third largest city in the UK, it is Scotland's chief commercial and industrial center. An important port with a tradition of ship building, Glasgow also has major engineering, textile, chemical, brewing, and whisky-blending industries. *History*: of early religious and educational importance (St Mungo's cathedral dates from the 12th century and the university was founded in 1451), Glasgow's wealth grew rapidly through trade after the union with England (1707), especially in tobacco and sugar from the New World, and through industry in the industrial revolution, having coal and iron ore nearby. Population (1991): 689,200.

glass A translucent and usually transparent noncrystalline substance that behaves as a solid although it has many of the properties of a liquid. Glass itself was known in the 3rd millennium BC and glass objects survive from Egypt's 18th dynasty (1570–1320 BC), but glassblowing was not invented until about 100 BC (in Syria) and windows, which were originally made of blown glass, were not in use until about 100 AD. Ordinary soda glass, used for windows, etc., consists of silica (sand), sodium carbonate, and calcium carbonate (limestone). Flint glass, used for crystal glassware, contains silica, potassium carbonate, potassium nitrate, and lead oxide. Heat-resistant glass also contains borates and alumina; optical glass contains additional elements to control the refractive index and other optical properties, homogeneity being obtained by repeated heating and slow cooling.

Blown glass is melted and blown inside a mold until it fills the mold; bottles and lightbulbs are made in this way by a fully automatic process. Flint glass is also blown to make glassware, but this is usually done by hand. Pressed glass, to make domestic bowls and headlight lenses, is made by pressing the molten glass into a mold. Plate glass, for windows, etc., was formerly made by pouring molten glass onto a flat table and rolling it through heated rollers into sheets, which were then polished. The last stage has now been replaced by floating the rolled sheet of glass on molten tin. This float-glass process was introduced in 1959. *See also* fiberglass; stained glass.

glasses Lenses worn in frames in front of the eyes to correct defective vision. Convex lenses bend parallel light rays inward; they are used by those unable to focus on close objects (*see* farsightedness). Concave lenses have the opposite effect and are used by those unable to focus on distant objects (*see* nearsightedness). *Astigmatism is treated by wearing lenses that produce a compensating distortion of the light rays. Bifocal glasses have convex lenses consisting of upper and lower parts of different curvatures, for focusing on distant and near objects, respectively; they are worn for presbyopia. *See also* contact lenses.

glassfish A fish of the family *Centropomidae* (about 24 species), especially the genus *Chanda,* having a transparent body and a cleft dorsal fin. Glassfish occur along coastlines, in estuaries, and in fresh waters from Africa to the Indian and Pacific regions. Order: *Perciformes.*

glass harmonica. *See* harmonica.

glass snake A legless lizard belonging to the genus *Ophisaurus,* occurring in Europe, S and E Asia, N Africa, and North America. Glass snakes live in loose soil and feed on insects, lizards, mice, and birds' eggs. Unlike true snakes, they have ears, eyelids, and rigid jaws. When attacked, they shed their tail, which breaks into several pieces. Family: *Anguidae.*

glasswort (*or* marsh samphire) An annual or perennial plant of the genus *Salicornia* (at least 7 species), native to European salt marshes, with jointed green succulent stems that turn red or purple in autumn. The fleshy leaves sheath the stem closely and the flowers are inconspicuous. It was once used in glassmaking as a source of soda. Family: *Chenopodiaceae.*

Glastonbury 51 09N 2 43W A market town in SW England, in Somerset. Here by tradition Joseph of Arimathea founded England's first Christian church; Glastonbury is also the reputed burial place of King Arthur. There are the ruins of an early Benedictine abbey and the site of an excavated Iron Age lake village. Population (1981): 6773.

glaucoma An eye disease caused by raised pressure inside the eye. Acute glaucoma is often caused by a sudden block to the drainage of the watery fluid (aqueous humor) inside the eye. It leads to pain and disturbed vision, which will result in blindness without urgent treatment. Chronic glaucoma—one of the commonest causes of blindness—comes on slowly and painlessly.

Glazunov, Aleksandr Konstantinovich (1865–1936) Russian composer and pupil of Rimsky-Korsakov. He became director of the St Petersburg conservatory in 1906 but left Russia in 1928 and died in Paris. Glazunov's works, which were influenced by Wagner and Liszt rather than by Russian musical nationalism, included eight symphonies, concertos, ballets, and string quartets.

Gleiwitz. *See* Gliwice.

Glendale 34 10N 118 17W A city N of Los Angeles in SW California. It was part of the first Spanish land grant, Rancho de San Rafael (1798), in California and became a town in 1887. It is largely residential, but there are airplane-parts, machine, and home-furnishings industries. Population (1990): 180,038.

Glendower, Owen (Welsh name: Owain Glyndwr; c. 1359–c. 1416) Welsh rebel. He led a Welsh rising that became a national war of independence. Allying with Henry IV's opponents, Glendower controlled most of Wales by 1404 but was subsequently defeated and turned to guerrilla warfare. He disappeared in 1416.

Glenn, John (Herschel), Jr. (1921–) US astronaut, the first from the US to orbit earth (1962), and senator. A pilot in the Marine Corps (1943–65), he served in World War II and Korea and was later a test pilot. As an astronaut (1959–64) he made three orbits of earth aboard *Friendship 7* on Feb 20, 1962. He served in the US Senate as a Democrat from Ohio (1975–). He was also an unsuccessful contender for the Democratic presidential nomination (1984).

gliders Light fixed-wing engineless aircraft, sometimes called sailplanes. They are launched into the air by a winch or catapult or by being towed by a car or powered aircraft. Once airborne a glider slowly loses height unless it is lifted by a rising air current created by warm air rising from the ground (a thermal), a ground contour, or a thunderstorm. These air currents enable a skillful pilot to remain airborne for several hours and to travel hundreds of miles.

Pioneered by Otto *Lilienthal in the US, gliders were used by the *Wright brothers in designing their powered aircraft. Gliders towed by aircraft were used in World War II to carry men and equipment. Since the 1920s gliding has been a popular sport and pastime in many countries. *See also* hang-gliding.

Glinka, Mikhail Ivanovich (1804–57) Russian composer. He studied with John Field, made many journeys abroad, and is regarded as the founder of Russian musical nationalism. He composed the first truly Russian opera *Ivan Susanin* (*A Life for the Tsar*; 1836), various works in a Spanish style, piano music, songs, and a second opera *Russlan and Ludmilla* (1842), influenced by oriental music.

Gliwice (German name: Gleiwitz) 50 20N 18 40E A city in S Poland. It is a heavy-industry center within Upper Silesia; industries include coal mining, steel processing, chemicals, and food processing. Population (1992 est): 215,000.

globe artichoke. *See* artichoke.

globefish. *See* puffer.

globeflower A herbaceous plant of the genus *Trollius* (about 15 species), found throughout Europe. It has lobed toothed leaves and solitary many-petaled globe-shaped flowers, yellow or orange, borne on stems 4–26 in (10–70 cm) high. Family: **Ranunculaceae*.

Globe Theatre An Elizabethan theater, in Southwark, England, in which most of Shakespeare's plays were first produced. A cylindrical wooden building open to the sky, it was built in 1598, burned down in 1613, rebuilt in 1614, and finally demolished in 1644.

globe thistle A stout perennial *thistle of the genus *Echinops* (about 15 species) of central and S Europe; 20–79 in (50–200 cm) high, it has lobed leaves, often white and wooly beneath, and large spherical flower heads, usually blue and sometimes woolly. Globe thistles are often planted in gardens.

Globigerina A genus of protozoan animals that are common components of marine plankton. Ranging in size from 0.01–0.08 in (0.3–2 mm), their chalky skeletons are a major constituent of the gray mud on some sea beds, forming globigerina ooze. Order: **Foraminifera*.

globular cluster. *See* star cluster.

globulin A type of protein that is generally insoluble in water. Serum (gamma) globulins of the blood include the immunoglobulins (antibodies), which are manufactured by the animal to combat infections. Newborn mammals receive these immunoglobulins in maternal milk. Other globulins occur in eggs, nuts, and seeds.

glockenspiel (German: bell play) A tuned percussion instrument having a keyboardlike arrangement of steel bars played with two small hammers. The notes of its two-and-a-half octave compass above bottom G of the bass stave sound two octaves higher.

Glomma River (Norwegian name: Glåma) A river in SE Norway and the longest river in Scandinavia. Flowing S from a small lake SE of Trondheim, it enters the Skagerrak at Fredrikstad. It is important for hydroelectric power and for transporting timber. Length: 365 mi (588 km).

Glorious Revolution (1688) The overthrow of James II of England and the establishment of his sister Mary and her husband William of Orange on the throne. The opposition to James' pro-Catholic and absolutist policies invited William and Mary to take the throne and James, offering no resistance, fled to France. As William III and Mary II, the joint monarchs accepted the *Bill of Rights, which established constitutional monarchy in England.

glory pea. *See* Clianthus.

glottis. *See* larynx.

Gloucester 51 53N 2 14W A market city in W England, the administrative center of Gloucestershire on the River Severn. First developed under the Romans (Glevum) in the 1st century AD, its principal building is its cathedral, noted for its inventions in the Perpendicular style. Gloucester has engineering (aircraft components, agricultural machinery), and match-making industries. Population (1983): 92,200.

Gloucester 42 41N 70 39W A town in NE Massachusetts, on S Cape Ann, NE of Boston. Settled in 1623 and historically a fishing town, it is a well-known resort area and fish processing center. Population (1990): 28,716.

Gloucestershire A county of W England, bordering Wales. It consists of three distinct regions: the Cotswold Hills, the Severn Valley, and the Forest of Dean. It is predominantly agricultural; wheat and barley are the chief arable crops and dairy farming is increasing in importance. Industry includes engineering and timber production. Coal is mined in the Forest of Dean. Area: 1019 sq mi (2638 sq km). Population (1987): 577,000. Administrative center: Gloucester.

glowworm. *See* firefly.

gloxinia An ornamental herb, *Sinningia speciosa,* native to Brazil. Gloxinias have rosettes of large simple velvety leaves and large bell-shaped velvety flowers, usually violet, purple, or pink. New plants can regenerate from the base of the leafstalks. There are many hybrids, which are popular house plants. Family: *Gesneriaceae.*

The genus *Gloxinia* (6 species) of the same family is not cultivated.

Glozel An archeological site SE of Vichy (central France). During the 1920s finds here included engraved pebbles and clay tablets with an alphabetic script. An international commission investigated the site (1927) and cast grave doubts on its authenticity. Scientific dating of Glozel artifacts in the 1970s revived the puzzle, as some objects are undoubtedly ancient.

glucagon A polypeptide hormone, produced by the *pancreas, that increases the level of glucose in the blood by stimulating the breakdown of *glycogen in body tissues and promoting the utilization of protein and fat as energy sources. At high levels in the blood glucagon stimulates the secretion of *insulin.

Gluck, Christoph Willibald (1714–87) German composer. He reformed *opera seria, making it less artificial. Inspired by Calzabigi's librettos, he composed the operas *Orfeo ed Euridice* (1762) and *Alceste* (1767) in which the music reflected the dramatic situation and merely musical repetition and vocal ornamentation were excluded. He composed over 40 dramatic works as well as other music.

glucose (*or* dextrose) A simple sugar ($C_6H_{12}O_6$) and an essential substance in the carbohydrate metabolism of living organisms. Carbohydrates (such as starch and glycogen) in food or tissue reserves are broken down to glucose, which is easily transported to cells where it undergoes *glycolysis to provide energy for the cell. Organisms can also manufacture glucose from fats and proteins. Glucose levels in blood are regulated by the hormones *insulin and *glucagon and small amounts of glucose are normally present in urine. Fruits and honey are good sources of glucose.

gluten A protein mixture derived from wheat. In bread making, dough rises because the gluten in wheat flour expands, trapping the carbon dioxide bubbles in an elastic network. The properties of gluten vary according to the mixture of the proteins, chiefly gliadin and glutenin. *See also* celiac disease.

glutton. *See* wolverine.

glycerol (*or* glycerine; $C_3H_8O_3$) A colorless syrupy liquid with a sweet taste. It is made from fats and oils or by fermentation and is used in explosives, cosmetics, and antifreeze solutions.

glycogen A starchlike carbohydrate found in animal tissues as a reserve energy source. Chemically, it consists of branched chains of *glucose molecules: when required to provide energy, glycogen is broken down to glucose under the influence of hormones, chiefly *adrenaline and *glucagon.

glycolysis The sequence of chemical reactions occurring in most living cells by which glucose is partially broken down to provide usable energy for the cell in the form of *ATP. Glycolysis can take place in the presence or absence of oxygen but only a small amount of the available energy is released, the major proportion being released via the *Krebs cycle.

Glyndebourne An estate near Lewes, England, home of an annual international festival of opera. The opera house was built on the estate by its owner, John Christie, who founded the Glyndebourne Festival in 1934 for his wife, the opera singer Audrey Mildmay (1900–53).

glyptodon An extinct giant *armadillo, whose remains have been found in South America. Glyptodons had a rigid bony shell (unlike the jointed modern armadillo shell) and some had a spiky macelike knob at the end of the tail. They became extinct about 100,000 years ago.

GMT. *See* Greenwich Mean Time.

gnat Any of the smaller delicate species of two-winged flies, the males of which fly in dancing swarms. The term is applied to the less virulent mosquitoes and phantom gnats (family *Culicidae*), winter gnats (family *Trichoceridae*), fungus gnats (family *Mycetophilidae*), craneflies (family *Tipulidae*), and several others.

gnatcatcher A small active songbird belonging to a family (*Polioptilidae*; 11 species) ranging from S Canada to Argentina; 4–5.5 in (10–14 cm) long, gnatcatchers have long wagging tails and fine pointed bills used to pick insects from leaves and crevices. The plumage is typically grayish blue above with lighter underparts and white outer tail feathers.

Gneisenau, August (Wilhelm Anton), Graf Neithardt von (1760–1831) Prussian field marshal, who was instrumental in effecting major reforms in the Prussian army following its defeat by Napoleon (1807). He subsequently played an important part in the wars of liberation (1813–14) and in the defeat of Napoleon at Waterloo (1815).

gneiss A coarse-grained metamorphic rock consisting predominantly of bands of quartz and feldspar alternating with bands of micas and amphiboles. These bands are often irregular or poorly defined. Gneisses are formed during regional metamorphism; those derived from igneous rocks are termed **orthogneiss**, those from sedimentary rocks **paragneiss**.

Gniezno 52 32N 17 32E A city in W central Poland. One of the oldest cities in Poland, it contains many notable historical buildings, including its 10th-century cathedral. It is a commercial center specializing in food processing. Population: 50,600.

Gnosticism A religious movement that flourished in the early Christian era. It manifested itself in many ways and contained many elements of pagan thought and magic, but is most fully recorded as a group of heretical Christian sects, attacked by Church Fathers, such as *Tertullian. The Gnostics' defining characteristic was their belief in *gnosis* (Greek: knowledge)—a special revelation from God to initiates, which would ensure their salvation (*compare* mysteries). Their world view was dualistic: God and the spirit were good and matter evil. They interpreted Christ (whose humanity they denied) as being sent to rescue particles of spirit (souls) entrapped in matter. Gnosticism influenced *Manichaeism and several medieval heresies. *See also* Mandaeanism.

GNP. *See* gross national product.

gnu A large ungainly antelope belonging to the genus *Connochaetes* (2 species), also called wildebeest, of African plains. The brindled gnu (*C. taurinus*) grows to 55 in (140 cm) high at the shoulder and is blue-gray with a long black mane, black facial tufts, and a black-tufted tail. The smaller white-tailed gnu (*C. gnou*) has a long white tail and is very rare, surviving only in game reserves.

go (*or* i-go) A board game that originated in China (as *Wei-ch'i*), possibly in the 3rd millennium BC, and is especially popular in Japan. The board is marked with a grid of 19 vertical and 19 horizontal lines, making 361 intersections. There are 361 counters: 181 black "stones" for one player and 180 white for the other. Black begins by placing a stone on any intersection of the empty board. Play alternates, one stone being placed at a time; once played a stone may not be moved except to remove it from the board. The object is to conquer territory by enclosing empty points with one's own stones. Opposing stones that are encircled are captured and removed. The score is calculated by deducting the number of stones a player has lost from the number of intersections he has captured.

Goa A state on the W coast of India, formerly part of the union territory of Goa, Daman, and Diu. A Portuguese overseas territory from 1510 until annexed by India in 1961, it has many fine examples of Portuguese colonial architecture, including the church in which St Francis Xavier is buried. Area: 1363 sq mi (3496 sq km). Population (1991): 1,168,622. Capital: Panaji.

Goa, Daman, and Diu A Union Territory of W India. Goa is on the central W coast; Daman lies inland N of Bombay; Diu is an island off the coast of Gujarat. Formerly Portuguese, they depend economically on agriculture, fishing, and tourism. Area: 1472 sq mi (3813 sq km). *See also* Daman and Diu.

goat A hoofed *ruminant mammal belonging to the genus *Capra* (5 species). Related to sheep, goats are 24–33 in (60–85 cm) tall at the shoulder and have hollow horns, less curled than those of sheep; males have a scent gland beneath the tail and a beard. Wild goats, found in mountainous regions of Eurasia, are grayish in winter, reddish in summer, and live in herds of 5–20 individuals. Goats were first domesticated over 10,000 years ago and are still used to provide milk, meat, and hides in many semiarid regions of the world. Family: *Bovidae*. *See also* ibex; markhor; Rocky Mountain goat; tahr.

goat moth A large moth, *Cossus cossus,* of Europe, Asia, and N Africa. Mottled gray and brown, it has a wingspan of 3 in (70 mm). The reddish caterpillar bores under the bark of trees and emits a characteristic strong odor. It may hibernate for up to four years.

goatsbeard A perennial herb, *Aruncus dioicus* (or *A. sylvestris*), native to N temperate wooded regions, especially Siberia. Often grown as a border plant, goatsbeard is 47–71 in (120–180 cm) tall and has fine compound leaves and branched plumes of small stalkless hay-scented creamy-white flowers. Family: *Rosaceae.*

Gobbi, Tito (1915–84) Italian baritone. He sang in all the world's major opera houses and was a well-known teacher. His most famous parts included the title roles in Mozart's *Don Giovanni* and Verdi's *Falstaff* and Scarpia in Puccini's *Tosca.* He also produced opera.

Gobelins, Manufacture nationale des A French state-controlled tapestry factory, founded in Paris as a dyeworks in the 15th century by Jean and Philibert

Gobelin. Manufacturing tapestries from 1529, it was incorporated by Henry IV in 1607. In 1662 Louis XIV purchased it and it was directed from 1663 to 1690 by his First Painter Charles *Le Brun. Since 1826 carpets have also been made here.

Gobi Desert A vast desert of SE Mongolia and N China, one of the largest in the world. On a plateau 2950–4920 ft (900–1500 m) high, it is largely rocky with salt marshes and streams that disappear into the sand. It is rich in prehistoric remains including fossils and stone implements. Area: about 500,000 sq mi (1,295,00 sq km).

Gobind Singh (*or* Govind S.; 1666–1708) The tenth and last Guru of the Sikhs (1675–1708). As a religious reformer he remodeled the Sikh religious belief and practice and renounced social inequality and caste distinctions. He was assassinated by a Muslim.

Gobineau, Joseph Arthur, Comte de (1816–82) French writer and diplomat. He wrote novels, notably *Les Pléiades* (1874), short stories, and scholarly studies, including *La Renaissance* (1877). His influential *Essai sur l'inégalité des races humaines* (1853–55) argued that the continuing strength of the Aryan race depended on its racial purity.

goblin shark A carnivorous *shark, *Scapanorhynchus owstoni.* Up to 14 ft (4.2 m) long, it has long upper teeth that overlap the lower set, a long paddle-shaped nose, and a very long tail fin. It has been found in deep water off Japan, India, and Portugal and is probably the only member of its family, *Scapanorhynchidae.*

goby A fish of the suborder *Gobioidei* (over 800 species), especially the family *Gobiidae* (true gobies). True gobies have smooth elongated bodies, two dorsal fins, and a suction disk formed from fused pelvic fins. Most are 2–4 in (5–10 cm) long, although *Pandaka pygmaea* of the Philippines is the smallest known vertebrate at under 0.51 in (13 mm) long. They are chiefly marine and inhabit sand or mud burrows in tropical coastal regions, sometimes in association with other animals. Order: *Perciformes.*

God The supreme being that is the creator and ruler of the universe. The concept of God perhaps originated in primitive animistic belief, which attributed souls to natural objects and phenomena. It may then have developed into *polytheism, as in India and ancient Greece and Rome. In some religions, principally Judaism, Christianity, and Islam, God is seen as not only the architect of the universe but also as being actively involved with its inhabitants and its destiny (*see* theism). In *deism, God is seen as the creator of the universe who leaves its destiny to natural forces and the will of its inhabitants. In *Hinduism, Brahman, the supreme spirit and ultimate reality, is conceived as operating through the triad Brahma, Vishnu, and Shiva (*see* Trimurti). *Buddhism is, strictly speaking, nontheistic, being concerned more with the attainment of *nirvana than with the nature of a supreme being. The concept of a single supreme deity (*see* monotheism) originated with the ancient Jews (*see* Yahweh). Jews, Christians, and Muslims believe that God reveals himself with supernatural authority in their holy scriptures (*see* Bible; Koran). However, theologians and philosophers have also tried to prove the existence of God by rational means or by means of observed facts about the universe (natural theology). Most of the traditional arguments are associated with St Thomas *Aquinas; these include: the argument from design or the teleological argument (there is an observable design, order, and regularity in the universe and therefore it must have been designed, which argues a designer); the cosmological argument (the mere fact that there is a universe demands further explanation); the degrees of perfection argument (if every thing or quality in the universe can be traced back to a more perfect thing or quality, there must be some ultimate perfect being, i.e. God); the First Cause argument (if everything is caused by something else, at the beginning there must have been an uncaused First Cause). Another important argument is the ontological argument (*see* Anselm of Canterbury, St).

Godard, Jean-Luc (1930–) French film director. During the 1950s he wrote for the magazine *Cahiers du Cinéma* and became a member of the *New Wave. His films, which are characterized by experimental narrative and editing techniques and by his Marxist political convictions, include *A bout de souffle* (1960), *Alphaville* (1965), *Week-End* (1967), *Tout va bien* (1972), and *Je vous salve, Marie* (1985).

Godavari River A river in central India. Rising in the Western Ghats, it flows ESE across the Deccan, through the Eastern Ghats, and into the Bay of Bengal. Its delta has an extensive canal irrigation system, which is linked to the Krishna delta. It is sacred to the Hindus. Length: 900 mi (1500 km).

Goddard, Robert Hutchings (1882–1945) US physicist. He was educated at Clark University, where he was appointed professor of physics in 1919. From early in his career, he was interested in the practical application of rocketry and published a scientific article, "A Method of Reaching Extreme Altitudes," that predicted orbital and lunar exploration by means of rockets. During World War I, Goddard took part in the US war effort and developed a prototype *bazooka that was extensively used in World War II. Goddard's greatest achievement came in 1926, when he launched a rocket powered by liquid fuel. By using a mixture of gasoline and liquid oxygen, he was able to improve the speed and reliability of his rockets in the following decade. In 1930 he launched a rocket that rose to a height of 2000 ft (610 m) at a speed of 500 mph (800 km per hr), and five years later, one of his rockets broke the sound barrier. Goddard supervised the jet propulsion program of the US Navy during World War II. He is generally considered to be the father of modern rocketry.

Gödel, Kurt (1906–78) US mathematician, born in Austria, who derived probably the most important proof in modern mathematics. Known as **Gödel's proof**, it states that, in a mathematical system based on a finite number of axioms, there will always exist statements that can be neither proved nor disproved. Gödel's proof, published in 1931, thus ended the search by mathematicians for a complete and self-consistent system.

Godfrey of Bouillon (c. 1060–1100) Crusader and Duke of Lower Lorraine. In 1096 Godfrey joined the first Crusade and played a major role in the siege and capture of Jerusalem. He then became defender of the Holy Sepulcher and effective King of Jerusalem. His exploits were celebrated in the medieval song cycle the *Chansons de Geste*.

Godiva, Lady (d. 1080?) The English woman who, according to the chronicler Roger of Wendover (d. 1236), rode naked through the marketplace of Coventry in order to persuade her husband Leofric, Earl of Mercia, to reduce the taxes he had imposed on the town. The story was later embellished with a Peeping Tom who, ignoring Godiva's request that the townspeople remain indoors, was struck blind.

Godolphin, Sidney, Earl of (1645–1712) British Whig politician; Lord Treasurer (1685–88, 1700–01, 1702–10). Under Anne (reigned 1702–14) he and *Harley were the most powerful men in politics until the unpopularity of their pursuit of the War of the *Spanish Succession caused their downfall.

Godoy, Manuel de (1767–1851) Spanish statesman; chief minister (1792–97, 1801–08) of Charles IV of Spain. He rose to power through the influence of Charles's wife María Luisa (1751–1819), whose lover Godoy became. He allied Spain with France during the Napoleonic War and, extremely unpopular, was overthrown together with Charles.

Godthåb 64 10N 51 40W The capital of Greenland, a port at the mouth of Godthåb Fjord. Founded in 1721, it is the site of a radio station, hospital, and college. Chief occupations are reindeer and sheep raising, hunting, and fishing. Population (1981): 9423.

Godunov, Boris (Fedorovich) (c. 1551–1605) Russian statesman and tsar (1598–1605). Godunov rose to power in the reign of *Ivan the Terrible and became regent for Fyodor I, whose younger brother and heir, Dimitrii, Godunov may have murdered in 1591. After Fyodor's death (1598), Godunov was elected tsar. His authority was challenged by the first False Dimitrii, a pretender who succeeded Godunov (*see* *Time of Troubles). Godunov was the subject of a play by Pushkin, on which Mussorgsky based his famous opera.

Godwin (*or* Godwine; d. 1053) Earl of Wessex. An Anglo-Danish noble, he rose to power under Canute, after whose death Godwin supported the accession of Edward the Confessor and became a dominant figure in royal government. In 1045 his daughter Edith married Edward. He was overthrown in 1051 but regained his position by force in 1052. He was succeeded by his son Harold (later Harold II).

Godwin, William (1756–1836) British political philosopher and novelist. A utilitarian with extreme radical beliefs, Godwin in *Political Justice* (1793) advocated anarchy and communism. As a determinist, he held that the notion of moral desert was irrelevant; Christianity was also a harmful influence, distracting humans with bogus promises of immortality. His major novel, *Caleb Williams* (1794), propagates his views on justice. He married Mary *Wollstonecraft (1797).

Godwin Austen, Mount. *See* K2.

godwit A long-legged long-billed migratory bird belonging to a genus (*Limosa*; 4 species) that breeds in N Eurasia and North America. The black-tailed godwit (*L. limosa*) is 16 in (40 cm) long and has a distinctive black-banded white tail, white wing stripe, and, in summer, a chestnut neck and breast. Family: *Scolopacidae* (plovers, sandpipers, etc.).

Goebbels, (Paul) Joseph (1897–1945) German Nazi politician. From 1926, when he became Nazi party leader in Berlin, he was well known for his skillful propagandist techniques. In 1928 he entered the Reichstag and in 1933 was appointed minister of propaganda by Hitler. He established a vast and complex machine for the control of public information, the arts, cinema, and theater, all of which he manipulated with a cynical disregard for truth to achieve Nazi aims. He committed suicide with his wife after taking the lives of his six children during the collapse of the Third Reich.

Goes, Hugo van der (c. 1440–82) Flemish painter, who worked in Ghent until about 1478. He spent the rest of his life in a monastery near Brussels. His *Portinari Altarpiece* (Uffizi), painted for a Florentine patron, is uncharacteristically large for Flemish paintings. The unharmonious colors and emotional intensity of his last work, *The Death of the Virgin* (Bruges), are perhaps related to mental illness, from which he suffered in the last years of his life.

Goethals, George Washington (1858–1928) US engineer and soldier. After graduating (1880) from West Point, he served in the Army Engineer Corps and in 1907 was made chief engineer of the Panama Canal project (1904–14). He had to deal with the health, housing, and feeding problems of about 30,000 workers, as well as the technical engineering problems of building the canal. He served as governor of the Canal Zone (1914–17) and was made quartermaster general during World War I.

Goethe, Johann Wolfgang von (1749–1832) German poet, scholar, and statesman. He studied law at Leipzig and Strasbourg, where his discovery of Shakespeare inspired him to write an epic drama, *Götz von Berlichingen* (1773). The autobiographical novel *The Sorrows of Young Werther* (1774) won him international fame. In 1775 he settled at the court of the Duke of Saxe-Weimar, whom he served as prime minister until 1785 as well as directing the state theater and scientific institutions. At Weimar he fell in love with Charlotte von Stein, who inspired some of his greatest lyric poetry. A visit to Italy (1786–88) made him an enthusiastic advocate of classicism, influencing such plays as *Iphigenia on Tauris* (1787) and *Torquato Tasso* (1790). After the novel *Wilhelm Meister's Apprentice Years* (1795–96) he published the first part of his greatest work *Faust* (1808), a poetic drama of the aspirations of man. Other novels and scientific publications followed, until in 1829 he published *Wilhelm Meister's Journeyman Years*. The second, more philosophical, part of *Faust* he completed shortly before his death. A friend of the dramatist Schiller, Goethe's wide interests included stagecraft, biology, physics, astrology, and philosophy both orthodox and occult; he knew six languages well and translated many works into German.

JOHANN WOLFGANG VON GOETHE *After a portrait by Friedrich Bury, drawn when Goethe was about 51 years old.*

Gog and Magog In Revelation and other books of the Bible, attendant powers of Satan. In British folklore they appear as the survivors of a race of giants destroyed by Brutus, the legendary founder of Britain. A famous pair of statues depicting them are located in the Guildhall, London.

Gogol, Nikolai Vasilievich (1809–52) Russian novelist and dramatist. Early ambitions to become a poet and an actor and to emigrate to the US all failed, but two volumes of stories based on his Ukrainian childhood won him acclaim from *Pushkin and other leading writers. To escape the controversy aroused by his satirical play *The Government Inspector* (1836) he went to Rome, where he wrote his best-known work, *Dead Souls* (1842), a grotesque lampoon of Russian feudalism. In his last years he became a depressive and a religious maniac.

Goiânia 16 43S 49 18W A city in central Brazil, the capital of Goiás state on the Pan-American Highway. Founded in 1933 to replace the old capital, it serves a cattle-raising and coffee-growing area and has two universities. Population (1980 est): 703,263.

Goidelic languages. *See* Celtic languages.

goiter Swelling in the neck caused by enlargement of the thyroid gland. A goiter is called simple if the thyroid is functioning normally; this occurs in areas where iodine is deficient in the water supply and it may occur sporadically in adolescent girls. A goiter may also be seen when the thyroid is overactive (*see* hyperthyroidism) or underactive (*see* cretinism; myxedema).

Golan Heights A range of hills in SW Syria, under Israeli administration. They are of great strategic importance; Syrian artillery positioned here was able to fire into the upper Jordan and Hula Valleys in Israel. Israeli forces stormed the heights in June 1967, when most of the local populace fled; Jewish settlements have since been established.

Golconda 17 24N 78 23E A ruined city in S India, in Andhra Pradesh near Hyderabad city. The impressive tombs of the Qutb Shahi dynasty and the fortress, built on a granite ridge, stand as reminders of the city's former status as capital of one of the five Islamic kingdoms of the Deccan (1518–1687).

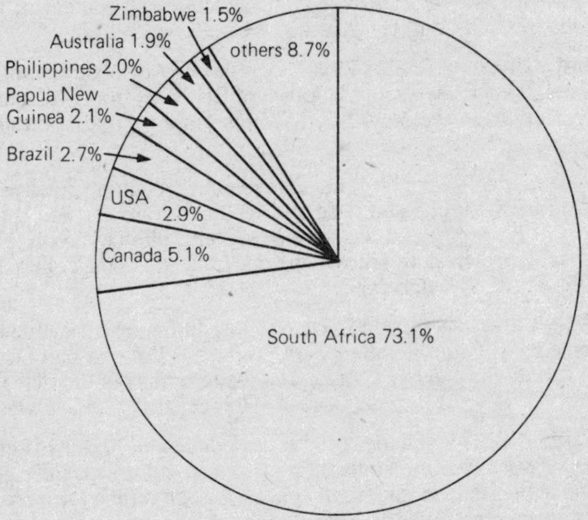

GOLD *World production.*

gold (Au) A soft dense yellow metal known and valued since ancient times. It occurs in nature as the element and in compounds with tellurium, in rock veins and alluvial deposits. The metal is the most malleable and ductile known. It alloys with other metals, is a good conductor of heat and electricity, and is chemically unreactive. The major uses for the element are for jewelry, electrical contacts, and as a currency standard (*see* gold standard). Gold dissolves in aqua regia (a mixture of one-third nitric acid and two-thirds hydrochloric acid) and the most common compound is the chloride ($AuCl_3$). Purity is measured in *karats. At no 79; at wt 196.967; mp 1950°F (1064.43°C); bp 5376°F (2966°C).

Gold, Thomas (1920–) Austrian-born astronomer, who spent 20 years in England before emigrating to the US in 1956 and becoming a professor at Cornell University. With *Bondi and *Hoyle he proposed the *steady-state theory of the universe in 1948. He also described pulsars as being neutron stars that are rapidly rotating.

Goldberg, Arthur J(oseph) (1908–90) US statesman, lawyer, and jurist; associate justice of the Supreme Court (1962–65). He practiced law in Chicago, eventually becoming general counsel of the *CIO (1948–55) and the newly merged *AFL-CIO (1955–61). Named secretary of labor (1961), he served until 1962, when he was appointed to the Supreme Court, a position he resigned in 1965 to become US ambassador to the UN (1965–68). He ran unsuccessfully for governor of New York (1970) and returned to private law practice.

Goldberg, Rube (Reuben, Lucius G.; 1883–1970) US cartoonist. In 1907 he joined the *New York Evening Mail,* where he created Professor Lucifer Gorgonzola Butts, who invented elaborate ways to perform simple tasks. Thereafter, any elaborate, complicated system, scheme, or device used to arrive at a simple end was called "a Rube Goldberg." In 1934 he began editorial cartooning, for which he was awarded the 1948 Pulitzer Prize.

Gold Coast The name applied by Europeans to the coastal zone in West Africa between Axim and the Volta River on the Gulf of Guinea. An important source of gold, it came under British control in the 19th century as part of the British colony of Gold Coast (present-day Ghana).

Gold Coast, City of 27 58S 153 20E A resort city of Australia, on the coast of Queensland. It stretches 20 mi (32 km) S of Brisbane, from Southport, the administrative center, to the New South Wales border. Population (1991 est): 274,200.

goldcrest A tiny agile songbird, *Regulus regulus,* occurring chiefly in coniferous woodland of N Europe and Asia and feeding on insects and spiders. It is about 3.5 in (9 cm) long and has a yellow-green plumage with white wing stripes and an orange crest, brighter in the male than the female. Family: *Muscicapidae* (Old World *flycatchers).

Golden Age, Latin The period (70 BC–18 AD) during which some of the highest achievements of Latin literature were produced. The first part of the period (70–43 BC) was dominated by *Cicero. The major writers of the subsequent Augustan age (43 BC–18 AD) include *Virgil, *Horace, *Livy, and *Ovid.

Golden Bull of 1222 A charter of liberties granted by Andrew II of Hungary (1175–1235) that curbed monarchical powers and confirmed the rights of the nobility. The nobles gained important concessions on military service, taxation, and the administration of justice. They had the right to resist if the king violated the Charter's articles.

golden calf An idol made by Aaron for the Israelites to worship when they believed that Moses would not return from Mt Sinai, where he was receiving the tables of the Law (Exodus 32). Moses destroyed the idol upon his return. A similar idol was made by King Jeroboam I (937–915 BC) and set up at Bethel and Dan (I Kings 12.28).

golden cat A small *cat of SE Asia and Sumatra, *Felis temmincki,* also called Temminck's cat. It is about 49 in (125 cm) long, with a plain golden coat and strikingly marked head; it lives among rocks preying on rodents and ground-dwelling birds. The closely related African golden cat (*aurata*) is found on the fringes of forests in West Africa.

golden chain (*or* golden rain). *See* laburnum.

golden eagle A large dark-brown *eagle, *Aquila chrysaetos,* occurring in mountainous regions of North America and Eurasia. It is 26–33 in (70–85 cm) long and has golden neck feathers, a gray beak, fully feathered legs, large yellow feet, and powerful talons. Golden eagles have a wingspan of up to 90 in (230 cm) and catch small mammals, rabbits, and gamebirds.

goldeneye A *diving duck, *Bucephala clangula,* that breeds in forested areas of N Eurasia and winters in more S regions. It is 16–18 in (41–45 cm) long and males are black and white with a greenish head and a circular white patch on the cheek; females are gray with white markings and a brown head.

Golden Fleece The fleece of a sacred winged ram, the recovery of which was the goal of *Jason and the *Argonauts. Athamas, King of Thebes, had two sons, Phrixus and Helle, by his first wife Nephele. His second wife, Ino, hated her stepsons and plotted their death. They escaped across the sea on the golden ram and, having reached Colchis, sacrificed the ram to Zeus and hung the fleece in a grove sacred to Ares, where it was guarded by a dragon.

Golden Fleece, Order of the A chivalric order founded by *Philip the Good, Duke of Burgundy, in 1430, taking as its badge the fleece captured by Jason in Greek mythology. When Burgundy was united to the Hapsburg empire (1477) the Order became increasingly aristocratic and was eventually confined to Austria and Spain.

Golden Gate bridge A suspension bridge for road traffic over the Golden Gate strait near San Francisco. Completed in 1937, its total length of 4200 ft (1280 m) made it the longest bridge in the world until the completion of the Verrazano Narrows bridge (1964) across New York Harbor.

Golden Horde The western part of the Mongol Empire following its fragmentation on the death (1227) of *Genghis Khan. The Horde, which adopted Islam, controlled all of Russia between the Urals and the Danube River until defeated by the Turk *Timur, in the late 14th century.

Golden Horn (Turkish name: Haliç) An inlet of the Bosporus in NW Turkey, on the N side of the peninsula upon which the old quarter of Istanbul stands. It is 4.5 mi (7 km) long and serves as the city's harbor.

golden mole A burrowing insect-eating mammal belonging to the African family *Chryochloridae* (15 species); 2.8–9 in (7–23 cm) long, they are stout-bodied, blind, and almost tailless, with two of the four digits on each forefoot greatly enlarged. Their fur is an iridescent golden-brown. Order **Insectivora.*

golden pheasant A small *pheasant, *Chrysolophus pictus,* native to mountainous regions of E Asia but widespread as an ornamental bird. Its plumage is gold, scarlet, black, and green and the male has a large ruff of broad feathers.

goldenrain tree. *See* lacquer tree.

golden retriever A large strongly built breed of □dog whose ancestors possibly included labradors, setters, and spaniels. The dense water-resistant wavy coat is gold or cream and these dogs are strong swimmers. They are used as gun dogs, guide gods, and police dogs. Height: 22–24 in (56–61 cm) (dogs); 20–22 in (51–56 cm) (bitches).

goldenrod A perennial herb of the genus *Solidago* (about 120 species), up to 8 ft (2.5 m) tall and mostly native to North America. The stem bears one-sided cylindrical heads of small yellow flowers, forming a branching plumelike inflorescence. Canadian goldenrod (*S. canadensis*) is often grown as a garden ornamental. Family: **Compositae.*

goldfinch, American A North American *finch, *Carduelis tristis.* About 5 in (12 cm) long, the male is bright yellow with a white rump, black forehead, and black tail and wings with white edges. The female is duller. It uses its pointed bill to extract seeds from thistles and dandelions and flocks of goldfinches are commonly seen on farmland.

goldfish A freshwater fish, *Carassius auratus,* also called golden carp, of E Asian origin but introduced elsewhere as an ornamental fish. In its natural state it is greenish brown or gray and up to 12 in (30 cm) long. However, the breeding of abnormal specimens, originally in China and Japan, has produced over 125 varieties, such as the "pop-eye," "veiltail," and "lionhead," often with a characteristic red-gold coloration. The goldfish requires cold well-oxygenated water and is omnivorous.

Golding, William (1911–93) British novelist. He served in the Royal Navy and subsequently became a schoolteacher. His best-known novel, *Lord of the Flies* (1954), concerns a group of schoolboys who are isolated on a desert island and revert to savagery. His other novels include *Pincher Martin* (1956), *The Spire* (1964), *Darkness Visible* (1979), *Rites of Passage* (1980), *A Moving Target* (1982), and *The Paper Men* (1984). He was awarded the Nobel Prize in 1983.

Goldoni, Carlo (1707–93) Italian comic playwright. A prolific writer of over 250 plays, he revolutionized the rigid conventions of the *commedia dell'arte with his realistic characters and witty dialogue. His plays include *The Liar* (1759), *Mine Hostess* (1753), and *The Fan* (1764). In 1762 he went to Paris, where he wrote his *Mémoires* (1787) and was from 1769 tutor to the daughters of Louis XV.

Gold Rush The transcontinental journey of eastern profiteers after the discovery of gold on John Sutter's land near Sacramento, Calif. (1848). Those (approximately 80,000) who arrived in the first year were called forty-niners. Harsh living conditions and the violent life of the gold fields took many lives and only a few forty-niners made fortunes. There were gold rushes in Australia, South Africa, and the Klondike, Canada, in the next half century.

Goldschmidt, Richard Benedict (1878–1958) US geneticist. His view of the chromosome as a large-chain molecule led to advances in genetic research. He demonstrated that differences between races were genetically determined and showed how drastic changes in environmental factors could cause changes in the external appearance of fruit flies.

Goldschmidt process The reduction of a metal oxide to the metal by reacting it with aluminum to form aluminum oxide and metal. The process, which produces a great deal of heat, is used to extract chromium from chromium ore. Named for Hans Goldschmidt (1861–1923).

Goldsmith, Oliver (1730–74) Anglo-Irish poet. Born in Ireland, he was sent to study medicine in Edinburgh and arrived penniless in London in 1756. A friend of Johnson and Boswell, he was inarticulate in conversation and a compulsive gambler. His best-known works are the poem "The Deserted Village"

(1770), the novel *The Vicar of Wakefield* (1776), and the play *She Stoops to Conquer* (1773).

gold standard A monetary system in which paper money was convertible on demand into gold. Banknotes were issued fractionally backed by gold (i.e. gold reserves were a fixed proportion of the value of the notes in circulation). Rates of exchange between countries were fixed by their currency values in gold. In classical economics imbalances in international trade were rectified automatically by the gold standard. A country in deficit would have depleted gold reserves and would therefore have to reduce its money supply. The resulting fall in demand would reduce imports and the lowering of prices would boost exports; thus the deficit would be rectified. Most financially important countries were on the gold standard from 1900 until its suspension during World War I because of the problems of transporting gold. It was reintroduced in 1925 but finally abandoned in 1931. *See also* International Monetary Fund.

Goldwater, Barry (Morris) (1909–) US political leader. A Republican senator from Arizona (1953–64; 1969–86), he served as a spokesman for right-wing, conservative America; he opposed a strong federal government and advocated US escalation in Vietnam. The Republican contender for the presidency (1964), he was defeated by Lyndon B. *Johnson. He wrote *The Conscience of a Conservative* (1960) and *Why Not Victory?* (1962).

Goldwyn, Samuel (S. Goldfish; 1882–1974) US film producer, born in Poland. In 1916 he cofounded Goldwyn Pictures, a production company that merged with other concerns to become Metro-Goldwyn-Mayer (MGM) in 1924. His many successful films as an independent producer include *Wuthering Heights* (1939) and *Guys and Dolls* (1955).

golem In medieval Jewish folklore, an image or automaton that can be brought to life by a charm. They were supposed to have been used as servants by rabbis. The word originally referred to anything incomplete or embryonic.

golf A club-and-ball game for two or four players played on a golf course. It was well established in Britain by the 15th century and almost certainly originated in Scotland. A standard course is usually between 4572 m (5000 yd) and 6400 m (7000 yd) and is divided into 18 holes (9 on a small course), each of which is between 90 m (100 yd) and 540 m (600 yd) long. A hole comprises the flat starting point, called the tee, a strip of mown grass about 27–90 m (30–100 yd) wide, called the fairway, and a smooth putting green. On the green is the actual hole. There are also obstacles around the course, such as trees, ditches, ponds, and sand bunkers. The object of the game is to hit the ball from each tee into each hole with as few strokes as possible (par for a hole is the standard number of strokes needed by a first-class player; one stroke less than par is called a birdie, and an eagle is two strokes less). To achieve this a player is allowed a set of 14 clubs of which there are three basic types: woods, irons, and putters.

Golgi, Camillo (1843–1926) Italian cell biologist, whose staining technique using silver nitrate revealed fine details of cells. Golgi distinguished different types of nerve cells in the brain (Golgi cells) and demonstrated a network of tubules and granules within cells (the *Golgi apparatus). He shared the 1906 Nobel Prize with *Ramon y Cajal.

Golgi apparatus (*or* Golgi complex) A structure present in the cytoplasm of nearly all □cells, composed of stacks of flattened sacs bounded by membranes and associated with vesicles. Discovered by Camillo *Golgi, it is thought to function in the synthesis and concentration of certain materials, especially secretory products, which are then packaged into the vesicles and transported within the cell.

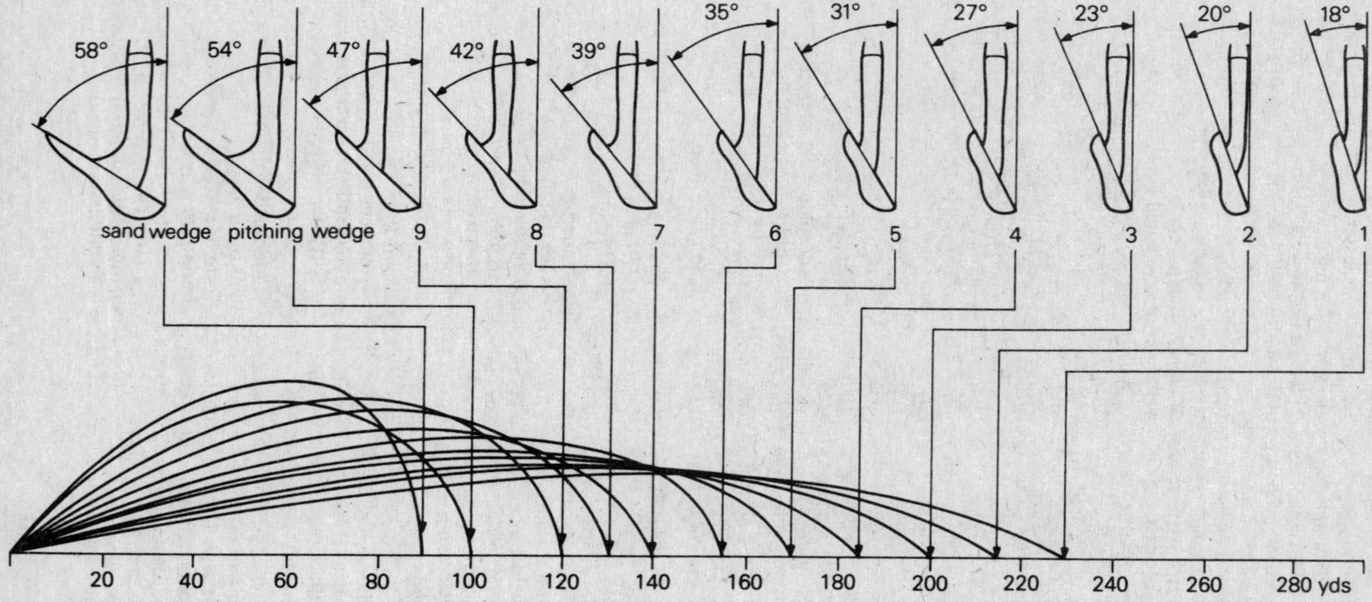

GOLF *Irons are numbered according to the angle of the face; the greater the angle of inclination, the higher the ball is hit into the air. Thus a good player, under normal conditions, knows the range of each iron. The Number One wood (driver) is used from the tee for the maximum distance and the putter is used on the green.*

Golgotha. *See* Calvary.

goliards Wandering scholars (often students or lesser clerics) of medieval Europe who were notorious for their scurrilous verses. Frequently condemned by the Church for their poetry and riotous behavior, by the 14th century the term had lost its earlier connotations, being applied to all minstrels. The largest collection of goliard poetry was published as the *Carmina Burana* in the 19th century.

goliath beetle A large beetle belonging to the group of flower chafers (*see* chafer). The African goliath beetle (*Goliathus giganteus*) has the largest body of all the insects, measuring about 4 in (96 mm) in length. It is white with bold black stripes and brown wing cases. The larvae are found in rotten logs.

goliath frog The largest known living frog, *Rana goliath,* which grows up to 14 in (35 cm) long. This rare shy frog inhabits deep river pools in Africa. Its bones are supposed to have magical properties.

Golovkin, Gavril Ivanovich, Count (1660–1734) Russian statesman. A relative of *Peter the Great, he accompanied the tsar on his early visits to W Europe. In 1706 he became foreign minister and in 1709, state chancellor. In the reign (1725–27) of Catherine I (?1684–1727), he became a member of the supreme privy council. In the 1730 accession crisis, he supported *Anna Ivanovna.

Gomel 52 25N 31 00E A port in Belarus on the Sozh River. It is an important railroad junction and industrial center, producing fertilizers, machinery, timber products, foodstuffs, and textiles. Population (1987 est): 406,000.

Gómez, Juan Vicente (1857–1935) Venezuelan soldier and statesman, who was brought to power in 1908 by a military coup. Elected president in 1910, he governed, either directly or through puppets, until his death. He did much to modernize Venezuela, simultaneously accumulating a vast personal fortune. His power base was in the army and he brutally suppressed all opposition to his regime.

Gomillion v. Lightfoot (1960) US Supreme Court decision that struck down an Alabama law. The law had allowed the redistricting of an area in such a way that most African-American voters were eliminated from the district.

Gompers, Samuel (1850–1924) US labor leader; born in London. As a young boy in the US he joined the Cigarmaker's Union (1863) and by 1877 had reorganized it. In 1886, when the American Federation of Labor (AFL) was organized, he served as its first president (1886–94; 1896–1924). He held a conservative view toward unions and believed in collective bargaining, a national union, and businesslike management of labor affairs.

Gomulka, Wladyslaw (1905–82) Polish statesman. Gomulka was secretary general of the Polish Workers' Party from 1945 until 1948, when his criticism of the Soviet Union led to his demotion and imprisonment (1951–54). Following the *Poznan Riots, which gave Poland more independence from the Soviet Union, Gomulka became first secretary of the Party. In 1970 he resigned after demonstrations over price increases.

gomuti A *palm tree, *Arenga pinnata* (or *A. saccharifera*), also called sugar palm, occurring in SE Asia. The sap yields palm sugar and the fermented juice (palm wine) is distilled to produce arrack. A form of sago is obtained from the pith and the leaf fibers are used to make cord, ropes, etc.

gonad. *See* ovary; testis.

gonadotrophin One of several hormones that control the activity of the testes and ovaries (the gonads) in mammals. The pituitary gland, under the influence of the hypothalamus, produces three gonadotrophins: luteinizing hormone (LH), which stimulates ovulation and *estrogen production by the ovaries and the production of *androgens by the testes; follicle-stimulating hormone (FSH), which promotes ovulation and sperm production; and *prolactin, which triggers lactation. LH and FSH are glycoproteins and are usually released together. Human chorionic gonadotrophin (HCG) is produced by the placenta, reaching a peak level in the urine in early pregnancy. Measurement of urinary HCG is the basis of pregnancy tests. Gonadotrophins are also used in *fertility drugs.

SAMUEL GOMPERS *Labor movement leader who advocated the use of peaceful, businesslike methods to achieve unionism's goals.*

Gonaïves 12 29N 72 42 W A port in W Haiti, on the Gulf of Gonaïves. Exports include coffee, bananas, and mangoes. Population (1992): 63,291.

Goncourt, Edmond de (1822–96) French writer, who collaborated with his brother **Jules de Goncourt** (1830–70) on art criticism, social histories of France, and a series of carefully researched naturalistic novels, most notably *Germinie Lacerteux* (1864) and *Madame Gervaisais* (1869). They are best known for their *Journal,* a lively record of French literary life from 1851–95, and for Edmond's legacy, the Académie Goncourt, which awards France's most prestigious annual literary prize, the Prix Goncourt.

Gondar 12 40N 37 45E A city in central Ethiopia. A former capital of Ethiopia, Gondar was built after the Portuguese Jesuits had been expelled in the 16th century and is now a tourist attraction. Population (1988 est): 95,000.

Gondwanaland The supercontinent in the S hemisphere believed to have existed prior to 200 million years ago, when the drift of the continents to their present positions began. It probably consisted of South America, Africa, Australia, Antarctica, Arabia, and India. *See also* Laurasia.

gong A percussion instrument of indefinite pitch. The orchestral gong (*or* tam-tam) is a disk of metal about 3 ft (1 m) in diameter with a turned-over edge, hanging in a wooden frame.

gong chimes A set of gongs tuned to different pitches, used in many countries of the Far East. The instrument exists in a number of forms, the most elaborate of which, found in Burma and Thailand, consists of 15–20 small gongs set in a circular wooden frame. The player kneels inside the frame and plays the gongs with hammers. □musical instruments.

Góngora y Argote, Luis de (1561–1627) Spanish poet. Son of a judge, he was court chaplain in Madrid from 1617. He wrote many conventional sonnets and satirical verses but is best known for his longer works, *Polifemo* (1612) and *Soledades* (1613), in which he used esoteric allusions and elaborate diction and syntax to create a deliberately obscure and artificial style.

gonorrhea An acute venereal infection caused by a bacterium (the gonococcus). It is now one of the commonest infections in developed societies. Symptoms in men are discharge from the penis and a burning pain on passing urine. Women may have vaginal discharge and pain on urinating, but half have no symptoms at all, which is one of the reasons the disease is so widespread. It can be treated with penicillin.

Gonzaga An Italian dynasty that ruled Mantua (1328–1707) and Montferrato and Casale (1536–1707). The family was established in Mantua by **Luigi Gonzaga** (c. 1268–1360). His distinguished successors included **Gianfrancesco Gonzaga** (?1394–1444), a soldier and patron of learning under whom *Vittorino da Feltre established a famous school at Mantua, and **Francesco Gonzaga** (1466–1519), who commanded Italian forces against the French invasion in 1494 and was the husband of the distinguished patron of arts Isabella d'Este (*see* Este).

González de Mendoza, Pedro (1428–95) Spanish churchman; cardinal, archbishop of Toledo, and primate of Spain (from 1482). He was the most powerful supporter of Isabella in her successful claim to the Spanish throne and in her subsequent attempts to strengthen the monarchy. He took part in the conquest of Granada.

Good Friday The Friday before *Easter, when Christ's crucifixion is commemorated. It is a fast day, and in the Roman Catholic Church the Mass is not celebrated.

Good Hope, Cape of. *See* Cape of Good Hope.

Goodman, Benny (Benjamin David G.; 1909–86) US clarinettist, prominent in the development of *swing. A versatile player and band leader, Goodman led big bands and played in small jazz groups from the 1930s to the 1980s. Also active in classical music, Bartok and Aaron Copland wrote works for him.

Good Neighbor Policy The US policy of cooperation and nonintervention in Latin American affairs. After decades of sporadic military involvement in South America, the US government began to change its policy in the late 1920s. This change to a policy of peaceful assistance to Latin American countries was detailed in the 1933 inaugural address of Pres. Franklin *Roosevelt. His Good Neighbor Policy included the withdrawal of American troops, the lifting of trade barriers, and the preparation of a common defense in case of war. In 1948, President *Truman continued this policy, helping to found the *Organization of American States (OAS).

Goodyear, Charles (1800–60) US inventor. He experienced financial difficulties early in his career that resulted in brief imprisonment in a debtors' prison. After his release, he became interested in developing a technique for treating raw India rubber to prevent its melting or stiffening with changing temperatures. In 1837, Goodyear patented his first rubber coating formula and by 1844 he had perfected the *vulcanization process. This method cured the raw rubber by treating it with sulfur at a high temperature making it strong and elastic. This development led to the use of rubber in many applications. Goodyear's financial difficulties plagued him in later years, and he was forced to sell his rights to his rubber patents.

Goolagong, Evonne. *See* Cawley, Evonne.

goosander A large migratory *duck, *Mergus merganser,* that breeds in North America and N Eurasia, also called sawbill because of its long toothed bill. The male is 30 in (75 cm) long and has a green head, black back, and white body; females are 22 in (57 cm) long and have a chestnut head and gray body. Goosanders feed chiefly on fish.

goose A large long-necked waterbird belonging to the family *Anatidae* (ducks, geese, and swans), occurring in the N hemisphere. Geese have short bills, humped at the base and tapering toward the tip, and short webbed feet. They chiefly feed inland on grass, grain, roots, etc., and are highly migratory, flying in characteristic V-formations and honking loudly in flight. The several breeds of domesticated goose are probably descended from the *graylag goose. Genera: *Anser* (gray geese), *Branta* (black geese); order: *Anseriformes. See also* barnacle goose; brent goose; Canada goose; Hawaiian goose; white-fronted goose.

gooseberry A fruit bush of the genus *Ribes,* especially *R. uva-crispa* (or *R. grossularia*), which is widely cultivated in the Old World for its hairy prickly-coated berries used (usually cooked) for preserves, wine, and in desserts. The bush, 40–60 in (1–1.5 m) high, may be upright, spreading, or drooping, with three-lobed toothed leaves and spiny stems. The small drooping greenish flowers arise in the axils of the leaves. Family: *Grossulariaceae.*

goosefish. *See* anglerfish.

goosefoot A herb or small shrub of the genus *Chenopodium* (110 species), of temperate regions, also called pigweed. The stem, 0.5–50 ft (0.5–15 m) high, is grooved or angular and the leaves are often fleshy. The whole plant may have a whitish mealy appearance. The small greenish flowers are borne on a branched inflorescence. Family: *Chenopodiaceae.*

goosegrass. *See* cleavers.

gopher. *See* pocket gopher; souslik.

Gorakhpur 26 45N 83 23E A city in N India, in Uttar Pradesh. It served as an army recruitment center for Gurkhas while under British rule. The main industries are sugar refining and fertilizer production and it has a university (1956). Population (1991): 489,850.

goral A small hoofed mammal, *Naemorhedus goral,* of mountainous regions in S Asia. About 26 in (65 cm) high at the shoulder, gorals have short conical horns and a coarse woolly coat, which varies from gray to foxy red. They graze in small herds at dawn and dusk. Family: **Bovidae*. *See also* serow.

Gorbachev, Mikhail Sergeyevich (1931–) Soviet political leader, general secretary of the Communist party (1985–91). He headed his region's Communist party by 1970 and was the youngest member of the Politboro from 1980. Succeeding Konstantin Chernenko as Soviet leader, he promoted *glasnost* (openness) and *perestroika* (economic restructuring). In 1986, he met President Reagan for a summit meeting on arms control. In 1987 a second meeting brought an agreement to limit nuclear arms. He met again with Reagan and US president-elect George *Bush in late 1988 and announced arms reductions in Europe. In the break-up of the Soviet Union in December 1991, he resigned.

Gordon, Charles George (1833–85) British general. Gordon earned the nickname Chinese Gordon after suppressing the *Taiping Rebellion (1864) in China. In 1874 he was employed by the Khedive of Egypt to open up the country and from 1877 to 1880 was British governor of Sudan. In 1884 he was sent back to the Sudan to evacuate Europeans and Egyptians, following al *Mahdi's revolt. Gordon was besieged for 10 months in Khartoum, which was taken two days before a relief force arrived. Gordon himself was murdered.

Gore, Albert Arnold, Jr (1948–) US vice president (1993–). A Democrat, he served under Pres. Bill Clinton. As a member of the House of Representatives (1977–85) and the Senate (1985–93), he concerned himself with environmental issues, for which he campaigned vigorously during the 1992 election. Born in Washington, D.C., where his father, Al Gore, Sr was a prominent senator from Tennessee, Gore graduated from Harvard University (1969) and was a journalist in the Army and on a Nashville, Tenn., newspaper (1971–76).

Gorgas, William Crawford (1854–1929) US physician and soldier. After becoming a doctor, he joined the Army Medical Corps (1880) and worked in Havana, Cuba (1898–1902). He was successful in controlling yellow fever and malaria outbreaks in Havana and later (1904–14) during the building of the Panama Canal. He was appointed surgeon general of the Army in 1914.

Gorgon In Greek legend, a monster inhabiting the underworld. Hesiod refers to three Gorgons, the sisters Stheno, Euryale, and *Medusa. They were usually portrayed as winged females with snakes for hair and boars' tusks for teeth.

gorilla The largest living *ape, *Gorilla gorilla,* of tropical African forests. Male gorillas can grow to 6 ft (1.8 m) with a weight of 661 lb (300 kg). They walk on their feet and knuckles, feeding on plant stems and also climbing to reach fruit. Troops are led by a dominant adult male and are generally not aggressive, preferring retreat to attack, although they will fight when cornered. Three races are recognized: the rare shaggy mountain gorilla and two lowland forms—light-colored in the West and black in the East.

Göring, Hermann Wilhelm (1893–1946) German Nazi politician. He became a Nazi in 1922, taking command of Hitler's Brownshirts. He was elected to the Reichstag in 1928 and became its president in 1932. When Hitler came to power in 1933, Göring was appointed air minister of Germany and prime minister of Prussia. He established the *Gestapo and *concentration camps and directed the development of the Luftwaffe. Hitler declared Göring his successor in 1939 but expelled him from the party shortly before the Nazi collapse. Condemned to hang at Nuremburg, Göring committed suicide.

Gorki, Maksim (Aleksei Maksimovich Peshkov; 1868–1936) Russian novelist. His hard nomadic early life is recounted in his autobiographical trilogy *Childhood* (1913–14), *In the World* (1915–16), and *My Universities* (1923). He established his literary reputation with romantic short stories and followed these with several novels and plays, including *Mother* (1906) and *The Lower Depths* (1906). He lived in exile in Italy from 1906–13 and again from 1921–28. He then returned to Russia, becoming first president of the Soviet Writers Union and an exponent of Stalinism.

Gorkii (Gorki *or* Gorky) *See* Nizhny Novgorod.

Gorky, Arshile (Vosdanig Adoian; 1905–48) US painter, born in Armenia, who emigrated to the US in 1920. He worked in most 20th-century styles before adopting, in about 1940, an individual and abstract form of *surrealism. Such works as *The Liver Is the Cock's Comb* (1944; New York) anticipate *action painting in their free application of paint. His promising career was cut short by his suicide.

Görlitz 51 11N 15 00E A city in Germany, on the *Neisse River where it marks the boundary with Poland. Famous since the Middle Ages for cloth making, its many industries also include vehicle and machinery manufacture and lignite mining. Population: 86,034.

Gorlovka 48 17N 38 05E A city in Ukraine in the *Donets Basin. It is one of the largest coal mining and industrial centers of the area. Population (1987): 345,000.

Gorno-Altai A region (*oblast*) in S Russia. Formed in 1922 for the Turkic-speaking Altaian peoples, it is now inhabited mostly by Russians. Gold and mercury are mined and livestock breeding is the main agricultural activity. Area: 35,740 sq mi (92,600 sq km). Population (1991 est): 197,000. Capital: Gorno-Altaisk.

Gorno-Badakhshan A region (*oblast*) in Tajikistan. It was formed in 1925 and its population consists mainly of *Tadzhiks. Chiefly agricultural, it produces wheat, fruit, and fodder crops; cattle and sheep are bred. Area: 24,590 sq mi (63,700 sq km). Population (1991 est): 167,000. Capital: Khorog.

gorse (*or* furze) A very spiny densely branched shrub, *Ulex europaeus,* up to 13 ft (4 m) high, with bright-yellow sweet-scented flowers. The leaves, which consist of three leaflets, are reduced to spines or scales on mature plants. The fruit is a black hairy pod that splits open explosively to release the seeds. Gorse is native to grassy areas and heaths throughout Europe and has been introduced elsewhere. Family: **Leguminosae.*

Gorton, Sir John Grey (1911–) Australian statesman; Liberal prime minister (1968–71). His administration was responsible for greater federal government intervention in the field of education, and he fostered Australia's involvement in the Vietnam War.

goshawk A large powerful *hawk, *Accipiter gentilis,* ranging throughout forests of the N hemisphere and formerly used in falconry. It is 24 in (60 cm) long with a wingspan of 51 in (130 cm) and a finely barred gray plumage. It feeds chiefly on birds.

Gospels (Old English: good news) The four New Testament accounts of Christ's life, ascribed to *Matthew, *Mark, *Luke, and *John. The word originally referred to the message of Christ's redemptive work rather than to the writings. The first three are known as the Synoptic Gospels, since they report approximately the same synopsis of the events. According to some biblical scholars Mark is the oldest of these and was used as a source by the authors of Matthew and Luke. Material that is not found in Mark but is common to Matthew and Luke is believed to derive from a single lost source, known as Q. The fourth Gospel, John, emphasizes the divinity of Christ and may presuppose a knowledge of the Synoptic Gospels.

Gosport 50 48N 1 08W A port in S England, on Portsmouth Harbour. It is a naval base, linked with Portsmouth by ferry, and has yacht-building and marine-engineering industries. Population (1981): 77,276.

Gossaert, Jan (c. 1478–c. 1532) Flemish painter, whose popular surname, Mabuse, derives from his birthplace Maubeuge. As one of the first Flemish artists to work in the Italian Renaissance style, after visiting Italy (1508) he painted sculptural nudes against Italian architectural backgrounds, e.g. *Neptune and Amphitrite* (Berlin). As a portraitist he was noted for his expressive treatment of hands.

Göta Canal A canal in S Sweden, linking Göteborg on the Kattegat in the W with Stockholm in the E. Opened in 1832, it enters the Baltic Sea near Söderköping. Length: 58 mi (93 km).

Göteborg (English name: Gothenburg) 57 45N 12 00E An important ice-free port in SW Sweden, at the mouth of the Göta River. Sweden's second largest city, it expanded through Napoleon's Continental System and with the opening of the Göta Canal (1832). Notable buildings include the town hall (1750), cathedral (1633), and university (1891). Industries include ship building, oil refining, and the manufacture of cars. Population (1992 est): 432,000.

Gotha 50 56N 10 42E A city in S Germany, on the N edge of the Thuringian Forest, former capital of the duchy of Saxe-Coburg-Gotha. It is noted for the *Almanac de Gotha* (an annual record of the royal and noble houses of Europe, published here from 1764–1944). Gotha manufactures machinery, vehicles, textiles, and chemicals. Population (1981 est): 57,600.

Gothenburg. *See* Göteborg.

gothic art and architecture The styles flourishing in Europe from the mid-12th to the end of the 15th centuries. "Gothic" originated as a derisory term used by Renaissance artists, who blamed the destruction of classical art on the Goths who invaded the Roman Empire. The gothic is most closely associated with church architecture, the hallmarks of gothic design being the rib and shaft ceiling, the pointed □arch, the flying buttress, and later great height and the impression of weightlessness. Gothic architecture was initiated in France in the chevet of the Abbey of Saint-Denis, near Paris. It was followed by the cathedrals of *Notre-Dame (begun 1163), Chartres (begun c. 1194), Reims (begun 1211), etc. (*see also* Flamboyant). Although used during the *romanesque period, *stained glass was only fully developed in the gothic period, being characterized by elaborate tracery, brilliant colors, and the reduction of stonework between the windows to very thin stone bars. Gothic sculpture mirrored the development of the architecture it adorned, renouncing its early naturalism for a stylized elegance and an emphasis on line and silhouette. In painting, the early gothic manifested itself chiefly in manuscript illumination. In the 14th century elements of it appear in the art of Simone *Martini, Rogier van der *Weyden, and others, but its full flowering in panel and manuscript painting came with the *international gothic style of the early 15th century. The gothic was revived in the 19th century by the Victorians, who considered it a perfect embodiment of religious intensity (*see* gothic revival).

gothic novel An English genre, popular in the late 18th and early 19th centuries, characterized by a prevailing atmosphere of mystery and terror and pseudomedieval—"gothic"—settings. Examples include Horace Walpole's *Castle of Otranto* (1765), Ann Radcliffe's *The Mysteries of Udolpho* (1794), and Matthew Gregory Lewis's *The Monk* (1796). The genre wilted under parodies, such as Jane Austen's *Northanger Abbey* (1818), but influenced later writers, among them the Brontë sisters, Poe, and Bram Stoker, in *Dracula* (1897).

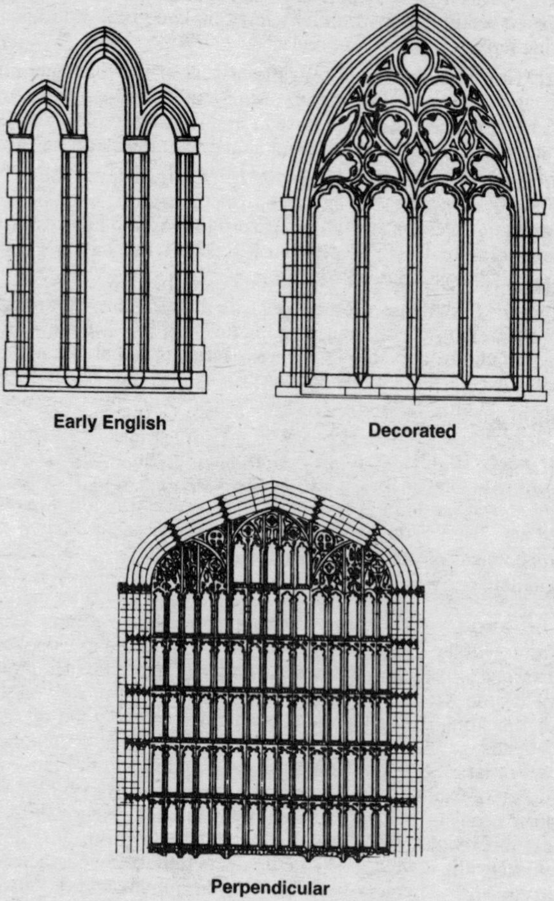

GOTHIC ART AND ARCHITECTURE *In England the three phases of gothic architecture are characterized by distinctive window designs.*

gothic revival An architectural style. Initially associated with *Romanticism, the revived popularity for *gothic architecture began in England in the late 18th century, with such buildings as Fonthill Abbey. Common throughout W Europe and the US, it was particularly dominant in Britain after 1818, when Parliament voted funds to build new Anglican churches. Over 170 were built in the gothic style. The culmination of the gothic revival was perhaps the new Houses of Parliament (1834–45). One of the last important gothic-revival buildings in London was the Law Courts (1882).

Goths Germanic peoples who originated in Scandinavia (Gotland) and had moved into the Ukraine by the end of the 2nd century AD. Shortly afterward they invaded the Roman Empire N of the Danube and expanded into the Balkans.

Converted to Arian Christianity (*see* Arianism) in the mid-4th century, their empire was soon destroyed by the *Huns and their two groups, the *Ostrogoths and *Visigoths, separated.

Gotland (Gothland *or* Gottland) The largest of the Swedish islands, in the Baltic Sea. Long disputed between Denmark and Sweden, it was finally ceded to Sweden in 1645. Its economy is based chiefly on agriculture (cattle and sheep raising) and tourism. Area: 1225 sq mi (3140 sq km). Capital: Visby.

Gottfried von Strassburg (13th century) German poet. Nothing is known of his life apart from what can be inferred from the erudition and poetic skill of his epic *Tristan und Isolde,* a retelling of the original Celtic legend according to the conventions of courtly love. It inspired Wagner's famous opera.

Göttingen 51 32N 9 57E A city in Germany in Lower Saxony. With its famous university, founded in 1734 by George II of Great Britain, and the Max Planck Association for the furtherance of science, it is a noted educational center. Its manufactures include precision instruments and aluminum goods. Population (1991 est): 122,000.

Gottsched, Johann Christoph (1700–66) German critic, who introduced French classical and rationalist critical principles into German literature. His dramatic academy in Leipzig and his own plays, such as *Der sterbende Cato* (1732), and translations helped to raise the literary standards of German theater.

gouache. *See* watercolor.

Gouda 52 01N 4 43E A city in the W Netherlands, in South Holland province. Its most notable church, the Grote Kerk (1552), has exceptional stained-glass windows (1556–1603). It is famous for its gouda cheese. Population (1988 est): 62,300.

Goujon, Jean (c. 1510–68) French Renaissance sculptor. His best-known works are the marble relief of the *Deposition, The Tribune of the Caryatids* supporting a gallery in the Louvre, and reliefs of nymphs for the Fontaine des Innocents. The first two were produced in collaboration with the architect Pierre *Lescot.

Gould, Jay (Jason G.; 1836–92) US businessman. With James *Fisk he caused the "Erie War" (1868) by illegally manipulating the Erie Railroad stock to prevent Cornelius *Vanderbilt from having full control of the line. His attempt to corner the gold market (1869) failed but was the cause of a stock market panic called Black Friday. His later dealings involved holdings in the Union Pacific, Kansas Pacific, Denver Pacific, Wabash, and Missouri Pacific railroads and brought him great profits, but upset the stability of the entire railroad system.

Gounod, Charles François (1818–93) French composer. He began serious composition after studying theology and deciding not to become a priest. His most successful works were the operas *Faust* (1852–59) and *Romeo and Juliet* (1864). Toward the end of his life he composed a large quantity of sacred music, including oratorios and masses.

gourami One of several freshwater tropical *labyrinth fishes, especially *Osphronemus goramy.* It has a brown or gray oval body, up to 24 in (60 cm) long, and a filamentous ray extending from each pelvic fin. Native to the E Indies, it has been introduced elsewhere and cultivated for food.

gourd The fruit of certain plants of the family *Cucurbitaceae,* especially the white-flowered bottle gourd (*Lagenaria siceraria*), a trailing annual herb widely grown in the tropics. Its fruits have woody shells used locally as bottles, pipes, and utensils. Other gourds are grown as ornamentals, having attractive shapes, colors, and surface patterns. The dishcloth gourd (*see* loofah) is used as a bath sponge and the *snake gourd is grown for food.

gout Sudden attacks of arthritis caused by the presence of uric acid crystals in the joints. The big toe is most commonly affected, becoming hot, red, and very painful. Gout is commonest in older men and tends to recur; if not treated (by drugs to reduce the uric acid in the blood) it may lead to destruction of the joint. Gout is associated with an increased incidence of heart disease.

Government Printing Office (GPO) US federal agency that is reponsible for all government printing and publishing. Established in 1860 and headed by the Public Printer, it carries out the printing and binding orders of Congress and the federal government departments through the Congressional Joint Committee on Printing. Certain printed materials are available to the public through mail-order catalogues, government bookstores, and selected libraries.

Govind Singh. *See* Gobind Singh.

Gowon, Yakubu (1934–) Nigerian statesman; head of state (1966–76). An army officer, in the 1966 military coup he became chief of staff and then head of state. He was ousted in a bloodless coup in 1976.

Goya (y Lucientes), Francesco (Jose) de (1746–1828) Spanish painter, born near Saragossa. After studying in Italy, he settled in Madrid (1775), where he painted gay scenes of Spanish life for the royal tapestry factory. As court painter from 1789 he produced realistic unflattering portraits of the royal family. He became deaf in 1792, and his works grew pessimistic and sometimes nightmarish, as in his etchings of *Los Caprichos* and *The Disasters of War,* condemning the French invasion of Spain. He settled in France in 1824. Among his best-known paintings are *Maja Clothed, The Shootings of May 3 1808,* and the so-called black paintings, such as *Satan Devouring His Children* (all Prado).

Goyen, Jan Josephszoon van (1596–1656) Dutch landscape painter and etcher, who was born in Leiden but after 1630 lived in The Hague. His river and winter scenes were characterized by large expanses of sky and near-monochrome colors.

Gozzi, Carlo (1720–1806) Italian dramatist. He opposed the theatrical reforms of *Goldoni and attempted to revive the techniques of the *commedia dell'arte. His plays, often including elements of fantasy and the grotesque, include *Turandot* (1762), on which Puccini's opera is based, and *L'Augellin Belverde* (1764).

Gozzoli, Benozzo (Benozzo di Lese; 1420–97) Florentine painter. His major works are the frescoes of the *Journey of the Magi* (Palazzo Medici-Riccardi, Florence), which are noted for their detailed landscapes, and portraits of his contemporaries.

Gracchus, Tiberius Sempronius (163–133 BC) Roman reformer, who as tribune (133) proposed land reforms intended to create a class of small landowners. He was killed in a riot. His brother **Gaius Sempronius Gracchus** (153–121 BC) was tribune in 123 and renewed Tiberius's attempts at land reform. He was killed in riots over his proposal to grant Roman citizenship to Latins. The Gracchi's attempts at reform polarized the aristocracy into hostile factions and thereafter change was difficult to achieve without violence.

grace In Christian theology, God's freely offered forgiveness to his sinful creatures. The nature of divine grace and the conditions on which it is offered and accepted were central to the controversy between *Pelagius and St *Augustine, and between the Calvinists and their opponents at the Reformation. *See also* free will; predestination.

Graces In Greek mythology, the three daughters of Zeus and Hera, representing beauty, grace, and charm. They were named Aglaia, Euphrosyne, and Thalia.

grackle An omnivorous black bird of the North American genus *Quiscalus*. Grackles are about 12 in (30 cm) long and have strong pointed bills used to dig for insect larvae, to kill small vertebrates, and to crack open nuts. They often feed in large flocks, causing damage to crops. Family: *Icteridae* (American orioles).

gradient A measure of the inclination of a slope, often expressed as the rise in height divided by the length of the slope, i.e. the sine of the angle of the slope. Mathematically, however, the gradient is the ratio of the vertical rise to the horizontal distance covered, i.e. the tangent of the angle. For gentle gradients the difference between the sine and the tangent is small. In *calculus the gradient is the slope of the *tangent at any point on a curve in a Cartesian *coordinate system. If the curve is represented by the function $f(x)$, then the gradient is the first derivative of this function.

Graf, Steffi (1969–) German tennis player. She won her first professional tournament in 1986 and by the end of 1987 was the top-ranked woman player. In 1988 she dominated the women's circuit, achieving the coveted Grand Slam by winning the Australian, French, Wimbledon, and US national open tournaments. She retained her titles at Wimbledon and the US open in 1989 and took Wimbledon again in 1991 before enduring a slump marked by injuries, personal problems, and the rise of other young stars. By mid-1992 she had nearly regained her old form, winning Wimbledon. In 1993, after her top rival, Monica Seles, was stabbed by a Graf fan, Graf won the French, Wimbledon, and US titles.

grafting **1.** (horticulture) The transfer of part of one plant, usually a shoot or a bud, onto another plant. It is often used as a means of vegetative propagation, particularly for fruit trees and roses. The *cambium (a region of actively dividing cells) of the transplanted piece (called the scion) is aligned with that of the recipient plant (called the stock): the wound tissue formed by the two cambia binds the graft together. Grafts will "take" only if the scion and stock are closely related. Genetically identical scions on different stocks may differ considerably, but this is due solely to environmental effects and there is no transfer of genetic material between stock and scion. Occasionally graft hybrids (*see* chimaera) arise from the graft junction, but these are mixtures of the two cell types rather than true hybrids. **2.** (surgery). *See* transplantation.

Graham, Billy (1918–) US evangelist. He began as an evangelist with the Youth for Christ movement before forming the Billy Graham Evangelistic Association (1950) and conducting worldwide crusades. His theatrical and carefully staged meetings, in which the audience is invited to "take a decision for Christ," have attracted very large crowds. His association with prominent personalities brought his movement increased attention.

Graham, Martha (1893–1991) US dancer and choreographer. She studied with Ruth St Denis and established her own dance academy in New York in 1927. She eventually became one of the most influential teachers of modern dance in America. Her ballets, often concerned with the psychological interpretation of mythological themes, include *Primitive Mysteries* (1931), *Night Journey* (1947), *Circe* (1963), and *Acts of Light* (1981).

Graham, Thomas (1805–69) British physicist, who investigated gaseous diffusion, discovering **Graham's law** (1831), which states that the rates at which gases diffuse are inversely proportional to the square roots of their densities. He continued to study diffusion, investigating the flow of solutions through semipermeable membranes. He coined the terms osmosis, crystalloids, and colloids.

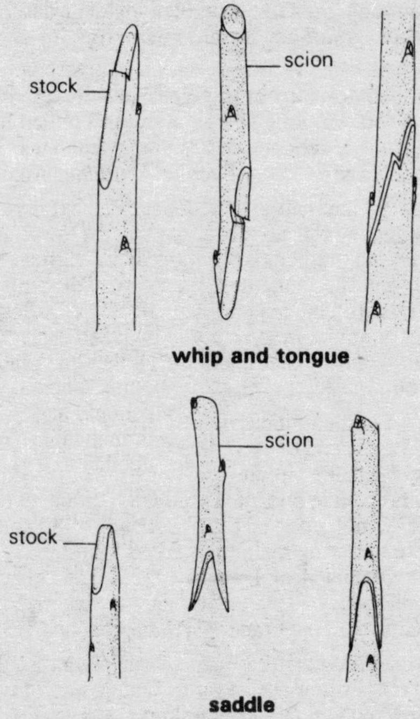

GRAFTING *Two commonly used grafting methods. After stock and scion are fitted together they are held securely by tape, string, etc., and protected from desiccation by covering the point of union with wax or moist material.*

Grahame, Kenneth (1859–1932) British children's writer. His best-known book is the children's classic *The Wind in the Willows* (1908), concerned with Toad, Mole, Rat, and other animal characters that inhabit an ideal riverside world. It was adapted as a play, *Toad of Toad Hall* (1929), by A. A. *Milne.

Graham Land A mountainous peninsula in Antarctica, bordering on the Weddell Sea and comprising part of *British Antarctic Territory. It was formerly a dependency of the Falkland Islands.

Graiae In Greek legend, three goddesses personifying old age, the sisters and protectors of the *Gorgons. They shared one eye and one tooth. *Perseus stole the eye to force them to tell him the whereabouts of the Gorgons.

Grainger, Percy Aldridge (1882–1961) Australian composer and pianist, trained in Germany. He lived in London and in 1914 went to the US, becoming a US citizen. Grainger was a friend of Grieg and Delius and studied and recorded English folk song. Many of his compositions incorporate folk-music intervals and rhythms; they include the orchestral *Shepherds' Hey* (1913), *English Dance* (1925), and *Harvest Hymn* (1933), as well as the "clog dance" *Handel in the Strand* (1913).

gram (g) A unit of mass equal to $^1/_{1000}$ of a *kilogram. The gram is itself one of the basic units in the *c.g.s. system, but in *SI units the basic unit is the kilogram.

grammar The study of the forms of the words of a language (morphology) and their relationships with one another (syntax). Until 1957 there were two basic types of grammar: **prescriptive grammar**, which expressed value judgments about the correctness of particular expressions, and **descriptive grammar**, which aimed to give an accurate account of the structures observable in recorded texts of a language. The earliest known descriptive grammar is by *Panini (c. 5th century BC) of *Sanskrit. Many grammars of the ancient Greek and Latin languages are still influential today; for example, the traditional parts of speech—noun, verb, adjective, etc.—were invented by Greek grammarians. Descriptive grammarians have been able to show that the judgments of prescriptivists are founded on no more objective basis than the willingness of the community to accept their judgments. Each language has its own patterns; attempts to resolve disputes or difficulties by appealing to authority, history, logic, or the structure of some other language are at best irrelevant, at worst confusing.

Publication in 1957 of *Syntactic Structures* by Noam *Chomsky introduced a new view of the study of grammar—namely that it should be predictive. Chomsky argued that, since the potential number of grammatical sentences in a language is literally infinite, a grammar must predict whether any given utterance is or is not a grammatical sentence of a particular language. Chomsky invented the concept of **generative grammar**, the finite set of linguistic rules that generate an infinite number of grammatical sentences in the language. Every speaker of a language acquires these rules at a very early age in a form to some degree idiosyncratic and different from those of other speakers. The raw material from which sentences are generated (words, phrases, etc.) form in a speaker's memory a store the exact nature of which is disputed. The concept of **transformational** (*or* transformational-generative) **grammar** seeks to explain the relationships among words in a sentence and among sentences themselves by logical structural analysis. Ambiguities and certain other problems are explained by postulating that behind the "surface structure" of a sentence lies a "deep structure," an abstract underlying form that determines the sentence's meaning. The surface structure is generated from the deep structure by generative rules, some of which are similar to the transformations of theoretical *logic.

Grampians A range of mountains in central Scotland. It extends generally SW–NE, bordered in the S by the Central Lowlands; the Cairngorm Mountains form a northerly extension. Its chief summits include Ben Nevis at 4406 ft (1343 m) and Ben Macdhui at 4296 ft (1309 m).

grampus A small toothed *whale, *Grampus griseus,* of warm and temperate waters, also called Risso's dolphin. About 146 in (3.7 m) long, dark-gray with a pale belly, grampuses live in small herds and migrate toward the Poles in summer and the equator in winter.

Gramsci, Antonio (1891–1937) Italian politician and Marxist theorist. In 1914 he joined the Italian Socialist party but, dissatisfied with its moderation, broke away in 1921 to form the Italian Communist party. In 1924 he became its leader in the chamber of deputies. The party was banned by the fascists in 1926 and Gramsci was imprisoned from 1928 until shortly before his death. His voluminous Marxist writings, mostly the work of his prison years, were published posthumously as *Prison Notebooks* (1947).

Granada 37 10N 3 35W A city in S Spain, in Andalusia. Formerly the capital of the kingdom of Granada, the last Moorish stronghold in Spain, it was conquered in 1492. Much frequented by tourists, its splendid architecture includes many Moorish buildings (notably the *Alhambra), a cathedral (1523–1703), and the 16th-century Capilla Real, containing the tombs of Ferdinand and Isabella. Population (1991): 254,034.

Granada 11 58N 85 59W A city in SW Nicaragua. It is the center of an area producing cotton, sugar, and coffee; manufactures include furniture, soap, and rum. Population (1985): 88,636.

granadilla. *See* passionflower.

Gran Chaco A vast plain in S central South America, mainly in N Argentina, E Bolivia, and Paraguay. It consists of a vast alluvial lowland region, drained by the W tributaries of the Paraguay and Paraná Rivers. It was the cause of the *Chaco War between Paraguay and Bolivia (1932–35). Area: 300,000 sq mi (780,000 sq km).

Grand Alliance, War of the (1689–97) The war in which a grand alliance led by England, Austria, Spain, and the Netherlands attempted to curb the expansionist policy of Louis XIV of France. Precipitated by the French invasion of the Palatinate (1688), the war was fought mainly in Flanders. Exhausted by the inconclusive but bloody battles, the participants accepted the Treaty of *Rijswijk in 1697. The conflict was renewed, however, in 1701, with the War of the *Spanish Succession.

Grand Banks A section of the North American continental shelf in the N Atlantic Ocean, extending SE of Newfoundland with a depth of about 130–330 ft (40–100 m). It is an internationally important fishing ground in which cod is especially plentiful. Area: c. 494,000 sq mi (c. 1,280,000 sq km).

Grand Canal (Chinese name: Da Yunhe) A canal in E China, the longest in the world, extending about 1000 mi (1600 km) N–S from Peking to *Wuhan. Begun possibly in the 4th century BC, it was built in sections over two millenniums; 100–200 ft (30–61 m) wide and 2–15 ft (0.6–4.6 m) deep, it is still used, chiefly in the S.

Grand Canyon A vast gorge in Arizona, on the Colorado River. It has been eroded through a varied series of virtually horizontal beds of multicolored rock, creating spectacular steps and rock formations. A popular tourist area, it was designated the **Grand Canyon National Park** in 1919. Length: 280 mi (451 km). Width: 4–18 mi (6–29 km). Greatest depth: over 1 mi (1.5 km).

Grand Coulee Dam A large gravity *dam on the Columbia River, in Washington. Completed in 1942, it is 4173 ft (1272 m) long at its crest, 354 ft (108 m) high, and has a reservoir capacity of 11,600 million cubic meters for irrigation, flood control, and hydroelectric power.

Grande Dixence Dam A gravity *dam on the Dixence River (Switzerland). Until 1970 it was the tallest dam in the world (932 ft [284 m] high). It is 2198 ft (670 m) wide at the crest and has a reservoir of 400 million cubic meters.

Grandfather Clause A clause in the constitutions of some southern US states (prior to 1915) that denied African Americans equal voting rights. It stated that anyone who had been able to vote before 1867 was exempt from the high literacy, property, and tax requirements for voting. Since the African-Americans' right to vote (15th Amendment) had not been granted until 1870, these clauses excluded most African Americans and included the poor whites. It was declared unconstitutional by the Supreme Court in 1915 (*Guinn and Beal* v. *US*).

Grand Guignol A type of popular sensational drama, exploiting situations of violence and terror, that flourished in Paris in the late 19th century. The term derives from the name of a theater at which these plays were performed, and from Guignol, a stock character in French puppet shows.

grand mal. *See* epilepsy.

Grand Pré A village in E Canada, in Nova Scotia. It was the center of French-speaking *Acadia until Britain deported its inhabitants for refusing to swear allegiance to the crown (1755), an event romanticized in Longfellow's *Evangeline.*

Grand Rapids 42 57N 86 40W A city in W central Michigan, on the Grand River. Founded in the 1820s, its industries include the manufacture of furniture, motor bodies, paper, and paint. Population (1990): 189,126.

Grand Remonstrance (1641) A list of grievances drawn up by the *Long Parliament on the eve of the English *Civil War. It itemized the past faults of Charles I, the reforms achieved by the Long Parliament, and grievances outstanding.

Grand Teton National Park A national park in NW Montana, on the E edge of the Rocky Mountains, just S of Yellowstone National Park. It encompasses part of the Teton Mountains, a part of Jackson Hole, and many lakes. The highest point is Grand Teton (13,766 ft; 4196 m). The original park was established in 1929, while the Jackson Hole area was added in 1950. Area: 500 sq mi (1295 sq km).

Grange, Red (Harold Edward G; 1903–91) US football player. He played running back for the University of Illinois (1923–25), where he was named All-American for three seasons. Nicknamed the "Galloping Ghost," he played professionally for the American Football League's New York Yankees (1925–28) and for the National Football League's Chicago Bears (1928–35); his success spurred the growth of professional football. He was elected to the Football Hall of Fame (1963).

Granger Movement US rural movement in the 1870s to obtain better business conditions for farmers. The goals of the movement were state regulation of the railroads and grain elevators, reduction of the role of middlemen, and an increase in cooperative buying and selling.

granite A coarse-grained plutonic rock of acid composition resulting from the high silica content. Granites contain quartz, feldspar (usually alkali), and mafic (dark-colored) minerals, usually muscovite and biotite (micas). Most granites crystallize from magma in large igneous intrusions known as batholiths, but some are produced by granitization, which is the transformation of preexisting rocks into granite by the action of granitic fluids rising from great depths. There are many different types of granite with different modes of formation and mineral content.

Gran Paradiso 45 33N 7 17E The highest mountain entirely in Italy, in the Alps. The surrounding area has been made into a national park. Height: 13,323 ft (4061 m).

Grant, Cary (Archibald Leach; 1904–86) US film actor, born in England. He went to Hollywood in 1932 and established his reputation as an actor of debonair sophistication in such films as *Holiday* (1938) and *The Philadelphia Story* (1940). He acted in more than 70 films, including *To Catch a Thief* (1955), and *North By Northwest* (1959), directed by Alfred Hitchcock.

Grant, Ulysses S(impson) (1822–85) US military and political leader; 18th president of the United States (1869–77). Born in Point Pleasant, Ohio, Grant graduated from West Point in 1843 and was decorated for gallantry during the *Mexican War. Personal problems forced his resignation from the army in 1854, and for the next six years he remained in private life, settling in Galena, Ill. At the outbreak of the *Civil War, he was commissioned as colonel of the 21st Illinois Volunteers. Grant proved to be an effective commander and won distinction in his capture of Fort Donelson, Tenn. in 1862. Promoted to the rank of major general, Grant won additional victories at *Shiloh, *Vicksburg, and Chattanooga in 1863. The following year, President *Lincoln appointed him commander-in-chief of the Union forces, and after defeating the Confederate forces in the *Wilderness Campaign and at the siege of *Petersburg, he accepted the surrender of Gen. Robert E. *Lee at Appomattox Courthouse, Va. on Apr 9, 1865. Following the war, he was named secretary of war in the administration of Pres. Andrew *Johnson.

ULYSSES S. GRANT *Commander of the victorious Union forces during the Civil War and then President (1869–77).*

In 1868 he was elected president as the candidate of the *Republican Party, and he won reelection in 1872. Among Grant's most important achievements as president were the reform of the civil service system and the ratification of the Treaty of Washington with Great Britain in 1871. The early phases of *Reconstruction were also initiated during his presidency. Charges of corruption and financial mismangement, however, marred Grant's second term. His autobiography, *Personal Memoirs,* was published in 1885.

Granville, John Carteret, 1st Earl (1690–1763) British statesman; prime minister (1742–44). A bitter opponent of Robert *Walpole, Granville became prime minister after Walpole's fall. His conduct of the War of the *Austrian Succession was criticized for putting George II's Hanoverian interests above Britain's and George was forced to dismiss him.

Granville-Barker, Harley (1877–1946) British theater director, critic, and dramatist. As comanager of the Royal Court Theatre (1904–07) he produced many plays by G. B. Shaw and by modern European dramatists. His most influential practical criticism is contained in *Prefaces to Shakespeare* (1927–47). His own plays include *The Voysey Inheritance* (1905) and *The Madras House* (1910).

grape The fruit of vines of the genus *Vitis* (about 60 species), especially *V. vinifera,* native to N Asia but cultivated throughout Mediterranean regions and in the US, especially California and New York. The grapevine is up to 90 ft (30 m) long, twining by means of tendrils, with lobed toothed leaves and dense clusters of small greenish flowers. The fruit—a berry—is green, red, or blue-black and used to make *wine, brandy, and liqueurs or eaten fresh or dried (in the form of raisins, sultanas, and currants).

grapefruit A tree, *Citrus paradisi,* 20–40 ft (6–12 m) high, cultivated throughout the tropics and subtropics. It has shiny oval leaves and clusters of white flowers that mature into fleshy yellow-skinned fruits, 4–6 in (10–15 cm) in diameter. Grapefruits are eaten fresh, canned, or crushed to make beverages. *See* citrus.

grape hyacinth A perennial herbaceous plant of the genus *Muscari* (50 species), mostly native to the Mediterranean region and widely grown as spring-blooming garden bulbs. The leaves are long and narrow and the blue, pink, or white urn-shaped flowers are borne in a dense cluster at the tip of a leafless flower stalk, up to 6 in (15 cm) high. *M. botryoides,* with blue flowers, is a popular species. Family: *Liliaceae.*

graph A method of providing a visual representation of relationships between quantities, usually in the Cartesian *coordinate system. In mathematics graphs are used to solve equations, represent functions, etc. Histograms, in which the height of columns represents the frequency of a result in each of a series of ranges, and pie charts, which show percentages as segments of a circle, are also sometimes referred to as graphs.

graphite An iron-gray to black form of pure carbon, found in many metamorphic rocks, especially metamorphosed coals or other carbonaceous sediments. It occurs in a laminar or massive form. It is very soft, flaky, and greasy to the touch. Graphite is used for making metallurgical crucibles, as a lubricant, in paint, rubber, and pencil leads, in batteries and for other electrical purposes, and as a moderator in nuclear reactors. It has often been called plumbago or black lead, since it was formerly mistaken for lead.

graptolite A small colonial marine animal belonging to the extinct class *Graptolithina,* possibly related to *coelenterates. Their fossils, in the form of carbonaceous impressions, occur in rocks of the Upper Cambrian to Carboniferous periods, about 420–250 million years ago. Graptolites were floating animals, individual polyps living in the cuplike tips of simple or branched hollow tubes.

grass A monocotyledonous annual or perennial herbaceous plant belonging to the family *Poaceae* (or *Gramineae*; 6000–10,000 species), distributed worldwide. The leaves consist of a basal sheath, which encircles the stem, and a long narrow blade. The flowering stems (culms) bear spikelets of inconspicuous flowers; each spikelet has two basal bracts (glumes) and each flower is enclosed by two other bracts—a lower lemma and an upper palea. The hard single-seeded fruit (the grain) is known botanically as a caryopsis, with the ovary wall (pericarp) and seed coat fused. Many species are important in agriculture as a source of food (*see* cereals; sugar cane) and as pasture grasses.

Grass, Günter (1927–) German novelist, poet, and political activist. He won international fame with his first novel, *The Tin Drum* (1959), an epic picaresque treatment of modern German history that established him as a moral spokesman for his generation. His other works include the play *The Plebeians Rehearse the Uprising* (1966), and the novels *Dog Years* (1963), *The Flounder*

(1978), *The Meeting at Telgte* (1981), and *Headbirths Or the Germans Are Dying Out* (1982).

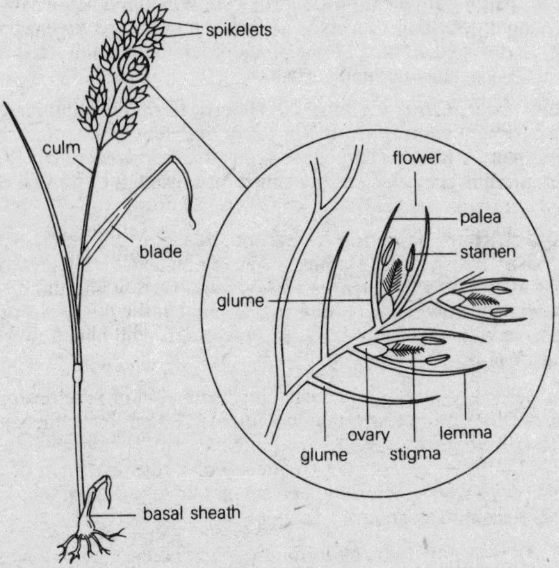

GRASS *The typical structure of a grass is seen in the meadow fescue* (Festuca pratensis). *The flowers are grouped into spikelets and each consists only of male and female parts; petals and sepals are absent.*

Grasse 43 40N 6 56E A city and resort in SE France, in the Alpes-Maritimes department. It is the center of the French perfume industry. Population (1975): 35,330.

grassfinch A songbird belonging to a subfamily of *weaverfinches, occurring chiefly in arid regions of Australasia. About 4 in (10 cm) long, grassfinches have long tails and stout bills. The group includes a number of colorful popular cage-birds, such as the Gouldian finch (*Poephila gouldiae*) and the *zebra finch.

grasshopper A jumping insect belonging to the family *Acrididae* (about 5000 species). Grasshoppers, 0.94–4 in (24–110 mm) long, are usually green or brown and have short stout antennae and tail appendages. Both sexes produce sound by rubbing the hind legs against the front wings. Some species can fly, sometimes forming dense migratory swarms (*see* locust). Grasshoppers live and feed on grass and low vegetation and the females lay eggs in the soil. Order: **Orthoptera.*

grass monkey A small African *guenon monkey, *Cercopithecus aethiops,* inhabiting thinly wooded regions. The West African green monkey, the East African grivet monkey, and the South African vervet or blue monkey are all local races of grass monkey.

grass of Parnassus A tufted perennial herb of the genus *Parnassia* (about 50 species), especially *P. palustris,* found in wet places throughout Europe and temperate Asia. The basal leaves are stalked and heart-shaped. The solitary white five-petaled flower is borne on an erect stalk with a single unstalked leaf near the base. Family: *Parnassiaceae.*

grass snake A nonvenomous snake, *Natrix natrix,* also called water snake, occurring throughout Europe, usually near ponds, streams, and marshes; 30–37 in (75–95 cm) long, it has a green back with two rows of black spots, vertical black bars along its sides, and a yellow neck patch. It can be distinguished from the *adder, which has a black zigzag line along its back. Its prey includes frogs, tadpoles, fish, lizards, and small mammals. Family: *Colubridae.*

grass tree A woody plant of the genus *Xanthorrhoea* (about 5 species), native to E Australia. They often have palmlike stems, 16 ft (5 m) tall, that end in a tuft of rigid grasslike leaves, from which extend flower spikes resembling those of the *reedmace, about 10 ft (3 m) tall. A red or yellow gumlike resin, used for varnishes, exudes from the bases of old leaves. Family: *Xanthorrhoeaceae.*

Gratian(us), Flavius (359–83 AD) Western Roman emperor (367–83). He was a Christian and abandoned (382) the pagan title *pontifex maximus* (supreme priest). He was deposed by Magnus Maximus (d. 388) and murdered.

Grattan, Henry (1746–1820) Irish politician, who with *Flood was one of the greatest orators in the Irish Parliament. From 1775 he led the patriot party and in 1782 obtained Irish free trade and legislative independence from Britain. He opposed, unavailingly, the union of England and Ireland and in 1805 sat in the British Parliament. For the remainder of his political career he pressed for *Catholic emancipation.

gravel Unconsolidated rock fragments ranging between 0.08–2 in (2–60 mm) in particle size, or between coarse sand and cobbles. The term is loosely used for any unconsolidated material coarser than sand, for instance river gravels and glacial gravels.

Gravenhage, 's. *See* Hague, The.

Graves, Robert (Ranke) (1895–1985) British poet, critic, and novelist. His early autobiography, *Goodbye to All That* (1929), recounts his experiences in World War I. In 1929 he emigrated to Majorca. He has published several editions of *Collected Poems,* historical novels including *I Claudius* (1934) and *Claudius the God* (1934), and studies of mythology, notably *The White Goddess* (1948). A more recent work is *They Hanged My Saintly Billy* (1980).

Gravesend 51 27N 0 24E A port in SE England, in Kent on the River Thames. It is a customs and pilot station for the Port of London and has printing, engineering, and paper-making industries. Population (1981): 52,963.

Gravettian A culture of the Upper *Paleolithic, succeeding the *Aurignacian in W Europe. Named for the cave at La Gravette in the Dordogne (SW France), the Gravettian is characterized by small pointed stone blades with one blunted edge (Gravette points) and dates from 26,000–20,000 BC. The well-known small female figurines called Venuses are of Gravettian origin. The term Eastern Gravettian is applied to similar material from mammoth hunters' campsites in Russia and E Europe. *Compare* Périgordian.

gravitation An attractive force that occurs between all bodies that possess mass. It was first described by Sir Isaac *Newton in a law stating that the force between two bodies is directly proportional to the product of their masses and inversely proportional to the square of the distance between them. The constant of proportionality is called the universal gravitational constant, *G,* which has the value 6.673×10^{-11} newton meter squared per kilogram squared. Gravitation is now more accurately described by the general theory of *relativity. In this theory a mass distorts the *space-time continuum around it so that the geometry of the space is locally no longer Euclidean. The force of gravity and the *acceleration of free fall are the result of the attractive force between a body and the earth.

gravitational collapse The sudden collapse of the core of a *star when thermonuclear fusion eventually ceases. The star's internal gas pressure can no longer support the weight of the star and the initial result may be a *supernova explosion. The gravitational pull of all the constituents of the star, or its remains, causes it to contract. The extent of the contraction depends on the mass of the object, producing a *white dwarf, *neutron star, or *black hole.

gravitational interaction One of the four kinds of interaction that occur between elementary particles (*see* particle physics) and by far the weakest (about 10^{40} times weaker than the *electromagnetic interaction). The interaction occurs between all particles with mass and can be explained as the exchange of *virtual particles called gravitons. Such particles have not yet been detected.

gray (Gy) The *SI unit of absorbed dose of ionizing radiation equal to the energy in joules absorbed by one kilogram of irradiated material.

Gray, Asa (1810–88) US botanist, who compiled *Flora of North America* (2 vols, 1838–43), a comprehensive taxonomic guide to the region's plants. He also wrote many popular books on botany, including a *Manual of the Botany of the Northern United States* (1848). Gray was a firm supporter of Darwin's theories of evolution, although he believed that the process of natural selection was controlled by God.

Gray, Elisha (1835–1901) US inventor. Early interested in electricity, he held about 70 patents, the first received in 1867 for an improved telegraph relay. In 1872 he established Gray and Barton Company, the predecessor of Western Electric Company, and in 1876 filed for a patent on his invention, the telephone, just hours after a similar patent application by Alexander Graham *Bell. Years of controversy and litigation followed, but the courts finally ruled in Bell's favor. From 1880 he taught electrical engineering at Oberlin College.

Gray, Thomas (1716–71) British poet. He spent most of his life in scholarly retirement. He published only a few odes apart from his most famous poem, *Elegy Written in a Country Churchyard* (1751), a classical meditation on the graves of the humble villagers of Stoke Poges, Buckinghamshire.

grayling A troutlike fish of the genus *Thymallus,* sometimes placed in a distinct family (*Thymallidae*). Graylings have a silver-purple scaly body, up to 20 in (50 cm) long, with a sail-like dorsal fin, and live in cold clear fresh waters of Eurasia and N North America, feeding on aquatic insects. They are important food and game fish. Family: *Salmonidae.*

graylag goose A grazing *goose, *Anser anser,* occurring in N and E Europe and central Asia; 30–34 in (75–87 cm) long, it has a heavy orange bill and is dark gray above with pale wings, a finely barred neck, and pink legs.

graywacke (*or* greywacke) A dark-colored sedimentary rock with sand-sized angular rock particles in a finer matrix. Graywackes display a wide range of sedimentary structures and are commonly found in geosynclines.

Graz 47 05N 15 22E The second largest city in Austria, the capital of Styria. Its numerous historical buildings include a cathedral (1438–62) and a notable clock tower (1561). It has a university (1586). An industrial center, it produces iron and steel, textiles, and chemicals. Population (1981): 239,404.

Great Artesian Basin An artesian basin of E Australia. The largest area of artesian water in the world, it extends S from the Gulf of Carpentaria in Queensland into South Australia and New South Wales, underlying the catchments of both the Darling River and Lake Eyre. Area: 676,250 sq mi (1,750,000 sq km).

Great Australian Bight A wide bay of the Indian Ocean, in S Australia situated between Capes Pasley and Carnot. Width: 720 mi (1159 km).

Great Awakening A religious revival in the American colonies in the 18th century. It began in the 1720s among members of the Dutch Reformed Church of New Jersey but flourished in New England in 1740–43, after which it spread to other colonies. It was largely inspired by the preaching of George *Whitefield and Jonathan *Edwards, who, however, disapproved of the excessive enthusiasm or hysteria that was often manifested by those claiming to be converted.

Great Barrier Reef The largest coral reef in the world, situated in the Coral Sea off the coast of NE Australia. Approximately 15,000 years old, it consists of a complex of coral reefs, shoals, and islets extending for 1250 mi (2000 km) from Breaksea Spit to the Gulf of Papua. Its many fish, crustaceans, birds, exotic plant life, and some 350 species of colorful corals make it popular with tourists.

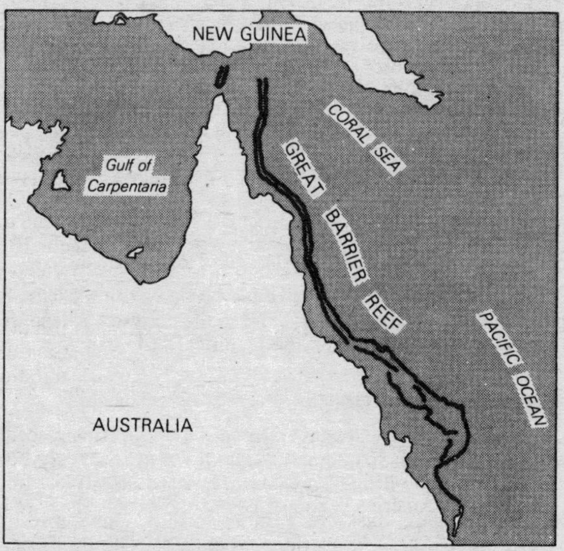

GREAT BARRIER REEF

Great Basin A large semiarid area in the US. Situated between the Sierra Nevada and the Wasatch Mountains, it extends over most of Nevada, Utah, and parts of California and Oregon. It consists of a series of basins, mountain ranges, deserts (including the *Mojave Desert), and salt lakes (including the *Great Salt Lake).

Great Bear. *See* Ursa Major.

Great Bear Lake A lake in N Canada, in Mackenzie district on the Arctic Circle. Frozen eight months of the year, it is the fourth largest lake in North America. It drains into the Mackenzie River via the Great Bear River, 70 mi (112 km) long. Area: 12,275 sq mi (31,792 sq km).

Great Belt (Danish name: Store Bælt) A channel between the Danish islands of Fyn and Sjælland, linking the Kattegat and the Baltic Sea.

Great Britain The largest island in the British Isles and in Europe, separated from the mainland of W Europe by the North Sea and the English Channel. Containing *England, *Scotland, and *Wales, it includes the islands governed with the mainland but excludes the Isle of Man and the Channel Islands. Area: 88,619 sq mi (229,523 sq km).

great circle A circle that is the intersection on the surface of a sphere of a plane passing through the center of that sphere. On the earth, each meridian of longitude is half of a great circle; the equator is the only parallel of lattitude that is a great circle.

great crested grebe A large *grebe, *Podiceps cristatus,* occurring in Eurasia. It is dark brown above with a white face, neck, and underparts, a black two-horned crest and neck frill, and chestnut patches at the sides of the face. Mating pairs perform an elaborate courtship display.

Great Dane A breed of large dog originating in Germany, where they were developed for hunting boar. The Great Dane has a large powerful frame with long legs and a large head with a square muzzle. The short sleek coat can be golden, black, streaked brown, blue-gray, or white with black patches. Height: 30 in (76 cm) minimum (dogs); 28 in (71 cm) minimum (bitches).

Great Dividing Range (Great Divide *or* Eastern Highlands) The E highlands of Australia, comprising a complex of mountains and plateaus. It extends for about 2300 mi (3700 km) from Cape York Peninsula to the Grampians of Victoria and includes the *Blue Mountains and Australian Alps, where it reaches 7316 ft (2230 m) at Mount *Kosciusko.

Greater Antilles The four largest West Indian islands, in the N Caribbean Sea, comprising Cuba, Hispaniola, Jamaica, and Puerto Rico.

Great Exhibition (1851) A display of the products of industrial Britain and Europe, planned by Prince Albert and held in the *Crystal Palace. It contained about 13,000 exhibits and showed the technical progress and industrial supremacy of Britain.

Great Indian Desert. *See* Thar Desert.

Great Lake A shallow freshwater lake in Australia. It lies on the central plateau of Tasmania, at an altitude of 3380 ft (1030 m), and is used as a storage reservoir for hydroelectric power. Area: 44 sq mi (114 sq km).

Great Lakes Five large lakes in E central North America, mostly along the US-Canadian border: Lakes *Superior, *Michigan, *Huron, *Erie, and *Ontario. The world's largest freshwater surface, they drain into the *St Lawrence River and form part of the *St Lawrence Seaway. Canals also link them to the Mississippi River, making them a major transportation route. Their basin is an important economic region, with agriculture, fishing, forestry, mining, hydroelectricity, manufacturing, commerce, and tourism. Recently water pollution has become a major problem, compounded by the many governments with jurisdiction over the lakes.

Great Leap Forward A nationwide campaign in China to promote economic and industrial growth. The movement started in 1958 and aimed to increase industrial production dramatically by using manpower rather than capital in large-scale rural communes and backyard steel furnaces and factories. Ambitious production targets were reached but it proved impossible to coordinate production and control quality, and the movement was revoked in 1960.

Great Ouse River (*or* R. Ouse) A river in E England, rising in Northamptonshire and flowing NE across the Fens to the Wash near King's Lynn. Length: 160 mi (257 km).

Great Plains An extensive area in North America. It consists of a system of rolling plains extending from the Mackenzie River Delta in Canada in the N to the Rio Grande in the S. It is chiefly agricultural with livestock raising and grain production. Length: about 3000 mi (4800 km). Average width: about 400 mi (645 km).

Great Red Spot An immense reddish oval feature in the atmosphere of *Jupiter, lying S of the equator. Observed for over a century, its prominence, color, and size (8694 mi [14,000 km] N–S by up to 24,840 mi [40,000 km] E–W) have been found to fluctuate. Pioneer planetary probes showed it to be a vortex of cold anticlockwise-rotating clouds elevated above the surrounding cloud layer and colored possibly by traces of phosphorus.

Great Rift Valley (*or* East African Rift System) An extensive rift valley in the Middle East and East Africa. It extends from the Jordan Valley in Syria along the Red Sea into Ethiopia and through Kenya, Tanzania, and Malawi into Mozambique. It is marked by a chain of lakes (Lakes Turkana [formerly Rudolf] and Natron) and volcanoes (Mount Kilimanjaro). Length: about 4000 mi (6400 km).

Great Salt Lake A salt lake in NW Utah, in the Great Basin. It is bordered by the Wasatch Mountains and the Great Salt Lake Desert and has no outlet. A salt extraction industry exists along its shores. Its area has fluctuated from less than 1000 sq mi (2500 sq km) to over 2000 sq mi (5000 sq km).

Great Sandy Desert A desert of N Western Australia. It consists of a vast arid region of sand dunes and salt marshes stretching SE from Eighty Mile Beach on the Indian Ocean to the Gibson Desert. Area: 160,000 sq mi (415,000 sq km).

Great Schism (1378–1417) The split in the Roman Catholic Church following the election of two rival popes to succeed Gregory XI. Criticisms of the residency of the papacy in Avignon (*see* Avignon papacy) forced its return to Rome and the election of an Italian, Urban VI. He determined to reform the College of Cardinals, which responded by electing an *antipope at Avignon, Clement VII. The Schism was ended by the Council of *Constance (1414–18) and the election of Martin V in 1417. (For the schism in 1054 between the E and W Christian churches, *see* Filioque.)

Great Slave Lake A very deep lake in N Canada, in Mackenzie district. The fifth largest lake in North America, it drains into the Mackenzie River. Area: 10,980 sq mi (28,438 sq km).

Great Smoky Mountains A mountain range, part of the Appalachians, in E Tennessee and W North Carolina, running NE from the Little Tennessee River to the Pigeon River. Most of the mountains comprise Great Smoky Mountains National Park. Clingmans Dome is the highest point (6643 ft; 2025 m). The mountains are thickly forested with nearly 100 kinds of trees. The hydrocarbons released from some of these trees create the haze that hangs over the mountains and gives them their name.

great tit The largest of the *tits, *Parus major*: a common European bird of woodland, farmland, and gardens feeding on caterpillars, aphids, scale insects, and other pests. It is about 5.5 in (14 cm) long and has a black head with white cheeks, a green back, and a black stripe down its yellow breast.

Great Trek The movement from the mid-1830s to mid-1840s of Dutch settlers (Afrikaners) in South Africa northward across the Orange and Vaal Rivers from the Cape. The so-called Voortrekkers, under such leaders as Andries *Pretorius, moved away from British rule at the Cape in search of more farmland that they could administer themselves. They are considered by Afrikaners to be the founding fathers of South Africa. They established the republics of the Transvaal and the Orange Free State.

Great Victoria Desert A desert of Western and South Australia, between the Gibson Desert and Nullarbor Plain. It consists of a vast arid region of sand hills and salt marshes. Area: 125,000 sq mi (323,750 sq km).

Great Wall of China A medieval defensive fortification in N China. Stretching from the Yellow Sea N of Peking nearly 1500 mi (2400 km) inland, the Great Wall is the world's largest building achievement. Originally begun in 214 BC as a defense against nomadic tribes, it was improved and largely rebuilt of stone in the 15th and 16th centuries. It is about 30 ft (9 m) high, with numerous higher watchtowers along its length.

Great Zimbabwe The largest of the ruined Bantu royal centers on the Zambezian plateau in Zimbabwe. The word *zimbabwe* is derived from the Bantu for "revered houses." Great Zimbabwe reached its zenith in the late 14th century but suffered abrupt decline after about 1440. Traces of widespread trade, based on local gold, have been discovered, including Chinese pottery. Parts of the so-called Elliptical Building (a compound enclosing now vanished huts) stand 35 ft (10.5 m) high and consist of regular dry stone courses of dressed granite.

GREAT ZIMBABWE *A picture of the ruins of a large round tower, part of the so-called Elliptical Building, published by Britain's Royal Geographical Society in 1892.*

grebe A bird belonging to a primitive family (*Podicipitidae*; 21 species) occurring in rivers and lakes worldwide. Grebes are adapted for swimming and diving by having short wings, a very small tail, and partially webbed feet with lobed toes. They have a long neck and a long pointed bill and feed chiefly on fish and aquatic invertebrates. Grebes are gray, black, or brown, usually with white underparts, and in the breeding season many have brightly colored erectile crests and ear tufts. Order: *Podicipediformes. See also* dabchick; great crested grebe.

Greece, Republic of (Greek name: Ellás) A country in SE Europe, occupying the S section of the Balkan Peninsula between the Mediterranean and Aegean Seas. Numerous islands, which comprise about one-fifth of the total area of Greece, lie to the S, E, and W, the largest being Crete. Crete as well as the other Greek islands, including Corfu, the Ionian Isles, the Cyclades, and the Dodecanese (especially Rhodes), are popular tourist spots, and tourism constitutes an important source of revenue for the country. About 75% of the terrain is mountainous, the highest point being Mt Olympus (rising to 9570 ft; 2917 m). In the S the Peloponnesus, a mountainous peninsula, is linked to the mainland by the Isthmus of Corinth. The mainland is largely mountainous, with plains in Thrace and Macedonia in the N and Thessaly in the center. *Economy*: since the early 1970s industry has replaced agriculture as the mainstay of the economy. The rapid expansion of the industrial sector (especially metallurgy, chemicals, textiles, rubber, plastics, and electrical machinery) began in the 1960s. Mineral resources, including lignite, bauxite, and iron ore, have been intensively exploited and processed and there has been a dramatic increase in electricity output. Recent plans include incentives for the decentralization of industry, which has led to a rapidly changing pattern of growth in N Greece aided by the discovery of natural gas and oil near the island of Thásos. There has been considerable diversification of agriculture and the principal crops include wheat, barley, maize, tobacco, sugar beet, tomatoes, and dried and fresh fruits. *History*: the centuries following the collapse of the *Mycenaean civilization (c. 1200 BC) saw the rise of the Greek city-states. From the 8th century, trading activities led to the establishment of colonies around the Mediterranean, in Asia Minor, N Africa, S Italy and Sicily, and in S France. The first half of the 5th century was dominated by the ultimately abortive attempt of the Persians to annex Greece (*see* Greek-Persian Wars) and the late 5th century, by the Peloponnesian War between rival Athens and Sparta. Sparta's subsequent supremacy in Greece lasted until its defeat by Thebes in 371. Greece fell to Philip of Macedon in 338 and was incorporated in the empire of his son Alexander the Great. Following the division of Alexander's possessions at his death (323), the Greek city-states remained within the Macedonian orbit but repeatedly attempted to assert their independence until the last Macedonian War (171–168) allowed Rome to dominate Greece. Roman rule lasted until 395 AD, when the Roman Empire was divided between W and E and Greece became part of the Byzantine (Eastern Roman) Empire, centered on Constantinople. In the Middle Ages Greece was subject to invasions by the Franks, Normans, and the Latin Crusaders. In the early 14th century Byzantium reasserted its control over the area but in 1453 Constantinople fell to the Ottoman Turks; by 1460 they controlled all Greece. Apart from a brief period (1686–1715) of partial Venetian occupation, Greece remained under Ottoman rule until achieving independence in 1829 (*see* Greek Independence, War of). The history of Greece since independence has been characterized by political instability. For over a century, warring republicans and monarchists threw the country into turmoil with monarchs successively toppled and restored in short order. In 1832 the Greek crown was offered to a Bavarian prince, who became Otto I (1815–67), but his despotic rule precipitated his deposition in 1862. In 1863 a Danish prince became king as George I (1845–1913). In the same year Greece acquired the Ionian Islands from Britain and in 1881, in the aftermath of the Congress of Berlin, Thessaly and part of Epirus from Turkey. Greek demands for Crete led to a disastrous war with Turkey in 1897, but in the Balkan Wars (1912–13) Greece gained the island together with territory in Thrace and Macedonia. In 1917 Venizelos took Greece into World War I on the Allied side and the immediate postwar period saw renewed territorial conflict with Turkey, in which Greece lost Smyrna. In 1924 Greece became a republic, which lasted until George II was restored in 1935. In World War II an unsuccessful Italian invasion (1940) was followed by the German occupation (1941–44), after which Greece was plunged into a civil war between monarchists and communists that lasted until 1949. The 1950s were dominated by the question of union with Cyprus, which Greece supported (*see* EOKA), and the 1960s saw a military coup (1967), which deposed Constantine II and established the rule of the colonels under Papadopoulos. He was overthrown in 1973 and succeeded by General Phaedon Ghizikis. The government's involvement in the coup against Makarios in Cyprus led to its collapse (1974). A new constitution (1975) saw the reintroduction of democratic government. Greece became a member of the EEC in 1981 and later in the same year the country's first socialist government was elected. The electoral victory of Andreas Papandreou and his Panhellenic Socialist Movement (Pasok) marked the end of 30 years of Western-style government in Greece. Seeking to assert Greek independence in foreign affairs, Papandreou's election campaign called for withdrawal from the EEC and NATO. Subsequently, however, more pragmatic strategies dominated Greece's relations with the West, resulting in dissatisfaction at home (especially within the Communist party) because of shelved campaign promises. In 1985, Socialist Christos Sartzetakis succeeded Karamanlis, and, in 1989, New Democrat Tzannis Tzannetakis succeeded Papandreou, who was acquitted of embezzlement in 1992. As a result of elections in 1990, Constantine Mitsotakis became the prime minister and Karamanlis the president again. The flood of Albanian refugees from 1991 further burdened Greece's already strained economy. Mitsotakis was reelected in 1992. Until 1993, Greece opposed the recognition of Macedonia's independence. Head of state: President Constantine Karamanlis. Prime minister: Constantine Mitsotakis. Official language: Greek. Official religion: Greek Orthodox. Official currency: drachma of 100 lepta. Area: 50,960 sq mi (131,986 sq km). Population (1990): 10,066,000. Capital: Athens. Main port: Piraeus.

Greek art and architecture The arts of ancient Greece from the 8th century BC until Greece's absorption in the Roman Empire after 27 BC, conventionally divided into three main periods: archaic (before c. 550), classical (550–323), and Hellenistic (323–27). Most extant paintings are on pottery. Nonfigurative all-over designs of the earliest period gradually gave way to the more naturalistic black-figure technique in the 7th and 6th centuries BC. The greatest achievements are the Athenian red-figure vases (530–400 BC). As is also the case with sculptors, the work of many Greek painters (e.g. *Zeuxis) is known only through Roman copies, but magnificent Hellenistic wall paintings have recently been uncovered at Vergina. In sculpture, the monumental Egyptian-influenced solidity of the early *kore and *kouros statues yielded to the idealized naturalism of the classical period (480–323 BC). This is exemplified in the *Elgin marbles and in the work of *Phidias and *Praxiteles. In the subsequent Hellenistic period sculpture is characteristically represented by dramatic subject matter and highly complex figure poses and groupings. The small-scale arts of coin engraving, gem carving, jewelry making, and the sculpting of bronze and terra-cotta figures (*see* Tanagra figurines) also reached a peak of perfection in the Hellenistic era. Greek architecture is perhaps the greatest legacy that the ancient Greeks have left us, for almost all subsequent European architecture is indebted to it. Although the Egyptians invented the colonnade (c. 2500 BC) and the Romans were the first to make use of arches, domes, and vaults as structural features, it was the Greeks who invented the entablature to surmount the colonnade in order to support a hipped roof. They also perfected the design of columns and created the concept of an architect as an artist, engineer, and town planner. Archaic Greek architecture had its roots in Crete (the first palace at Knossos was built about 2000 BC) and in Mycenae (the famous Lion Gate was erected about 1450 BC). Classical (*or* Hellenic) Greek architecture, however, did not emerge until about 700 BC, when the Greeks began to build in stone (limestone or marble) instead of wood, rubble, and mud bricks. This development followed slightly different courses on opposite sides of the Aegean Sea. During the 6th century BC the Doric order (*see* orders of architecture; □architecture) emerged as a consistent style in mainland Greece; at about the same time the Ionic order developed on the E shores of the Aegean. Both styles reached their zenith in the time of Pericles (490–429 BC); on the Athenian Acropolis the *Parthenon is the prime example of a Doric temple, while the Erechtheum (built by Mnesicles in 405 BC) contains three different Ionic orders. During the Hellenistic period the Doric gave way to the Ionic, and this in turn yielded to the third order of Greek architecture, the Corinthian. This style is exemplified by the Olympieium at Athens, built by Cossutius in 174 BC.

GREEK ART *An Attic black-figure cup (c. 550 BC). The names on it are those of Epiketus, the painter, and Hischylos, the maker.*

Greek Independence, War of (1821–32) The war that established a Greek state independent of the Ottoman Empire. The rebels had some initial success until in 1825 the Ottomans were strengthened by Egyptian help. The UK, France, and Russia offered to mediate and when rebuffed by the Ottomans defeated the Ottoman and Egyptian fleet at the battle of *Navarino (1827). The Ottomans fought on briefly but peace negotiations were begun in London in 1829 and independence was proclaimed, being recognized by the Ottoman Empire in 1832, when a Greek monarchy was established. European sympathy for the Greek cause had been encouraged by Lord Byron's championship.

Greek language An Indo-European language spoken chiefly in Greece and the E Mediterranean islands. Well documented since the 14th century BC (*see* Linear B), ancient Greek was a highly complex inflected language. It had many dialect forms, the main groupings being Ionic (E Greece and Asia Minor), Aeolic (Boeotia and Thessaly), and Doric (the Peloponnese). From Ionic developed the Attic dialect, centered on Athens, which became the chief literary language of classical Greece. When the Greek city-states lost their independence (4th century BC), their dialects gave way to a new common dialect (*koine*), which became the language of Hellenistic Greece and the New Testament. During the Byzantine Empire, Greek increasingly diverged from classical forms, with simplified pronunciations and foreign borrowings. Modern Greek has two widely differing forms: the classically based Katharevusa (purified tongue) used in official publications, and Demotic, the living language of speech, poetry, and fiction.

Greek literature The epics of *Homer date from the 8th century BC, though their echoes of *Mycenaean civilization suggest that they may have existed in oral form for considerably longer. A little later (c. 700) *Hesiod's poems portray the lives and concerns of farmers. *Archilochus of Paros and Alcman (both 7th century) were early masters of lyric verse; they were followed by *Alcaeus, *Sappho, *Solon, and *Anacreon in the 6th century and *Pindar in the early 5th century. Incipient philosophical speculation in 6th-century Ionia stimulated the development of prose, but the earliest prose work to survive intact is the mid-5th-century history of *Herodotus. After the defeat of the Persians (480 BC) Attic writers brought about the flowering of classical Greek literature; major figures were the tragedians *Aeschylus, *Sophocles, and *Euripides, the comedian *Aristophanes (*see* Old Comedy), and the historian *Thucydides. Prose achieved its acme in the 4th century with the works of *Plato, *Xenophon, and the orators *Isocrates and *Demosthenes. During the Hellenistic age Alexandria became the cultural center of the Greek world; it was the home of the poets *Apollonius of Rhodes and *Callimachus, as well as of mathematicians, astronomers, and others who enhanced the status of Greek as a scientific and scholarly medium. Notable among Hellenistic writers elsewhere were the Sicilians *Theocritus and Moschus (c. 150 BC). Under the Roman Empire, Greek remained an international literary language, as the works of *Marcus Aurelius, *Plutarch, and the Greek Church Fathers testify. After the 6th century AD, when Byzantium became the center of Greek culture, histories (*see* Procopius), theological works, and scholarly commentaries became the main output. The 10th-century compilation known as the Greek Anthology comprises over 6000 poems ranging in date from the 7th century BC to the 10th century AD. A popular (demotic) tradition also survived, which expressed itself in folk song and epic (e.g. the late 10th-century epic, *Digenìs Akritas*) and led eventually to the birth of modern Greek literature. *See also* Greek language.

Greek Orthodox Church Strictly, the Orthodox Church in Greece, although the term is often applied to the Orthodox Churches as a whole, to distinguish them from the Latin Church of the West. The Church in Greece dates from the 1st century and St Paul's activities, especially at Corinth. Under the patriarchate of Constantinople Greece was, from the acceptance of Christianity by *Constantine, one of the main Christian centers. With the eventual fall of Constantinople to the Turks, it ceased to be identified with the Byzantine Empire and is now a self-governing Church, the see of Athens holding a primacy of honor after the separation from the patriarchate of Constantinople in 1833.

Greek-Persian Wars An intermittent conflict between the Greeks and Persians. Persian encroachment on Greek territory began in 499 BC, when the Greek cities of *Ionia revolted against their Persian overlords and were crushed by *Darius I. In 490 the Persians were defeated by a small force of Athenians at *Marathon. Darius died in 486 and in 480 *Xerxes I crossed the Hellespont with a large force. The Greeks and Persians fought at *Thermopylae, where the Spartans (under *Leonidas I) heroically held the pass. Xerxes now attacked Attica and Athens was evacuated. At the battle of *Salamis the Persians were defeated by the Greek fleet commanded by *Themistocles and were again defeated at *Plataea (479). Intermittent warfare continued until 449, when the Persians abandoned hope of annexing Greece.

Greek religion The polytheistic religion of ancient Greece. From at least the time of Homer (8th century BC) the myths and deities of the various Greek states were integrated into a more or less coherent system, with a pantheon of 12 anthropomorphic gods who lived on Mount Olympus: *Zeus, *Hera, *Poseidon, *Athena, *Apollo, *Artemis, *Hephaestus, *Aphrodite, *Ares, *Demeter, *Hermes, and *Hestia. All these had appropriate festivals and observances throughout Greece. The orgiastic rites of *Cybele and *Dionysus were slightly later imports from Asia Minor. Deified heroes, such as *Heracles, were also worshiped and there were innumerable local cults for lesser supernatural beings, such as the *nymphs. For those who found the traditional eschatology of *Hades unsatisfactory, the *mysteries held a powerful attraction. During the Hellenistic age king-worship, another oriental import, became important. Religious centers honored throughout Greece included *Delphi, *Delos, Dodona, *Epidaurus, and *Olympia. The forms of the ancient religion were not finally abolished until the Christian emperors closed these shrines (4th century AD), and even today local saints sometimes retain some of the attributes of the pagan gods.

Greeley, Horace (1811–72) US political journalist, who in 1841 founded the *New York Tribune,* championing temperance, liberal reforms, and protectionism. Among his contributors were many well-known people, including, for a time, Karl Marx. In the 1860s he vigorously opposed slavery. After the war he advocated amnesty and suffrage for all males in the South. He made several attempts to enter politics, unsuccessfully running as presidential candidate for the Liberal Republican Party in 1872.

green algae *Algae of the division *Chlorophyta* (about 6000 species), which are bright green, owing to the predominance of the green pigment chlorophyll. Green algae range from simple unicellular plants, for example *Chlamydomonas,* to complex seaweeds, for example *sea lettuce. They are aquatic (mainly freshwater) or terrestrial in moist areas. Reproduction can be sexual or asexual.

Greenaway, Kate (1846–1901) British artist and book illustrator. The daughter of an engraver and draftsman, she is famous for her charming representation of children in such books as *Kate Greenaway's Birthday Album* and *The Language of Flowers.*

Greenback Party (Independent National Party, Greenback Labor Party, National Greenback Party; 1875–84) A US political party in favor of issuing unlimited paper currency to boost the economy. Backed by farmers and workers, it advocated an eight-hour working day, a graduated income tax, the continued circulation of paper money, government controlled interstate commerce, and women's suffrage. It opposed the gold standard and national banks. When the gold standard returned in 1879, the party steadily declined and in 1884 was absorbed by the Anti-Monopoly Party.

Green Bay 44 32N 88 00W A city and port in E Wisconsin, at the head of an inlet of Lake Michigan. Its main industries are paper manufacture and food and dairy processing. Green Bay is the home of the National Railroad Museum and a professional football team, the Green Bay Packers. Population (1990): 96,466.

greenbrier A green-stemmed often evergreen vinelike plant, *Smilax rotundifolia,* that grows in North American woods and thickets, also called catbrier. The leaves are heart-shaped and leathery, and the plant climbs by means of tendrils. The six-part flowers are borne in stalked clusters in the leaf axils and produce blue-black berries. Family: *Liliaceae.*

Greene, (Henry) Graham (1904–91) British novelist. After the publication of his first novel, *The Man Within* (1929), he devoted himself to full-time writing. He was converted to Roman Catholicism in 1927, and an intense concern with questions of morality is central in many of his novels, including *Brighton Rock* (1938), *The Power and the Glory* (1940), *The End of the Affair* (1951), *The Human Factor* (1978), *Dr Fischer of Geneva or The Bomb Party* (1980), and *Monsignor Quixote* (1982). He also wrote a number of literary thrillers, which he labeled "entertainments," including *The Ministry of Fear* (1943), *The Third Man* (1950), and *Our Man in Havana* (1958). His other works include plays, film scripts of several of his books, short stories, and essays.

Greene, Nathaniel (1742–86) US military leader. He served in the RI General Assembly (1770–72) and was appointed brigadier general in the Continental Army in 1775. After serving as commander of the army of occupation in Boston, he was promoted to the rank of major general and took part in the battles of *Trenton (1776) and Germantown (1777). In 1778, at *Valley Forge, George Washington named him quartermaster general and Greene successfully organized the supplies to the American troops at the battles of Monmouth and Newport in the same year. Greene was chosen by Washington to succeed Gen. Horatio Gates as commander of the Army of the South in 1780, and he ultimately forced the British army under Lord *Cornwallis to relinquish its occupation of the Carolinas.

greenfinch A Eurasian *finch, *Carduelis chloris,* about 5.5 in (14 cm) long with an olive-green body and a pale bill. The male has a bright yellow-green breast and both sexes show bright-yellow wing flashes in flight.

greenfly. *See* aphid.

greengage A bush or small tree, *Prunus italica,* related to the *plum, probably native to Asia Minor and widely cultivated. It bears round green fruits, often tinged with red, which are scented and sweet flavored and used in preserves and for canning.

greenheart An evergreen South American lumber tree, *Nectandria rodiaei,* native to Guiana, also called sweetwood or bebeeru. Up to 98 ft (30 m) tall, it has branching clusters of inconspicuous flowers and the fruit is surrounded by an acornlike cup. The wood, which is extremely dense and hard, is used for underwater construction and ships. Family: *Lauraceae* (laurel family).

greenhouse effect An atmospheric effect in which some of the energy of ultraviolet radiation and visible light from the sun is retained by the earth as heat. The radiation is transmitted through the atmosphere to the earth's surface, where it is reradiated as longer wavelength infrared radiation. The atmosphere only partially transmits the infrared back into space and so a heating effect occurs. The phenomenon takes its name from a greenhouse, in which a similar effect occurs.

Greenland (Danish name: Grønland) A large island off NE North America bounded by the N Atlantic Ocean and the Greenland and Norwegian Seas. Lying chiefly within the Arctic Circle, it is largely covered by a vast ice cap through which nunataks protrude around its rim. Many glaciers emerge from this, including the Humboldt Glacier, breaking off to form icebergs along the coast. Eskimos form about 80% of the population, the remainder being chiefly Danish. *Economy*: fishing is the chief occupation, principally for cod and halibut but other catches include shrimps and sea trout. Whaling and seal hunting have declined in recent years. The harsh environment makes agriculture difficult but sheep are reared in the SW. Greenland possesses potentially important mineral resources, notably lead and zinc, which have been exploited since the early 1970s; uranium is also present. *History*: in about 986 AD the Norwegian Eric the Red discovered the island, which he named Greenland to attract settlers. Norse colonies on the island disappeared during the 15th century and until 1721, when a new Danish settlement was established, the Eskimos were the sole inhabitants. A Danish colony from 1721, Greenland became an integral part of Denmark in 1953. In 1979 it gained self-government under Danish sovereignty with its own Parliament. Prime minister: Jonathan Motzfeldt. Official language: Greenland Eskimo. Official currency: Danish krone of 100 øre. Area: 840,000 sq mi (2,175,600 sq km). Population (1989 est): 55,500. Capital: Godthaab.

Greenland Sea An extension of the Arctic Ocean, between Greenland, Svalbard, and Iceland. Covered by drifting ice, it links with the Atlantic Ocean.

Greenland shark A large omnivorous *shark, up to 23 ft (7 m) long, *Somniosus microcephalus,* found usually in shoals in the deeper waters of the N Atlantic and Arctic Oceans. Family: *Squalidae.*

green monkey disease An acute, often fatal, viral infection first described in Marburg, Germany, and therefore sometimes called Marburg disease. It occurs in vervet monkeys and may be transmitted to laboratory workers by contact with infected animals.

Green Mountain Boys A volunteer militia formed in 1764 to protect the property rights of the settlers of N New England. In response to attempts by the province of New York to annex portions of Vermont, the Green Mountain Boys, under the command of Ethan *Allen after 1770, successfully defended their land grants. With the outbreak of the *Revolutionary War, they joined forces with the Continental Army, participating in the capture of Fort *Ticonderoga (1775) and in the Battle of Bennington (1777). Their original purpose was attained in 1791 when Vermont was granted statehood.

Green Mountains A mountain range, part of the Appalachians, that extend from N Massachusetts, through central Vermont to S Canada. Mt Mansfield in NW Vermont is the highest point and rises to 4393 ft (1339 m). The mountains yield granite for Vermont's quarrying industry, lumber, and recreation areas, especially for winter sports.

Greenock 55 57N 4 45W A city in W central Scotland, on the Clyde estuary. Ship building is its principal industry; others include engineering, sugar refining, and chemicals. James Watt was born here. Population (1981): 57,324.

Greenough, Horatio (1805–52) US neoclassical sculptor. A pupil of *Thorvaldsen, Greenough worked mainly in Rome. His most important sculpture was of George Washington in a toga commissioned by Congress in 1832.

Green Revolution. *See* agriculture; arable farming.

Greensboro 36 04N 79 47W A city in N central North Carolina, E of Winston-Salem and NW of Durham. The Battle of Guilford Courthouse, a Revolutionary War battle in 1781, was fought near here. Industries include clothing, tobacco, petroleum-related products, drugs, and building materials. Population (1990): 183,521.

greenshank A bird, *Tringa nebularia,* that breeds in N Eurasian moorland and tundra and winters in South Africa and S Eurasia. It is 12 in (30 cm) long and grayish in color with greenish legs, a white rump, and a long slightly upturned blue-gray bill. Family: *Scolopacidae* (sandpipers).

green turtle A large brown-green marine turtle, *Chelonia mydas,* which has green fat and is used to make turtle soup. Up to 40 in (1 m) long and weighing up to 309 lb (140 kg), they occur in warm Atlantic coastal waters feeding on marine algae and migrate long distances to lay their eggs on Central American beaches. □reptiles.

Greenwich A borough of E Greater London, on the S bank of the River Thames. It has important royal and maritime connections. The Greenwich Royal

Hospital, designed by *Wren, became the Royal Naval College in 1873. Wren also designed the original *Royal Greenwich Observatory. Population (1981): 212,001.

Greenwich Mean Time (GMT) The local time at Greenwich, London, located on the 0° meridian (*see* longitude), from which the standard times of different areas of the globe are calculated, 15° longitude representing one hour in time.

Greenwich Village A residential section of New York City, in Manhattan. It became a favorite haunt of authors and artists early in the 20th century, acquiring a reputation for bohemianism. It is the site of the main campus of New York University.

Gregorian calendar. *See* calendar.

Gregorian chant The official liturgical plainchant of the Roman Catholic Church as codified during the papacy of Gregory I (590–604 AD). It consists of single unaccompanied melodic lines based on a system of *modes and sung to flexible rhythms. *See* plainchant.

Gregory I, St (c. 540–604 AD) Pope (590–604), known as Gregory the Great. Of senatorial rank, he gave himself to charitable works and was a monk before becoming a papal official. As pope he reorganized and increased papal power in Italy, making peace with the Lombards and limiting imperial authority over the Church. He reformed the papal states and sponsored *Augustine (of Canterbury) in his mission to convert England. Gregory's many pastoral and doctrinal works were of considerable influence, and he introduced the use of *Gregorian chant into the liturgy. He was canonized on his death. Feast day: Mar 12.

Gregory VII, St (Hildebrand; c. 1021–85) Pope (1073–85). Before his election he worked closely with *Leo IX and Alexander II to reform the Church. As pope, he condemned simony, lay investiture, and clerical marriage. He was ultimately largely successful in asserting the independence of the Church from lay control but during his lifetime he created considerable opposition, especially in France and Germany, where Emperor *Henry IV declared his deposition (1076). He in turn excommunicated Henry and released his subjects from allegiance. Henry was soon forced to accept the pope's reforms and submitted to him at Canossa (1077). The conflict continued, however, when the emperor appointed Wibert, Archbishop of Ravenna, antipope (1080), invaded Italy, and captured Rome (1084). Gregory was rescued by Norman troops whom he had summoned but was nevertheless forced to flee from Rome. He died at Salerno. Feast day: May 25.

Gregory IX (Ugolino of Segni; c. 1148–1241) Pope (1227–41). He was employed as a papal legate by his uncle, *Innocent III, and preached the fifth Crusade (1217). On his election as pope, he immediately excommunicated Emperor *Frederick II for his delay in fulfilling crusading vows. His papacy was marked by conflict with the emperor, and he died while Frederick was besieging Rome. He was a noted canon lawyer and was a friend of St *Francis of Assisi, whom he canonized.

Gregory XIII (Ugo Buoncompagni; 1502–85) Pope (1572–85). His pontificate was marked by support of the *Counter-Reformation and the sponsorship of colleges and reformed orders, especially the *Jesuits and the Oratorians. He founded the English College at Rome (1579) and was responsible for instituting the Gregorian *calendar (1582).

Gregory, Lady Augusta (1852–1932) Irish theater patron and dramatist. With W. B. Yeats, in 1899 she founded the Irish Dramatic Movement, a national theater company that moved into the Abbey Theatre in 1904. She collaborated with Yeats on *The Pot of Broth* (1902) and *Cathleen ni Houlihan* (1902) and wrote many comedies and translations, notably of Molière.

Gregory of Nazianzus, St (c. 330–c. 389 AD) Cappadocian Father of the Church, son of the Bishop of Nazianzus. He was educated in Athens, where he became a friend of St *Basil the Great. With Basil and St *Gregory of Nyssa he became a leading defender of orthodox Christianity against *Arianism. He was Bishop of Caesarea from 370 to 379 and briefly served as Patriarch of Constantinople in 380. Feast Day: May 9.

Gregory of Nyssa, St (c. 335–c. 394 AD) Cappadocian Father of the Church. A leader of the orthodox party, which opposed *Arianism, he was made Bishop of Nyssa in 372 by his brother, St *Basil the Great. He was deposed in 376 but reinstated in 378 on the death of the Arian emperor, Valens. He wrote many theological works. Feast day: Mar 9.

Gregory of Tours, St (c. 538–594 AD) French churchman and historian; Bishop of Tours (573–94). He is best known for his *Historia Francorum,* which is a history of the world from its creation to the 6th century AD. It is a valuable source of information on early European history. Feast Day: Nov 17.

Grenada, State of An island country in the West Indies, in the Windward Islands in the E Caribbean Sea off the NE coast of Venezuela. It is the smallest nation state in the Western Hemisphere. It also includes some of the Grenadine Islands, the largest of which is Carriacou. The majority of the population is of mixed European and Indian descent. *Economy*: largely agricultural, the chief products are cocoa, bananas, citrus fruits, sugar, and nutmeg (the main export). *History*: discovered by Columbus in 1493, it was colonized by the French and ceded to the British in 1763. In 1967 it became an Associated State under the West Indies Act and in 1974, an independent state within the Commonwealth of Nations. In March, 1979, the government of Sir Eric Gairy (1922–) was overthrown in a nearly bloodless coup by the New Jewel Movement (NJM) led by Maurice Bishop (1944–83), who subsequently became prime minister. Following an uprising of armed forces in 1983, during which Bishop was killed, the US invaded the country to take out US nationals. Bishop, a moderate socialist, formed close ties with Cuba and the Soviet Union. In October 1983 Bishop was deposed and executed by rebels under the leadership of Bernard Coard and the military seized control of the government. Later in October Pres. Ronald Reagan ordered an invasion of the island by US forces, supported by troops from several Caribbean nations, that quickly overcame resistance and imposed a stable government. Viewing Grenada as a strategic threat, Reagan cited the presence of Soviet military equipment on the island and Soviet and Cuban assistance in building an airport at Point Salines as evidence that the two countries were using the island as a forward base. Elections were held in 1984 and Herbert Blaize became prime minister. Blaize died in December 1989 and was succeeded by Ben Jones, who was succeeded by Nicholas Brathwaite in 1990 elections. Official language: English. Official currency: East Caribbean dollar of 100 cents. Area: 133 sq mi (344 sq km). Population (1990 est): 84,000. Capital and main port: St George's.

grenadier A carnivorous bottom-dwelling fish, also called rat-tail or torpedo, belonging to a family (*Macrouridae*; about 300 species) found in deep warm and temperate marine waters. It has a stout body, usually 12–24 in (30–60 cm) long, with a long ratlike tail and a large head.

Grenadine Islands A chain of West Indian islets, extending for about 60 mi (100 km) between St Vincent and Grenada and administratively divided between the two.

Grenoble 45 11N 5 43E A city in SE France, the capital of the Isère department. The capital of the Dauphiné until 1341, it has a cathedral (12th–13th centuries) and a university (1339). It is the principal tourist center of the French Alps and has metallurgical, textile, cement, and paper industries. Population (1982): 160,000.

Grenville, William (Wyndham), Baron (1759–1834) British statesman; prime minister (1806–07). As prime minister he led the coalition Ministry of All the Talents, which was notable for its abolition of the slave trade (1807). His government fell owing to royal opposition to the Catholic Relief bill. His father **George Grenville** (1712–70) was prime minister from 1763–65. His government was noted for its *Stamp Act (1765) and prosecution of John *Wilkes.

Gresham, Sir Thomas (c. 1519–79) English financier and philanthropist. He founded Gresham College and the Royal Exchange, both in London, but is best known for the so-called **Gresham's Law**, attributed to him in the 19th century, that "bad money drives out good": if there are two different types of coin in circulation, and one sort of coin is suspected of being debased and is falling in value relative to the other, the more valuable coin will be hoarded and will eventually disappear from circulation.

Greuze, Jean-Baptiste (1725–1805) French painter, born in Tournus. Settling in Paris, he achieved early acclaim with his *Father Reading the Bible to His Children* (1755; Louvre). After an unsuccessful attempt at history painting (1769), he concentrated on sentimental and vaguely erotic portraits of girls, e.g. *The Broken Pitcher* (Louvre).

Grey, Charles, 2nd Earl (1764–1845) British statesman, who as Whig prime minister (1830–34) secured the passage of the parliamentary *Reform Act of 1832 by persuading William IV to create sufficient new peers to carry the bill through the House of Lords.

Grey, Lady Jane (1537–54) Queen of England for nine days (1553) and the great-granddaughter of *Henry VII. The Duke of *Northumberland had her proclaimed queen when Edward VI died but Mary, the rightful heiress, had popular support and Jane abdicated. She was executed for treason with her husband Lord Guildford Dudley, Northumberland's son.

Grey, Zane (1875–1939) US author. Although he graduated from dentistry school, he practiced for only six years before turning to writing novels, mostly about the Old West. His works include *Spirit of the Border* (1905), *The Heritage of the Desert* (1910), *Riders of the Purple Sage* (1912), *Desert Gold* (1913), *Wildfire* (1917), *To the Last Man* (1922), *The Call of the Canyon* (1924), and *Western Union* (1939). A noted fisherman, he also wrote sports and outdoor life books for boys.

greyhound An ancient breed of dog used for hare coursing and racing. It has a slender deep-chested streamlined body with long legs and a long muscular neck. The short smooth coat can be of various colors. Greyhounds can reach speeds of up to 45 mph (70 km per hour). Height: 28–30 in (71–76 cm) (dogs); 27–28 in (68–71 cm) (bitches).

greyhound racing (*or* dog racing) A form of racing popular for betting, in which greyhounds pursue an electrically propelled mechanical rabbit around a circular or oval track. The sport evolved from *coursing in the US in the early 20th century and is especially popular in the US, Britain, and Australia. Races may be on the flat or over hurdles, with distances ranging from 220–1200 yd (200–1100 m).

gribble A wood-boring marine crustacean of the genus *Limnoria* (about 20 species). It feeds on algae, driftwood, and the submerged sections of docks and piers. *L. lignorum,* common in the N hemisphere, has a gray body up to 0.20 in (5 mm) long. Order: **Isopoda.*

Grieg, Edvard Hagerup (1843–1907) Norwegian composer, who studied in Leipzig and Copenhagen. He spent the latter part of his life in a house near the Troldhaugen fjord and was buried there. The influence of Norwegian folk music is apparent in many of his works, which include the *Lyric Pieces* (for piano; 1867–1901), a very popular piano concerto (1868), incidental music to Ibsen's play *Peer Gynt* (1876), chamber music, and many songs.

griffin A mythological creature with the head and wings of an eagle, the body of a lion, and often a serpent's tail. It is common in many ancient eastern mythologies.

Griffith, Arthur (1872–1922) Irish journalist and nationalist, who organized *Sinn Féin in 1905. He was imprisoned three times (1916, 1918–19, 1920–21) by the British authorities. In 1918 Sinn Féin won the majority of parliamentary seats in Ireland and declared a republic, which Griffith headed from 1919–20. In 1921 he led the Irish delegation to the conference that determined the treaty establishing the Irish Free State. On *De Valera's rejection of the terms, Griffith was elected (1922) president of the Irish assembly (the Dáil Éireann) but died later that year.

Griffith, D(avid) W(ark) (1875–1948) US film director. His intuitive understanding of the artistic potential of the cinema and his innovations in editing and narrative techniques made him the most influential pioneer of the US cinema. His major films include *The Birth of a Nation* (1915), an ambitious epic concerning the Civil War, *Intolerance* (1916), *Broken Blossoms* (1919), and *Isn't Life Wonderful* (1924).

griffon (dog) A breed of toy dog originating in Belgium and of terrier ancestry. It has a square compact body, a docked tail, and a large head covered with long coarse hair. The coat is either rough and wiry or short and tight and may be red, black, or black and tan. Weight: 4–11 lb (2–5 kg).

griffon vulture One of the largest Old World *vultures, *Gyps fulvus.* It is 40 in (100 cm) long and occurs in mountainous regions of S Europe, South Africa, and Asia. It is gray-brown with darker wingtips, a white head and ruff, and whitish downy patches on the neck.

Grignard reagents Organomagnesium compounds, discovered by F. A. V. Grignard (1871–1935) and usually prepared by adding an organic halide to magnesium under ether. They are invaluable in a host of organic syntheses, giving addition products with almost all groups.

Grimm, Brothers German philologists and folklorists. After early work on medieval German texts, **Jakob** (1785–1863) and **Wilhelm** (1786–1859) set about collecting German folktales, published in 1812–14 as *Kinder- und Hausmärchen.* The *Deutsche Grammatik* (1819, 1822) is a historical and descriptive German grammar containing observations on the regularity of sound changes in Indo-European languages, known as **Grimm's law**. Their *Deutsches Wörterbuch* is a historical and descriptive German dictionary. A new Grimm brothers tale was found in 1983.

Grimsby 53 35N 0 05W A seaport in NE England, near the mouth of the Humber estuary. Although it is the largest fishing port in England, the extension of Iceland's fishing limits (1975–76) combined with overfishing in many of the traditional grounds led to a considerable reduction in the size of the fishing fleet. Population (1981): 92,147.

Gris, Juan (José Victoriano González; 1887–1927) Spanish-born cubist painter, who worked in Paris from 1906. In contrast to *Picasso and *Braque, his approach to *cubism was mathematical; his starting points were abstract shapes from which he developed real objects in geometrically constructed still lifes, landscapes, and portraits. He also promoted the art of collage and wrote an influential study of painting entitled *Les Possibilités de la peinture* (1924).

Grisham, John (1955–) US author, whose legal-adventure best-sellers set in the Deep South catapulted him to fame. He practiced law in Oxford, Miss., before turning to writing. The success of *The Firm* (1991) was followed by *The Pelican Brief* (1992) and *The Client* (1993). *A Time to Kill* (1988) was republished to acclaim in 1993. His first four books all had enormous sales in paperback, and *The Firm* and *The Pelican Brief* were made into successful films.

grison A mammal belonging to the genus *Grison* (2 species) of Central and South America. Grisons are about 24 in (60 cm) long and grayish black, hunting through forest and grassland for invertebrates and small mammals. Family: **Mustelidae* (weasels, stoats, etc.).

Grissom, Virgil ("Gus"; 1926–67) US astronaut. He was a member of the Mercury space team. His 1961 space flight made him the second American in space. A fire on board a ground-training spaceship took his life.

Griswold v. Connecticut (1965) US Supreme Court decision that upheld right of privacy and struck down a Connecticut law banning the dissemination of information about birth control and sale of birth control devices. Written by Justice William O. *Douglas, aided by Justice Arthur *Goldberg, the decision established the "penumbra theory"—that privacy in marriage was protected in the Bill of Rights (*see* Constitution, US), implied in the 1st, 3rd, 4th, 5th, and 9th amendments.

Grivas, Georgios (1898–1974) Greek general, born in Cyprus. Known as Dighenis, he was the leader of *EOKA, which fought for the union of Cyprus with Greece.

grizzly bear. *See* brown bear.

Grodno 53 40N 23 50E A port in Belarus, on the Neman River. Possessed by Lithuania and then by Poland, it has many historic buildings, including a medieval castle and *Stephen Báthory's 16th-century palace. It is an important railroad center and major industrial city, producing fertilizers, textiles, food products, and tobacco. Population (1987): 263,000.

Gromyko, Andrei (1909–89) Soviet diplomat; foreign minister (1957–85) and president (1985–88). Gromyko began his diplomatic career in 1939 and served as ambassador to the US (1943–46) and the UK (1952–53). He was Soviet representative at the UN between 1946 and 1949.

Groningen 53 13N 6 35E A city in the N Netherlands, the capital of Groningen province. It has a notable church (the 15th-century Martinikerk) and a university (1614). An important commercial and market center, its industries include textiles, clothing, and sugar refining. Population (1988 est): 168,000.

Groningen A province in the Netherlands, bordering on the North Sea and Germany. Low lying and fertile, it is intensively cultivated and agriculture forms the chief occupation. Natural gas is extracted at Slochteren. Area: 900 sq mi (2350 sq km). Population (1989): 555,200. Capital: Groningen.

Groote Eylandt 12 20S 135 15E An Australian island, in the Gulf of Carpentaria off the coast of the Northern Territory. It forms part of the Arnhem Land Aboriginal Reserve. Manganese deposits have recently been discovered and exploited. Area: 950 sq mi (2460 sq km).

Gropius, Walter (1883–1969) German architect, one of the pioneers of the international modern style of architecture. Gropius was influenced by William *Morris and Frank Lloyd *Wright and trained under *Behrens until 1910. His first major building, a factory at Alfeld (1911) is a very early example of the new style. As director of the *Bauhaus (1919–28) he was able to greatly influence all aspects of contemporary design. The rise of Nazi power forced him to leave Germany (1934) for England. In 1937 he moved to America, where he spent 14 influential years teaching at Harvard. He continued to design a few buildings, for example the US Embassy in Athens (1960), and to influence European architecture.

Gros, Antoine Jean, Baron (1771–1835) French painter. A pupil of *David, he later traveled with Napoleon's armies, painting such scenes as *Napoleon Visiting the Plague-Stricken at Jaffa* (1804; Louvre). Although initially successful under the restored Bourbons, he fell into obscurity in the 1820s and finally drowned himself. His style, influenced by *Rubens, anticipates the work of *Delacroix and *Géricault.

grosbeak A finch with a particularly heavy bill used to crack open hard seeds and nuts. The name is given to birds of several genera found in N Eurasia, America, and the tropics. The reddish-brown Eurasian pine grosbeak (*Pinicola enucleator*) uses its bill as a hammer to obtain seeds from pine cones.

gross domestic product. *See* gross national product.

Grossglockner 47 05N 12 44E The highest mountain in Austria, in the Alps. The Grossglockner Road (built 1930–35) crosses it, rising to 7852 ft (2576 m). Height: 12,457 ft (3797 m).

gross national product (GNP) A measure of the total annual output of a country, including net income from abroad, it provides a measure of the economic strength of that country. GNP can be calculated in three ways: based on income, output, or expenditure. If income is used as the basis, all incomes accruing to residents of the country as a result of economic activity (excluding, for instance, pensions) are summed (national income is thus synonymous with GNP calculated in this way). On the basis of output, the value added to a product at each stage of production is summed. If expenditure is used, the value of all consumption products is calculated. All three methods should give the same result. **Gross domestic product** (GDP) is GNP excluding net income from abroad and gives some indication of the strength of industry within a country. **Net national product** differs from GNP in that it makes a provision for *depreciation, i.e. the using up of the country's capital stock.

Gros Ventres Algonkian-speaking North American Indian tribe found in Montana and Saskatchewan, Canada. Originally of the Arapaho, they had broken away and established their own name (meaning "big bellies"), customs, and rituals, which were similar to the Arapaho's. They warred against the Crow and Dakota and, eventually, were defeated by the Blackfoot (1867). The remaining Gros Ventres reside on Fort Belknap reservation in Montana. The Hidatsa, a Siouan-speaking tribe, were also known as Gros Ventres.

Grosz, George (1893–1959) German painter and draftsman, born in Berlin. A member of the *Dada art movement, he is famous for his bitter satirical depictions of war, the bourgeoisie, the church, and German social evils. He was fined and charges of blasphemy were brought against him because of his work. He emigrated to the US in 1932.

Grotefend, Georg Friedrich (1775–1853) German philologist. He did important work on ancient *Italic languages, but after 1800 was increasingly occupied with attempts to decipher Persian *cuneiform inscriptions. He established several facts, including the alphabetic (as opposed to syllabic) nature of the characters, which facilitated their successful decipherment by *Rawlinson.

Grotius, Hugo (*or* Huig de Groot; 1583–1645) Dutch jurist and diplomat, the founder of international law. Sentenced to life imprisonment in 1619 by Prince Maurice of Nassau for his support of the Arminian faith in the religious controversies of the time, he escaped to France in 1621. There he wrote his famous *De jure belli et pacis* (1625), arguing that natural law should be applied to nations as well as individuals and that war should only be waged for justified causes. He was Swedish ambassador to France from 1635 until his death.

Groton 41 19N 72 12W A city in SE Connecticut, on Long Island Sound at the E mouth of the Thames River. It is a major submarine-building center and is home to a US Navy submarine base. The first nuclear-powered submarine, *Nautilus* (1954), was constructed there. Population (1990): 9,837.

ground beetle A heavily armored long-legged beetle belonging to a family (*Carabidae*; 25,000 species) that is particularly common in temperate regions. Ground beetles are dark in color or have a metallic sheen and are from 0.08–3 in (2–85 mm) long. Most are nocturnal and can be found under stones, logs, and debris during the day. The adults and most larvae are active carnivores, preying on insects, slugs, and snails. *See also* bombardier beetle.

ground bug A *plant bug belonging to the worldwide family *Lygaeidae* (about 3000 species). Ground bugs have elongated brown or black bodies, 0.12–0.59 in (3–15 mm) long, often with red markings. They live in moss or rubbish or under stones or low bushes and feed on a variety of plants, in many cases becoming serious pests (*see* chinch bug).

ground elder A perennial herbaceous plant, *Aegopodium podagraria,* also called goutweed, bishop's weed, or herb Gerard, common in Europe on waste ground and as a garden weed; 19–40 in (49–100 cm) tall, it has compound leaves with three leaflets (like those of elder) and umbrella-like clusters of small white flowers. The leaves may be eaten as a salad or vegetable. Family: **Umbelliferae.*

groundhog. *See* marmot.

ground ivy A creeping perennial herb, *Glechoma hederacea* (or *Nepeta glechoma*), found in woods and grasslands across Eurasia. It has long-stalked heart-shaped toothed leaves and its stems, 4–12 in (10–30 cm) high, bear groups of tubular violet two-lipped flowers. Family: **Labiatae.*

groundnut The fruit of *Arachis hypogea,* also called peanut or earthnut, native to tropical South America but widely cultivated in the tropics. The plant is an erect or creeping annual, 12–18 in (30–45 cm) high, with compound leaves and yellow flowers. After fertilization the flower stalk elongates, pushing the developing pod below the soil to ripen underground. The pod has a thin spongy wall and contains one to three seeds (the nuts), which are highly nutritious. They are used in cooking, canned, and made into peanut butter and peanut oil (used in margarine). Family: **Leguminosae.*

groundsel A weedy herbaceous plant of the genus *Senecio,* especially *S. vulgaris,* 3.1–18 in (8–45 cm) high and common in Eurasia and N Africa. It has lobed toothed leaves and small yellow flower heads, which lack ray florets and are almost enclosed by the sepals. Family: **Compositae.*

ground squirrel A *squirrel that lives in an underground burrow rather than in a tree. Ground squirrels have short strong legs, small ears, and shorter tails than tree squirrels, inhabiting open country in North America, Eurasia, and Africa. Chief genera: *Citellus* (34 species), *Lariscus* (2 species), *Xerus* (4 species). *See also* prairie dog; chipmunk; souslik; marmot.

groundwater Water that has percolated into the ground and become trapped within pores, cracks, and fissures. It is important in *weathering processes through its chemical effects. With depth the *water table is reached, below which all pore spaces are filled.

grouper One of several sedentary food and game fish of the family *Serranidae* (*see* sea bass), especially the genera *Epinephelus* and *Mycteroperca,* widely distributed in warm seas. Groupers have a dull-green or brown heavy body, up to or exceeding 7 ft (2 m) long, and a large mouth. Some are poisonous when consumed.

Group of Seven (also, G–7) Association of the world's seven leading industrialized democratic nations: Canada, France, Germany, Italy, Japan, the UK, and the US. Through frequent meetings, the G–7 nations attempt to plan global financial and economic policies and to encourage democracy, as in the 1993 aid package for Russia and other former Soviet republics, which was tied to economic reform.

group therapy A form of *psychotherapy in which several patients meet together to understand and overcome their problems, usually with the help of a therapist. There are many forms of group therapy: sometimes the aim is to increase patients' insight in psychoanalytic terms, sometimes to teach social skills, sometimes to act out distressing events from the past, and sometimes to support one another in overcoming a common problem (such as alcoholism).

grouse A fowl-like game bird, 12–35 in (30–88 cm) long, belonging to a family (*Tetraonidae*; about 18 species) of the N hemisphere. Grouse are mostly ground-living, with short round wings, a short strong bill, and feathered legs. They are noted for their spectacular courtship displays (called *leks*). The family includes the *black grouse, *red grouse, and *capercaillie of N Europe (including Britain); the *ptarmigans; and the North American ruffed grouse (*Bonasa umbellus*) and *sage grouse. Order: *Galliformes. See also* gamebird.

Grove, Sir George (1820–1900) British musicologist, founder and first editor of *Grove's Dictionary of Music and Musicians* (1879–89). His interest in the arts led to extensive musical and biblical research during which he traveled widely. He was founder and first director (1883–94) of the Royal College of Music and was knighted in 1883. *The New Grove Dictionary of Music and Musicians* was published in 1980.

growth hormone (*or* somatotrophin) A protein hormone that promotes the metabolic processes involved in growth of bone and muscle. It is secreted by the pituitary gland and stimulates protein synthesis, mobilizes fat reserves, increases glucose levels in the blood, and affects mineral metabolism. Lack of growth hormone in children causes dwarfism.

Groznyi 43 21N 45 42E A city in Azerbaijan, the capital of the Checheno-Ingush republic. It is one of the country's oldest and richest oil-producing areas. Population (1987): 404,000.

Grub Street A street, now renamed Milton St, in London, England, associated in the 18th century with writers of little talent, who earned their livings by whatever literary work they could obtain. *Pope satirized such hacks in *An Epistle to Dr. Arbuthnot* (1755) and the name is referred to in the title of George Gissing's novel *New Grub Street* (1891).

GROUSE *The male sage grouse* (Centrocercus urophasianus) *in courtship display, during which it fans out its tail and inflates a pouch on its chest to attract females.*

Grünewald, Matthias (Mathis Gothardt; d. 1528) German painter, born in Würzburg. His earliest known work is *The Mocking of Christ* (c. 1503; Alte Pinakothek, Munich). For much of his career, he was court painter at Mainz. His favorite subject was the crucifixion, of which perhaps his most tragic treatment is the *Isenheim Altarpiece* (Colmar, France), noted also for its dazzling color. His style, characterized by a distortion of form, influenced 20th-century German expressionists (*see* expressionism).

grunt A small food fish, belonging to the family *Pomadasyidae* (about 75 species), that can produce piglike grunts. It has a colorful elongated body and a large mouth; it occurs in the warm and tropical coastal waters. Order: *Perciformes.*

Gruyère A district in Switzerland, in the middle Saane Valley, famed for its cheese and cattle.

G–7 *See* Group of Seven.

Guadalajara 20 30N 103 20W The second largest city in Mexico, at an altitude of 5413 ft (1650 m). Founded by the Spanish (1530), it has several notable buildings including the cathedral (16th–17th centuries) and the Governor's Palace (begun 1763); there are two universities (1792, 1935). Its key position as a communications center across the Sierra Madre Occidental has led to its rapid expansion in recent years and it now has a large industrial complex. Its handicraft industries (especially glassware and pottery) also remain important. Population (1990): 1,628,617.

Guadalcanal 9 30S 160 00E The largest of the Solomon Islands, in the S Pacific Ocean. During World War II the first major US offensive in the Pacific against the Japanese took place here; it was captured after six months of jungle fighting (1942–43). Copra, rubber, and some gold are produced. Area: 2500 sq mi (6475 sq km). Population (1991 est): 60,700. Chief settlement: Honiara.

Guadalquivir River The main river of S Spain. It flows mainly WSW from the Sierra de Segura to the Gulf of Cádiz and is navigable to Seville by ocean-going vessels. Length: 348 mi (560 km).

Guadalupe Hidalgo (name from 1931–71: Gustavo A. Madero) 19 29N 99 07W A city in central Mexico, a NE suburb of Mexico City. The Basilica of the Virgin of Guadalupe, which was built after an Indian convert reported seeing a vision of the Virgin Mary there in 1531, is a famous place of pilgrimage. The Treaty of *Guadalupe Hidalgo was signed there.

Guadalupe Hidalgo, Treaty of (1848) The treaty that ended the *Mexican War. In exchange for $15 million and the payment of the claims of US citizens, the US received what are now the states of California, Nevada, Utah, parts of Colorado, Wyoming, and Arizona and most of New Mexico.

Guadalupe Mountains National Park A national park in W Texas, E of El Paso that includes part of the Guadalupe Mountain Range, a part of the Rockies. Established in 1966, the park includes the highest point of the range, Guadalupe Peak (8751 ft; 2668 m), a large earth fault, and many examples of limestone fossil reef. Area: 82,280 acres (33,299 hectares).

Guadeloupe A French overseas region in the West Indies, in the E Caribbean Sea. It comprises two main islands, Grande Terre and Basse Terre, together with the island dependencies of Marie Galante, La Désirade, Îles des Saintes, St Barthélemy, and the N part of *St Martin. The economy is based on agriculture; sugar cane is the chief crop. Area: 657 sq mi (1702 sq km). Population (1991 est): 395,000. Capital: Basse-Terre.

guaiacum A small evergreen tree of the genus *Guaiacum,* especially *G. officinale* of tropical America, also called lignum vitae. It has blue flowers, yellow heart-shaped fruits, and very dense hard wood, used to make pulleys, axles, and bowling balls. The greenish resin is distilled for medicinal use. Family: *Zygophyllaceae.*

Guam 13 30N 144 40E An island and US unincorporated territory in the West Pacific Ocean, the largest of the Mariana Islands. Mountainous in the S, it is mantled by jungle. Spanish from 1565 to 1898, it was occupied by the Japanese (1941–44). It is a major naval and air base, especially important during the Vietnam War. Industries include ship repairing. Tourism became a major industry from the 1980s. Area: 210 sq mi (450 sq km). Population (1990): 133,152. Capital: Agaña.

guanaco A hoofed mammal, *Lama guanacoe,* closely related to the *llama and found at altitudes of up to 16,404 ft (5000 m) in W South America. Red-brown with a pale face and pale underparts, guanacos grow up to 43 in (110 cm) high at the shoulder and live in small herds on open grassland. Family: *Camelidae.*

Guan Di (*or* Kuan Ti) In Chinese mythology, the god of war. A historical figure and hero of numerous romantic exploits, he was captured and executed in 219 AD. His popularity with both common people and the aristocracy grew until he was pronounced a god in 1594. Various professions and trades, including writers, adopted him as patron and hundreds of temples were built in his honor.

Guangdong (Kuang-tung *or* Kwangtung) A mountainous province in S China, including Hainan and other islands. Heavily populated, it produces rice, sugar cane, tobacco, silk, fish, timber, and minerals. *History*: Chinese from 222 BC, it only came under Chinese cultural influence in the 12th and 13th centuries AD. As China's main trading area, it later had considerable contact with the West and from the mid-19th century overpopulation led to overseas emigration. During the 19th and early 20th centuries it was a center of revolutionary movements. Area: 90,246 sq mi (231,400 sq km). Population (1990): 62,829,236. Capital: Canton.

Guangxi Zhuang Autonomous Region (*or* Kwangsi Chuang AR) A mountainous administrative division in S China, on the N Vietnamese border. It has seen great economic growth since 1949, producing sugar cane, rice, timber, manganese, and tin. *History*: its non-Chinese minorities have rebelled periodically and the *Taiping Rebellion started here (1851). It became a center of communist opposition to *Chiang Kai-shek's government and heavy fighting against the Japanese invasion took place here during World War II. Area: 85,956 sq mi (220,400 sq km). Population (1990): 42,245,765. Capital: Nanning.

Guang Xu (*or* Kuang-hsü; 1871–1908) The title of Cai Tian (*or* Tsai-t'ien) of the Qing dynasty, who became emperor (1875) at the age of four with his aunt *Zi Xi as regent. When after coming of age he sponsored the *Hundred Days of Reform she imprisoned him for the rest of his life.

Guangzhou. *See* Canton.

guano The accumulated excrement of certain animals, especially seabirds, seals, and bats. It contains 10–18% nitrogen, 8–12% phosphoric acid, and 2–3% potash, according to the age and origin of the deposit. Large amounts have been found on islands off the Peruvian and other coasts and it has been widely used as a fertilizer.

Guantánamo 20 09N 75 14W A city in SE Cuba, N of Guantánamo Bay. It is the center of an agricultural area producing sugar cane and coffee. Industries include coffee roasting, sugar refining, and chocolate manufacture. Population (1989): 197,868.

Guan Yin (*or* Kuan Yin) In Chinese Buddhism, the goddess of compassion. She is the same *bodhisattva who was worshiped in India in male form as Avalokiteshvara and in Japan as the multiheaded or multiarmed Kannon. In Chinese art Guan Yin only took on female form during the 12th and 13th centuries.

guarana A climbing plant, *Paullinia cuparia,* of the Amazon Basin, with large compound leaves and clusters of short-stalked flowers. The fruit is about 0.8 in (2 cm) long and contains one seed. The seeds are roasted to produce a stimulant drink containing more caffeine than coffee or ground to make bread. Guarana is also a source of starch, gum, saponin, oils, and drugs. Family: *Sapindaceae.*

Guarani A group of South American Indian peoples of Paraguay and neighboring areas of Brazil and Argentina who speak languages of the Tupian group. About a million Paraguayans speak Guarani. Few now retain their original culture, typical of the tropical forest, based on hunting and maize cultivation, warfare, and cannibalism.

Guardi, Francesco (1712–93) Venetian painter, who studied under and sometimes collaborated with his elder brother, **Giovanni Antonio Guardi** (1699–1760). His souvenir views of Venice were sometimes copied from *Canaletto but they are distinguished by their romantic style and impressionistic technique.

guardian angels Divine beings that figure in several religions. They derive from the belief that every individual has an angel assigned by God as his guardian. In the Roman Catholic Church they may be invoked as intercessors. Feast day: Oct 2.

FRANCESCO GUARDI *An architectural caprice, depicting the vaulted arcade of the Doge's Palace in the artist's native city of Venice (c. 1780).*

Guarini, Giovanni Battista (1538–1612) Italian poet. He served at the court of the Duke of Ferrara and in Rome and Florence. His best-known work, *The Faithful Shepherd* (1590), emulating Torquato *Tasso's *Aminta* (1573), helped to establish the genre of pastoral drama.

Guarini, Guarino (1624–83) Italian baroque architect, philosopher, and mathematician. Most of Guarini's work was done in his native Piedmont. Although influenced by *Borromini, his work shows great originality and technical skill. Probably his most successful building is the church of S Lorenzo, Turin (1668–87).

Guarneri An Italian family of violin makers, famous in the 17th and 18th centuries. The first of the line was **Andrea Guarneri** (d. 1698), who was a pupil (with Stradivari) of Amati in Cremona. Andrea's grandson **Giuseppe Guarneri** (1698–1744), known as "del Gesù," was the most famous member of the family; influenced by the makers of the Brescian school, he produced violins with a characteristically powerful tone, signing them "Guarnerius."

Guatemala, Republic of A country in Central America, on the Pacific Ocean, with a small outlet on the Caribbean Sea. The tropical forests of the

Petén in the N and a narrower plain on the Pacific rise to a central mountainous region, containing a fertile plateau. The country is subject to hurricanes and earthquakes, which have caused havoc throughout its history. About half the population are *Maya Quiché Indians and most of the rest are of mixed Spanish and Indian descent. *Economy*: mainly agricultural, the land being fertile but subject to erosion. Since the 1950s a new system of land development has been introduced, largely on a cooperative basis. The main crops are coffee, sugar, bananas, and cotton, which are the principal exports. Rubber and essential oils are being developed as well as forest products (chicle and timber). Minerals include zinc and lead concentrates, and nickel mining is being introduced. Oil was discovered in 1974 and production is increasing. Efforts are being made to promote industrial growth in plastics, as well as the more traditional food processing and textile industries. *History*: there is extensive archeological evidence of pre-Spanish civilizations, especially that of the Maya, and, from the 12th century, the Aztecs. From 1524–1821 the area was part of the Spanish captaincy general of Guatemala, which included most of Central America. It formed the nucleus of the Central American Federation until 1839, when it became independent. In recent years periods of democratic government have alternated with military dictatorships, accompanied by considerable political unrest. In 1976 a serious earthquake in the center caused further damage to the economy. Guatemala's claims to Belize have intensified in recent years. Following a military coup in 1983, Gen. Oscar Humberto Mejìa Victores succeeded the previous president, Gen. Efraín Ríos Montt. Jorge Serano, elected president in 1991, was ousted by the military amid political and economic turmoil in 1993 after he had assumed dictatorial powers and dissolved the legislature. He was succeeded by Ramiro de Leon, who launched an anticorruption drive. Official language: Spanish. Official religion: Roman Catholic. Official currency: quetzal of 100 centavos. Area: 42,042 sq mi (108,889 sq km). Population (1990 est): 9,340,000. Capital: Guatemala City. Main port: Puerto Barrios.

Guatemala City 14 38N 90 22W The capital of Guatemala, situated in the S of the country in a high valley. Founded in 1776, it was the capital of the captaincy general of Guatemala and later of the Central American Federation. It has four universities; the oldest was founded in 1776. Population (1992 est): 1,115,000.

guava A tropical American tree, *Psidium guajava,* about 33 ft (10 m) tall. Its white four-petaled flowers develop into yellow pear-shaped fruits with white or pink pulp containing many small seeds. Guava fruits, rich in vitamin C, are used to make jam and jelly, stewed for desserts, or canned. Family: *Myrtaceae* (myrtle family).

Guayaquil (*or* Santiago de Guayaquil) 2 13S 79 54W The largest city and chief port of Ecuador, on the Guayas River. It is a major commercial center; industries include food processing, tanning, and textile manufacture. Its university was founded in 1867. Population (1974): 823,219.

gudgeon A freshwater shoaling fish, *Gobio gobio,* related to *carp, found in Europe and N Asia. It has a slender greenish or grayish body, up to about 8 in (20 cm) long, with a row of blackish spots along each side and a pair of barbels at the corners of the mouth. It is used as food and bait.

guelder rose A small tree or shrub, *Viburnum opulus,* 13–16 ft (4–5 m) high, found throughout Eurasia. It has three-lobed leaves and flat-topped clusters of flowers, 2–4 in (5–10 cm) across, in which the outer flowers are large and sterile and the inner ones are small and fertile. The fruits are clusters of red translucent berries. The cultivated form, grown as a garden shrub, is sterile: it has rounded heads of flowers and is called snowball tree. Family: *Caprifoliaceae* (honeysuckle family).

Guelfs and Ghibellines The propapal and proimperial factions respectively in medieval Germany and Italy. Commencing in a German struggle between rival claimants to the Holy Roman Empire, the Guelfs (named for Welf, the family name) and Ghibellines (after Waiblingen, a *Hohenstaufen castle), their conflict acquired an Italian context because of papal opposition to the Hohenstaufen. The Italian city-states were led by Florence (Guelf) and Pisa (Ghibelline). Both sides, however, had factions within each city. Defeat of the Hohenstaufen (1268) contributed to Ghibelline decline, while the Guelfs espoused the *Angevin cause in Italy. By the end of the 14th century the factions had only local significance, reflecting urban rivalries.

Guelph 43 34N 80 16W A city in central Canada, in SW Ontario. Founded in 1827, it is an agricultural research and farming center, especially at the University of Guelph (1964). Numerous factories produce electric motors, wire, metal and rubber products, and many other goods. Population (1991): 87,976.

guenon An *Old World monkey belonging to the genus *Cercopithecus* (10 species), of African forests. They are 33–63 in (83–160 cm) long including the tail (20–35 in [50–88 cm]) and move through the trees in troops, feeding on leaves, fruits, insects, and snails. The mona monkey (*C. mona*), dark with creamy-white underparts and rump patches, is a strikingly marked guenon. *See also* grass monkey.

Guercino (Giovanni Francesco Barbieri; 1591–1666) Italian painter, born at Cento, near Bologna. His masterpiece, the ceiling frescos in the Casino Ludovisi, Rome, commissioned by Pope Gregory XV in 1621, were influenced by the *Carracci, under whom he had studied. While in Rome (1621–23) he also painted the *Burial of St Petronilla* (Capitoline Museum, Rome), which his later work never equaled.

Guericke, Otto von (1602–86) German physicist, renowned for his investigation of vacuums. In 1650 he invented the air pump, which he used to perform a series of experiments culminating in a demonstration in which two teams of horses failed to separate a pair of large hemispheres (called the Magdeburg hemispheres after his hometown) placed together and evacuated. When air was admitted to the hemispheres they fell apart on their own.

Guernica 43 19N 2 40W A historic Basque town in N Spain, on the Bay of Biscay. During the Spanish Civil War it was bombed and virtually destroyed by German planes supporting the Nationalists on Apr 27, 1937. This is depicted in a painting by Picasso.

Guernsey 49 27N 2 35W The second largest of the Channel Islands, in the English Channel. Roughly triangular in shape, it is low lying in the N and hilly in the S with rugged coastal cliffs. Agriculture and horticulture are important, especially dairy farming (the Guernsey breed of cattle originated here) and the production of tomatoes and flowers for export. Guernsey's mild climate, scenery, and beaches contribute to its popularity as a tourist resort. Area: 24.5 sq mi (63 sq km). Population (1981): 53,303. Capital: St Peter Port.

Guernsey cattle A breed of dairy cattle originating from Guernsey. They have a yellowish coat with a white tail switch and produce high-quality creamy milk.

guerrilla warfare (Spanish: small war) Military action by small irregular armed forces, often supported by a hostile foreign power, intended to erode the war potential and political stability of a country. Relying on hit-and-run techniques and avoiding combat with better equipped regulars, guerrillas usually attempt to gain local support rather than territory. The word was first adopted in reference to the Spanish-Portuguese action against the French conquest in the

*Peninsular War. In the 20th century, guerrilla warfare has been employed by many movements, including the Vietnamese in the Vietnam War.

Guesclin, Bertrand du (c. 1320–80) French commander in the *Hundred Years' War. As constable of France from 1370 he was instrumental in recovering the territory previously lost to the English in S and W France.

Guevara, Che (Ernesto G.; 1928–67) Argentine revolutionary and theorist of guerrilla warfare, who became the hero of left-wing youth in the 1960s. A doctor by training, he joined *Castro's invasion of Cuba (1956) and became one of his chief lieutenants in the subsequent guerrilla war. After Castro's victory, Che Guevara influenced Cuba's procommunist foreign relations and directed the land-reform policies. Guevara was an exponent of exporting revolution and in 1967 he was captured and killed by government troops while attempting to instigate a revolt in Bolivia.

Guicciardini, Francesco (1483–1540) Florentine statesman and historian. He was Florentine ambassador to Aragon (1512–14) and then active in Florentine politics before entering the service of the papacy and becoming governor of Modena (1516) and Reggio (1517). After the sack of Rome (1527) by the imperial army Guicciardini concentrated on his writings, including his famous *Storia d'Italia,* which deals with contemporary events in Italy between 1494 and 1534.

guided missiles Rocket-powered missiles without wings or other lift surfaces that are guided throughout their flight. They comprise a power unit, a guidance system, and a warhead. In most, propulsion is by solid-fuel rocket. Of the many guidance systems the most common methods of controlling the missile depend on a trailing wire or a radio, radar, or laser beam. Some have preset on-board computers, others depend on *inertial guidance, and some home on sources of infrared radiation. Warheads range from relatively small antitank high explosives to nuclear devices in the kiloton range. All missiles are vulnerable to electronic countermeasures (ECM), although cruise missiles, driven by turbofan engines, have a range of over 2000 miles (3000 km) and can change course and direction according to a preset-computer program to confuse defense measures. Missiles may be launched from aircraft (air-to-air or air-to-surface) or from the land or sea (surface-to-air or surface-to-surface). *See also* Polaris missile.

Guido d'Arezzo (c. 990–c. 1050) Italian monk and musical theorist. He developed the hexachord, a six-note scale used to facilitate sight-singing. The notes of the hexachord were named for the first syllables of the first six lines of a Latin hymn: ut, re, mi, fa, sol, and la. The hexachord became the basis of later systems of *solmization. Guido also developed the Guidonian hand, a mnemonic device that gave note names to the tips and joints of the fingers, and popularized the use of colored lines in written music to indicate pitch.

Guildford 51 14N 0 35W A city in SE England, in Surrey on the River Wey. A market and residential town, it is the site of the University of Surrey (1966), and Guildford Cathedral. Population (1981): 56,500.

guilds (*or* gilds) Associations formed in medieval Europe to further their members' common purposes. Originally religious or social in character, the first such guilds are recorded in the 9th century. Merchant guilds were created in many towns in the 11th century to organize local trade and became a powerful force in local government. Craft guilds, confined to specific crafts or trades, were formed from the 12th century and these too became very powerful, exercising a monopoly over both production and trade and controlling recruitment by the apprenticeship system. In the later Middle Ages and beyond, their activities were largely superseded by the development of capitalism.

Guilford Courthouse, Battle of (1781) American Revolutionary War battle in N North Carolina. American General Nathanael *Greene's troops made a stand at the Guilford Courthouse against Lord *Cornwallis's British forces. Although the Americans retreated, the British, far more depleted, withdrew to Wilmington in the S of the state and thereafter abandoned the Carolinas.

Guillaume de Lorris (13th century) French poet, author of the first 4000 lines of the verse allegory *Roman de la rose* (c. 1230–40), one of the most influential of medieval poems, translated into English by *Chaucer. Nothing certain is known about Guillaume.

guillemot A bird, *Uria aalge,* occurring in coastal regions of the N hemisphere. It is 16 in (40 cm) long and has a dark-brown plumage with a white belly and wing stripe and a slender bill, feeding on fish, shellfish, and worms. The eggs are shaped so that they do not roll off the cliff ledges where they are laid. Family: *Alcidae* (auks).

guillotine A device with which a person may be beheaded. It consists of two vertical posts and a horizontal knife that is dropped onto the victim's neck. Invented by Joseph Ignace Guillotin (1738–1814), it was introduced as a method of capital punishment in France in 1792, during the French Revolution.

Guinea, Gulf of A large inlet of the E Atlantic Ocean, bordering on the *Guinea Coast of West Africa, between Cape Palmas, Liberia, and Cape Lopez, Gabon.

Guinea, People's Republic of A country on the coast of West Africa. A coastal plain, partly swamp, rises steeply to plateaus and mountains. The population is mainly Fulani and Mandingo. *Economy*: chiefly agricultural, now largely collectivized. The chief crops are rice and palm oil and nuts, as well as coffee, peanuts, and fruits. Livestock, especially cattle, is also important. The principal mineral resources are diamonds, iron ore, and bauxite (alumina is the principal export). Most trade and industry are now nationalized. *History*: the N formed part of Ghana from the 5th–8th centuries AD and of the Mali empire in the 16th century. From the mid-15th century European traders were active along the coast. In 1849 the French established a protectorate over part of Guinea, which became a colony in 1891. In 1895 it became part of French West Africa. In 1958 French Guinea became an independent republic, with Ahmed Sékou Touré as its first president, rather than joining the French Community. A treaty of cooperation reestablished economic relations with France in 1963. Touré died in 1984 and was succeeded by Col. (now Gen.) Lansana Conté, who headed a military regime. In recent years accusations have been made of violations of human rights. Official language: French and the languages of eight ethnic groups. Official currency: syli of 100 cauris. Area: 95,000 sq mi (245,857 sq km). Population (1990 est): 7,269,000. Capital and main port: Conakry.

Guinea-Bissau, Republic of (name until 1974: Portuguese Guinea) A small country on the coast of West Africa, including the archipelago of Bijagós. It consists chiefly of a coastal plain, cut by wide river estuaries and rising to savanna-covered plateau inland. The majority of the population are Fulani, Mandyako, and Mandingo. *Economy*: chiefly agricultural, the principal crops being groundnuts (the main export), rice, and palm oil and nuts. Cattle breeding is important in the interior, and there are plans to diversify crops in order to increase self-sufficiency in food. Land has been nationalized and cooperative farming introduced. Important bauxite deposits have been discovered and there are plans for a major hydroelectric scheme to power an aluminum plant. Other smaller industries are also being developed. *History*: explored by the Portuguese in the mid-15th century, the area became a center of the slave trade. It became a

Portuguese colony in 1879 and an overseas province of Portugal in 1951. In 1974 it became an independent republic. Luis de Almeida Cabral became the first president; he was replaced by Joao Vieira following a coup in 1980. Vieira was reelected in 1984 and 1989. One-party rule ended in 1991. Official language: Portuguese; Crioulo is widely spoken. Official currency: Guinea-Bissau peso of 100 centavos. Area: 13,948 sq mi (36,125 sq km). Population (1989 est): 929,000. Capital: Bissau.

Guinea Coast The coastlands of West Africa extending from Gambia to Cape Lopez in Gabon.

guinea fowl A bird belonging to an African family (*Numididae*; 7–10 species). About 20 in (50 cm) long, domesticated guinea fowl are descended from the helmet guinea fowl (*Numida meleagris*), which has a large bony crest, a bare face with red and blue wattles, and a gray white-spotted plumage. Guinea fowl scratch for seeds and insects, especially termites. Order: *Galliformes* (pheasants, turkeys, etc.).

guinea pepper The spicy aromatic fruit of a West African tree, *Xylopia aethiopica,* source of the condiment "Negro pepper." The tree has simple leaves with a metallic sheen arranged in two ranks along the branches and fragrant flowers producing aggregates of berries. Family: *Annonaceae.*

guinea pig A domesticated rodent, *Cavia porcellus,* descended from the *cavy. Guinea pigs were originally bred for food but are now popular as pets. They should be fed on grain, roots, green food, and hay.

guinea worm A parasitic *nematode worm, *Dracunculus medinensis,* that is a serious parasite of man in Africa, India, and the Middle East. The larvae are carried by water fleas (genus *Cyclops*) often present in drinking water. When swallowed by the human host, they burrow into the tissues and grow to maturity: the females reach a length of up to 47 in (120 cm), causing ulcers on the feet and legs.

Guinevere In *Arthurian legend, the wife of King Arthur and lover of *Lancelot. She is featured in various medieval romances. Malory's *Morte d'Arthur* (1485) describes her abduction by Mordred, Arthur's nephew, and her adulterous love for *Lancelot, which triggered the decline of Arthur's chivalric society.

Guinness, Sir Alec (1914–) British actor. He established his reputation as a stage actor in repertory in the late 1930s and played Hamlet in modern dress in 1938. After World War II he achieved success as a character actor in films, including *Oliver Twist* (1948), *Kind Hearts and Coronets* (1949), *The Bridge on the River Kwai* (1957), for which he received an Academy Award, *The Comedians* (1967), *Star Wars* (1977), and *A Passage to India* (1985).

Guiscard, Robert (c. 1015–85) Norman knight, who took part in the invasions of S Italy and extended Norman power into Sicily. He established himself in Calabria and gained papal recognition as Duke of Apulia (1059). He died while campaigning in the Balkans. His brother and nephew later ruled Sicily as Roger I (1031–1101; reigned c. 1071–1101) and *Roger II.

Guise A French noble family prominent during the 16th century. The duchy of Guise was the reward (1528) of **Claude I, Duke of Aumale** (1496–1550) for services to France. His daughter **Mary of Guise** (1515–60) married James V of Scotland and was the mother of Mary, Queen of Scots. Claude's sons **François, 2nd Duke of Guise** (1519–63) and **Charles, Cardinal of Lorraine** (1524–74) became the most powerful men in France and the leaders of the Roman Catholic party in the French *Wars of Religion. François was assassinated by a Huguenot and the Catholic leadership passed to his son **Henri I, 3rd Duke of Guise** (1550–88), who directed the *St Bartholomew Day's Massacre of Huguenots in 1572. Following Henri's assassination the Guise's influence on French politics diminished.

guitar A plucked stringed instrument of Moorish origin, which came to Europe via Spain. The modern Spanish guitar has a flat back, a round sound hole, a fretted fingerboard, and six strings tuned chiefly in fourths. It has a range of over three octaves from the E below the bass stave. Music for it is written an octave higher than it sounds. Guitar technique was developed by Fernando Sor (1778–1839) and in the 20th century by Andrés *Segovia.

guitar fish A *ray fish, belonging to the family *Rhinobatidae*, that has a pointed flattened head with fused pectoral fins and a long muscular sharklike tail. Guitar fish live in shallow waters of tropical and temperate seas and feed on bottom-dwelling animals, especially crustaceans.

Guitry, Sacha (1885–1957) French actor and dramatist. He wrote many light comedies, often concerning the lives of famous men, such as Napoleon and Mozart. He acted in these and occasionally in films, including *Le Comédien* (1949) and *Napoléon* (1955).

Guiyang (*or* Kuei-yang) 26 35N 106 40E A city in S China, the capital of Guizhou province. Industries, developed since 1949, include steel, machinery, and aluminum. Population (1990): 1,018,619.

Guizhou (Kuei-chou *or* Kweichow) A province in S China, a rather infertile high plateau. There were frequent rebellions among the minority non-Chinese groups, which have rich folk cultures. Rice, maize, tobacco, tea, and timber are grown and silk and minerals produced. Area: 69,278 sq mi (174,000 sq km). Population (1990): 32,391,066. Capital: Guiyang.

Guizot, François (Pierre Guillaume) (1787–1874) French statesman and historian. As a professor of history at Paris University (1812–30) he became the chief supporter of constitutional monarchy in France. He was prominent in the revolution that brought Louis Philippe to the throne in 1830 and served as foreign minister (1840–48). The most prominent figure in the government, Guizot was forced by the Revolution of 1848 to resign and devoted the rest of his life to historical writing.

Gujarat A state in W India, on the Arabian Sea SE of Pakistan. Lowlands merge into hills in the S and E and into marshes in the NW. Cotton, tobacco, peanuts, and other crops are raised. An industrial area, Gujarat produces textiles, machinery, and chemicals. *History*: a flourishing area under Muslim princes (13th–17th centuries), Gujarat was conquered by the Maratha in the 18th century before passing to Britain. Area: 75,650 sq mi (195,984 sq km). Population (1991): 41,174,343. Capital: Gandhinagar.

Gujarati An Indo-Aryan language spoken by 20 million people in Gujarat and Maharashtra in India. It is related to Rajasthani, uses a modified Devanagari script, and has a long literary tradition.

Gujranwala 32 06N 74 11E A city in NE Pakistan. The Sikh ruler Ranjit Singh was born here. Manufactures include textiles and leather goods and it has a famous ceramics industry. Population (1981): 658,753.

Gulf States The nations situated on the Persian Gulf. They are Oman, the United Arab Emirates, Qatar, Bahrein, Saudi Arabia, Kuwait, Iraq, and Iran. They comprise the world's major oil-producing area.

Gulf Stream One of the major ocean currents of the world, flowing from the Florida Strait parallel to the North American coast as far as the Newfoundland banks. It bears NE across the Atlantic as the North Atlantic Drift, branching into two main directions, one flowing N toward Spitsbergen and the other flowing S to form the Canary Current. Water from the North and South Equatorial Currents builds up in the Gulf of Mexico and escapes with force through the Florida Strait as the Florida Current, one of the strongest major ocean currents. The water is warm and although as the Gulf Stream progresses it mixes with cooler waters, the ameliorating effect on the climate of NW Europe is significant.

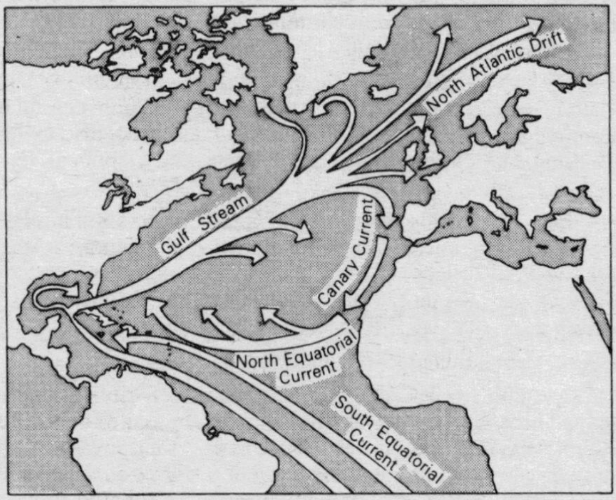

GULF STREAM

gulfweed Tropical *brown algae, also called rockweed or sea holly, of the genus *Sargassum,* especially *S. natans,* which forms huge free-floating masses of seaweed in the Sargasso Sea. They have highly branched serrated fronds, with berrylike gas-filled floats or bladders, and most reproduce sexually.

gull A seabird belonging to the subfamily *Larinae* (about 40 species), ranging throughout the world's coastal regions and also found inland. Up to 30 in (75 cm) long, gulls are well built and have long pointed wings and a strong slightly hooked bill. Gulls are typically gray and white, often with dark markings, and some have a dark mask or hood in summer. Some gulls feed on fish but most are scavengers, feeding on invertebrates, eggs, chicks, and refuse. Family: *Laridae* (gulls and terns); order: *Charadriiformes* (gulls, plovers, etc.).

gullet. *See* esophagus.

gum arabic. *See* gums.

gums Adhesive substances exuded by plants. They are odorless tasteless amorphous *carbohydrates that form either clear liquid solutions or gelatinous mixtures with water. **Gum arabic** (*or* gum acacia), the most widely used of the water-soluble gums, is obtained from trees of the genus *Acacia,* although the name is also applied to substitute gums from other plants. It is used for making candies, cosmetics, gummed labels, and textile finishes. **Gum tragacanth** is extracted from shrubs of the genus *Astragalus*: it is not completely water-soluble, but forms a thick mucilage. It is used as an adhesive in pills and as a sauce thickener.

gum tree A tree of the genus *Eucalyptus* (about 600 species), so called because the whole tree is rich in resin and aromatic oils.

gun metal A type of *bronze containing about 90% copper and sometimes a little zinc. Being easy to cast, it was originally used for making cannons. Admiralty gun metal (88% copper, 10% tin, 2% zinc) is used in shipbuilding.

Gunn effect The effect used in solid-state *semiconductor microwave generators (Gunn diodes). When a sufficiently high steady electric field (typically several thousand volts per centimeter) is applied across a sample of n-type gallium arsenide, microwave frequency current oscillations are set up. Named for J. B. Gunn (1928–).

gunnel An eel-like fish of the family *Pholididae* (about 8 species), found usually among seaweed or rocks in N Atlantic and N Pacific coastal waters, feeding on invertebrates. The rock gunnel (*Pholis gunnellus*), also called butterfish, is 12 in (30 cm) long and brownish with 9–13 black spots along the dorsal fin. Order: *Perciformes.*

gunpowder An explosive mixture of saltpeter (potassium nitrate), sulfur, and powdered charcoal. Invented by the Chinese many centuries before its description by Roger *Bacon in the 13th century it has had a profound and far-reaching effect on human conflict (*see* firearms). It has now been replaced for most purposes by safer explosives, but is still used in fireworks.

Gunpowder Plot. *See* Fawkes, Guy.

guns *Artillery firearms that discharge high-velocity shells with a relatively flat trajectory. A modern breech-loading gun has a rifled barrel. Its sliding or interrupted screw-thread breech blocks contain linked levers activating the firing pin, which strikes the primer, located either in the round or the block. Buffers absorb the firing shock and recuperators return the barrel to its firing position. Controls elevate and traverse the gun, sometimes electronically. Most ammunition is fused to burst before, on, or after impact. Specialized shells are used in *antitank guns and *anti-aircraft guns. Some shells have nuclear warheads. Guns may be towed or mounted on vehicles or in aircraft or ships. *See also* small arms.

Gunter's chain. *See* chain.

Gunther, John (1901–70) US author. An overseas correspondent (1924–36) for the Chicago *Daily News,* he wrote accounts of his interviews, travels, and experiences in a series of books, including *Inside Europe* (1936), *Inside Asia* (1939), *Inside Latin America* (1941), *Inside U.S.A.* (1947), *Inside Africa* (1955), *Inside Russia Today* (1958), and *Inside South America* (1968). *Death Be Not Proud* (1949) is an account of his son's losing battle with cancer.

Guntur 16 20W 80 27E A city in S India, in Andhra Pradesh. It is an agricultural trading and processing center. Population (1971): 269,991.

Guomindang (*or* Kuomintang) The National People's Party of *Taiwan (Republic of China). Organized in 1912, following the overthrow of the imperial government, from *Sun Yat-sen's Alliance Society, it formed, under Soviet influence, an alliance with the new Chinese Communist Party (CCP) in 1924 (*see* United Fronts). Following Sun's death (1925), the Guomindang was led by *Chiang Kai-shek and with the CCP had gained control of most of China from the *warlords by 1926. A break between the two parties (1927) led to civil war until Japanese conquests in China (*see* Sino-Japanese Wars) necessitated renewed cooperation in 1937. After Japan's defeat (1945), civil war was resumed until a communist victory in 1949 drove Chiang Kai-shek and his Guomindang followers into exile in Taiwan.

guppy A freshwater fish, *Lebistes reticulatus,* native to N South America and the West Indies. Male guppies are up to 1.6 in (4 cm) long and brightly colored, marked with black eyespots and having variably shaped and colored fins. Females, slightly larger and less colorful, are prolific breeders, producing live young (rather than eggs) at monthly intervals. Guppies are popular aquarium fish and—in their native regions—are used to control mosquitoes. Family: *Cyprinodontidae.*

Gupta A powerful Indian dynasty founded in the late 4th century AD. Its founder *Chandra Gupta I was succeeded by *Samudra Gupta and the throne then passed to *Chandra Gupta II. His son Kumara (d. 455; reigned c. 415–55) was followed by Skanda Gupta (reigned 455–67), during whose reign foreign invaders began to conquer parts of the empire. The early Gupta kings fostered Buddhism and presided over a golden age of artistic and cultural achievement. The dynasty was overthrown by the Huns in the 6th century.

Gurdjieff, George Ivanovitch (1873–1943) Russian occultist of Greek parentage, who traveled widely in Europe and Asia before establishing a teaching center near Paris in the 1920s. Believing that man is not usually fully conscious, his students were required to perform a stylized dance to assist them to attain a higher level of perception. Part mystic, part bon viveur, and reputedly part charlatan, this enigmatic man had a considerable following, including P. D. Ouspensky, whose books have outlived Gurdjieff's own *All and Everything, Beelzebub's Tales to his Grandson.*

gurdwara A Sikh place of worship, housing a copy of the *Adi Granth. Although every Sikh home contains one, public gurdwaras are used for meetings, weddings, and services. The most sacred is the Golden Temple or Harimandir at Amritsar.

gurnard A carnivorous bottom-dwelling fish, also called sea robin, belonging to a family (*Triglidae*; about 40 species) found in temperate and tropical seas. It has a tapering body, up to 26 in (70 cm) long, a large armored head, and fingerlike pectoral fin rays and produces sound by vibrating its swim bladder. The flying gurnards belong to the family *Dactylopteridae.* Order: *Scorpaeniformes.*

guru In *Hinduism, a venerated spiritual teacher who personally instructs and guides the disciple. In Tibetan Buddhism the guru embodies the Buddha himself and is correspondingly revered. In Sikhism, guru is the title of the first 10 patriarchs (*see* Nanak).

Gustavus II Adolphus (1594–1632) King of Sweden (1611–32), who displayed military genius in the *Thirty Years' War. He inherited wars with Denmark, Russia, and Poland, which he successfully terminated in 1613, 1617, and 1629 respectively. He simultaneously, with the help of his chancellor *Oxenstierna, consolidated his internal position and in the 1620s instituted important administrative and educational reforms. In 1630 he entered the Thirty Years' War on the Protestant side, inspired by religious aims as well as a desire for Sweden to dominate the Baltic. He defeated Tilly at *Breitenfeld (1631) and at the Lech (1632) and Wallenstein at *Lutzen, in which Gustavus Adolphus was mortally wounded.

Gustavus I Vasa (1496–1560) King of Sweden (1523–60), who achieved Swedish independence of Denmark and founded the Vasa dynasty. He was taken captive in the 1517–18 war against Denmark but escaped and on returning to Sweden led a successful rebellion against the Danes (1521–23). As king, he dealt effectively with the political and economic consequences of war and established Lutheranism as the state religion (1527–29).

Gutenberg, Johann (c. 1400–c. 1468) German printer, who invented the method of printing with movable metal type (*see* typesetting). Gutenberg worked on his printing process from the 1430s. In 1448 he received the financial backing of *Fust and by 1455 had produced his great 42-line Bible (the Gutenberg Bible). Fust successfully sued Gutenberg in 1455 for the repayment of his loan and the impoverished Gutenberg was forced to relinquish his machinery, with which Fust set up a printing business. He produced a famous psalter (1457), which was largely Gutenberg's work.

Guthrie, (William) Tyrone (1900–71) British theater director. He directed the Old Vic and other British companies and frequently worked abroad, notably at Stratford, Ontario, where he founded the Shakespeare Festival in 1953. He was best known for his inventive productions of Shakespeare, often in modern dress.

Guthrie, Woody (Woodrow Wilson G.; 1912–67) US folksinger and songwriter, many of whose songs reflected the social injustice of the Depression. His most famous song was "This Land Is Your Land." His style and compositions strongly influenced other young musicians. His son, **Arlo** (1947–) is also a singer and songwriter. His best-known song is the satirical "Alice's Restaurant."

gutta percha A brownish leathery material obtained from the *latex of various trees of the family *Sapotaceae,* especially those of the SE Asian genus *Palaquium.* It was once extensively used, for example, as an electrical insulator, in golf balls, and in chewing gum, but it has now largely been replaced by synthetics.

Guyana, Cooperative Republic of (name until 1966: British Guiana) A country in the NE of South America, on the Atlantic Ocean. Narrow fertile coastal plains give way to higher undulating areas, rich in minerals and forests. The main rivers, the Demerara, Essequibo, and Berbice give their names to its three counties. Most of the population is of African and East Indian descent. *Economy*: agriculture is important, the main crops being rice and sugar. Fishing, livestock, and cotton growing are being developed as part of a campaign to "feed, house, and clothe" the nation. The most important minerals were formerly gold and diamonds, but these have now been overtaken by bauxite. By 1976 nearly all foreign economic interests had been nationalized. Most power comes from hydroelectric sources. *History*: the coast was first explored by the Spanish in 1499 and settlements were founded by the Dutch in the 17th century. The area was occupied by the British (1796–1802, 1803–14) and then formally ceded to Britain, becoming a colony as British Guiana in 1831. In 1961 it gained internal self-government under *Jagan. In 1966, as Guyana, it became independent within the British Commonwealth. It is also a member of CARICOM. Marxist forces in political life led to the formation of a Cooperative Republic in 1970. In 1978 an agricultural commune (Jonestown) 150 mi (240 km) NW of Georgetown was the scene of the mass suicide of some 900 members of the People's Temple sect led by James Warren Jones. A new constitution was formulated in 1980. In 1992, former president Cheddi Jagan, a former Marxist, won the presidential election. Official language: English. Official currency: Guyana dollar of 100 cents. Area: 83,000 sq mi (210,000 sq km). Population (1989 est): 846,000. Capital and main port: Georgetown.

Guyenne A former region of SW France. Ruled by the English kings in the late Middle Ages, it was regained by France after the Hundred Years' War. The scene of fierce fighting in the 16th-century Wars of Religion and the 17th-century Fronde, Guyenne was later merged with Gascony.

Guzmán Blanco, Antonio (1829–99) Venezuelan statesman. He was president three times (1870–77, 1879–84, 1886–88) but retained despotic power throughout the period 1870–88. He helped Venezuela's economy, encouraging foreign investment and building public works, including the country's first railroad.

Gwalior 26 12N 78 09E A city in India, in Madhya Pradesh. Strategically important, it developed around its impressive fortress, which is believed to date from the 6th century AD. Gwalior is an important commercial and industrial center manufacturing a variety of goods. Jiwaji University was established here in 1964. Population (1991): 693,000.

Gweru (former name: Gwelo) 19 25S 29 50E A city in central Zimbabwe. It is the center of a mining area (with chrome-ore and asbestos deposits) and a cattle-rearing area. Industries include ferrochrome processing. Population (1987 est): 79,000.

Gwyn, Nell (1650–87) English actress. Originally an orange seller in Drury Lane, she achieved fame as an actress and became Charles II's mistress, bearing him two sons. "Let not poor Nellie starve" are said to have been his last words. She helped to establish the Royal Hospital at Chelsea.

Gyandzha (name until 1813 and from 1920–35: Gandzha; name from 1813–1920: Yelisavetpol; from 1920–91: Kirovabad) 40 39N 46 20E A city in NW Azerbaijan. A medieval commercial center, it is now an important industrial center, producing especially textiles, building materials, and wine. Population (1987 est): 245,000.

gymnastics Exercises designed to perfect balance, strength, and coordination, popular as a sport for individual performers and teams. The modern sport developed in Germany and Sweden in the 19th century from **calisthenics**, rhythmical exercises performed without apparatus or weights. The ancient Persians, Chinese, Indians, Greeks, and Romans also exercised in this way. Competitions consist of prescribed programs of exercises and optional routines, the apparatus being for men the horizontal bar, parallel bars, pommel horse, vaulting horse, and rings, and for women the balance beam, asymmetrical bars, and vaulting horse; both men and women do floor exercises. The sport's popularity increased dramatically, especially among girls, after the victories of Olga Korbut (1972) and Nadia Comaneci (1976) in the Olympics. The strong showing of the US men's and women's teams in the 1984 Los Angeles Olympics further spurred the sport's growth in the US. The world governing body is the Fédération internationale de Gymnastique (founded in 1881).

gymnosperms A group of plants, most of which are trees, forming one of the two classes of seed-bearing plants (*compare* angiosperms). The sole consistent characteristic of this variable class is that their seeds are not enclosed within a fruit but are borne naked, in many species on *cone scales. Gymnosperms originated in the late Devonian period (about 380 million years ago) and the principal orders are as follows: *Coniferales* (*see* conifer); *Ginkgoales* (*see* ginkgo); *Cycadales* (*see* cycad); *Gnetales* (e.g. *welwitschia); and several extinct orders, including the *Pteridospermales* (*see* seed fern) and the **Cordaitales*.

gymnure An insectivorous mammal belonging to the family *Erinaceidae* of SE Aisa, also called hairy hedgehog. There are four species, including the *moon rat. Short-legged and flat-footed, 6–24 in (15–60 cm) long, they resemble *hedgehogs without spines. They are shy, usually living in thick undergrowth and hunting mainly at night.

gynecology The branch of medicine and surgery concerned with diseases of women and girls, particularly those affecting the reproductive system. The closely related specialty of **obstetrics** deals with the care of women during pregnancy, childbirth, and the period immediately after delivery. Doctors specializing in these fields (gynecologists and obstetricians) work in close association: a gynecologist is usually also an obstetrician.

Györ 47 41N 17 40E A city in NW Hungary, near the confluence of the Rába and Danube Rivers. Györ has many old buildings, including a 12th-century cathedral (rebuilt in the 18th century). It has heavy engineering and lies in an area famous for horse breeding. Population (1991 est): 130,000.

Gypsies A wandering people found on most continents. The name "Gypsy" is derived from "Egyptian," but they probably originated in India. One group is thought to have migrated through Egypt and North Africa and another through Europe reaching NW Europe during the 15th and 16th centuries and North America in the 19th century. They travel by motorized caravan and live largely by seasonal work, itinerant trade, entertaining, and fortune telling. They have frequently been persecuted, with half a million killed by Nazis in World War II. Their native language is *Romany.

Gypsophila A genus of slender annual or perennial herbs (about 120 species), native to the Mediterranean area. Up to 5 ft (1.5 m) high, they have gray-green strap-shaped leaves and large clusters of white or pink flowers. Some species are grown in rock gardens; others are popular for flower arrangements. Family: *Caryophyllaceae* (pink family).

Gypsum A colorless or white mineral consisting of hydrated calcium sulfate found in clays, shales, and limestones. It occurs mainly as a result of the evaporation of saline water. Rock gypsum is often red-stained, granular, and found in layers. Gypsite is impure and earthy, occurring as surface deposits. *Alabaster is a pure compact fine-grained translucent form. Satin-spar is fibrous and silky. Selenite occurs as transparent crystals in clays and mudstones. Gypsum is used in the manufacture of cement, rubber, paper, plaster of Paris, and blackboard chalk.

gypsy moth A moth, *Lymantria dispar,* distributed throughout the N hemisphere. Males are brownish gray and females white. The grayish larvae, which feed on a variety of trees, were introduced to North America in 1869 and have become a serious pest. *See also* tussock moth.

gyrfalcon The largest *falcon, *Falco rusticolus,* which breeds in N Eurasia, North America, and mountainous regions of Asia. It is 24 in (60 cm) long and its plumage varies from pure white speckled with black to dark gray with dense black barring. It hunts for hares, rodents, and ground-dwelling birds.

gyrocompass. *See* compass.

H

Haakon IV Haakonsson (1204–63) King of Norway (1217–63), who added Iceland and Greenland to Norwegian territories (1262). He subdued rebellions and strengthened the monarchy by improving royal administration and by extensive legislation. In 1247 he was crowned by the pope's legate. He died in an invasion of the Isle of Man and the Hebrides.

Haakon VII (1872–1957) The first king of Norway (1905–57) following the restoration of Norwegian independence. His refusal to abdicate during the German occupation (1940–45), during which he was in England, encouraged Norwegian resistance.

Haarlem 52 23N 4 38E A city in the W Netherlands, the capital of North Holland province. Surrounded by flower fields, it is a major trade center for bulbs. Industries include textiles and printing. It is noted for its Frans Hals museum and its fine cathedral (14–15th centuries). Population (1991 est): 149,500.

Habakkuk An Old Testament prophet of Judah, who lived at the time when a Babylonian invasion was imminent (c. 605 BC). **The Book of Habakkuk** records his perplexity that a just God should make use of an evil nation to inflict punishment on his own people, but the prophet is told to trust in God, who will see to it that all evil will eventually be punished.

habeas corpus (Latin: have the body) A remedy against unlawful confinement, which takes the form of a writ ordering the person having custody of a prisoner to produce him before the court issuing the writ and to submit to whatever the court directs. There are a variety of such writs, the most important being that of *habeas corpus ad subjiciendum* (have the body to submit to whatever the court directs), used to test the legality of imprisonment but not to appeal against a conviction or sentence. The writ is not to determine a prisoner's guilt or innocence; the only issue it presents is whether the liberty of the prisoner is restrained pursuant to the laws of due process.

Haber, Fritz (1868–1934) German chemist and inventor of the Haber process (*see* Haber-Bosch process). The Haber process, developed in 1908, enabled atmospheric nitrogen to be combined with hydrogen to form ammonia, which could then be converted into nitrates. The process was essential to Germany's supply of explosives and fertilizers during World War I. For this work, Haber was awarded the 1918 Nobel Prize. *See also* Bosch, Carl.

Haber-Bosch process A method for the bulk production of ammonia from nitrogen and hydrogen. The pure gases are passed over an iron catalyst at about 933°F (500°C) and a pressure of 500 atmospheres. Ammonia is chiefly used in the manufacture of fertilizers and *explosives. The process was devised by Fritz *Haber and adapted by Carl *Bosch, who added a process for making the hydrogen from *water gas and steam.

Habsburgs. (*See* Hapsburgs).

Hackney horse An English breed of trotting horse developed from Norfolk trotters. It has a compact body with strong short legs and powerful shoulders, a full tail, and a fine chestnut bay, brown, or black coat. Hackneys were once fashionable carriage horses and are now used mainly for shows. Height: 14⅓–15⅓ hands (1.50–1.60 m).

hadal zone. *See* abyssal zone.

haddock A carnivorous food fish, *Melanogrammus aeglefinus,* related to *cod, that usually occurs in shoals near the bottom of N Atlantic coastal waters. It has an elongated body, up to 40 in (1 m) long, gray or brown above and silvery below with a black spot behind each pectoral fin, two anal and three dorsal fins, a small chin barbel, and a dark lateral line. It is eaten both fresh and smoked, Finnan haddock from Scotland being especially well known.

Hades (*or* Pluto) The Greek god of the dead; also the name of the underworld he ruled. He was the brother of Zeus and Poseidon and husband of *Persephone, whom he abducted. The souls of the dead were ferried to Hades across the River Styx by *Charon.

Hadhramaut A region in central South Yemen. It consists of a mountain range parallel to the coast rising to over 6562 ft (2000 m) and the valley, further inland, of an intermittent stream that turns toward the sea E of the mountains. With irrigation, the production of dates, grain, and tobacco is the main industry, and the chief town is Mukalla, on the coast.

Hadith (Arabic: tradition) Traditional records of sayings and deeds attributed to Mohammed that are not contained in the Koran but are accepted as authoritative sources of moral, ritual, and religious law. Extensive compilations of such traditions were made after the Prophet's death. The chief collection is that made by al-*Bukhari.

Hadrian (76–138 AD) Roman emperor (117–38). He was admitted to the imperial household as *Trajan's ward in 85 and a successful military career included special responsibility in Trajan's Parthian campaign. On Trajan's death he became emperor, crushed a conspiracy against him (118), and from 120 to 131 toured the provinces. His foreign policy was generally defensive (he sponsored the building of *Hadrian's Wall in Britain) but he subdued a Jewish revolt (132–35) with considerable severity. From 131 until his death he lived in Rome, instigating building projects, including the *Pantheon and the mausoleum (Castel Sant' Angelo) in which he was buried.

Hadrian IV. *See* Adrian IV.

Hadrian's Wall A Roman frontier defense work. Begun in 122 AD, it was the N frontier of Roman Britain for 250 years. Designed to control the Scottish tribes, it stretched 85 mi (120 km) from the Tyne River to Solway Firth. Temporarily superseded by the Antonine Wall and several times overrun and rebuilt, it was finally abandoned in 383 AD. Substantial portions still stand.

hadron Any elementary particle that takes part in *strong interactions. The group thus includes all baryons and mesons but not leptons or the photon. *See* particle physics.

Haeckel, Ernst Heinrich (1834–1919) German zoologist, noted for his speculative theories concerning the origin of life and evolution. A firm advocate of *Darwin's theories, Haeckel went even further. He suggested that life originated through spontaneous combination of the elements and he drew genealogical trees to represent the course of evolution. His recapitulation theory (i.e. that stages in the embryological development of an individual reflect stages in the evolution of the species) did much to stimulate embryological research, although the theory is now regarded as unsound.

Ha-er-bin (English name: Harbin) 45 45N 126 41E A port in NE China, the capital of Heilongjiang province on the Songhua River. A trading and industrial center, the site of Heilongjiang University, it was developed by Russia and was a haven for refugees from the Russian Revolution (1917). Population (1990): 2,443,398.

HADRIAN'S WALL

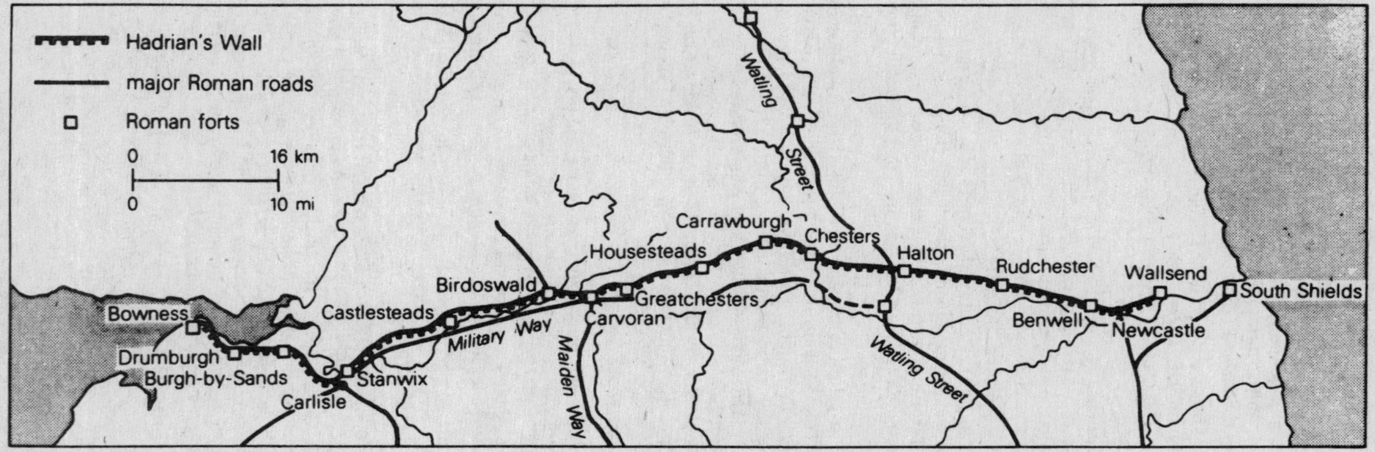

HADRIAN'S WALL *Constructed by the Romans in Britain as a defense against the Scottish tribes.*